Constitutional Law in Malta

Constitutional Law in Malta

Kevin Aquilina

This book was originally published as a monograph in the International Encyclopaedia of Laws/Constitutional Law.

Founding Editor: Roger Blanpain
General Editor: Frank Hendrickx
Volume Editors: André Alen & David Haljan

Wolters Kluwer

Published by:
Kluwer Law International B.V.
PO Box 316
2400 AH Alphen aan den Rijn
The Netherlands
E-mail: international-sales@wolterskluwer.com
Website: lrus.wolterskluwer.com

Sold and distributed in North, Central and South America by:
Wolters Kluwer Legal & Regulatory U.S.
7201 McKinney Circle
Frederick, MD 21704
United States of America
Email: customer.service@wolterskluwer.com

Sold and distributed in all other countries by:
Air Business Subscriptions
Rockwood House
Haywards Heath
West Sussex
RH16 3DH
United Kingdom
Email: international-customerservice@wolterskluwer.com

Printed on acid-free paper

ISBN 978-90-411-9560-9

e-Book: ISBN 978-90-411-9561-6
web-PDF: ISBN 978-90-411-9563-0

Printed in the United Kingdom.

The Author

Kevin Aquilina is Professor and Dean of the Faculty of Laws at the University of Malta where he is also the Head of the Department of Media, Communications and Technology Law. He holds a Doctor of Philosophy (PhD) in Law from the London School of Economics and Political Science of the University of London, a Doctor of Law (LLD) from the University of Malta and a Master of Laws (LLM) in International Maritime Law from the International Maritime Organization's International Maritime Law Institute. He currently lectures on Constitutional Law, Administrative Law, Human Rights Law, Media Law and the Maltese Legal System at the Faculty of Laws at the University of Malta. Professor Aquilina has held the office of Chief Executive of the constitutionally established Maltese audiovisual broadcasting regulator – the Broadcasting Authority – for over ten years. He also served as Chairman of the Press Ethics Commission – the self-regulatory media body which hears and decides complaints against journalists. Professor Aquilina served for eleven years as Chairman of the Planning Appeals Board, and subsequently as Legal Advisor to the Planning Appeals Board and Member of the Environment and Planning Review Tribunal.

Professor Aquilina has authored various books, written several reports for Maltese and foreign institutions, drafted many primary and subsidiary laws and has published papers in edited books and articles in peer reviewed journals apart from various contributions to the print, broadcasting and new media. His books include: *A List of Maltese Maritime Legislation Together with a Subject Index* (Mid-Med Bank, Malta: June 1992, i + 88 pp.); *Development Planning Legislation: The Maltese Experience* (Malta: Mireva Publications, May 1999, xciii + 616 pp.); a six-volume compilation of *Decisions of the Planning Appeals Board* (Malta: Legal Publishing (Enterprises) Ltd., 1995–1998 consisting of 1,208 pp. in all). Apart from having authored all the Annual Reports of the Broadcasting Authority for the period 1999–2008, Professor Aquilina has co-authored in 2007 a publication and compact disk entitled *Maltese Broadcasting Legislation: Salient Documentation* as part of the Broadcasting Authority's *Broadcasting Studies Series*. In 2013 he co-authored *Il Sistema Ambiente, Tra Etica,*

The Author

Diritto Ed Economia, published in Italy by CEDAM, Casa Editrice Dott. Antonio Milani. His latest international book is *Media Law in Malta* in the *International Encyclopaedia of Laws Series* (The Netherlands: Wolters Kluwer Law and Business, September 2014, 240 pp.).

Professor Aquilina's papers have been published in international peer reviewed journals such as *Computer Law & Security Review*, *International Journal of Private Law, Journal of Civil Law Studies, Cambrian Law Review, Commonwealth Law Bulletin, International Journal of Public Law and Policy, Journal of Medical Ethics, Dike Kai Nomos, EUCRIM: The European Criminal Law Associations' Forum*, *Comparative Law Review*, *European Journal of Comparative Law and Governance*, *International Human Rights Law Review, Global Journal of Comparative Law, International Human Rights Law Review, International Journal of Legislative Drafting and Law Reform* and Maltese peer reviewed journals such as *Mediterranean Journal of Human Rights*, *Malta Medical Journal, Melita Historica, Melita Theologica, BOV Review*, *Law and Practice*, *Future Generations Journal, European Law Students Association (ELSA) Malta Law Review* and *Id-Dritt Law Journal*. Professor Aquilina is the Maltese regular contributor to *IRIS – Legal Observations of the European Audiovisual Observatory,* of the Council of Europe. He has served as the editor of the Broadcasting Authority's *Broadcasting Studies Series*.

Table of Contents

The Author	3
List of Abbreviations	21
General Introduction	23
Chapter 1. Historical Outline of the Constitution of Malta	23
§1. An Introduction to Maltese Constitutional History	23
§2. The 1964 Independence Constitution of Malta	24
Chapter 2. The Demographic and Population Features of the Maltese Republican Constitution	25
§1. Demographics and Population	25
§2. Characteristics of the Maltese State	25
I. Constitutionalism	25
A. The Juridical Status of the Constitution of Malta	25
B. The Supremacy of the Constitution of Malta	26
1. Section 6 of the Constitution of Malta	27
2. Section 46(2) of the Constitution of Malta	29
3. Section 47(9) of the Constitution of Malta	29
4. Section 65(1) of the Constitution of Malta	30
5. Section 66 of the Constitution of Malta	30
6. Section 95(2)(e) of the Constitution of Malta	32
7. Section 116 of the Constitution of Malta	32
II. The Rule of Law	32
III. The Separation of Powers	33
IV. The Independence of the Judiciary	34
V. National Sovereignty	35
A. Making of Extra-Territorial Legislation	36
B. Meaning of Sovereignty	36
C. Limitations on Sovereignty	37
§3. State Territory	38

I. Definition of 'State' 39
II. Definition of 'Malta' 39

§4. Features of the Republican Constitution 40

I. Constitutional State Symbols 41
A. The National Religion 41
B. The National Flag 41
C. The George Cross Award 41
D. The National Language 42
E. The National Anthem 43
II. General Principles of Constitutional Law 43
III. A Typology of the Constitution 43
IV. Constitutional State Affiliations and Diplomatic Representation 44
V. Constitutional Multi-Level Government 45
A. Prior to EU Accession 45
1. Central Government 45
2. Local Self-Government 45
B. Following EU Accession 45
VI. Constitutional Organs, Institutions and Public Offices 46
A. Organs of the State 46
B. State Institutions 46
C. Public Offices of the State 46
VII. Constitutional Review Mechanisms of Legislative and Executive Action, Including Investigatory Functions 47

Part I. Sources of Law 49

Chapter 1. Introduction 49

Chapter 2. External Sources: International Law 50

§1. Incorporation of International Law into Domestic Law 50

§2. Incorporation of International Customary Law 51

§3. Incorporation of International Treaties 51

Chapter 3. European Sources 55

§1. The Incorporation of EU Law into Domestic Law 56

§2. The Reception of EU Law into the Maltese Legal System 56

§3. European Union Directives 58

Chapter 4. Domestic Sources 59

§1. Introduction 59

§2. The Relevance of Sources to a Study of Maltese Constitutional Law 59

§3. Definition and Classification of Maltese Constitutional Law 59

§4. Characteristics of Maltese Constitutional Law 60

§5. The Sources of Maltese Constitutional Law in Concrete Form 61

I. Legal Sources of Maltese Constitutional Law 61
A. Legislation 61
1. Maltese Primary Constitutional Legislation 62
2. Maltese Subsidiary Constitutional Legislation 63
3. Maltese Constitutional Legislation 64
4. Foreign National Constitutional Legislation 66
5. European Legislation 68
6. International Legislation 68
B. Judicial Decisions 69
C. Official Publications Setting Out Rules and Procedures 70
D. General Principles of Maltese Constitutional Law 72
II. Non-legal Sources of Maltese Constitutional Law 72
A. Authoritative Works 72
B. Constitutional Practice 72

§6. Constitutional Annulment of Laws 73

I. The Actio Popularis 73
II. Section 6 of the Constitution 73
III. Section 46 of the Constitution 74
IV. Section 47 of the Constitution 74
V. Section 95 of the Constitution 74
VI. Emergency Powers Act 74
VII. European Convention Act 74
VIII. European Union Act 75
IX. Diplomatic Immunities and Privileges Act 75
X. Ultra vires Delegated Legislation 75

Chapter 5. Forms of Direct Democracy and Abrogative Referenda 76

§1. Popular Sovereignty 76

I. The Consultative Referendum 76
II. The Abrogative Referendum 77
III. The Constitutional Amendment Referendum 77
IV. Local Council Referenda 77

§2. Public Consultation 77

Part II. Form of Government 79

Chapter 1. Introduction to the Maltese System of Government 79

§1. The Maltese System of Government: An Outline 79

§2. The Political System 79

§3. The Social Forces 80

Chapter 2. The President of Malta 81

§1. The Election of President of Malta 81

§2. The Electoral Procedure 82

§3. Qualifications for Appointment 82

§4. Presidential Oath and Term of Office 83

I. President's Oath of Office 83
II. President's Term of Office 83

§5. The Status of the President: Holder of Multiple Roles 84

§6. The President as Guardian of the Constitution 84

§7. Temporary and Permanent Incapacity and Other Cases of Early Conclusion of the Presidential Term of Office 84

I. Dual or Multiple Citizenship 85
II. Infirmity of Body or Mind 85

§8. Replacement of President 85

§9. Reappointment of President 86

§10. Salary of the President of Malta 86

§11. Responsibility of the President 86

§12. President to Act Either on Advice or on Own Deliberate Judgment 87

I. Acting on Advice of the Government 87
II. Acting on Own Deliberate Judgment 88

§13. Powers Concerning the Parliamentary System 89

§14. Powers of Participation in the Activities of the Government 91

§15. Powers of Participation in the Activities of the Judiciary 96

§16. Functions Concerning International Relations 98

§17. Functions Concerning the Armed Forces of Malta 98

§18. Power to Confer Honours 101

§19. Functions of President under Other Laws 102

§20. President's Fora and Foundations 103

§21. The President and Philanthropy: The Community Chest Fund Foundation 103

§22. Concluding Remarks on the Presidency 104

Chapter 3. The Structure of Parliament 105

§1. The Unicameral System: An Introduction 105

§2. The Electoral System 107

§3. Electoral Divisions 107

§4. Suspension of a General Election 109

§5. Provisions Related to Conduct of Elections 109

§6. The Election of the House of Representatives 110

§7. Election Campaign Laws 113

§8. Qualifications of Members of Parliament 114

§9. Tenure of Office of MP 116

§10. Officers of the House of Representatives 117

§11. Parliamentary Privilege 118

§12. Standing Orders 119

§13. Pairing of Members of Parliament 120

§14. House Committees 120

§15. Visitors to the House of Representatives 121

§16. Direct Broadcasting of Parliamentary Sittings 122

§17. International Relations 123

Chapter 4. Parliament Its Activities 124

§1. The Pre-parliamentary Stage 124

§2. The Passing of Laws 124

§3. The Incorporation of Laws in a Revised Edition of the Laws of Malta 124

§4. The Different Procedures for Considering Bills 125

§5. The Promulgation and Publication of Laws 125

I. Postponement of Coming into Operation 125
II. Laws with Retrospective Effect 126

§6. The Legislative Process of Constitutional Laws 127

§7. Laws Delegating Legislative Powers 128

§8. Subsidiary Legislation Made under the Constitution 128

§9. Language of Laws 128

§10. Conflict Between Texts of the Law 129

§11. Political Control on the Government's Political Activities in Parliament 129

§12. Parliamentary Enquiries 129

§13. Parliamentary Hearings 130

§14. Links Between the House, the EU and Other International Organizations 130

Chapter 5. The Executive 131

§1. The Government: An Introduction 131

§2. Structure of Government 132

I. The Cabinet of Ministers 132
II. The Prime Minister 133
III. Ministers 133
IV. Acting Prime Minister 134
V. Temporary Ministers 134
VI. Parliamentary Secretaries 134
VII. Permanent Secretaries and Heads of Government Departments 135
VIII. Secretary to the Cabinet 136
IX. Cabinet Committees 137

§3. Government Formation 137

I. Caretaker Government 139
II. Recall of Parliament 139

§4. The Status and Responsibilities of Government Members 139

§5. Government Competencies 139

§6. Government and Political Parties 140

Chapter 6. Confidence in Parliament: The Relationship of Confidence 144

§1. A Motion of No Confidence 144

§2. A Contrary Vote on Government's Proposal 145

§3. The Question of Confidence 146

Chapter 7. The Judicial Power 147

Table of Contents

§1. The Judiciary is Subject Only to the Constitution, Laws and Customs of Malta 147

§2. The 'External' Independence of the Judiciary: Composition and Functions of the Commission for the Administration of Justice 148

§3. The Internal Independence of the Judiciary 149

§4. The Powers of the Minister Responsible for Justice 149

§5. The Organization of Justice in Malta: Civil and Criminal Jurisdiction 150

§6. Citizen Participation in the Administration of Justice 152

§7. Special Courts and Tribunals 153

§8. Officers of the Criminal Justice Sector 156

I. The Inquiring Magistrate 156
II. The Attorney General 156
III. The Advocate for Legal Aid 157

§9. Military Courts 157

§10. The Revisionary Function of Special Tribunals 158

§11. Judicial Activities and Constitutional Rights of Citizens 158

§12. Principles of Good Administrative Behaviour 159

Chapter 8. Judicial Control of Administrative Action 161

§1. Introduction 161

§2. Evolution of the Principle of Administrative Justice in Malta 161

§3. Powers and Limits of the Ordinary Judge Over the Public Administration 161

I. Section 32(2) of the Code of Organization and Civil Procedure 161
II. Section 469A of the Code of Organization and Civil Procedure 162

A. General Issues Relating to Judicial Review of Administrative Action 164
B. What Constitutes an 'Administrative Act'? 165
C. What Constitutes Any 'Measure Intended for Internal Organization or Administration Within the Said Authority' 165
D. What Constitutes a 'Public Authority'? 166
E. Section 469A(3) 166
F. Section 469A(4) 166
G. Section 469A(5) 166
H. Section 469A(6) 167

Chapter 9. The Constitutional Court 168

§1. Functions of the Constitutional Court 168

§2. Composition of the Constitutional Court 168

§3. The Origins of Constitutional Review of Legislation 170

§4. The Constitutional Reference 170

§5. The Constitutional Application 171

§6. Effects of the Constitutional Court's Decision 172

§7. Interpretative and Manipulative Judgments 172

§8. Disputes Between State Powers 172

§9. Decisions on the Admissibility of Referenda 173

Chapter 10. The Public Administration in the Constitution 174

§1. Duties and Powers of the Public Administration 174

§2. The Constitutional Principles Regulating Public Administration Activities 174

I. The Principle of Legality 174
II. The Principle of Full Respect to International Law 175
III. The Principles of Public Finance Law 175
IV. The Principle of Acting in the Public Interest 177

§3. Administrative Organs with Advisory and/or Control Functions 178

I. Advisory Administrative Organs 178
II. Control Administrative Organs 178
III. Advisory and Control Administrative Organs 178

§4. Independent Administrative Authorities 179

§5. Hierarchy of Independence of Regulators 179

Chapter 11. The Budget Process 180

§1. Fiscal Law versus Finance Law 180

§2. The Budget 181

§3. Other Financial Laws 181

§4. The Financial Institutional Framework: The Competent Authorities in Constitutional Public Finance Law 182

§5. Public Procurement 182

§6. Relevant EU Law to Public Procurement 182

§7. Remedies: Review and Supervisory Authorities 183

Part III. The State and Its Subdivisions 185

Chapter 1. Local Government 185

§1. The Origins of Maltese Local Self-Government 185

§2. Legal Principles Inspiring Local Self-Government Law 187

§3. Local Self-Governing Authorities in the Maltese Constitution 189

§4. Local Self-Government Authorities in the Local Councils Act 190

§5. The Creation of Regional Committees and Local Councils 191

§6. Organizational Structure of Local Self-Government 191

§7. The Organization of the Regions, Local Councils and Communities 191

I. Organization of Regional Government 191
II. Organization of Local Councils 192
III. Organization of Communities 192

§8. Competence of Regional Committees, Local Councils and Administrative Communities 193

I. Functions of Regional Committees 193
II. Functions of Local Councils 194
III. Functions of Communities 194

§9. General Aspects of Regional and Local Legislative Autonomy 195

§10. The Administrative Autonomy of Regional Committees and Local Councils from Central Government 196

I. The Administrative Autonomy of Regional Committees 196
II. The Administrative Autonomy of Local Councils 196
III. The Administrative Dependence of Administrative Committees on Local Councils 197
IV. Regulation of Human Resources 197

§11. The Financial Autonomy of the Regions and of Local Councils and Audit Functions 198

I. Financial Autonomy of Regional Committees 198
II. Financial Autonomy of Local Councils 198
III. Financial Autonomy of Administrative Committees 199
IV. Local Self-Government Financial Regulations 199

§12. The Relationship Between Central Government and Regional Committees, Local Councils and Administrative Committees 200

§13. The Electoral Process for Local Self-Government 200

§14. Local Self-Government Complaints Mechanism 201

§15. Local Self-Government Twinning Agreements 202

§16. Delegation of Functions to Local Self-Government 203

§17. Dissolution of Regional Committees and Local Councils 203

§18. Joint Committees of Local Councils 204

§19. LOCAL SELF-GOVERNMENT ENFORCEMENT SYSTEM 204

§20. LOCAL SELF-GOVERNMENT MACHINERY OF JUSTICE 205

§21. LOCAL COUNCILS ASSOCIATION 206

§22. LOCAL COUNCILS AND THE DEVELOPMENT PLANNING PROCESS 206

§23. PROHIBITION OF BROADCASTING BY LOCAL COUNCILS 207

§24. THE EU DIMENSION OF LOCAL SELF-GOVERNMENT: THE COMMITTEE OF THE REGIONS 207

§25. CONCLUDING REMARKS ON LOCAL SELF-GOVERNMENT 207

Part IV. Citizenship and Fundamental Rights 209

Chapter 1. Citizenship 209

§1. INTRODUCTION TO MALTESE CITIZENSHIP LAW 209

§2. THE CONSTITUTIONAL REGULATION OF CITIZENSHIP 210

§3. ACQUISITION OF CITIZENSHIP 211

I. Birth 211
A. On or After the Appointed Day 211
B. Before the Appointed Day 212
II. Marriage 212
A. On or after the Appointed Day 212
B. Before the Appointed Day 213
III. Illegitimate Children, Adopted Children and Foundlings 213
IV. Descent 213
V. Registration 214
VI. Naturalization 215

§4. POSSESSION OF CITIZENSHIP 216

§5. RENUNCIATION OF CITIZENSHIP 216

§6. DEPRIVATION OF CITIZENSHIP 216

I. Grounds for Deprivation of Citizenship 217
II. Procedure for Deprivation of Citizenship 217

§7. STATELESSNESS 218

§8. Dual or Multiple Citizenship 218

§9. Commonwealth Citizens 219

§10. Criminal Liability of Commonwealth Citizens 219

§11. European Union Citizenship 220

§12. The Individual Investor Programme 220

Chapter 2. The General Aspects of Fundamental Rights and Freedoms 223

§1. Introduction 223

§2. The Preambular Status of Section 32 of the Constitution 225

§3. The Inviolability of Constitutional Rights and Freedoms 226

§4. The Beneficiaries of Fundamental Rights and Freedoms 227

I. Physical Persons and Legal Persons 227
II. Citizens and Non-nationals 228

§5. The European Convention Act: An Adjunct to the Constitution 228

§6. Fundamental Rights under the Maltese Constitution and International Legal Norms 228

§7. European Multi-Level System for the Protection of Fundamental Rights and Freedoms 229

§8. Fundamental Rights and the European Convention of Human Rights 230

§9. The Principle of Equality 230

§10. Two Instruments for the Protection of Fundamental Rights and Freedoms 230

§11. Judicial Remedies for the Protection of Fundamental Rights and Freedoms 231

Chapter 3. Key Rights Enshrined in the Constitution 232

Table of Contents

§1. Introduction 232

§2. Historical Evolution and Sources of Chapter IV of the Constitution 233

§3. Preamble: Fundamental Rights and Freedoms of the Individual 233

§4. Structure of the Human Rights and Fundamental Freedoms Provisions: The Clawback Clause 234

§5. Protection of Right to Life 235

§6. Protection from Arbitrary Arrest or Detention 235

§7. Protection from Forced Labour 238

§8. Protection from Inhuman Treatment 238

§9. Protection from Deprivation of Property without Compensation 239

§10. Protection for Privacy of Home or Other Property 240

§11. Provisions to Secure Protection of Law 241

§12. Protection of Freedom of Conscience and Worship 243

§13. Protection of Freedom of Expression 243

§14. Protection of Freedom of Assembly and Association 244

§15. Prohibition of Deportation 245

§16. Protection of Freedom of Movement 245

§17. Protection from Discrimination on the Grounds of Race, Etc. 246

Part V. Specific Issues 249

Chapter 1. Relations Between the State and Religious Denominations 249

§1. Equality of Religious Denominations and Their Different Relations with the State 249

§2. Relations Between the State and the Catholic Church 249

I. Canon Law Influence on the Legal Relationship Between Church and State 249
II. The Constitution 250
III. Ordinary Laws 251
IV. Recent Trends in State: Church Relations 252
V. Agreements with the Vatican 253

§3. Relations Between the State and Other Religious Denominations 253

Chapter 2. The Economic Constitution 254

§1. The Way to a Mixed Economy 254

§2. Economic Principles in the Constitution 254

I. The Encouragement of Private Economic Enterprise 255
II. The Protection of Artisan Trades 255
III. The Encouragement of Co-operatives 255

§3. Freedom of Private Economic Enterprise 255

I. The Business Promotion Act 256
II. The Small Enterprises (Loan Guarantee) Act 256
III. The Malta Enterprise Act 256
IV. The Small Business Act 257

§4. Co-operative Societies and Handicraft 258

I. Co-operative Societies 258
II. Crafts 259

§5. Ownership in the Maltese Constitution 260

§6. Public Ownership 261

§7. Private Ownership 263

§8. Expropriation and Partial Expropriation 263

Chapter 3. Constitutional Principles Relating to the Armed Forces 265

§1. The Maltese Constitution and the Deployment of the Armed Forces 265

§2. Military Service 265

§3. The Organization of the Armed Forces 266

§4. The Command Structure 266

§5. Police Powers 267

§6. Parliamentary Control of the Armed Forces of Malta 268

Selected Bibliography 269

Index 281

List of Abbreviations

AD	Alternattiva Demokratika (Green Party)
CHOGM	Commonwealth Heads of Government Meeting
CJEU	Court of Justice of the European Union
Constitution	Constitution of Malta
DOI	Department of Information
EAW	European Arrest Warrant
ECHR	European Convention on Human Rights
ECtHR	European Court of Human Rights
ETC	Employment and Training Corporation
EU	European Union
EU Charter	European Union Charter of Fundamental Rights
FSS	Final Settlement System
Gazette	The Malta Government Gazette
House	House of Representatives
ICJ	International Court of Justice
LESA	Local Enforcement Systems Agency
LLD	Doctor of Laws
LP	Labour Party (otherwise known as 'Malta Labour Party' MLP)
LNTS	League of Nations Treaty Series
LOSC	United Nations Law of the Sea Convention 1982
MEP	Member of the European Parliament
MEPA	Malta Environment and Planning Authority
MLP	Malta Labour Party
MP	Member of Parliament
PAC	Public Accounts Committee
PEG	Publishers Enterprises Group
PhD	Doctor of Philosophy
PN	Nationalist Party
President	President of Malta

PSC	Public Service Commission
Speaker	Speaker of the House of Representatives
TFEU	Treaty on the Functioning of the European Union (Lisbon Treaty)
UK	United Kingdom
UNTS	United Nations Treaty Series
USA	United States of America

General Introduction

Chapter 1. Historical Outline of the Constitution of Malta

§1. An Introduction to Maltese Constitutional History

1. To write the history of the Constitution of Malta deserves a book in its own right. However, in brief, Malta has been a colony of several great powers such as the Romans, the Arabs, the Normans, the Knights of St John, the French and, more recently, the British.[1] The historical journey of Malta as an independent state culminates on 21 September 1964, the date which was appointed by Queen Elizabeth II of the United Kingdom (UK) for Malta's independence. Prior to attaining independence, Malta was a United Kingdom colony. The British came to Malta in 1800 following a request to that effect by the local inhabitants and they held control over Malta till 20 September 1964. Malta is thus a relatively newcomer to the international community of states with a life history of fifty-three years. However, although from a historical perspective, fifty-three years might seem to constitute too short a time span, these fifty-three years have proved to be quite eventful. Landmark dates include 13 December 1974 when Malta became a republic and 1 May 2004 when Malta acceded to the European Union (EU). Malta had also joined, earlier, the United Nations and several of its specialized agencies, the Council of Europe, other international and regional institutions, including courts and tribunals, whilst it established various bodies and offices which did not exist in colonial times such as an elaborate national system of local self-government, an Ombudsman and a Central Bank of Malta, a thriving maritime, financial services, gaming and aircraft registration, and film industry. It also strengthened other institutions which existed under British rule such as the Broadcasting Authority, the Director of Audit (subsequently re-designated in the Constitution as 'Auditor General'), developed a myriad of Standing and Select Committees for the House of Representatives, set up several corporations, commissions, boards, quasi-judicial tribunals and other institutions which were inexistent fifty-three years ago.

1. *See* Hugh W. Harding, 'Law', in Henry Frendo and Oliver Friggieri (eds), *Malta: Culture and Identity*, Ministry of Youth and the Arts, Floriana, 1994, pp. 205–217; and Kevin Aquilina, 'Rethinking Maltese Legal Hybridity: A Chimeric Illusion or a Healthy Grafted European Law Mixture?', *Journal of Civil Law Studies*, Vol. 4, 2011, pp. 261–283.

§2. THE 1964 INDEPENDENCE CONSTITUTION OF MALTA

2. The independence Constitution of Malta of 1964 was made up of eleven chapters and two Schedules as follows:

(1) Chapter I The State
(2) Chapter II Declaration of Principles
(3) Chapter III Citizenship
(4) Chapter IV Fundamental Rights and Freedoms of the Individual
(5) Chapter V The Governor-General
(6) Chapter VI Parliament
(7) Chapter VII The Executive
(8) Chapter VIII The Judiciary
(9) Chapter IX Finance
(10) Chapter X The Public Service
(11) Chapter XI Miscellaneous
(12) First Schedule [The Five Codes][2]
(13) Second Schedule Oath of Allegiance.

2. The five codes are the Criminal Code, Chapter 9 of the Laws of Malta, the Code of Police Laws, Chapter 10 of the Laws of Malta, the Code of Organization and Civil Procedure, Chapter 12 of the Laws of Malta, the Commercial Code, Chapter 13 of the Laws of Malta, and the Civil Code, Chapter 16 of the Laws of Malta.

Chapter 2. The Demographic and Population Features of the Maltese Republican Constitution

§1. Demographics and Population

3. Malta is the smallest Member State in the EU in terms of both geography and demography. The total area of Malta is 246 square kilometres.[3] It is situated in the centre of the Mediterranean and, in this respect, forms part of two geographic regions: Europe and the Mediterranean. Insofar as Europe is concerned, Malta is situated at the southernmost part of Europe next to Sicily. The distance between Malta and the nearest point in Sicily is 93 kilometres. On the other hand, the nearest point on the North African mainland is 288 kilometres.

4. The population of Malta is 425,384 as at 2013.[4] The Maltese are very much of a homogenous people all speaking one language. The majority of the population – 94.1% – is Maltese.[5]

§2. Characteristics of the Maltese State

I. Constitutionalism

A. The Juridical Status of the Constitution of Malta

5. The Constitution is the highest law of the archipelago.[6] All other laws are subservient thereto.[7] The Constitution is considered to be supreme law because it establishes the principal organs of the State of Malta – the Legislature (Parliament), the Executive (Government) and the Judiciary (Courts). Primarily, it is these three organs of the state which govern Malta. The Constitution further establishes a number of Constitutional Commissions – Electoral Commission, PSC, Employment Commission and Commission for the Administration of Justice – and the Broadcasting Authority, Public Service, Officers of Parliament (Auditor General, Deputy Auditor General and

3. Stanley J.A. Clews, *Malta Year Book 2003*, De La Salle Brothers Publications, Sliema, 2003, p. 50.
4. National Statistics Office, *Demographic Review 2013*, National Statistics Office, Valletta, 2015, p. ix.
5. *Ibid.*
6. The text of the Constitution of Malta (hereinafter 'Constitution') is available at http://www.justiceservices.gov.mt/DownloadDocument.aspx?app=lom&itemid=8566&l=1. Last accessed on 31 March 2016.
7. All the Laws of Malta are published on the Ministry responsible for justice's website http://www.justiceservices.gov.mt/LOM.aspx?pageid=24. Last accessed on 31 March 2016.

Ombudsman) and several public officers (Attorney General, Secretary to the Cabinet, Permanent Secretaries, and Ambassadors including High Commissioners and Permanent Representatives. It also establishes a system of local government. The part dealing with Parliament establishes the House of Representatives, and the offices of Speaker, Deputy Speaker and Clerk to the House; the part dealing with the Executive establishes the offices of Prime Minister, Ministers and Parliamentary Secretaries; the part dealing with the Judiciary establishes judicial offices of Chief Justice, Judges and Magistrates. The Constitution also establishes the office of President of Malta, the highest ranking officer serving the Republic. In a nutshell, the most important institutions and offices of state for the governance of Malta are established by the Constitution together with their respective powers and functions. In turn, the Constitution is supplemented by various laws of a constitutional nature even if it remains the most important constitutional document. It is also supreme to all other laws, and these laws have to give in should there be a conflict between them and the Constitution.[8] Parliament, even if the most supreme of all the organs established by the Constitution, is still subject to the Constitution. This emerges from the constitutional provisions and from the doctrine of the rule of law. It is the Constitution which establishes Parliament, regulates its powers and functions, and limits its supremacy with regard to the other organs and institutions of the state. Although it is Parliament which ultimately has the power to alter the Constitution it can do so *only* subject to the provisions of the Constitution.[9] At certain instances, its powers cannot be exercised independently: there are indeed cases where Parliament's sovereignty is restricted by the Constitution as two particular provisions can be amended following a referendum.[10] In those cases where it is only Parliament which can alter the law, there is a procedure which has to be followed so that the necessary alterations can be approved.[11] There are also other instances where the exercise of its law-making powers is subject to judicial review by the Courts,[12] not to mention situations where the law-making power is vested in the Executive, even if this is done with Parliament's assent.[13] Finally, there are cases where the people, through an abrogative referendum, can repeal certain laws or provisions made by Parliament itself.[14]

B. The Supremacy of the Constitution of Malta

6. The main provisions of the Constitution of Malta which render Parliament subservient to the Constitution of Malta are the following:

(a) section 6;
(b) section 46(2);
(c) section 47(9);

8. Constitution, sections 6, 46(2), 47(9), 95(2)(e) and 116.
9. *Ibid.*, section 66.
10. *Ibid.*, section 66(3).
11. Constitution, section 66.
12. *Ibid.*, sections 6, 46(2), 47(9), 95(2)(e) and 116.
13. *Ibid.*, section 78(3).
14. Referenda Act, Chapter 237 of the Laws of Malta, sections 13–20.

(d) section 65(1);
(e) section 66;
(f) section 95(2)(e); and
(g) section 116.

7. Other provisions exist in the Constitution where Parliament's legislative functions are totally taken over by other entities established by the Constitution or else established by ordinary law but conferring overriding powers over Parliament.

1. Section 6 of the Constitution of Malta

8. Section 6 of the Constitution of Malta states that: 'Subject to the provisions of subsections (7) and (9) of section 47 and of section 66 of this Constitution, if any other law is inconsistent with this Constitution, this Constitution shall prevail and the other law shall, to the extent of the inconsistency, be void.'

9. First, section 6 does not restrict itself only to inconsistency with any provision of Chapter IV of the Constitution dealing with human rights and fundamental freedoms. On the contrary, section 6 subjects all laws (other than the Constitution) to consistency with all the provisions of the Constitution except for those contained in section 47(7) and (9) and section 66. 'Law' is defined in the Constitution as 'any instrument having the force of law and any unwritten law'. 'Law' thus includes subsidiary legislation (regulations, rules, orders, bye-laws, schemes, warrants, etc.) and customary law such as usages of trade.

10. Second, once the competent courts of constitutional competence – the Constitutional Court and the Civil Court, First Hall, sitting in its constitutional competence – come to the conclusion that another law is inconsistent with the Constitution of Malta, such courts are bound, in terms of section 6, to note that the other law is void. The term 'note' not 'declare' is used because it is not the court's judgment which renders void the inconsistent law: it is the Constitution in section 6 that does so. The marginal note to section 6 reads: 'Constitution to be supreme law.' Although at law normally marginal notes are not used for interpretation purposes, the marginal note in question is a very apt and faithful synopsis of the provision in question.

11. Third, the concept of a 'void' law has to be contrasted with that of an 'invalid' law. Section 116 of the Constitution allows a 'right of action for a declaration that any law is invalid on any grounds other than inconsistency with the provisions of sections 33 to 45 of this Constitution'. A similar provision is found in section 95(2)(e). Invalidity, to have effect, requires an express declaration to that effect in a court judgment. However, this is not the case with a void law because the inconsistent law is void *ab initio* and *ipso jure*. The Constitution establishes a hierarchy of nullity of laws – the most superior being void laws followed by invalid laws. Void laws and invalid laws therefore produce different effects at law. The Constitution uses four terms: 'inconsistency', 'void', 'invalid' and 'in contravention of'.[15] The term 'nullity' is not used (although the term 'annulled' is used with regard to elections).[16] Void, in law, has more serious

15. For the distinction between the expressions 'inconsistent with' and 'in contravention of', *see* Kevin Aquilina, 'Constitutional Symbols', *The Times of Malta*, 14 August, 2015, p. 16.
16. Constitution, section 56(6) and (7).

consequences than 'invalid' because in the case of section 6, the inconsistent law is *ex lege* void without necessarily requiring a pronouncement by a court of constitutional jurisdiction declaring the inconsistent law to be void. The inconsistent law is inherently void by its very own nature: although it remains on the statute book, once it is inconsistent with the Constitution, even if no court has taken note of such a state of affairs, it has *ipso jure* no legal effect, nor can it produce any such legal effect: it is unenforceable and is a dead letter. Therefore, such law has no binding effect and nobody (courts, government, public administration, any person) should follow its command. As the Roman adage runs: *quod nullum est, nullum producit effectum.*

12. Void implies that the provision is by its very own ontological essence an absolute nullity. Once a law is void, it binds nobody and does not require a court declaration to that effect. If there is a court judgment noting that such inconsistent law is void, that court judgment obviously binds the parties thereto in terms of section 237 of the Code of Organization and Civil Procedure,[17] and that same judgment also binds third parties, not by virtue of section 237 but, insofar as third parties are bound by the operation of section 6 of the Constitution. In law, a distinction is made between 'void' and 'voidable': the latter term means that a law or a provision in a law is valid until it is annulled. Whilst voidable requires a pronouncement by a court so that a provision or a law is declared by a court judgment to be void, what is inherently void requires no court pronouncement other than the word of the law to that effect. In this respect, an inconsistent law is void *ab initio* and not when it is so declared by the competent constitutional court. The court's pronouncement that an inconsistent law is void is an indication of the legal status of that inconsistent law. Indeed, it is not the court's judgment that makes the provision void even though this has practical relevance as it is through such authoritative pronouncement that the community gets to know that an inconsistent law is void. The court's decision simply takes note of a situation of fact as it obtains when the judgment is delivered.

13. However, the court's judgment is retroactive in effect as it recognizes that the inconsistent law was void not only at the time of the delivery of the judgment but also at the time the inconsistent law was enacted (*ab initio*). This is but a manifestation of the Constitution's supremacy over Parliament. The Constitution uses its inbuilt defensive mechanism to strike down any law enacted by Parliament which is inconsistent with the Constitution and without, in reality, needing to have recourse to the judicial organ of the state to declare the inconsistent law void. So although the other law can be inconsistent and void – and these are two different concepts – they are closely interlinked to each other from a constitutional point of view: inconsistency with the Constitution makes a law void; the inconsistency has to do with the juridical nature of the norm whilst a void law concerns the effects of the inconsistency of the norm. The supremacy of the Constitution over Parliament is further manifested through the court's declaration of invalidity of a law in terms of sections 95(2)(e) and 116 of the Constitution.

14. Fourth, foreign courts and authors have adopted this same interpretation. The German Federal Constitutional Court has held that an unconstitutional law is

17. Article 237 reads as follows: 'A judgment shall not operate to the prejudice of any person who neither personally nor through the person under whom he claims nor through his lawful agent was party to the cause determined by such judgment.'

'inconsistent with the Basic Law and therefore invalid'.[18] As Klaus Schlaich states an 'unconstitutional law is from its inception (*ex tunc*) and without need for any further act (*ipso iure*) inoperative ... The German view is that the Federal Constitutional Court does not annul a statute, (the Court) does not invalidate: it merely establishes the invalidity (in a declaratory way).'[19] By the same token, the South African Constitutional Court has declared that 'laws are objectively valid or invalid depending on whether they are or are not inconsistent with the Constitution. The fact that a dispute concerning inconsistency may only be decided years afterwards, does not affect the objective nature of the invalidity'.[20]

2. Section 46(2) of the Constitution of Malta

15. The courts of constitutional competence, if they use their powers under the Constitution judiciously, are in a very strong position to safeguard human rights because the Constitution gives them full powers to do so including, if need be, ordering the disobedience of a law made by Parliament.[21] Such wide powers are found in section 46(2) of the Constitution which reads as follows:

> The Civil Court, First Hall, ... may make such orders, issue such writs and give such directions as it may consider appropriate for the purpose of enforcing, or securing the enforcement of, any of the provisions of the said articles 33 to 45 (inclusive) to the protection of which the person concerned is entitled.

3. Section 47(9) of the Constitution of Malta

16. Section 47 of the Constitution relates to protection from deprivation of property without compensation. It provides in sub-Article (9) that:

> Nothing in article 37 of the Constitution shall affect the operation of any law in force immediately before 3rd March 1962 or any law made on or after that date that amends or replaces any law in force immediately before that date (or such a law as from time to time amended or replaced in the manner described in this sub-article) and that does not –
>
> a. add to the kinds of property that may be taken possession of or the rights over and interests in property that may be acquired;

---

18. Klaus Schlaich, *Das Bundesverfassungsgericht*, 3rd edn, Verlag C.H. Beck, Munich, 1994, pp. 220–221.
19. *Ibid.*
20. *Ibid.*
21. For a list of measures adopted by the court of constitutional jurisdiction short of annulling a law, *see* Kevin Aquilina, 'Remedies under Maltese Law for Wrongful State Action in Breach of EU Law: A Case of Crying Over Spilt Milk?', in Eugène Buttigieg (ed.), *Enforcing One's Rights Under EU Law*, Gutenberg Press, Tarxien, 2011, especially p. 103.

b. add to the purposes for which or circumstances in which such property may be taken possession of or acquired;

c. make the conditions governing entitlement to compensation or the amount thereof less favourable to any person owning or interested in the property; or

d. deprive any person of any right such as is mentioned in paragraph (b) or paragraph (c) of article 37(1) of this Constitution.

4. Section 65(1) of the Constitution of Malta

17. Section 65(1) of the Constitution concerns Parliament's law-making function It is this provision of the Constitution which defines Parliament's *vires* in enacting laws. In particular, it directs Parliament to make laws 'for the peace, order and good government of Malta'. The latter concept of 'good government' is applicable to Parliament, but there is no corresponding provision whereby Cabinet is bound by a system of good governance even though the Ombudsman has championed this principle.

18. If Parliament's primary law-making function is curtailed by the Constitution as provided in section 65(1), it is more than evident that Parliament is subservient to the Constitution. Parliament's law-making function is limited by all the other provisions of the Constitution and by all the qualifiers in section 65(1). Hence the laws enacted by Parliament must comply with these qualifiers as otherwise they can be annulled by a court of constitutional jurisdiction.

5. Section 66 of the Constitution of Malta

19. Section 66 of the Constitution prescribes its amending mechanism:

1. Subject to the provisions of this article, Parliament may alter any of the provisions of this Constitution and (in so far as it forms part of the law of Malta) any of the provisions of the Malta Independence Act, 1964.

2. In so far as it alters -

a. this article; or

b. Article 1, sub-article (2) of Article 2, sub-article (1) of Article 3, sub-article (1) of Article 5, Article 6, Articles 32-48 (inclusive), Articles 51, 52, 56, 57, 60, 61 and 64A, sub-article (3) of Article 65, sub-article (2) of Article 75, Article 76 (other than sub-article (2) thereof), Articles 77 and 78, Article 80, Article 91,

Articles 95-100 (inclusive), Articles 102-110 (inclusive), Articles 113, 114, 115A, 118, 119 or 120 of this Constitution; or

c. Article 124 of this Constitution in its application to any of the provisions specified in paragraph (a) or (b) of this sub-article,

a bill for an Act of Parliament under this article shall not be passed in the House of Representatives unless at the final voting thereon in that House it is supported by the votes of not less than two-thirds of all the members of the House.

3. In so far as it alters -

a. this sub-article or sub-article (4) of this article; or

b. sub-article (2) of article 76 of this Constitution,

a bill for an Act of Parliament under this article shall not be presented to the President for his assent unless not less than three nor more than six months after its passage through the House in the manner specified in sub-article (2) of this article it has been submitted to the electors qualified to vote for the election of members of the House of Representatives and the majority of the electors voting have approved the bill.

20. In this section, Parliament's hands are tied down as how to alter the Constitution. Parliament is so much subservient to the Constitution that, apart from the requirement of an absolute or at least a two-thirds majority vote to change the Constitution, there are two provisions which can be amended *only* following popular support where a majority has to be garnered in a referendum. Nevertheless, it must be observed that whilst in the independence Constitution there were by far more provisions which required popular endorsement for alteration, in the republican Constitution these have shrunk to two instances – the duration of the lifespan of Parliament[22] and the provision regulating the alteration of the deeply entrenched provision of the Constitution.[23] The deeply entrenched provision also regulates the procedure to be adopted by voters when called upon to vote on such bill, that is, voting has to be by ballot, by secret vote, without recourse to voting by proxy and in such manner as Parliament may prescribe.

22. Constitution, section 76(2).
23. *Ibid.*, section 66(3).

6. Section 95(2)(e) of the Constitution of Malta

21. The Constitution empowers the Constitutional Court to strike down laws made by Parliament:

> 2. One of the Superior Courts, ... shall be known as the Constitutional Court and shall have jurisdiction to hear and determine ...
>
> e. appeals from decisions of any court of original jurisdiction in Malta on questions as to the validity of laws other than those which may fall under article 46 of this Constitution.

22. Whilst Parliament may repeal laws, an abrogative referendum can, in certain specified cases, also abrogate a law. The Constitutional Court can declare laws invalid, and such invalidity need not necessarily relate to constitutional invalidity such as when the Constitutional Court declares regulations made by a constitutional commission to lack the necessary *vires* to make such regulations, thereby rendering them *ultra vires*.

7. Section 116 of the Constitution of Malta

23. The *actio popularis* (the people's action) is enshrined in section 116 of the Constitution:

> A right of action for a declaration that any law is invalid on any grounds other than inconsistency with the provisions of articles 33 to 45 of this Constitution shall appertain to all persons without distinction and a person bringing such an action shall not be required to show any personal interest in support of his action.

24. Through the institution of this action, a court of constitutional competence may declare a law enacted by Parliament invalid.[24]

II. The Rule of Law

25. Although the Constitution does not expressly refer to the doctrine of the rule of law, it is embedded within it. The rule or supremacy of law in its present formulation gained currency through the work of Albert Venn Dicey's *An Introduction to the Study of the Law of the Constitution.*[25]

---

24. A case where the popular action has been resorted to, though unsuccessfully, is *Darryl Francis Grima pro et noe v. Prime Minister et noe*, Constitutional Court, 21 June 1988.
25. Albert Venn Dicey, *An Introduction to the Study of the Law of the Constitution,* 10th edn, The Macmillan Press Ltd., London, 1959. *See* David Joseph Attard with the assistance of Kevin Aquilina and Patricia Mallia, *The Maltese Legal System, Volume II, Constitutional and Human Rights Law*, Part A, Malta University Press, Msida, 2015, pp. 8–14.

26. Tom Bingham, on the other hand, considers the key components of the rule of law to be the following:

(a) the law must be accessible and so far as possible intelligible, clear and predictable;
(b) questions of legal right and liability should ordinarily be resolved by application of the law and not the exercise of discretion;
(c) the laws of the land should apply equally to all, save to the extent that objective differences justify differentiation;
(d) ministers and public officers at all levels must exercise their powers conferred on them in good faith, fairly, for the purpose for which the powers were conferred, without exceeding the limits of such powers and not unreasonably;
(e) the law must afford adequate protection of fundamental human rights;
(f) means must be provided for resolving, without prohibitive cost or inordinate delays, bona fide civil disputes which the parties themselves are unable to resolve;
(g) adjudicative procedures provided by the state should be fair;
(h) the rule of law requires compliance by the state with its obligations in international law as in national law.[26]

27. If the above were to be applied to Malta, it is clear that a constitutional tenant is that the rule of law is fundamental to the governance to the state and that the rule of law can be implied from a reading of the Constitution's provisions, not because the Constitution, by express words, states so but because this can be deduced by necessary intendment. For instance, the Judicial Committee of the Privy Council has held, with regard to similar Westminster Constitutions like the Maltese, that Westminster Constitutions are based on the rule of law.[27]

III. The Separation of Powers

28. Aristotle is said to have come up with the political doctrine of the separation of powers when he wrote in *The Politics* that:

> There are three elements in each constitution in respect of which every serious lawgiver must look for what is advantageous to it; if these are well arranged, the constitution is bound to be well arranged, and the differences in constitutions are bound to correspond to the differences between each of these elements. The three are, first the deliberative, which discusses everything of common importance; second, the officials ...; and third, the judicial element.[28]

---

26. *See* Tom Bingham, *The Rule of Law*, Penguin Books, London, 2011.
27. *See Ahnee, Sydney Selvon and Le Mauricien Ltd. v. Director of Public Prosecutions (Mauritus)* [1999] UKPC 11 (17 March 1999) and *Brantley and Others (Appellants) v. Constituency Boundaries Commission and Others (Respondents) (Saint Christopher and Nevis)* [2015] UKPC 21, 11 May 2015.
28. Aristotle (384–322 BC), *The Politics*, Bk iv, xiv, 1297b35.

29. It was however Charles Louis de Secondat, otherwise known as Baron de Montesquieu, who in his 1748 *L'Esprit des Lois*[29] conceived the doctrine as a stratagem to prevent the abuse of power through the concentration of power itself into one or more organs of the state without any adequate form of checks and balances by the other organs of the state. As Montesquieu succinctly put it:

> When the legislative and executive powers are united in the same person, or in the same body of magistrates, there can be no liberty; because apprehensions may arise, lest the same monarch or senate should enact tyrannical laws, to execute them in a tyrannical manner.
>
> Again, there is no liberty, if the judicial power be not separated from the legislative and executive. Were it were joined with the legislature, the life and liberty of the subject would be exposed to arbitrary control; for the judge would be then the legislator. Were it were joined to the executive power, the judge might behave with violence and oppression. There would be an end of everything, were the same man or the same body, whether of the nobles or of the people, to exercise these three powers, that of enacting the laws, that of executing the public resolutions, and of trying the causes of individuals.[30]

30. The doctrine of the separation of powers is more of a political rather than a legal concept. This is because the Constitution of Malta, a Westminster-modelled Constitution, does not refer explicitly to this doctrine. Nevertheless, there are aspects thereof which are enshrined in the Constitution even if one has to search all over the constitutional document to figure out where they are found and even if the Constitution has not adopted to the letter Montesquieu's theory as the separation of powers as adopted in Malta is more in the form of a system of checks and balances rather than a strict separation of powers. Evidence of the doctrine is found in the fact that the Constitution establishes three principal organs of the state: the Legislature, the Executive and the Judiciary. It further sets out their distinct composition and functions and their inter-relationship.[31]

IV. The Independence of the Judiciary

31. As David Joseph Attard maintains, 'the independence of the judiciary is a constitutional doctrine and its elements are found in the Constitution itself'.[32] It is ascertained from a number of provisions set out in the Constitution as evidenced below:

29. Translation: 'The Spirit of the Laws'. Charles-Louis de Secondat, Baron de Montesqieu, *The Spirit of Laws*, New York, Prometheus Books, 2002.
30. *Ibid.*, Volume I, Book XI, Chapter 6, pp. 151–152.
31. For a discussion of the doctrine of the separation of powers, *see* David Joseph Attard, *supra* note 25, pp. 4–8.
32. David Joseph Attard, *supra* note 25, p. 62 and pp. 63–66.

(a) a judge of the Superior Courts and a Magistrate of the Inferior Courts cannot be removed from office except by 'the President upon an address by the House of Representatives supported by the votes of not less than two-thirds of all the members thereof and praying for such removal on the ground of proved inability to perform the functions of his office (whether arising from infirmity of body or mind or any other cause) or proved misbehaviour';[33]
(b) there can be no abolition of office in the case of the higher judiciary, though not in the case of the lower judiciary;[34]
(c) the salaries and allowances payable to judges and magistrates constitute a charge on the Consolidated Fund;[35]
(d) the salary (other than allowances) payable to a judge or a magistrate, and his/her terms of office, cannot be altered to his/her disadvantage after his/her appointment;[36]
(e) the provisions in the Constitution related to appointment, removal and discipline over public officers do not apply to judges and magistrates[37] even though the judiciary are public officers in terms of the Constitution;[38]
(f) the concurrence of the PSC is not required for the removal from office of judges and magistrates who have been found guilty of misbehaviour so as not to subject the judiciary to the PSC;[39]
(g) no person or authority may require a judge or magistrate to retire from the public service;[40] and
(h) the Constitution allows the judiciary to carry out their constitutional and legal duties independently of any other person or body when it vests in them the final say in determining the functions listed in, *inter alia*, sections 6, 46, 55, 56, 63, 95, 101A and 116 of the Constitution.

V. National Sovereignty

32. The State of Malta exercises its sovereignty in various ways. First, it enacts laws which bind over its own territory.[41] Second, it also enacts extra-territorial legislation.[42] Third, it has its own sovereign national institutions which are responsible

33. Constitution, sections 97(2) and 100(4).
34. *Ibid.*, section 95(6).
35. Constitution, section 107(2).
36. *Ibid.*, section 107(3).
37. *Ibid.*, section 110(5)(a).
38. *Ibid.*, section 124(2).
39. *Ibid.*, section 114(2).
40. *Ibid.*, section 124(7) proviso (a).
41. The expression 'Malta' is defined by section 124(1) of the Constitution as meaning 'the Island of Malta, the Island of Gozo and the other islands of the Maltese Archipelago, including the territorial waters thereof'.
42. For example, section 5(1) of the Criminal Code, Chapter 9 of the Laws of Malta, section 27 of the Official Secrets Act, Chapter 50 of the Laws of Malta; section 19 of the Civil Aviation Act, Chapter 232 of the Laws of Malta; and sections 5 and 8 of the Extradition Act, Chapter 276 of the Laws of Malta.

for the governance of the state – the three principal organs of the state and other state organs established by the Constitution or by ordinary law.

A. Making of Extra-Territorial Legislation

33. Although the Constitution mentions the making of laws for Malta, the UK Malta Independence Act 1964 has a provision which reads as follows:

> The legislature of Malta shall have full power to make laws having extra-territorial operation.[43]

B. Meaning of Sovereignty

34. Sovereignty implies that Malta possesses independence from other states and can exercise its right to self-determination, that is, 'the right of all peoples to govern themselves'.[44] Being sovereign means that Malta is equal and at par to other states,[45] and that it is empowered to exercise acts of dominion over its territory and over its subjects, in the latter case, also wherever they might be, whether in Malta or abroad. A characteristic feature of sovereignty is that Malta, like any other state, has exclusive control over its domestic affairs and, in terms of Article 2(7) of the United Nations Charter, the United Nations cannot 'intervene in matters which are essentially within the domestic jurisdiction of any state or shall require the members to submit to such matters to settlement under the present Charter'.[46] However, being sovereign does not mean that the state or its organs and institutions are above the law; otherwise, sovereignty would end up in conflict with the doctrine of the rule of law which pervades Maltese Constitutional Law. Nevertheless, sovereignty does admit of immunities such

---

43. United Kingdom, Malta Independence Act 1964, Schedule 1, paragraph 3.
44. Patrick Thornberry, 'The Principle of Self-Determination', in Vaughan Lowe and Colin Warbrick (eds), *The United Nations and the Principles of International Law: Essays in Memory of Michael Akehurst*, Routledge, London, 1994, pp. 175–203 at p. 175.
45. Colin Warbrick, 'The Principle of Sovereign Equality', in Vaughan Lowe and Colin Warbrick (eds), *supra* note 44, pp. 204–229.
46. Bruno Simma (ed.), *The Charter of the United Nations: A Commentary*, Oxford, Oxford University Press, 1994, pp. 139–154. Vaughan Lowe, 'The Principle of Non-intervention: Use of Force', in Vaughan Lowe and Colin Warbrick (eds), *supra* note 44, pp. 66–84 and Dominic McGoldrick, 'The Principle of Non-intervention: Human Rights', in Vaughan Lowe and Colin Warbrick (eds), *supra* note 44, pp. 85–119.

as those enjoyed by diplomats,[47] Members of Parliament,[48] the President of Malta[49] and the judiciary.[50]

35. Once Malta is sovereign within its territory, it has the power to admit and to expel aliens. The Constitution states in section 43(3) that: 'No citizen of Malta shall be removed from Malta except as a result of extradition proceedings or under any such law as is referred to in Article 44(3)(b) of this Constitution.' This means that whilst Maltese citizens cannot be deported, aliens can. Further, the Immigration Act[51] allows for the deportation of non-citizens whilst the Extradition Act[52] and the European Arrest Warrant (EAW)[53] regulate the transfer of both Maltese and foreign citizens.

36. Being sovereign in one's territory ensures that a state enjoys jurisdiction over crimes committed within its territory. The Criminal Code, in section 5(1)(a), provides, in this respect that:

> 5. (1) Saving any other special provision of this Code or of any other law conferring jurisdiction upon the courts in Malta to try offences, a criminal action may be prosecuted in Malta -
>
> a. against any person who commits an offence in Malta, or on the sea in any place within the territorial jurisdiction of Malta.

37. Sovereignty does however impose a number of duties which a state owes to its citizenry and which it exercises over its territory. One of these duties is that it has to protect its citizens wherever they might be and not to refuse them entry when travelling back home.

C. *Limitations on Sovereignty*

38. Although Malta is a sovereign state, there are a number of limitations imposed upon its sovereignty. These limitations are self-imposed and normally arise

47. The Diplomatic Immunities and Privileges Act, Chapter 191 of the Laws of Malta, and the Consular Convention Act, Chapter 144 of the Laws of Malta.
48. Section 65(2)-(5) of the Constitution and the House of Representatives (Privileges and Powers) Ordinance, Chapter 113 of the Laws of Malta.
49. Section 5(1) of the Criminal Code, Chapter 9 of the Laws of Malta, and Article 742A of the Code of Organization and Civil Procedure, Chapter 12 of the Laws of Malta.
50. The judiciary enjoy immunity from civil suit in certain cases. *See* Kevin Aquilina, *supra* note 21, pp. 98–101 whilst certain judicial proceedings are considered to be privileged publications (Press Act, Chapter 248 of the Laws of Malta, section 33(d) and the Judicial Proceedings (Regulation of Reports) Act, Chapter 60 of the Laws of Malta, section 5).
51. Chapter 217 of the Laws of Malta.
52. Chapter 276 of the Laws of Malta.
53. Extradition (Designated Foreign Countries) Order, Subsidiary Legislation 276.05. *See also* Stefano Filletti, *Significant Developments in EU Criminal Law and Their Impact on Maltese Criminal Law*, PhD thesis, Faculty of Laws, University of Malta, Msida, November 2015, pp. 93–96, 163–181 and 212–228.

as a result of adherence to a treaty or other similar agreements. Once Malta opts to adhere to a treaty, then its sovereignty is restricted by the provisions of that treaty. Malta is a member of the United Nations, the Commonwealth of Nations, the Council of Europe and the EU apart from several other United Nations specialized agencies and other international and regional organizations which have their own rules and regulations to follow. Malta is also under the jurisdiction, *inter alia*, of several other international courts and tribunals such as the ECtHR, the Court of Justice of the EU, the General Court, the International Court of Justice (ICJ), the International Criminal Court and the International Tribunal for the Law of the Sea. Each time Malta enters into a treaty arrangement, it cedes a portion of its sovereignty with regard to the subject matter of that treaty. But even the other states which are parties to that treaty lose correspondingly their sovereignty as well. Perhaps it might be more precise to state that in such cases, Malta shares its sovereignty with other states and/or with the institutions that such treaty establishes. In this sense, Malta's sovereignty is incrementally augmented and strengthened insofar as it is proportionately multiplied by the number of states with which it shares its sovereignty. Being a sovereign state, Malta can exercise its sovereignty in a way to renounce or condition its own sovereignty.

39. On the other hand, sovereignty has to be distinguished from sovereign rights. In the case of Malta, it enjoys both sovereignty and sovereign rights.[54]

40. An expression of Malta's national sovereignty is found in the Foreign Interference Act which is 'intended to regulate the limitations on the political activities of aliens, and this in accordance with Article 16 of the Convention of Rome (1950) for the Protection of Human Rights and Fundamental Freedoms'. Another expression of sovereignty is found in the National Interest (Enabling Powers) Act[55] and in the Ratification of Treaties Act.[56]

§3. State Territory

41. One of the four characteristics[57] of statehood, in terms of Article 1 of the Montevideo Convention of 1933 on the Rights and Duties of States,[58] is a defined territory. Malta does not form part of mainland Europe or North Africa but is geographically situated at the centre of the Mediterranean and in southern Europe. It is an archipelago with the islands of Malta, Gozo, Comino and Manoel Island being inhabited.

---

54. The concept of 'sovereign rights' is included in Article 2 of the Geneva Convention on the Continental Shelf 1958 and in Article 77 of the LOSC. *See* E.D. Brown, *The International Law of the Sea*, Volume I – *Introductory Manual*, Dartmouth Publishing Company Limited, Aldershot, 1994, pp. 255–256 and p. 258.
55. Chapter 365 of the Laws of Malta.
56. Chapter 304 of the Laws of Malta.
57. The other three characteristics being: (a) a permanent population; (b) a Government; and (c) the capacity to enter into international relations with other states. Although Malta is a small island state, it satisfies all the four characteristics of statehood.
58. 165 LNTS 19.

I. Definition of 'State'

42. Malta is a state. It is no longer a colony of the UK. Although on independence Malta became a sovereign state, it was still referred for a very limited period of time under colonial times as a state even though Malta was a colony of the UK. Indeed, the Blood Commission[59] had recommended in their report[60] that 'it would be fitting in view of the new status which Malta will achieve under the new [1961] constitution, that it should be described as the State of Malta, and we recommend that the new constitution should so provide'.[61]

II. Definition of 'Malta'

43. According to section 1(2) of the Constitution of Malta, '[t]he territories of Malta consist of those territories comprised in Malta immediately before the appointed day, including the territorial waters thereof, or of such territories and waters as Parliament may from time to time by law determine'. This definition is more far reaching than that given in the Constitution of the same expression in section 124(1). The expression 'Malta' is defined in the latter provision as meaning 'the Island of Malta, the Island of Gozo and the other islands of the Maltese Archipelago, including the territorial waters thereof'. On the other hand, section 1(2) of the Constitution gives a more extensive definition than the above. It states that:

> The territories of Malta consist of those territories comprised in Malta immediately before the appointed day, including the territorial waters thereof, or of such territories and waters as Parliament may from time to time by law determine.

44. The definition of section 124(1) does not include, for instance, the contiguous zone of Malta or any exclusive economic zone which Malta might declare in the future. Such maritime zones are however comprised under section 1(2), as Parliament has made laws to regulate such zones in the Territorial Waters and Contiguous Zone Act[62] and the Fishing Waters (Designation) and Extended Maritime Jurisdiction Act.[63] Parliament has also defined its continental shelf in the Continental Shelf Act[64] and its exclusive fisheries zone in the Fisheries Conservation and Management Act.[65] Section 2 of the Fishing Waters (Designation) and Extended Maritime Jurisdiction Act empowers the Prime Minister to extend Malta's jurisdiction to territory beyond its territorial waters.

---

59. The UK appointed Blood Commission consisted of Sir Hilary Blood, Sir Alfred Roberts, Mr Edward St. John and Mr Fred Hayday.
60. *Report of the Malta Constitutional Commission*, 1960, Her Majesty's Stationery Office, London, February 1961, Cmnd. 1261.
61. *Ibid.*, p. 22.
62. Chapter 226 of the Laws of Malta.
63. Chapter 479 of the Laws of Malta.
64. Chapter 535 of the Laws of Malta.
65. Chapter 425 of the Laws of Malta.

45. The Interpretation Act has also its own definition of 'Malta' in section 3(2) thereof:

> 2. In this Act, and in every Act passed either before or after the commencement of this Act, 'Malta' means the Island of Malta, the Island of Gozo and other islands of the Maltese Archipelago, including the territorial waters thereof.

46. This definition is not as extensive as that of section 1(2) of the Constitution which applies also to territories beyond the territorial waters of Malta though it was a reproduction of section 124(1) of the Constitution.

47. Parliament has indeed determined, through ordinary law, other territories belonging to Malta. The seaward waters of Malta comprise:

(a) the internal waters;
(b) the territorial waters;[66]
(c) the contiguous zone;[67]
(d) the continental shelf;
(e) the exclusive fisheries zone; and
(f) the extended maritime zone.[68]

48. Insofar as the seaward territories of Malta are concerned, Malta is bound by the provisions of the United Nations Law of the Sea Convention 1982 (LOSC).

§4. Features of the Republican Constitution

49. Kenneth C. Wheare in *Modern Constitutions*[69] has adopted a fivefold classification of constitutions:

(a) written or unwritten;
(b) flexible or rigid;
(c) federal or unitary;
(d) presidential or parliamentary;
(e) republican or monarchical.

50. Hilaire Barnett[70] opts for a sixfold classification of constitutions:

(a) written and written;

---

66. *See* Kevin Aquilina, 'Territorial Sea and the Contiguous Zone', in Malgosia Fitzmaurice and Norman Martínez Gutiérrez (eds), *The IMLI Manual of International Maritime Law, Volume I, The Law of the Sea*, Oxford University Press, Oxford, 2014, pp. 26–70.
67. *Ibid.*
68. Chapter 479 of the Laws of Malta.
69. Kenneth C. Wheare, *Modern Constitutions*, Oxford University Press, Oxford, 1951, pp. 14–31.
70. Hilaire Barnett, *Constitutional and Administrative Law*, 10th edn, Routledge, London, 2013, pp. 8–14.

(b) rigid and flexible;
(c) supreme and subordinate;
(d) federal and unitary;
(e) separated powers and fused powers;
(g) republican and monarchical.

I. Constitutional State Symbols

51. The Constitution, in its first Chapter, encompasses the state symbols of the Constitution which bestow national identity upon the Maltese population. These are: the national religion, the national flag, the George Cross Award, the national language and the national anthem.

A. The National Religion

52. The Constitution is confessional because one of the state symbols it establishes, in its very opening chapter, is the state religion. It declares that 'the religion of Malta is the Roman Catholic Apostolic Religion'.[71] It recognizes that 'the authorities of the Roman Catholic Apostolic Church have the duty and the right to teach which principles are right and which are wrong'[72] and mandates that religious teaching 'of the Roman Catholic Apostolic Faith shall be provided in all State Schools as part of compulsory education'.[73]

B. The National Flag

53. When referring to the national flag of Malta, the Constitution restricts itself to provide that the 'National Flag of Malta consists of two equal vertical stripes, white in the hoist and red in the fly'.[74] Although the Constitution describes the colours of the flag, it fails to protect it. Yet, the national flag is afforded protection by ordinary law according to the Emblem of Malta Act[75] and the Press Act.[76]

C. The George Cross Award

54. The Constitution provides that 'a representation of the George Cross awarded to Malta by His Majesty King George the Sixth on 15 April 1942 is carried, edged with red, in the canton of the white stripe' on the Maltese national flag.[77] Once again,

71. Constitution, section 2(1).
72. Constitution, section 2(2).
73. *Ibid.*, section 2(3).
74. Constitution, section 3(1).
75. Chapter 253 of the Laws of Malta, section 6.
76. Chapter 248 of the Laws of Malta, section 5(2).
77. Constitution, section 3(2). On the Maltese language, *see* Geoffrey Hull, *The Maltese Language Question: A Case Study in Cultural Imperialism*, Said Publications Ltd., Valletta, 1993.

protection is afforded to the George Cross,[78] as in the case of the national flag, through ordinary law – the George Cross (Restriction of Use) Ordinance.[79] This Ordinance regulates the use of the emblem of the George Cross disallowing any person 'to use for the purposes of his trade or business, or for any other purpose whatsoever, without the authority of the Prime Minister, the emblem of the George Cross or any colourable imitation thereof or the words "George Cross" whether alone or in combination with any other word or words'. Failure to comply with this provision entails the punishment of a fine.[80]

D. *The National Language*

55. The national language of Malta is the Maltese language.[81] It is also the language of the courts and of the House.[82] However, the official languages of Malta are the Maltese and the English languages and the public administration 'may for all official purposes use any of such languages'. The public administration nevertheless is bound to reply in the official language in which it is addressed.[83] Parliament may also prescribe other national languages in addition to the Maltese and English languages, though to date it has failed to do so.[84] Moreover, insofar as the courts are concerned, 'Parliament may make such provision for the use of the English language',[85] and such provision has indeed been made by means of the Judicial Proceedings (Use of English Language) Act.[86] The House is also empowered to 'determine the language or languages that shall be used in Parliamentary proceedings and records'.[87] The Interpretation Act[88] further provides that an Act of Parliament 'may be enacted in whole or in part, in the Maltese or in the English language only if the bill for that Act of Parliament, or part of such bill, is presented to the Clerk of the House and published in one only of the said languages and if the Act when passed contains a provision authorizing the enactment thereof, or any one or more of its parts, as the case may require, in that language only'.[89]

---

78. For the award of the George Cross to Malta, *see* John Frayn Turner, *The Awards of the George Cross 1940-2009*, Pen & Sword Military, South Yorkshire, 2010, pp. 54–67; and Mario Spiteri, *The National Day, Standard and Flag in Maltese Legislation, 1849 to 1964*, LL.D. thesis, Faculty of Laws, University of Malta, Msida, May 2006, pp. 103–142.
79. Chapter 115 of the Laws of Malta.
80. George Cross (Restriction of Use) Ordinance, section 2.
81. Constitution, section 5(1). For the historical evolution of the Maltese language, *see* Joseph M. Brincat, *Maltese and Other Languages: A Linguistic History of Malta*, Midsea Books Ltd., Sta. Venera, 2011; and Alexander Borg, 'Language', in Henry Frendo and Oliver Friggieri (eds), *supra* note 1, pp. 27–49.
82. Constitution, section 5(3).
83. *Ibid.*, section 5(2) proviso.
84. *Ibid.*, section 5(2).
85. *Ibid.*, section 5(3) proviso.
86. Chapter 189 of the Laws of Malta. As to legal Maltese, *see* Geoffrey Hull, *supra* note 77, and Joseph Felice-Pace, 'Maltese Legal Jargon', *Symposia Melitensia*, Msida, University of Malta Junior College, No. 5, 2008, pp. 99–110.
87. Constitution, section 5(4).
88. Chapter 249 of the Laws of Malta.
89. Interpretation Act, section 14.

The Constitution further provides that 'every law shall be enacted in both the Maltese and English languages and, if there is any conflict between the Maltese and the English texts of any law, the Maltese text shall prevail'.[90] The provisions of the Constitution on the national language are supplemented by the Maltese Language Act.[91]

E. The National Anthem

56. Although section 4 of the Constitution proclaims the national anthem to be the poem written by Reverend Karm Psaila, the national poet, and composed by Professor Robert Samut, entitled *L-Innu Malti*,[92] it does not provide the text of the anthem in a Schedule, nor does it provide details as to its author and composer, nor does it proscribe its vilification either in the constitutional provision or through ordinary law. The text of the national anthem is instead found in non-legally binding Maltese literature books.[93]

II. General Principles of Constitutional Law

57. A study of the Constitution reveals that it enshrines a number of principles or doctrines, some expressly, others by necessary intendment or implication. These comprise: the supremacy of the Constitution, the rule of law, the separation of powers, the independence of the judiciary, the principle of accountability, the principle of pluralism, the principle of subsidiarity, the principle of decentralization of the state, the principle of constitutionality, the principle of double construction, the principle of judicial review of legislation, the principle of financial accountability, the principle of investigation of government action, the principle of majority rule, the principle of due impartiality and fair apportionment of broadcasting facilities and time, the principle of allegiance to the Republic of Malta and its Constitution, the principle of a state centric constitution, and the principle of collective and individual ministerial responsibility.

III. A Typology of the Constitution

58. Diverse authors have come up with their own typology of a Constitution. Leslie Wolf-Phillips has identified thirteen such features:

90. Constitution, section 74.
91. Chapter 470 of the Laws of Malta.
92. Translation: The Maltese Hymn.
93. For the genesis of the Maltese anthem, *see* Oliver Friggieri, *Dun Karm il-Bniedem fil-Poeta* (Translation: Rev. Carm The Man in the Poet), Valletta, *Edizzjoni Klabb Kotba Maltin* (Translation: Maltese Book Club Edition), 1980, pp. 62–65; *Il-Versi tal-Innu Malti* (Translation: The Lyrics of the Maltese Anthem) in Philip E. Said (ed.), *Dun Karm: Patrimonju Malti u Żebbuġi* (Translation: Rev Carm: Maltese and Zebbugian [from the village of Żebbuġ] Patrimony), Ħaż-Żebbuġ Local Council, 2012, pp. 65–78; and *L-Istorja tal-Innu Malti: Kif Sar U Xi Jfisser* (Translation: The History of the Maltese Anthem: Its Formulation and Meaning), Valletta, *Klabb Kotba Maltin* (Translation: Maltese Book Club), 2014. The latter publication also provides the text of the national anthem at p. 114.

(a) codified/uncodified;
(b) conditional/unconditional;
(c) superior/subordinate;
(d) rigid/flexible;
(e) indigenous/adventitious;
(f) manifest/latent;
(g) Presidential Executive/Parliamentary Executive;
(h) monarchical/republican;
(i) bicameral/unicameral;
(j) competitive/consolidatory;
(k) programmatic/confirmatory;
(l) justiciable/nugatory; and
(m) federal/unitary.[94]

59. The Constitution of Malta favours an indivisible government, an anonymous Public Service, a liberal Constitution, a proportional representative electoral system, a Cabinet system of government, a two-party political system, a bipolar House of Representatives, an austere party discipline snubbing free votes, a constitutionally recognized parliamentary opposition, a codified constitution, a written constitution, a rigid constitution, a controlled constitution, a conditional constitution, a superior constitution, an adventitious constitution, a latent constitution, a competitive constitution, a justiciable-nugatory constitution, a unitary constitution, a parliamentary government, a representative government, a prime ministerial government, a responsible government, a Westminster constitution, a Whitehall constitution, a unicameral parliament, a sovereign state, an independent state, a confessional state, a republican state, a democratic state, a neutral state, a non-aligned state, a state which refuses to participate in any military alliance, a state which enjoys territorial integrity, a state founded on work, a state founded on the respect for inviolable human rights and fundamental freedoms, a monist state and a dualist state.

IV. Constitutional State Affiliations and Diplomatic Representation

60. The Constitution recognizes Malta's membership of international bodies. Such is the case of:

(a) the Commonwealth of Nations;
(b) the United Nations; and
(c) the EU.

61. In terms of section 111(1) of the Constitution, the President – acting in accordance with the advice of the Prime Minister – may appoint Ambassadors, High

94. *See* Leslie Wolf-Phillips, *Comparative Constitutions*, The Macmillan Press Ltd., London, 1972, pp. 32–47.

Commissioners and other principal representatives[95] of Malta in any other country. Section 65(1) of the Constitution stipulates that Parliament has to enact legislation with full respect for Malta's international and regional obligations. These include its obligations under the Vienna Convention on Diplomatic Relations and the Vienna Convention on Consular Relations.[96]

V. Constitutional Multi-Level Government

A. Prior to EU Accession

62. Prior to EU accession, Malta was divided into two tiers of government: central government and local self-government. Power resided and continues to reside in central government, and local self-government had got and continues to have restricted powers. For instance, local councils could not, and still cannot, levy local taxes.[97]

1. Central Government

63. The central government main organs – the Legislature, the Cabinet and the Courts – are established by the Constitution.

2. Local Self-Government

64. The local self-government institutions enshrining subsidiarity and decentralization established by the Local Councils Act[98] are Regional Committees,[99] Local Councils[100] and Administrative Committees.[101]

B. Following EU Accession

65. Following EU accession, the two-tier type of government has developed into a multi-level type of government whilst still retaining within it the two-tier levels. As Godfrey Baldacchino explains:

95. For the case of the removal from office of a principal representative by the House, *see* Kevin Aquilina, 'Ambassadors at the Bar', *The Times of Malta*, 29 June 2012, p. 11.
96. Done at Vienna on 18 April 1961, 500 UNTS 95.
97. *See* Kevin Aquilina and Isabelle Calleja, 'Local Government in Malta', in Ángel Manuel Moreno (ed.), *Local Government in the Member States of the European Union: A Comparative Legal Perspective*, Madrid, National Institute of Public Administration, Spain, 2012, pp 435–458 at p. 448.
98. Chapter 363 of the Laws of Malta.
99. Local Councils Act, section 37A.
100. *Ibid.*, section 3.
101. *Ibid.*, section 47A.

The concept of multi-level governance (MLG) gives expression to the idea that there are many interacting authority structures at work in the emerged global political economy. It is an approach in political science and public administration theory that has emerged from studies on European integration, and particularly from the various structures that were introduced by and in the EU via the Maastricht Treaty (1992). Multi-level governance refers to the deep and messy entanglement between various domestic, local, regional and international levels of authority. MLG is a dynamic three-dimensional concept that blurs and renders problematic three analytical distinctions that have hitherto been central to the conventional understanding of the contemporary European state: (1) that between centre and periphery, (2) that between state and society, and (3) that between the domestic and the international.[102]

VI. Constitutional Organs, Institutions and Public Offices

A. Organs of the State

66. The three principal organs of the State are Parliament, Cabinet and the Courts. These three organs have already been discussed above in the context of the separation of powers doctrine.[103]

B. State Institutions

67. The Constitution, apart from establishing the three principal organs of government, establishes other institutions in the form of Commissions (Electoral Commission,[104] Commission for the Administration of Justice,[105] PSC,[106] and Employment Commission)[107] and an Authority (the Broadcasting Authority).[108]

C. Public Offices of the State

68. The Public Offices established by the Constitution are: President of Malta, Acting President of Malta, Speaker of the House of Representatives, Deputy Speaker of the House of Representatives, MP, Clerk of the House, Ombudsman, Auditor General, Deputy Auditor General, National Audit Office, Chief Electoral Commissioner, Leader of the Opposition, Prime Minister, Acting Prime Minister, Ministers, Temporary

102. *See* Godfrey Baldacchino, 'Malta Transformed by Multi-Level Governance: More Than Just an Outcome of Europeanisation', *Reflections of a Decade of EU Membership: Expectations, Achievements, Disappointments and the Future*, Occasional Paper No 3, Institute for European Studies, University of Malta, Msida, 2014.
103. *See supra* paragraphs 28–30.
104. Constitution, section 60(1).
105. *Ibid.*, section 101A(1).
106. *Ibid.*, section 109(1).
107. *Ibid.*, section 120(1).
108. *Ibid.*, section 118(1).

Ministers, Parliamentary Secretaries, Attorney General, Permanent Secretaries, Acting Permanent Secretaries, Heads of Department of Government, Secretary to the Cabinet, public officers, Ambassadors, High Commissioners, Principal Representatives, Chief Justice, Acting Chief Justice, Judges, Acting Judges, Magistrates and Local Councils.

VII. Constitutional Review Mechanisms of Legislative and Executive Action, Including Investigatory Functions

69. Various review mechanisms are established by the Constitution. These comprise the Constitutional Court[109] and the Civil Court, First Hall, constitutional jurisdiction, the Employment Commission, the Ombudsman, the Auditor General and the Commission for the Administration of Justice.

109. Constitution, section 95(2).

Part I. Sources of Law

Chapter 1. Introduction

70. As Malta is a mixed legal system,[110] it takes its sources from a plurality of legal systems. In identifying the sources of the Maltese mixed legal system, the sources of law are divided as follows:

(a) sources originating from the civil law (ius civile) legal system (including Canon Law);
(b) sources originating from the common law legal system;
(c) sources originating from the EU legal system;
(d) sources originating from public international law;
(e) sources originating from the national law of individual Member States of the EU;
(f) sources originating from the national law of third-country non-EU Member States;
(g) sources originating from the regional law of Mediterranean states;
(h) sources originating from the regional law of the Council of Europe Member States; and
(i) sources originating from Maltese autochthonous law.

110. For a discussion of Malta as a mixed legal system, *see* Kevin Aquilina, 'Non-Autochthonous Law Influences on the Maltese Legal System', *Id-Dritt*, Vol. XXII, 2011, 265–278; 'The Nature and Sources of the Maltese Mixed Legal System: A Strange Case of Dr Jekyll and Mr Hyde', *Comparative Law Review*, Vol. No. 4, Issue No. 1, 2013, pp. 1–38.

Chapter 2. External Sources: International Law

71. Malta has two systems of law: its national law and its public international law.[111] For international law to become part of Maltese Law, a process has to take place. Indeed, International Law does not, when created, automatically become part and parcel of Maltese municipal law. The incorporation of international treaty law into Maltese domestic law which makes Malta a dualist state, at least insofar as international law is concerned because with regard to EU law, Malta is both a monist and a dualist state: it is dualist insofar as EU directives are concerned as these need to be transposed into national law, and it is monist insofar as EU regulations and council decisions are concerned as they become part and parcel of the Laws of Malta on their adoption by the competent EU institutions. Thus, unless an international law is incorporated into Maltese state law, international law cannot have legal effect in Malta even if it can have and does have international effect against Malta and Malta can end up actionable before an international court or tribunal or even amenable to the imposition of sanctions against Malta by the international community. Insofar as EU Law is concerned, if Malta consistently and persistently fails to transpose an EU directive into Maltese national law, then the European Court of Justice will, when called upon by the EU Commission, have to rule against Malta.

72. The sources of public international law are authoritatively laid down in Article 38 of the Statute of the ICJ, namely:

(a) international conventions, whether general or particular, establishing rules expressly recognized by the Contesting States;
(b) international custom, as evidence of a general practice accepted as law;
(c) the general principles of law, recognized by civilized nations;
(d) subject to the provisions of Article 59, judicial decisions and the teachings of the most highly qualified publicists of the various nations, as subsidiary means for the determination of rules of law.[112]

§1. Incorporation of International Law into Domestic Law

73. The public international law of Malta is highly influenced by the public international law of the UK in the light of the principle that where there is a *lacuna* in

111. For a study of generally accepted principles of international law and Malta's international and regional obligations, *see* Kevin Aquilina, 'The Parliament of Malta versus the Constitution of Malta: Parliament's Law Making Function under Section 65(1) of the Constitution', *Commonwealth Law Bulletin*, Vol. 38, No. 2, June 2012, pp. 217–249, at pp. 238–244.

112. The Statute is annexed to the Charter of the United Nations. *see* Bruno Simma (ed.), *supra* note 46, pp. 661–678.

Maltese Public Law, reference is made to English Public Law.[113] Malta incorporates public international law into its legal system not in a uniform manner but depending on the nature of the source of international law. In the case of treaties, for instance, these have to be incorporated into domestic legislation in order to bind. A departure from this dualist principle however occurred in 2004 when Malta became a EU Member State where EU Law, with the exception of directives which still have to be transposed into state law, form automatically part and parcel of Maltese Law on their adoption by the competent EU authorities and entry into force.[114] But of course this is done through national law.[115]

§2. Incorporation of International Customary Law

74. Once again, Malta follows English public international law on this matter which, nonetheless, tends to be incoherent and unsettled as two theories abound in this respect, the doctrine of incorporation – which is generally more favoured by English courts in the absence of a statutory provision laying down which doctrine ought to apply – and the doctrine of transformation.

75. The prevalent view in the UK continues to be the doctrine of incorporation.[116] Malta has to respect customary international law unless it has persistently objected thereto once this is allowed by customary international law. In the latter case, Malta will, as a persistent objector, not be bound by the emergence of a new custom in its respect. Otherwise, Malta will, on an international law plane, be bound by such custom.

§3. Incorporation of International Treaties

76. As Malta is primarily a dualist state, all treaties have to be incorporated into national law. Malta's dualism emerges from section 3(3) of the Ratification of Treaties Act which provides that: 'No provision of a treaty shall become, or be enforceable as, part of the law of Malta except by or under an Act of Parliament.' The matter is regulated by a plurality of laws, namely:

113. This point was made in *D. J. Low v. M. Low*, Collection of Decisions of the Superior Courts of Malta, 27 June 1892, *Aula Civile*, Vol. XIII, p. 243; *Marquis James Cassar Desain v. James Louis Forbes, C.B.E. nomine*, 7 January 1935, Collection of Decisions of the Superior Courts of Malta, Part I, Vol. XXVIIII, p. 43; *Anthony M Callus et v. Dr Antonio Paris et*, Constitutional Court, 7 July 1966, *Decizjonijiet Kostituzzjonali 1964-1978* (Translation: Constitutional Decisions 1964-1978), Vol. 1, p. 188 at p. 195; and *Frank Pace et v. Commissioner of Police et*, Court of Appeal, 28 January 2005. *See also* David Joseph Attard with the assistance of Kevin Aquilina and Patricia Mallia, *The Maltese Legal System, Volume I: A General Introduction*, Malta University Press, Msida, 2012, pp. 31 and 83–84.

114. For a discussion on the direct effect of directives, *see* Josephine Steiner, Lorna Woods and Christian Twigg-Flesner, *EU Law*, 9th edn, Oxford University Press, Oxford, 2006, pp. 94–104.

115. The European Union Act, Chapter 460 of the Laws of Malta, sections 3 and 4.

116. Malcolm N. Shaw, *International Law*, 3rd edn, Cambridge, Grotius Publications Limited, 1991, pp. 107–113.

(a) section 65(1) of the Constitution;
(b) the Ratification of Treaties Act;[117]
(c) special laws which incorporate treaties into national laws through verbatim reproduction in a schedule;[118] and
(d) special laws which incorporate treaties into national laws through adaptation within the text of the law.[119]

77. In terms of the Ratification of Treaties Act, the expression 'ratification' is defined in section 2 of the Ratification of Treaties Act as including 'a reference to such treaty and to any other act or manner in which such treaty may be brought into force'. The term 'treaty' is also defined in section 2 as 'an international agreement concluded between States in written form and governed by international law, whether embodied in a single instrument or in two or more related instruments and whatever its particular designation'. This definition is lifted *verbatim* from Article 1(a) of the Vienna Convention on the Law of Treaties 1969.[120]

78. The Ratification of Treaties Act does not encompass all treaties to which Malta is or might eventually be a party thereto. On the contrary, the said enactment applies only to certain treaties listed in section 3(1), that is, to those falling within the following three categories which affect or concern:

(a) the status of Malta under international law or the maintenance or support of such status; or
(b) the security of Malta, its sovereignty, independence, unity or territorial integrity; or
(c) the relationship of Malta with any multinational organization, agency, association or similar body.

79. For a treaty which falls under any of the matters referred to in paragraphs (a) and (b) above, such treaty can enter into force with respect to Malta only if it is authorized or approved in terms of the Ratification of Treaties Act.[121]

80. Ratification comes in two forms. It can be through an Act of Parliament or through a Resolution of the House of Representatives. In the case of treaties listed in paragraphs (a) and (b) above, an Act of Parliament is required for the treaty to enter

---

117. Chapter 304 of the Laws of Malta.
118. Such is the case with the Diplomatic Immunities and Privileges Act, Chapter 191 of the Laws of Malta; Malta Membership of the International Monetary Fund, Chapter 209 of the Laws of Malta; Membership of International Financial Organisations Act, Chapter 235 of the Laws of Malta; European Convention Act, Chapter 319 of the Laws of Malta; the International Criminal Court Act, Chapter 453 of the Laws of Malta; International Carriage of Goods by Road Act, Chapter 486 of the Laws of Malta; and Malta Membership of the Asian Infrastructure Investment Bank Act, Chapter 548 of the Laws of Malta.
119. Such is the case with the Criminal Code, Chapter 9 of the Laws of Malta; Territorial Waters and Contiguous Zone Act, Chapter 226 of the Laws of Malta; Merchant Shipping Act; Chapter 234 of the Laws of Malta, and the Continental Shelf Act, Chapter 535 of the Laws of Malta.
120. 1155 UNTS 331.
121. Ratification of Treaties Act, section 3.

into force.[122] In the case of the matters listed in paragraph (c) above, the authorization or approval is given by a Resolution of the House.[123]

81. Section 3(3) of the Ratification of Treaties Act provides that: 'No provision of a treaty shall become, or be enforceable as, part of the law of Malta, except by or under an Act of Parliament.' This provision raises a number of issues. First, if Malta joins an international organization but has to incorporate into national law certain international obligations arising from that relationship, authorization by resolution of the House is not, by itself, sufficient to incorporate those international obligations into municipal law for an Act of Parliament is still needed to cater for such purpose. This makes the whole process too rigid for two separate and distinct procedures have to be resorted to. Second, as the law stands, in the case of the relationship between Malta and a multinational organization which imposes international obligations upon Malta, a twofold procedure has to be followed: first, ratification of the treaty arrangement by resolution of the House and second, incorporation of the treaty obligations through an Act of Parliament. All this procedure could have been easily carried out in one step through an Act of Parliament catering for the authorization to ratify the treaty arrangement and to incorporate the international obligations therein. Third, what happens if notwithstanding ratification Parliament does not enact the necessary law? How can Parliament be coerced to comply with its international duties? Apart from coercive measures available under international law, Malta would be embarrassed to attract criticism by other states which have adhered and implemented the treaty but which it has not done so, notwithstanding that it is a party thereto.

82. It is the Minister responsible for foreign affairs who issues the instrument of ratification under his/her signature and who has to deposit that instrument with the competent depositary.[124]

83. From the above, certain conclusions can be drawn with regard to incorporation of treaties into Maltese Law:

(a) Not all treaties require Parliamentary ratification to be effective in Malta. Indeed, it is only the three categories mentioned in section 3(1) of the Ratification of Treaties Act that require such ratification.
(b) In those matters not listed in the three categories listed in paragraph 78 above, a contrario sensu, the executive may pass on to ratify a treaty without the need of obtaining parliamentary approval.
(c) Even in those cases where Government approves a treaty, that treaty becomes part of Maltese Law and is enforceable in Malta 'by or under an Act of Parliament'. This clearly indicates that Malta is a dualist state insofar as the incorporation of treaties is concerned. Section 5 of the Ratification of Treaties Act states that: 'Nothing in this Act shall be construed as in any way affecting the powers of the Government with respect to treaties to which sub-article (1) of article 3 of this Act does not apply.'
(d) The Ratification of Treaties Act applies to the ratification, accession or other forms of adherence which brings a treaty into force with respect to Malta. It does

122. *Ibid.*, section 3(2)(a).
123. *Ibid.*, section 3(2)(b).
124. *Ibid.*, section 3(4).

not, therefore, apply to a denunciation of a treaty. This matter is made quite clear in sections 4 and 5 of the Ratification of Treaties Act which state that:

> 4. Where Malta ceases, or does any act whereby it will cease, to be a party to a treaty affecting or concerning any of the matters mentioned in paragraphs (a), (b) or (c) of sub-article (1) of article 3 of this Act, the Minister responsible for foreign affairs shall inform the House of the fact, giving the reasons therefor, at the earliest opportunity and in no case later than the second sitting of the House after the expiration of one month from the date of the denunciation or other act whereby Malta ceases or will cease to be a party to a treaty as aforesaid.
>
> 5. Nothing in this Act shall be construed as in any way affecting the powers of the Government with respect to treaties to which subsection (1) of section 3 of this Act does not apply.

84. While Parliament has to authorize or approve the ratification of certain treaties, Parliament does not have to authorize or approve the denunciation of those same treaties. The Government, in the case of denunciation, has only the duty to inform the House of such denunciation. But such denunciation might still require the passing of amendments to existing laws to free Malta from the provisions incorporating the treaty which has been denounced by Malta.

85. In terms of Maltese Law, it is not possible to resort to an abrogative referendum with respect to 'any legislation giving effect to any treaty obligation undertaken by Malta'.[125] Although no definition is afforded of the term 'treaty' in the Referenda Act, it is safe to apply the corresponding definition of 'treaty' in the Ratification of Treaties Act. Hence, no abrogative referendum may be called to annul a law which is incorporating a treaty into national law once, as stated above, that would place Malta in breach of its international obligations and in conflict with Article 26 of the Vienna Convention on the Law of Treaties 1969.

125. Referenda Act, section 13(2)(g).

Chapter 3. European Sources

86. EU Law is a sui generis type of law. It cannot be considered at par with international law because Malta, like any other EU Member State, is bound by it. In the case of International Law, Malta – like any other state member of the international community – can decide which conventions to adhere to or not, which provisions of that convention it does not want to be bound by, the period by which it wants to be bound by those provisions and other considerations which International Law allows out of deference to the universally accepted principle of the sovereignty of states. On the contrary, in the case of EU Member States they have to adopt all EU Law in an *à la carte* approach. There is really no choice: once Malta is an EU Member State, it is expressly bound by the Union's laws unless Malta has been, is, or will be, allowed some form of derogation from a specific provision of EU Law though this is the exception not the rule and such derogation has to be allowed by EU Law. Furthermore, contrary to International Law, EU Law has direct applicability and direct effect within Maltese national law and, in those cases where transposition of a directive is required, consequences will abound if Malta, or any other Member State, were not to transpose, transpose badly or incompletely or transpose by far after the due date. In addition, EU Law is supreme and overrides Maltese Law. This point was well made by the ECJ in *Costa v. ENEL*[126] where the Court held as follows:

> By creating a Community of unlimited duration, having … powers stemming from a limitation of sovereignty, or a transfer of powers from the States to the Community, the Member States have limited their sovereign rights, albeit within limited fields, and thus have created a body of law which binds both their nationals and themselves.

87. P.P. Craig opines that:

> The Community's supremacy was given added force by the ECJ's ruling in the Simmenthal case[127] where the Court made it clear that Community law would take precedence even over national legislation which was adopted after the passage of the relevant EC norms. The existence of Community rules rendered automatically inapplicable any contrary provision of national law, and precluded the valid adoption of any new national law which was in conflict with the Community provisions.[128]

88. One exception to this rule, at least theoretically, is when the Constitution of Malta might run counter to EU Law. Strictly speaking this is possible – though it is very remotely probable that it will materialize – because of the provisions of section 65 of the Constitution which obliges Parliament to make laws 'in conformity with full

126. Case 6/64 [1964] E.C.R. 585, at 593.
127. Case 106/77, *Amministrazione delle Finanze dello Stato v. Simmenthal Spa* [1978] E.C.R. 629.
128. P.P. Craig, Administrative Law, 5th edn, Sweet & Maxwell, London, 2003, p. 304. For a discussion of supremacy within the EU legal order, *see* pp. 303–308.

respect for ... the treaty of accession to the European Union signed in Athens on the 16 April 2003'. Of course, mistakes do happen and one cannot exclude beforehand the possibility of the Constitution being or ending up in breach of EU Law. In such a case, Malta will have to amend the Constitution to bring it in full compliance with EU Law.

§1. The Incorporation of EU Law into Domestic Law

89. EU Law is incorporated into Maltese Law through the European Union Act.[129] It specifically provides that EU Law is 'binding on Malta' and 'part of the domestic law thereof under the conditions laid down in the Treaty'.[130] Furthermore, any law in Malta which is incompatible with EU Law is, to the extent that such law is incompatible with EU Law, 'without effect and unenforceable'.[131] In addition, EU Law is 'recognized and available in Law, and be enforced, allowed and followed accordingly'.[132]

§2. The Reception of EU Law into the Maltese Legal System

90. As EU Law is part of Maltese legislation, Malta is bound by all the sources of EU Law, that is, by both primary and secondary sources of EU Law. The primary source of EU Law is the EU Treaties, as amended over time, which, in turn, confer law-making powers upon the Union's institutions. According to Article 288 of the Treaty on the Functioning of the European Union (TFEU) – better known as the 'Lisbon Treaty' – the subsidiary sources of EU Law come in the form of regulations, directives and decisions, though it must be pointed out that EU institutions may also adopt non-binding instruments such as a recommendation or an opinion. As to the three types of secondary sources of EU Law, the Lisbon Treaty does afford a definition of this key terminology as follows:

> A regulation shall have general application. It shall be binding in its entirety and directly applicable to all Member States.
>
> A directive shall be binding, as to the result to be achieved, upon each Member State to which it is addressed, but shall leave to the national authorities the choice of form and methods.
>
> A decision shall be binding in its entirety. A decision which specifies those to whom it is addressed shall be binding only on them.

129. Chapter 460 of the Laws of Malta.
130. European Union Act, section 3(1).
131. *Ibid.*, section 3(2).
132. *Ibid.*, section 4(1).

91. Their main characteristics are reproduced below:

(a) a regulation and a decision are both binding in their entirety upon Member States;
(b) a regulation has general application;
(c) a decision binds only those Member States to which it is addressed;
(d) a directive is also binding upon that Member State to which it is addressed but only as to the result to be achieved;
(e) a directive – contrary to a regulation and a decision – requires transposition into national law. The choice and form or method of transposition is left to the national authorities; and
(f) a contrario sensu, a regulation and a decision do not require transposition into national law as they both become binding upon Member States from the relative date of entry into force. Hence, a distinction has to be drawn between 'direct applicability' and 'direct effect'. Hilaire Barnett carefully distinguishes the two terms:

> Direct applicability: an EU provision/measure is automatically legally effective from the relevant date, without any legislative action on the part of the Member State's legislature.[133]

92. To put it differently, a measure is directly applicable because it is self-executing, that is, it does not require the intervention of national institutions such as Parliament or the taking of a national measure such as the enactment of a law or the making of a subsidiary legislation to make the EU measure applicable and enforceable in Malta:

> Direct effect: an EU provision automatically confers legal rights on individuals which are enforceable against the Member State government and other bodies. Direct effect may be vertical or horizontal … Where a provision does not have direct effect, it may be indirectly effective as a result of a national court's duty to interpret law in a manner which gives effect to EU law.[134]

93. Direct effect allows individuals to bring court proceedings in their own name in national courts in order to enforce rights granted to them by the Treaty.[135]

---

133. *See* Hilaire Barnett, *supra* note 70, p. 173.
134. *Ibid.* For a discussion of vertical and horizontal effects of EU Law and the principle of indirect effect, *see* pp. 173–183.
135. *See* P.P. Craig, *supra* note 128, pp. 308–324.

§3. European Union Directives

94. As a directive needs to be transposed into national law, Malta has in practice adopted four methods how to transpose directives.[136] First, a directive can be transposed into a newly enacted Act of Parliament. Second, a directive can be transposed through an amendment to a primary law, be it an Act of Parliament, a Code or an Ordinance. Third, an Act of Parliament, Code or Ordinance may be amended so as to allow a Minister or some other person, body or authority, to make subsidiary legislation under that Act, Code or Ordinance transposing the directive in question. Fourth, it is also possible for the Prime Minister, in the absence of a law authorizing a Minister, person, body or other authorities to make subsidiary legislation, to make such subsidiary legislation under the EU Act[137] which acts as an umbrella provision for making subsidiary legislation under that enactment to transpose any EU directive on whatever subject it might be. Indeed, this approach is possible through section 4(2) of the EU Act.

136. *See* David Fabri, 'Transposition Tables, Toil and Tears … True Tales from the Accession', in Peter G. Xuereb (ed.), *Malta in the European Union: Five Years On and Looking to the Future*, The European Documentation and Research Centre, Jean Monnet Centre of Excellence, University of Malta, Msida, 2009, pp. 85–95; and *From Application to Accession: The Interplay between the EC Consumer Directives and Selected Areas of National Consumer Law and Policy – A Case Study From Malta (1990-2004)*, PhD thesis, Faculty of Laws, University of Malta, Msida, 2015.

137. Chapter 460 of the Laws of Malta.

Chapter 4. Domestic Sources

§1. Introduction

95. Although one might consider a chapter discussing the sources of Maltese Constitutional Law to be relatively straightforward, this might not be necessarily the case. Indeed, one should appreciate the difficulty in ascertaining the richness in terms of breadth and diversity of the sources of Maltese Constitutional Law. Thus the aim of this chapter is to identify the diverse sources both of Maltese Constitutional Law in general and of the organic law of the land in particular.

§2. The Relevance of Sources to a Study of Maltese Constitutional Law

96. Sources are of the utmost importance to unravel the DNA of Maltese Constitutional Law. Through the application of such sources to a particular provision or to a plurality of provisions of Maltese Constitutional Law, one can really comprehend the intended meaning of that provision. Sources are, undoubtedly, an aid to interpretation and it is through the application of these sources that the meaning of a provision (or a set of provisions) is clarified. However, one must appreciate which source to use within a precise given context, whether there exists a hierarchy amongst sources which has to be invariably followed, and the correct identification of the proper legal system from which that source originates. This is because, as is the case with Maltese Constitutional Law, the legal systems which have influenced Maltese Constitutional Law are multiple and varied, even if, predominantly it is the English legal system which prevails in this respect in order to construe a specific provision of Maltese Constitutional Law; yet there are other legal systems such as the civil law (ius civile), international law and European law traditions which influence the Maltese legal system, including Maltese Constitutional Law.

§3. Definition and Classification of Maltese Constitutional Law

97. No law obtaining in Malta defines Maltese Constitutional Law. Foreign jurists have attempted a definition. For instance, Ian Loveland sums up the writings of other jurists on this point as follows:

> Colin Turpin suggests that the constitution is 'a body of rules, conventions and practices which regulate or qualify the organisation and operation of government in the United Kingdom'; de Smith's classic introductory text regards the constitution as 'a central, but not the sole feature, of the rules regulating the system of government'. A longer version is offered by Vernon Bogdanor, for whom the

constitution is: 'a code of rules which aspire to regulate the allocation of functions, powers and duties among the various agencies and officers of government, and defines the relationship between these and the public'.[138]

98. A working definition which this author favours is that provided by Owen Hood Philips, Paul Jackson and Patricia Leopold. It reads as follows:

> The word 'constitution' is used in two different senses, the abstract and the concrete. The Constitution of a state in the abstract sense is the system of laws, customs and conventions which define the composition and powers of organs of the state, and regulate the relations of the various state organs to one another and to the private citizen. A 'constitution' in the concrete sense is the document in which the most important laws of the constitution are authoritatively ordained. A country, such as our own [the United Kingdom], which has no 'written' constitution ..., has no constitution in the concrete sense of the word. It should be clear from the context which meaning is being employed.[139]

99. Insofar as the Constitution is concerned, it distinguishes itself from ordinary primary legislation in the manner that amendments to the Constitution are passed. It is, therefore, this special qualified majority which differentiates amendments to the Constitution from amendments to other primary constitutional laws which only require a simple majority vote to be passed in the House. Nonetheless, there are several constitutional laws which are passed by the House following a simple majority vote and are therefore not entrenched in terms of section 66 of the Constitution.[140] The ensuing difficulty which arises is how are these ordinary primary laws distinguished from other non-constitutional ordinary primary laws. One way of achieving such a purpose is by identifying the characteristics of Maltese Constitutional Law.

§4. Characteristics of Maltese Constitutional Law

100. A way of defining Maltese Constitutional Law is by examining its characteristics.

101. A characteristic of Maltese Constitutional Law is that it establishes the three principal organs of the state and other state institutions (both in terms of bodies and offices). It defines their functions, powers, duties, and procedure, and, insofar as persons occupying high office, their appointment, renewal (where allowed by law), discipline, resignation and removal. Constitutional Law also regulates the relationship *inter se* between these state organs, institutions and offices as well as their relationship with citizens. Constitutional Law governs the elections for a democratically elected

138. Ian Loveland, *Constitutional Law, Administrative Law, and Human Rights: A Critical Introduction*, 5th edn, Oxford University Press, Oxford, 2009, pp. 3–4.

139. Owen Hood Phillips, Paul Jackson and Patricia Leopold, *O. Hood Phillips and Jackson, Constitutional and Administrative Law,* 8th edn, Sweet & Maxwell, London, 2001, p. 5.

140. The entrenchment mechanism applies only to the Constitution and to ordinary law referred to in section 56(8) of the Constitution.

legislature and makes provision for the granting and withdrawal of citizenship. It is Constitutional Law which bestows upon persons – both legal and physical – human rights and fundamental freedoms and proclaims the rights and duties of these persons vis-à-vis state organs, institutions and officers of the State as well as the rights and duties of state organs, institutions and officers of the State vis-à-vis these persons. Constitutional Law also sets out the applicable rules related to government finance, the public service, local self-government, and judicial review of legislation and serves to supplement the provisions of the fundamental law, the Constitution.

§5. The Sources of Maltese Constitutional Law in Concrete Form

102. The sources of Maltese Constitutional Law are manifold. Broadly speaking, they can be divided under two general headings:

(a) legal; and
(b) non-legal sources.

I. Legal Sources of Maltese Constitutional Law

103. The *legal* sources of Maltese Constitutional Law consist in:

(a) legislation;
(b) judicial decisions;
(c) official publications setting out rules and procedures; and
(d) the general principles of Maltese Constitutional Law.

104. The non-legal sources of Maltese Constitutional Law consist in:

(a) constitutional practice; and
(b) authoritative works comprising both the writings of jurists and of non-jurists.

A. Legislation

105. The first source of Maltese Constitutional Law is legislation. Constitutional legislation is divided into:

(a) Maltese constitutional legislation;
(b) foreign national constitutional legislation; and
(c) international (including European) constitutional legislation.

106. Maltese constitutional legislation is divided into:

(a) primary constitutional legislation; and
(b) subsidiary (or delegated or secondary) constitutional legislation.

1. Maltese Primary Constitutional Legislation

107. Maltese primary constitutional legislation, in turn, is also divided into two sources:

(a) the Constitution of Malta, as the highest law of the archipelago; and
(b) other ordinary primary constitutional legislations.

108. In terms of section 65 of the Constitution, Parliament may make laws. The term 'law' is defined in section 124(1) of the Constitution as 'any instrument having the force of law'. The practice has been, since independence, for Parliament to enact solely laws in the form of Acts of Parliament though there are still on the statute book pre-independence laws in the forms of Codes and Ordinances. Thus primary legislation comes in four forms:

(a) the Constitution;
(b) Acts of Parliament;
(c) Codes; and
(d) Ordinances.

109. While there are Acts of Parliament which can be classified as falling under the category of 'primary constitutional legislation' such as the General Elections Act[141] and there are also Ordinances which can also be classified under the same category such as the House of Representatives (Privileges and Powers) Ordinance,[142] the same cannot be said for Codes. However, the Criminal Code and the Code of Organization and Civil Procedure, though not 'primary constitutional legislation' in their own right do have a bearing on primary constitutional legislation insofar as they supplement the provisions of the Constitution in certain respects. Such is the case, for instance, with section 117 of the Constitution on prohibition of certain associations which is supplemented by section 83 of the Criminal Code[143] and with section 46(6) and (7) of the Constitution which are developed by the Code of Organization and Civil Procedure[144] and Rules of Court made thereunder.[145]

a. The Constitution

110. The Constitution is the supreme law of Malta. Even Parliament is subdued by the Constitution.[146] It establishes the principal organs of the state and other state institutions and public offices. It sets out their composition and functions, their manner

141. Chapter 354 of the Laws of Malta.
142. Chapter 113 of the Laws of Malta.
143. Chapter 9 of the Laws of Malta. Section 83 of the Criminal Code concerns the 'promotion of political object by use or display of physical force'.
144. Chapter 12 of the Laws of Malta. *See* , for instance, sections 32, 45 and 46 of the said Code.
145. *See* section 29 of the said Code and the Court Practice and Procedure and Good Order Rules, Subsidiary Legislation 12.09.
146. *See supra* paragraphs 6–24.

of appointment, disqualification from membership, dismissal and, where applicable, their security of tenure. The Constitution further regulates Maltese citizenship, human rights and fundamental freedoms, the principles to be followed in the governance of the state and financial regulation. It allows for judicial review of legislation and establishes a Constitutional Court with powers to apply and interpret the provisions of the Constitution. A number of public offices are established in the Constitution ranging from that of President of Malta to that of Speaker of the House, Auditor General to Ombudsman, and Attorney General to Secretary to the Cabinet. The Constitution establishes Malta as a parliamentary democracy, a republic and a neutral and non-aligned state. Local government is also established by the Constitution, but its detailed regulation is set out in an ordinary primary law, the Local Councils Act.[147]

b. Constitutional Laws

111. Constitutional Laws (other than the Constitution) serve two purposes: first, to amend the Constitution in terms of the amending provision of the Constitution – section 66; second, to supplement the provisions of the Constitution either through laws which are specifically mentioned for that purpose in the Constitution or through other laws not specifically mentioned in the Constitution though of a constitutional nature. The Constitution does mention instances where Parliament is authorized by it to make laws to give better effect to the provisions of the Constitution. These provisions all indicate that Parliament is subordinate to its master and creator – the Constitution. An example in point is section 119(2) of the Constitution which provides as follows:

> The function of the Broadcasting Authority referred to in sub-article (1) of this article shall be without prejudice to such other functions and duties as may be conferred upon it by any law for the time being in force in Malta.

112. Moreover, there are other constitutional laws which supplement the provisions of the Constitution but which are not specifically referred to in the Constitution itself.

113. Finally, it is also possible for the Constitution to be amended not by an Act of Parliament but by a subsidiary law. Indeed, in terms of section 23(4), the President may amend, add to, revoke or substitute the list of countries in the Fourth Schedule to the Constitution, that is, the list of Commonwealth countries other than Malta.

114. The Constitution cannot be subject to an abrogative referendum in terms of section 13(2)(a) of the Referenda Act,[148] including any regulations made under the Constitution.

2. Maltese Subsidiary Constitutional Legislation

115. Maltese subsidiary constitutional legislation is divided into two:

(1) national subsidiary constitutional legislation; and

147. Chapter 363 of the Laws of Malta.
148. Chapter 237 of the Laws of Malta.

(2) local self-government constitutional legislation.

116. Subsidiary legislation – like primary legislation – comes in different forms. These are listed, though not defined, in section 7 of the Interpretation Act as follows:

(a) regulations;[149]
(b) rules;[150]
(c) orders;[151]
(d) bye-laws;[152]
(e) warrants;[153]
(f) schemes;
(g) notices;[154] and
(h) other instruments.

117. Although the Interpretation Act[155] does not list nor define the category 'other instruments' having the force of law, a proclamation and resolutions of the House of Representatives are examples of other instruments having the force of law.

118. Local self-government subsidiary constitutional legislation takes only two forms, that of bye-laws[156] and regulations.[157]

3. Maltese Constitutional Legislation

119. Maltese Constitutional Legislation consists in:

149. For example, the Public Service Commission Regulations, Subsidiary Legislation 0.01; and the Disciplinary Procedure in the Public Service Commission Regulations, Subsidiary Legislation 0.03.
150. For instance, Her Majesty's Constitutional Court Rules of Court, 1964, Legal Notice 49 of 1964 (the latest version of the rules of court is the Court Practice and Procedure and Good Order Rules, Subsidiary Legislation 12.09), and the Commission for the Administration of Justice (Election of Members) Rules, Subsidiary Legislation 0.04.
151. *See* Standing Orders of the House of Representatives Order, Subsidiary Legislation 0.02.
152. Such is the case of Advertisements on Street Furniture (Pembroke Local Council) Bye-Laws, Subsidiary Legislation 363.11; Use of Facilities (Floriana Local Council) Bye-Laws, Subsidiary Legislation 363.165; and Control of Pigeons (Paola Local Council) Bye-Laws, Subsidiary Legislation 363.169.
153. Warrants by the Minister responsible for finance issued in terms of sections 27(2), (3) and (4); 31(3); and 37 of the Financial Administration and Audit Act, Chapter 174 of the Laws of Malta.
154. A case in point is the Expiry Date of Certain Identity Cards Notice, Subsidiary Legislation 258.02.
155. Chapter 249 of the Laws of Malta.
156. Bye-laws are made by a Local Council in terms of sections 34(1) and 60 of the Local Councils Act, Chapter 363 of the Laws of Malta; and in terms of section 37(6) of the Local Councils Act, by a Regional Committee.
157. Regulations are made by the Minister responsible for local government in terms of, for instance, section 34(2) of Local Councils Act, Chapter 363 of the Laws of Malta.

(a) the Constitution itself;[158]
(b) the amendments made, since 1964, to the Constitution;[159]
(c) the primary legislation made under the powers of a specific provision of the Constitution[160] or, though not made under such a specific provision, is referred to by the Constitution[161] or supplement a specific provision of the Constitution;[162]
(d) the subsidiary legislation made under the powers of a specific provision of the Constitution or, though not made under such a provision, is referred to by the Constitution;[163]
(e) provisions in the Constitution, though few in number, which are autochthonous, that is home-grown. It is not that easy to identify a specific source for these provisions, even though this is not excluded. Examples comprise the provision

---

158. Contained in the Schedule to The Malta Independence Order, 1964 of 2 September 1964 (Statutory Instrument 1964 No 1398) published in *The Malta Government Gazette* No 11,688 of 18 September 1964.
159. At the moment of writing The Malta Independence Order, 1964, has been amended by Acts Nos: XLI of 1965, XXXVII of 1966, IX of 1967, XXVI of 1970, XLVII of 1972, LVII, LVIII of 1974, XXXVIII of 1976, X of 1977, XXIX of 1979, IV of 1987, XXIII of 1989; Proclamations Nos II and VI of 1990; Acts XIX of 1991, IX of 1994; Proclamations IV of 1995 and III of 1996; Acts: XI of 1996, XVII of 1997, III of 2000, XIII of 2001, V of 2003, XIV and XXI of 2007, XX of 2011, VII and X of 2014, XXIV of 2015 and XLIV of 2016.
160. Primary legislation made under the provisions of the Constitution comprises the following: the Petroleum (Production) Act, Chapter 156 of the Laws of Malta; the Territorial Waters and Contiguous Zone Act, Chapter 226 of the Laws of Malta; the Fisheries Management and Conservation Act, Chapter 425 of the Laws of Malta; the Fishing Waters (Designation) and Extended Maritime Jurisdiction Act, Chapter 479 of the Laws of Malta; and the Continental Shelf Act, Chapter 535 of the Laws of Malta, in so far as section 1(2) of the Constitution is concerned.
161. Primary legislation referred to in the Constitution, though not by name of the enactment but by its subject matter, includes the Maltese Citizenship Act, Chapter 188 of the Laws of Malta, in relation to sections 22 and 23 of the Constitution; the Judicial Proceedings (Use of English Language) Act, Chapter 189 of the Laws of Malta, in relation to section 5(3) proviso of the Constitution; the General Elections Act, Chapter 354 of the Laws of Malta, in relation to section 52(1) of the Constitution; and the Commission for the Administration of Justice Act, Chapter 369 of the Laws of Malta, in relation to sections 91(5), 97(3), and 100(4) of the Constitution.
162. Primary legislation which supplements a provision of the Constitution includes the European Convention Act, Chapter 319 of the Laws of Malta with regard to sections 1(1) and 65(1) of the Constitution; and the Education Act, Chapter 327 of the Laws of Malta, with regard to section 2(3) of the Constitution.
163. Such is the case of resolutions of the House of Representatives which are referred not only in the Constitution's provisions but also in various other laws such as section 3(2)(b) of the Ratification of Treaties Act, Chapter 304 of the Laws of Malta; sections 2 and 3(1)(c)(d)(e)(f)(ii), (4) and (5) of the Disposal of Government Land Act, Chapter 268 of the Laws of Malta; section 5 of the Participating and Granting of Financial Stability Support under the European Stability Mechanism, Chapter 523 of the Laws of Malta; section 50(3) of the Fiscal Responsibility Act, Chapter 534 of the Laws of Malta; and section 5 of the Participation within the Single Resolution Fund and granting of financial support under the Single Resolution Mechanism Act, 2015, Chapter 547 of the Laws of Malta. The Court Practice and Procedure and Good Order Rules, Subsidiary Legislation 12.09, give effect to the provisions of section 46(7) of the Constitution.

on neutrality and non-alignment in section 1(3); the 1991 amendment made to section 45 to include reference to discrimination on the basis of sex; the 2014 amendments made to sections 32 and 45 to include reference to discrimination on the basis of sexual orientation and gender identity; the electoral corrective mechanism in section 52(1); the appointment of an Ombudsman in terms of section 64A; the regulation of local self-government according to section 115A; the Employment Commission in section 120; the automatic constitution of the Constitutional Court in terms of section 95(5); and the amendment made in 2003 to section 65(1) with regard to accession to the EU and the constitutional limitation imposed upon Parliament to make laws, *inter alia,* in conformity with 'the treaty of accession to the European Union signed in Athens on the 16th April, 2003';

(f) Constitutional Law which preceded the independence Constitution which is still relevant as an aid to interpretation of the 1964 Constitution. This can be done by comparing the current version of the Constitution – the 1964 Constitution as amended to date – with earlier Constitutions under imperial rule, both as to provisions which are similar and to provisions which are dissimilar. For instance, the provision which does not require practice at the bar in the 1964 Constitution (section 97(2) in the original version; since then renumbered as section 96(2) in the current version of the Constitution) is identical to section 96(2) of the 1961 Constitution.[164] Both constitutional provisions require a person to have practised as an advocate in Malta or served as a magistrate in Malta, or partly so practised and partly so served in Malta for a period of, or periods amounting in the aggregate to, not less than twelve years, to be appointed Judge of the Superior Courts. Yet the 1936,[165] 1939,[166] 1947[167] and 1959[168] Constitutions required such practice in Malta to be 'at the bar'. Hence, by comparing the text of these six constitutions, it is evident that the independence Constitution does not require practice to be 'at the bar'.[169]

4. Foreign National Constitutional Legislation

120. Maltese Constitutional Law is primarily influenced by the Constitutional Law of England. Yet it has adopted provisions from the Constitutions of other jurisdictions as is the case with the USA, New Zealand and Italy.

a. Foreign National Constitutional Legislation: The UK

121. Foreign national constitutional legislation of the UK which constitutes a source of Maltese Law comprises the following:

---

164. The Malta (Constitution) Order in Council 1961.
165. Section 10(2) of Malta Letters Patent of 1936.
166. Section 52(2) of the Malta Letters Patent 1939.
167. Section 43(1) of the Malta (Constitution) Letters Patent 1947.
168. Section 27(2) of the Malta (Constitution) Order in Council, 1959.
169. A study of these six constitutions in relation to appointment of judges is found in Kevin Aquilina, 'Judicial Appointment in Malta: A Historico-Legal Perspective', *Melita Historica*, Vol. XV, No. 3, 2010, pp. 233–254.

(a) imperial Maltese constitutions whose provisions have been retained, with or without amendments, and whose text is reproduced, with or without amendments, in the 1964 Constitution;[170]
(b) subsidiary Legislation made under Imperial Maltese Constitutions whose provisions have been retained, with or without amendments;[171]
(c) English national ordinary primary constitutional laws such as the UK Malta Independence Act;
(d) English national ordinary subsidiary constitutional legislation such as the Malta Independence Order 1964;[172] and
(e) English Constitutional Conventions which have been written down within the text of, and incorporated within, the Constitution of Malta.

b. Foreign National Constitutional Legislation: Other States

122. Foreign national constitutional legislation, other than that of the UK, states which are a source of Maltese Constitutional Law include the following:

(a) imperial Commonwealth colonies' and states' constitutions whose provisions have been emulated by, with or without amendments, and are reproduced in, the 1964 Constitution such as in the case of the Constitutions of Nigeria and Sierra Leone. The 1964 Constitution is heavily modelled on the 1960 Nigerian Constitution, and Chapter IV of the 1964 Constitution derives its source from the 1961 Sierra Leone Constitution;
(b) foreign constitutions whose provisions have been emulated by, with or without amendments, and are reproduced in, the 1964 Constitution such as in the case of the Constitutions of the USA and Italy. The President of Malta's oath of office is lifted from Article 1, paragraph 2, of the Constitution of the USA Article II, Section I, whilst section 1(1) and Chapter II of the Constitution are influenced by the Constitution of Italy; and
(c) foreign national ordinary primary constitutional laws which have been emulated by, with or without amendments, and are reproduced in, the 1964 Constitution as in the case of the Irish Law on the proportional representation by means of the

170. *See* the reference to the 1961 Constitution with regard to the qualifications for judgeship. On the effect of English Public Law on Maltese Public Law, *see* David Joseph Attard, *supra* note 25, pp. 83–84 and *supra* note 113, p. 31 and Kevin Aquilina, *supra* note 1, pp. 271–276.

171. Such is the case of the Standing Orders of the Legislative Assembly established under the Malta (Constitution) Order in Council, 1961.

172. Sections 23(2) and 24(2) of the Constitution refer to the UK British Nationality Act, 1948; section 124(14) of the 1964 Constitution referred to the UK Interpretation Act 1889. Standing Order 173 of the Standing Orders of the House of Representatives Order, Subsidiary Legislation 0.02, states that in all cases not provided for in the Standing Orders, the rules, forms, usages and practice of the House of Commons of the United Kingdom are to be followed in Malta. The Malta Independence Order 1964 refers to the following enactments of the United Kingdom Parliament: the Malta Independence Act 1964; the Malta Constitution Act 1932; the Malta (Letters Patent) Act 1936; the Malta (Constitution) Order in Council 1959; and the Malta (Constitution) (Modification) Order in Council 1963.

single transferable vote; the Freedom of Information Act has its source in the New Zealand and Australian Freedom of Information Acts; the Ombudsman Act is largely influenced by the New Zealand Ombudsman Act 1975; and the Public Administration Act draws upon the Australian Public Service Act 1999.

5. European Legislation

123. European legislation includes:

(a) EU Law; and
(b) Council of Europe Conventions.

a. European Union Law

124. Since its accession to the EU on 1 May 2004, Malta is bound by EU Law. The legislation of the EU is divided into two:

(a) legal sources; and
(b) non-legal sources.

125. The legal sources are, in turn, also subdivided into two:

(a) primary sources; and
(b) secondary sources.

126. The primary sources consist in the treaties founding the EU whilst the secondary sources consist in regulations, directives and decisions.

127. The non-legal secondary sources consist in:

(a) opinions; and
(b) recommendations.

b. Council of Europe Treaties

128. Malta has ratified and acceded to a number of conventions of the Council of Europe which can be classified under Constitutional Law, foremost amongst which is the European Convention for the Protection of Human Rights and Fundamental Freedoms and its Protocols. This Convention is, indirectly, the source of Chapter IV of the Constitution.

6. International Legislation

129. International Law as referred to in the Constitution includes:

(a) the Charter of the United Nations with regard to 'measures or actions decided by the Security Council of the United Nations';[173]
(b) international conventions setting out human rights;[174]
(c) regional conventions setting out human rights;[175]
(d) international conventions setting out generally accepted principles of international law;[176]
(e) regional conventions setting out generally accepted principles of international law;[177]
(f) international conventions setting out Malta's obligations thereunder;[178]
(g) regional conventions setting out Malta's obligations thereunder;[179] and
(h) the treaty of accession to the EU signed in Athens on 16 April 2003.[180]

B. Judicial Decisions

130. Judicial Decisions are divided into:

(a) decisions of the Courts in Malta;
(b) decisions of the Courts in England;
(c) decisions of the Courts in other national States;
(d) decisions of European courts and tribunals; and
(e) decisions of international courts and tribunals.

131. The decisions of the Courts in Malta comprise the following courts:

(a) the Civil Court, First Hall, sitting in its Constitutional Competence;
(b) the Court of Appeal; and
(c) the Constitutional Court.

132. The decisions of the Courts in England comprise the Judicial Committee of the Privy Council. These decisions can be divided under two headings:

(a) decisions applicable to Malta where Malta was the respondent state; and
(b) decisions applicable to Malta where Malta was not the respondent state but the decision relates to an identical or similar provision of a Commonwealth Constitution to the Maltese Constitution.

133. The decisions of:

173. Constitution, section 1(3)(b)(i).
174. *Ibid.*, section 65(1).
175. *Ibid.*
176. *Ibid.*
177. *Ibid.*
178. *Ibid.*
179. *Ibid.*
180. *Ibid.*

(a) the Supreme Court of the UK,[181] since 1 October 2009;
(b) the House of Lords before 1 October 2009; and
(c) other English inferior courts,

may also be relevant when they are interpreting English constitutional legislation which acts as a source to Maltese Constitutional Law in homage to the principle that where there is a lacuna in Maltese Public Law, reference can be had to English Public Law.

134. The decisions of the Courts in other States comprise those Commonwealth ex-Colonies/States the constitutional provisions whereof are identical or similar to those of Malta and the case law of the Supreme Court of the USA which allows judicial review of legislation.[182]

135. The decisions of European courts comprise the decisions of:

(a) the ECtHR;[183]
(b) the European Commission of Human Rights;[184]
(c) the Court of Justice of the EU;[185] and
(d) the General Court.[186]

136. The decisions of international courts comprise the decisions of:

(a) the International Criminal Court;[187]
(b) the ICJ;[188]
(c) the Tribunal for the Law of the Sea;[189] and
(d) the Nuremberg and Tokyo Tribunals, the International Criminal Tribunal for Former Yugoslavia and the International Criminal Tribunal for Rwanda, amongst other international courts and tribunals, to the extent that they are relevant to the interpretation of International Criminal Law as incorporated into Maltese Law.

C. *Official Publications Setting Out Rules and Procedures*

137. Regard has also to be had to Maltese official publications which set out rules and procedures to be followed by constitutional organs, institutions and offices. These comprise:

---

181. The Supreme Court of the United Kingdom was established by Part 3 of the Constitutional Reform Act 2005, c. 4.
182. *William Marbury v. James Madison*, 5 U.S. 137 (1803). For a discussion of this case, *see* Robert A. Carp and Ronald Stidham, *Outline of the American Legal System*, Bureau of International Information Programs, United States Department of State, Washington, 2004, pp. 24–26.
183. Constitution, section 65(1).
184. *Ibid.*
185. *Ibid.*
186. *Ibid.*
187. *Ibid.*
188. *Ibid.*
189. *Ibid.*

(a) *il-Manwal tal-President*;[190]
(b) *il-Manwal ta' Proceduri tal-Kabinett*[191] and other Cabinet approved documents such as that related to positions of trust;
(c) various Codes of Ethics;[192]
(d) *Is-Sedja Titkellem* insofar as parliamentary practice and procedure is concerned;[193]
(e) guidelines issued by the PSC;[194]
(f) guidelines and case notes issued by the Office of the Ombudsman;[195]
(g) other information contained in annual reports compiled by constitutional organs, institutions and officers of the state either in terms of law such as by the PSC,[196] the Broadcasting Authority,[197] the Auditor General,[198] and the Ombudsman,[199] or in terms of administrative practice such as by the House of Representatives and the Foreign and European Affairs Committee of the House, in the various papers laid on the Table of the House and in press releases issued by constitutional organs, institutions and offices of the state; and
(h) materials relevant to the interpretation of the Constitution of the British Parliament and Government such as command papers and official publications, including

---

190. Translation: *The President's Manual*. A translation into English of *The Manual of the President of the Republic*, is printed in David Joseph Attard, *supra* note 25, Appendix III, pp. 249–281.
191. Translation: *Cabinet Manual of Procedures*. Cabinet Office, *Cabinet Manual of Procedures*, Cabinet Office, Valletta, August 2014.
192. Codes of Ethics approved by the Cabinet Office include: (a) the Code of Ethics for Ministers and Parliamentary Secretaries (January, 1994); the Code of Ethics for Employees in the Public Sector (October 1994); the Code of Ethics for Board Directors in the Public Sector (November 1994); and the Code of Ethics for Local Councillors (July 1995). All four codes are published by the Cabinet Office, Office of the Prime Minister, Valletta.
193. Translation: The Chair Speaks Out. *Is-Sedja Titkellem, Collection of Decisions Delivered Between April 2013 and March 2014*, Vol. I, 2014; *Is-Sedja Titkellem, Collection of Decisions Delivered Between April and December* 2014, Vol. II, 2015; *Is-Sedja Titkellem, Collection of Decisions Delivered Between December 2014 and October 2015*, Vol. III, 2015, Office of the Speaker of the House of Representatives, Valletta; *Is-Sedja Titkellem, Collection of Decisions Delivered Between November 2015 and April 2016*, Vol. IV, 2016, Office of the Speaker of the House of Representatives, Valletta. *See also* Raymond Mangion (ed.), *Speakers' Rulings in the Parliament of Malta, First Volume, Part One, The Legislative Assembly, 1921-1924*, House of Representatives, Valletta, and Malta University Press, 2012.
194. These comprise *Guidelines to Selection Boards*, available at https://opm.gov.mt/en/PSC/Documents/Selection%20Process/Instructions%20to%20Selection%20Boards%202014%20_2_.pdf; and *Brief Guidelines to Disciplinary Boards*, available at http://opm.gov.mt/en/PSC/Documents/Discipline/Brief%20Guidelines%20for%20Disciplinary%20Boards.pdf. Last accessed on 31 March 2016.
195. *Guidelines for Good Governance* available at http://www.ombudsman.org.mt/wp-content/uploads/2014/10/Guidlines-for-Good-Governance.pdf; and *Case Notes*, available at http://www.ombudsman.org.mt/category/case-notes/. Last accessed on 31 March 2016.
196. Available at: https://opm.gov.mt/en/PSC/Pages/Documents/Annual-Reports-.aspx. Last accessed on 31 March 2016.
197. Available at: http://www.ba-malta.org. Last accessed on 31 March 2016.
198. Available at: http://www.nao.gov.mt/page.aspx?id=38. Last accessed on 31 March 2016.
199. Available at: http://www.ombudsman.org.mt/category/annual-reports/. Last accessed on 31 March 2016.

files deposited at the National Archives of the UK and of Malta and, generally, materials relevant to the interpretation of the UK Constitution and Commonwealth constitutions similar to the Maltese.

138. Although not necessarily binding or serving as a precedent, these official publications serve to set out constitutional practice followed by the above persons, bodies and by other persons or bodies to whom they are addressed and are considered to be authoritative in nature.

D. *General Principles of Maltese Constitutional Law*

139. The general principles of Maltese Constitution Law derive from the previous three sources of Maltese Constitutional Law. The Constitution contains several constitutional principles discussed in this monograph, whilst case law also applies constitutional principles when interpreting Maltese Constitution Law. Such is the case with regard to the supremacy of the Constitution over Parliament enunciated in *Mintoff v. Borg Olivier*.[200] Equity, justice, proportionality and fairness are considered to be general principles of law. The same applies to the principles of natural justice.

II. Non-legal Sources of Maltese Constitutional Law

140. Non-legal sources of Maltese Constitutional Law comprise authoritative works and constitutional practice.

A. *Authoritative Works*

141. Authoritative works are those works which are cited by the Courts in their decisions, by the Speaker and MPs in the business transacted in the House and in Government official documents. Works which are not cited by the above-mentioned persons or bodies do not make these works less 'authoritative'; it however makes it more difficult to establish their authoritativeness. Authoritative works are works written by jurists and consist in commentaries on constitutional law, elucidation of a particular legal query or elaboration upon an unclear provision of constitutional law. The decisions of the Constitutional Court are replete with references to the writings of publicists. Insofar as public international law is concerned, 'the teachings of the most highly qualified publicists of the various nations' is considered to be a source, though a subsidiary one, 'for the determination of the rules of law'.[201]

B. *Constitutional Practice*

142. In the Maltese Constitution, English conventions are part and parcel of the Constitution and are, where possible, enforceable. But the conventions, once reduced

---

200. *Dom Mintoff v. Giorgio Borg Olivier noe*, Her Majesty's Constitutional Court, 5 November 1970.

201. *See* Statute of the International Court of Justice, Article 38(1)(d).

into writing within the text of a law, lose their soft law status of law and become now hard law. If these Conventions were to change through constitutional practice, it is still the norm written down in the Constitution which prevails over the new practice. This is because by being grounded in the Constitution, the British Conventions have lost their conventional status and became law binding and, where possible, enforceable. The words 'where possible' enforceable are resorted to because there are situations where these conventions, notwithstanding that they have been incorporated into the organic law, are unenforceable. A case in point is where it is not possible to institute legal proceedings against the President as envisaged by section 742A of the Code of Organization and Civil Procedure even though the point might arise as to whether it is constitutional for an ordinary law, not being the Interpretation Act in terms of section 124(14) of the Constitution, to be allowed to restrict, limit or qualify a constitutional provision. But, in the absence of a provision in the Constitution, prohibiting the enforcement of a specific provision of the constitution, the Constitution is enforceable.

§6. Constitutional Annulment of Laws

I. The Actio Popularis

143. One way how to impugn a law, apart from an abrogative referendum, is through an action for a declaration of invalidity of a law. Section 116 of the Constitution allows for such an action.

II. Section 6 of the Constitution

144. Section 6 of the Constitution has been discussed in the case of *The Hon. Dom Mintoff v. The Hon. Dr Giorgio Borg Olivier in his capacity as Prime Minister of Malta*[202] where the Constitutional Court held that the Parliament of Malta was not absolutely sovereign as the Parliament of the UK which was omnipotent and whose actions could not be enquired into any court because: (a) the Constitution of Malta is a rigid constitution and its provisions can only be amended in terms of the Constitution where certain provisions are entrenched by at least a two-thirds majority vote for their alteration and others also require in addition to the two-thirds vote a majority vote in a referendum to be able to be altered; and (b) the principle of judicial review of legislation has been expressly recognized in sections 46 and 116 of the Constitution. In the instant case, the Court held that a House resolution could not validate retrospectively an invalid Act of Parliament. The latter could only be cured through the passing of a valid enactment which validates the invalid Act of Parliament.

202. *See supra* note 200.

III. Section 46 of the Constitution

145. Section 46(2) of the Constitution is also pertinent to a discussion of constitutional annulment of laws. Its text has been reproduced above.[203]

IV. Section 47 of the Constitution

146. The text of section 47(9) of the Constitution is reproduced in paragraph 16 above.

V. Section 95 of the Constitution

147. Section 95(2)(e) of the Constitution provides that the Constitutional Court has jurisdiction to hear and determine '(e) appeals from decisions of any court of original jurisdiction in Malta on questions as to the validity of laws other than those which may fall under article 46 of this Constitution'.

VI. Emergency Powers Act

148. Section 7 of the Emergency Powers Act[204] provides that any provision of a law which is inconsistent with a delegated legislation made under the Emergency Powers Act will have no effect once it is inconsistent with that delegated legislation.

VII. European Convention Act

149. In terms of section 4(2) of the European Convention Act, the Civil Court, First Hall, has 'original jurisdiction to hear and determine any application made by any person' to enforce the ECHR in domestic courts, and 'may make such orders, issue such writs and give such directions as it may consider appropriate for the purpose of enforcing, or securing the enforcement, of the Human Rights and Fundamental Freedoms to the enjoyment of which the person concerned is entitled'.[205]

---

203. *See supra* paragraph 15.
204. Chapter 188 of the Laws of Malta.
205. For the genesis of the European Convention Act, *see* 'The author and his creation: An interview with Giovanni Bonello in Mark A. Sammut, Patrick Cuignet and David A. Borg', *Malta at the European Court of Human Rights 1987-2012,* Birkirkara, *ius melitae*, 2012, pp. 26–37.

VIII. European Union Act

150. Section 3(2) of the European Union Act[206] makes a similar provision to the above ensuring that any Maltese law which derogates from any right under the Treaty of accession to the European Union is 'without effect and unenforceable'.

IX. Diplomatic Immunities and Privileges Act

151. Section 13 of the Diplomatic Immunities and Privileges Act is discussed above.[207]

X. Ultra vires Delegated Legislation

152. Delegated legislation which runs counter to the provisions of the parent law is declared null and void by the court.[208]

206. Chapter 460 of the Laws of Malta.
207. Chapter 191 of the Laws of Malta
208. *Louis F. Cassar and Christian Holland in their name and on behalf of and in representation of the Association Youth for the Environment v. The Hon. Prime Minister and Minister of the Interior*, Civil Court, First Hall, per Mr Justice Victor Borg Costanzi, 20 July 1988. For a summary of this case, *see* Kevin Aquilina, *supra* note 111, p. 218, note 5.

Chapter 5. Forms of Direct Democracy and Abrogative Referenda

§1. Popular Sovereignty

153. Although the Constitution enshrines indirect democracy as its form of government,[209] it cannot be said that this is the sole method of democracy prevalent in Malta. This is because there is also, though to a lesser extent, an element of direct democracy such as that of a referendum.[210] Recourse to the referendum is had in the following instances:

(a) as a tool of public consultation – the consultative referendum;
(b) as a tool of abrogating laws – the abrogative referendum;
(c) as a tool of amending the Constitution – the Constitution alteration referendum; and
(d) as a tool of local government consultation and abrogation of bye-laws.

I. The Consultative Referendum

154. In terms of section 3(1)(a) of the Referenda Act, persons entitled to vote in a referendum may be called upon to declare 'whether they approve proposals set out in a resolution passed for that purpose by the House and published in the *Gazette*'. Not much consultative referenda have been held in Malta. Indeed, only seven referenda have been held over a time span of 144 years since the holding of the first referendum in 1870.[211] These seven referenda took place as follows:

(a) in 1870 which dealt with whether clerics should be allowed to act as candidates for the Council of Government;
(b) in 1956 to decide whether Malta should be integrated in the UK;
(c) in 1964 to approve the independence Constitution;
(d) in 1973 to determine whether the Gozo Civil Council should continue in existence;
(e) in 2003 to decide whether Malta should join the EU;
(f) in 2011 to decide whether to introduce divorce in Malta; and
(g) in 2015 to decide whether spring hunting should be abolished.

209. The Maltese system of government is based on popular representation in the House of Representatives with general elections scheduled once every five years.

210. *See* David Joseph Attard, *supra* note 25, pp. 92–95.

211. *See* Maria Carmen Debono, 'The Development of the Law on Referenda in Malta', LL.D. thesis, Faculty of Laws, University of Malta, Msida, 2008, and Michael J. Schiavone, *L-Elezzjonijiet F'Pajjiżna Fl-Isfond Storiku 1800-2013* (Translation: Elections in our Country within a Historical Background 1800-2013), Independence Publications – PIN, Pjetà, 2013.

II. The Abrogative Referendum

155. Section 3(1)(b) of the Referendum Act allows for the calling of a referendum to determine whether the electorate 'agrees that a provision of law should be abrogated in accordance with the provisions of Part V of this Act'. Although the abrogative referendum is a more recent phenomenon, the relative legislation dating back to 1996, only one abrogative referendum has been held since then dealing with the abolition of spring hunting though it procured a negative outcome.

III. The Constitutional Amendment Referendum

156. Section 3(2) of the Referenda Act provides that:

> Persons entitled to vote in a referendum under the Constitution will be called upon to declare whether they approve a bill for an Act of Parliament submitted to them for the purposes of article 66(3) of the Constitution.

157. Indeed, the Constitution may be amended in two instances only through the participation of the electorate via a referendum. If a majority of votes cast is not obtained in such a referendum, then the Bill to amend the Constitution cannot become law. This provision applies to extending the lifetime of Parliament currently set for 'five years from the date of its first sitting after any dissolution'[212] and to the provision which requires a referendum for the extension of the lifetime of Parliament.[213]

IV. Local Council Referenda

158. In 1996, the Local Councils Act was amended to allow a referendum to be called within a locality with regard to any bye-law made by the local council of that locality. A referendum was held by the Gharb Local Council in Gozo on 8 December 2010 where the residents of Gharb were asked whether they agreed or not with the construction of a new fireworks factory in Gharb.[214] However, to be precise, this was a consultative referendum.[215]

§2. Public Consultation

159. Although referenda are both a form of public consultation[216] and an exercise in law-making, the law provides for other mechanisms where the people are consulted

212. Constitution, section 76(2).
213. *Ibid.*, section 66(3) and (4).
214. *See* http://gozonews.com/15832/gharb-council-releases-the-official-results-of-the-referendum/print. Last accessed on 31 March 2016.
215. For a list of consultative referenda, *see* paragraph 154 above.
216. *See* Kevin Aquilina, 'The Consultation Process', *The Times of Malta*, 4 February 2013, p. 16.

even if the final say does not vest in them. Several consultation processes are carried out by the public administration where public consultation is mandated by law or is decided through an executive decision. For instance, the Environment and Development Planning Act[217] requires public consultation in the formulation of planning policy. In the latter case, government consults through Green Papers,[218] White Papers[219] and other types of consultation documents.[220]

217. Chapter 504 of the Laws of Malta.

218. For example, Ministry for Infrastructure, Transport and Communications, *Next Generation Access Infrastructure Green Paper*, Ministry for Infrastructure, Transport and Communications, Valletta, July 2008.

219. For example, Ministry for Social Dialogue, Consumer Affairs and Civil Liberties, *Towards the Establishment of the Human Rights and Equality Commission*, Ministry for Social Dialogue, Consumer Affairs and Civil Liberties, Valletta, December 2014.

220. The Commission for the Holistic Reform of the Justice System, *The First Document for Public Consultation*, Parliamentary Secretariat for Justice, Valletta, 31 May 2013 and *The Second Document for Public Consultation*, Parliamentary Secretariat for Justice, Valletta, 29 July 2013. Consultation documents are uploaded on socialdialogue.gov.mt/en/Public_Consultations/Pages?Home.aspx. Last accessed on 31 March 2016.

Part II. Form of Government

Chapter 1. Introduction to the Maltese System of Government

§1. The Maltese System of Government: An Outline

160. The State of Malta is governed by three principal organs of the State and various institutions, public offices and other bodies. The three principal organs of state are:

(a) the Legislature or Parliament, composed of the President of Malta and the House of Representatives (consisting in the Speaker, Deputy Speaker and Members of Parliament);
(b) the Executive or Government, composed of Cabinet Ministers, Parliamentary Secretaries (equivalent to junior ministers) and the non-public offices referred to in section 110(6) of the Constitution; and
(c) the Judiciary or the judicial organ composed of the Chief Justice, Judges and Magistrates.

161. The Prime Minister and Ministers are appointed from amongst sitting Members of Parliament and not from outside the House. The same applies to Parliamentary Secretaries.

162. The Head of State is the President of Malta. Malta is a parliamentary democracy where all MPs are elected except in very exceptional circumstances where they may be co-opted. As far as the system of central government is concerned, the following points are noteworthy.

§2. The Political System

163. The political system does not comprise only Parliament and the government, even if these are the two main *dramatis personae* involved in the political system. It also includes political parties – whether represented in Parliament or otherwise – social forces such as the Roman Catholic Apostolic Church, civil society, campaign movements and lobby groups as well as non-governmental organizations.

164. With regard to political parties, the last general election of 2017 was contested by the two major political parties: the PN; and the PL; and three small parties, AD, the Alliance for Change and the Maltese Patriot Movement.

§3. The Social Forces

165. The social forces or interest groups[221] comprise the private sector, trade unions, employers' associations, the church and non-governmental organizations. Trade unions and employers' associations are regulated by the Employment and Industrial Relations Act,[222] the Catholic Apostolic Church is not established by the Laws of Malta but is regulated by the Code of Canon Law,[223] whilst non-governmental organizations are regulated by the Voluntary Organisations Act[224] and the Second Schedule of the Civil Code.[225] Civil society[226] is represented in the Malta Council for Economic and Social Development[227] and in the Malta-EU Steering & Action Committee. The latter is not established by law but by administrative decision.

221. For a discussion of interest groups in Malta, *see* Mario Thomas Vassallo, *The Europeanization of Interest Groups in Malta and Ireland: A Small State Perspective*, Palgrave Macmillan, Hampshire, 2015.
222. Chapter 452 of the Laws of Malta.
223. For a discussion of church-state relations, *see infra* paragraphs 568–575.
224. Chapter 492 of the Laws of Malta.
225. Chapter 16 of the Laws of Malta.
226. Civil society is defined in the Malta Council For Economic and Social Development, Chapter 431 of the Laws of Malta, as including 'all those organizations of persons established to seek the common good and whose main aims are neither to generate profits nor to seek executive power'. Chapter 431 of the Laws of Malta also establishes in section 6 a Civil Society Committee.
227. Chapter 431 of the Laws of Malta.

Chapter 2. The President of Malta

166. Chapter V of the Constitution of Malta establishes and regulates the office of President of Malta. This Chapter is not an all-embracing chapter which deals with the President of Malta in his/her multifarious duties as the supreme officer of the State. This is because the President is referred to in other provisions of the Constitution as well as in other laws[228] including the Standing Orders of the House of Representatives Order.[229] Thus to understand better the functions, powers and duties of the President of Malta, one has to go through all these laws as well as other administrative structures in which the President is involved such as the Community Chest Fund Foundation, the President's Foundation for The Wellbeing of Society and the Trade Union Forum.

§1. The Election of President of Malta

167. Although the President is not elected directly by the people like MPs, he/she is elected by the House. The electoral college from which a President is chosen is very limited in number, and MPs have to vote to appoint a President. Indeed, the Constitution does not even use the term 'election', but 'appointment' as the former term is reserved for Members of Parliament who are elected by popular suffrage.[230] Yet the Speaker[231] and Deputy Speaker[232] of the House, who are also elected from amongst MPs, are said to be elected (not appointed, notwithstanding that the same procedure for appointing the President is used in electing the Speaker and Deputy Speaker). Nonetheless, in the case of the President, although he/she is appointed by resolution of the House, he/she is in reality elected by the people's representatives. Now it might happen that all MPs agree with the appointment of President and the resolution is approved unanimously by all MPs.

168. In terms of section 48(1) of the Constitution, the President is 'appointed by resolution of the House'. But the Constitution does not state what percentage vote is required for the Resolution to be carried successfully. Should the resolution obtain a two-thirds majority vote as in the case of the appointment of Auditor General,[233] Deputy Auditor General,[234] or Ombudsman[235] or should it obtain an absolute or a simple majority? The provision is silent on this matter. This dilemma is resolved by reference to section 71(1) of the Constitution which provides that:

228. *See* Ugo Mifsud Bonnici, *supra* note 190, for a discussion of ordinary laws which assign functions upon the President.
229. For instance, Standing Orders of the House of Representatives Order, Subsidiary Legislation Const. 02, Standing Orders 6, 7, 120 and 184–193.
230. Constitution, section 52(1).
231. *Ibid.*, section 59(1).
232. *Ibid.*, section 59(3).
233. Constitution, section 108(2).
234. *Ibid.*, section 108(9)(a).
235. *Ibid.*, section 64A(2) and Ombudsman Act, Chapter 385 of the Laws of Malta, section 3.

> Save as otherwise provided in this Constitution, all questions proposed for decision in the House of Representatives shall be determined by a majority of the votes of the members thereof present and voting.[236]

169. Thus, in terms of this provision, the resolution to appoint the President has to enjoy 'the vote of the members thereof present and voting', that is, a simple majority. This is quite strange when one bears in mind that parliamentary officers such as the Auditor General, the Deputy Auditor General and the Ombudsman are all appointed with at least a two-thirds majority vote in the House of Representatives but this is not the case with the President.

§2. The Electoral Procedure

170. When the President's term of office comes to an end, the Prime Minister moves a motion in the House for the appointment of a new President. Like any other motion in the House, a vote is taken thereupon. As the motion requires a simple majority of MPs present and voting, and the Prime Minister normally enjoys the support of a majority of MPs in the House, the Prime Minister's motion is expected to be carried and the ensuing resolution would have appointed the person proposed by the Prime Minister to fill in the office of President. Prior to moving such a motion consultation takes place between the Prime Minister and the Leader of the Opposition as to the candidate whom the Prime Minister is proposing to that office.

§3. Qualifications for Appointment

171. Any person can be appointed President except persons who:

(a) are not citizens of Malta;[237]
(b) hold or have held the office of Chief Justice or other Judge of the Superior Courts;[238]
(c) are not eligible for appointment to or to act in any public office in accordance with section 109 with regard to the PSC, section 118 regarding the Broadcasting Authority and section 120 concerning the Employment Commission.[239]

172. With regard to holding the office of Chief Justice, it is relevant to observe that whilst a Chief Justice cannot be appointed President, he/she can carry out the duties, in terms of the Constitution, of Acting President.[240]

236. Not even an absolute majority is required for the appointment of President.
237. Constitution, section 48(2)(a).
238. *Ibid.*, section 48(2)(b).
239. *Ibid.*, section 48(2)(c).
240. *Ibid.*, section 49.

173. Being the highest office of the Republic, it is protected by law. Such is the case, for instance, with sections 5 and 55 of the Criminal Code,[241] section 742A of the Code of Organization and Civil Procedure,[242] and sections 4 and 5 of the Press Act.[243]

§4. Presidential Oath and Term of Office

I. President's Oath of Office

174. A person who is appointed President or who assumes that office in an acting capacity (i.e., an Acting President),[244] has to take and subscribe the oath of office before entering upon that office.[245] The text of the oath of office of President is set out in the Second Schedule to the Constitution and reads as follows:

> I .... solemnly swear/affirm that I will faithfully execute the office of President (perform the functions of the President) of Malta, and will, to the best of my ability preserve, protect and defend the Constitution of Malta. (So help me God).

175. The oath of office has to be taken both by the President and an Acting President. However, in the case of President, the oath has to be taken before the House whilst in the case of an Acting President, there is no requirement for the oath to be taken before the House.[246] The practice evolved that the oath of Acting President is taken in the hands of the Attorney General. The Constitution places no requirement upon the President or the Acting President to subscribe to the oath of allegiance set out in the Third Schedule to the Constitution.

II. President's Term of Office

176. As to the President's term of office, this is set out in section 48(3)(a) of the Constitution which states that the office of President becomes vacant 'on the expiration of five years from the date of the appointment to that office'. Of course, the President can be removed from office during that period, he/she may resign altogether or die in office; admittedly, none of these have happened since Malta became a republic.

177. It might happen that the President travels abroad on official duties or takes his/her vacation or is sick or unable to perform the functions of office. In such an

---

241. Chapter 9 of the Laws of Malta.
242. Chapter 12 of the Laws of Malta.
243. Chapter 248 of the Laws of Malta.
244. Mr Paul Xuereb served as Acting President between 1987 and 1989. For a biography of Mr Paul Xuereb, *see* the entry 'Paul Xuereb', in Michael J. Schiavone (ed.), *Dictionary of Maltese Biographies, Volume II, G-Z*, Pubblikazzjonijiet Indipendenza, Pjetà, 2009, pp. 1649–1650.
245. Constitution, section 50.
246. Constitution, section 50.

eventuality, section 49 of the Constitution allows for the appointment of an Acting President. This is because in Malta, contrary to say the USA, there is no Deputy or Vice-President who can step in the shoes of the indisposed President when the latter cannot perform the functions of office.

178. The Prime Minister, following consultation with the Leader of the Opposition, appoints an Acting President.

§5. The Status of the President: Holder of Multiple Roles

179. The Constitution does not prohibit the President from holding multiple roles apart from that of Head of State. This is because the Constitution allows the President to partake in all three organs of the state in his/her capacity as President. First, he/she is the head of the Executive;[247] second, he/she forms part of the Legislature;[248] third, he/she presides over the Commission for the Administration of Justice.[249] As President, the incumbent holds multiple roles conferred upon him/her by the Constitution.

§6. The President as Guardian of the Constitution

180. A function of the President is that of guardian of the Constitution. The Constitution does not use this term but instead states that the President has the duty 'to preserve, protect and defend the Constitution of Malta' in terms of the oath of office. Such duty is undefined and the Constitution does not provide the President with powers to comply with this constitutionally imposed duty.

§7. Temporary and Permanent Incapacity and Other Cases of Early Conclusion of the Presidential Term of Office

181. The presidency can come to an end in different ways. These are:

(a) resignation from office;
(b) removal from office;
(c) loss of Maltese citizenship;
(d) appointment to certain offices of state such as the office of Chief Justice, Judge or any of the offices mentioned in sections 109, 118 and 120 of the Constitution;[250]
(e) when five years from the date of appointment have elapsed;
(f) when the incumbent is unable to perform the functions of office due to infirmity of body or mind.

247. *Ibid.*, section 78(1).
248. *Ibid.*, section 51.
249. *Ibid.*, section 101A(1).
250. *See supra* paragraph 171(c).

I. Dual or Multiple Citizenship

182. In the case of loss of Maltese citizenship, the incumbent has no further claim on the office of President. But it can happen that the President – apart from being a Maltese national – can also enjoy dual or multiple citizenship of other states. Is this prohibited by the Constitution?[251] Strictly speaking, the answer is in the negative. However, one must remember that when the Constitution was enacted in 1964, persons could enjoy only one citizenship – Maltese. At that time, section 28 of the independence Constitution disallowed dual or multiple citizenship. Hence, the President had to be of pure Maltese breed who could never hold dual or multiple nationalities. This provision is no longer on the statute book. Instead in 2000,[252] section 22 of the Constitution was amended to provide, in subsection (2), that:

> Dual or multiple citizenship is permitted in accordance with any law for the time being in force in Malta.

II. Infirmity of Body or Mind

183. Although the Constitution states in section 48(3)(b) that the holder of the office of President can be removed in the case of infirmity of body or mind or any other cause which enables the said office holder from performing the functions of office of President, it does not provide further details. For instance, which types of infirmity of mind or body has the Constitution in mind and who is to certify such infirmity? Apart from being removed from office because of inability to perform the functions of office, a President may also be removed from office due to misbehaviour.

§8. Replacement of President

184. Situations might arise where the President needs to be replaced. In such cases, an Acting President is appointed. The Acting President has to satisfy all the eligibility criteria for appointment as President, but the Acting President can continue exercising his/her profession, trade, art, business or other office he/she may hold.

185. In terms of section 49 of the Constitution, a President is replaced in the following cases:

(a) when the office is temporarily vacant and until a new President is appointed;
(b) when the office holder is absent from Malta;
(c) when the office holder is on vacation;
(d) when the office holder is unable to perform the functions conferred upon him/her by the Constitution.

---

251. The Constitution of Malta (Amendment) Act, 2000 replaced section 22 of the Constitution by removing the restriction on dual and multiple citizenship.
252. Act No. III of 2000.

186. In all these four cases, an Acting President is appointed by the Prime Minister after consultation with the Leader of the Opposition.

187. If there is no person in Malta who is appointed Acting President and able to perform those functions, such duty falls upon, by express provision of the Constitution, the Chief Justice.[253] There is however no provision in the Constitution which states how long can the office of President remain vacant until the Chief Justice is so appointed by the Prime Minister.

§9. Reappointment of President

188. The Constitution does not allow the same person to be reappointed President both for a full term and in an acting capacity. Section 123(2) of the Constitution expressly excludes such a reappointment.

§10. Salary of the President of Malta

189. Although the Constitution does not state the exact amount of salary which the holder of the office of President should enjoy, the matter is regulated by the President of Malta and Other Officers (Salaries) Act.[254]

190. What the Constitution however provides for is that the salary payable to the President is a charge on the Consolidated Fund.[255] The President's salary and his/her term of office cannot 'be altered to his disadvantage after his appointment, and for the purposes of this sub-article, in so far as the salary or the terms of service of any person depend upon the option of that person, the salary or terms for which he opts shall be deemed to be more advantageous to him than any others for which he might have opted'.[256]

§11. Responsibility of the President

191. Section 5(1) of the Criminal Code[257] provides that 'no criminal action shall be prosecuted against the President of Malta in respect of acts done in the exercise of the functions of his office'; where, however, the criminal action relates to an act which is not done in the exercise of the functions of his/her office, the office holder of President does not enjoy any immunity. In those cases where the President enjoys immunity, that immunity cannot be waived as the Criminal Code does not allow for such waiver. On the other hand, section 742A of the Code of Organization and Civil Procedure states that 'no civil proceedings whatsoever shall be taken against the President of Malta in respect of acts done in the exercise of the functions of his office'. This provision

253. Constitution, section 49.
254. Chapter 186 of the Laws of Malta.
255. Constitution, section 107(2) and (4).
256. *Ibid.*, section 109(3).
257. Chapter 9 of the Laws of Malta.

was added to the Code of Organization and Civil Procedure in 1995.[258] Although the Code was promulgated in 1854, it did not contain such a provision between 1854 and 1995.

§12. President to Act Either on Advice or on Own Deliberate Judgment

192. Section 85 of the Constitution concerns the exercise of the functions of President. According to the Constitution, the President either acts on advice or on his/her own initiative. A study of the Constitution reveals that the rule is that the President acts on the advice of Government, and it is only in a handful of situations that he/she acts on his/her deliberate judgment.

I. Acting on Advice of the Government

193. Section 85(1) of the Constitution states that:

> In the exercise of his function the President shall act in accordance with the advice of the Cabinet or a Minister acting under the general authority of the Cabinet except in cases where he is required by this Constitution or any other law to act in accordance with the advice of any person or authority other than the Cabinet.

194. The general rule is that the President is bound by the Constitution to act on the advice of the Government, that is, either on the advice of Cabinet or a Cabinet Minister or on the advice of any other person or authority other than Cabinet or a minister.[259] Instances which can be cited from the Constitution where the President does not act on the advice of Cabinet or a Cabinet Minister but on the advice of another person or authority are few and far between. Such instances are when removing a member of the Commission for the Administration of Justice or any of its Committees, in accordance with the advice of the body or the holder of the office appointing such member[260] and when appointing the Auditor General,[261] the Deputy Auditor General[262] and the Ombudsman[263] in accordance with a resolution of the House supported by at least a two-thirds majority vote of all MPs.

---

258. By section 284 of the Code of Organization and Civil Procedure (Amendment) Act, 1995, Act No. XXIV of 1995.
259. *See* David Joseph Attard, *supra* note 25, pp. 47–48, provides a list of instances where the President acts on the advice of the Prime Minister.
260. Constitution, section 101A(9).
261. *Ibid.*, section 108(2).
262. *Ibid.*, section 108(9)(b).
263. *Ibid.*, section 64A(2) and Ombudsman Act, Chapter 385 of the Laws of Malta, section 3.

II. Acting on Own Deliberate Judgment

195. The situations where the President acts in accordance with his/her own deliberate judgment are listed in section 85(2) of the Constitution. They are the following:

(a) in the exercise of the powers relating to the dissolution of Parliament.[264] Indeed:

- 'if the House of Representatives passes a resolution, supported by the votes of a majority of all the members thereof, that it has no confidence in the Government and, the Prime Minister does not within three days either resign from his office or advise a dissolution, the President may dissolve Parliament';[265]
- 'if the office of Prime Minister is vacant and the President considers that there is no prospect of his being able within a reasonable time to appoint to that office a person who can command the support of a majority of the members of the House of Representatives, the President may dissolve Parliament';[266] and
- 'if the Prime Minister recommends a dissolution and the President considers that the Government of Malta can be carried on without a dissolution and that a dissolution would not be in the interests of Malta, the President may refuse to dissolve Parliament'.[267]

(b) when appointing or removing a Prime Minister from office;[268]
(c) when exercising the powers which relate to the performance of the functions of Prime Minister during absence, vacation or illness for appointing an Acting Prime Minister. Although the Constitution states in section 83(2) that when appointing an Acting Prime Minister, the President should exercise his/her power in accordance with the advice of the Prime Minister, the said provision further provides that 'if the President considers that it is impracticable to obtain the advice of the Prime Minister owing to his absence or illness he may exercise those powers without that advice';
(d) when appointing or revoking the appointment of Leader of the Opposition in terms of section 90 of the Constitution; and
(e) when approving his/her personal staff in terms of section 110(4) of the Constitution.

---

264. *Ibid.*, section 85(1), proviso, paragraph (a). Former Speaker Michael Frendo states that when President George Abela was in the process of deciding whether to dissolve Parliament following a request to that effect by Prime Minister Lawrence Gonzi whose government was defeated during the budget vote (*see* Michael J. Schiavone, *supra* note 211, pp. 980–983), the President had taken the initiative to carry out a consultation exercise with – amongst others – the Speaker before deciding to dissolve Parliament (*See* Andrew Azzopardi, *George Abela: Qalb in-Nies* (Translation: George Abela: The Heart of, and Amongst, the People), Kite, B'Kara, 2014, p. 77).
265. Constitution, section 76(5), proviso, paragraph (a).
266. *Ibid.*, section 76(5), proviso, paragraph (b).
267. *Ibid.*, section 76(5), proviso, paragraph (c).
268. *Ibid.*, section 85(1), proviso, paragraph (b) and sections 80(1) and 81.

§13. Powers Concerning the Parliamentary System

196. There are several inter-relationships between the President and the parliamentary system. These consist in the following:

(a) the President forms part of Parliament. This is because in terms of the Constitution, Parliament consists of the President and a House of Representatives;[269]
(b) on appointment by resolution of the House, the President takes the oath of office before the House;[270]
(c) the President has to assent to bills passed by the House so that those bills become law;[271]
(d) the President reads out the speech prepared by the Government on the opening of a new legislature;[272]
(e) the President recommends to the House, on the advice of a Minister, the adoption of certain financial measures, such as the budget, that is, before proceeding:

 - 'upon any bill (including any amendment to a bill) that, in the opinion of the person presiding, makes provision for any of the following purposes, that is to say, for imposing or increasing any tax, for imposing or increasing any charge on the revenues or other funds of Malta or for altering any such charge otherwise than by reducing it, or for compounding or remitting any debt due to Malta;
 - upon any motion (including any amendment to a motion) the effect of which, in the opinion of the person presiding, would be to make provision for any of the purposes aforesaid; or
 - to receive any petition which, in the opinion of the person presiding, requests that provision be made for any of the purposes aforesaid'.[273]

(f) the House may present an Address to the President to which the latter may reply;[274]
(g) the President, in terms of Standing Orders, can communicate with the House;[275]
(h) the President summons Parliament by proclamation at such time and place/s as he/she proclaims.[276] In summoning Parliament, the President shall ensure that it is summoned 'not later than two months after the publication of the official result of any general election by the Electoral Commission';[277]
(i) the President summons Parliament when the House is adjourned or prorogued;[278]

269. Constitution, section 51.
270. *Ibid.*, section 50 and Second Schedule.
271. *Ibid.*, section 72(2).
272. Standing Orders of the House of Representatives Order, S.L. Const. 02, standing order 6.
273. Constitution, section 73.
274. Standing Orders of the House of Representatives Order, Subsidiary Legislation Const. 02, Standing Orders 187–193.
275. *Ibid.*, Standing Orders 184–186.
276. Constitution, section 75(1).
277. *Ibid.*, section 75(3).
278. *Ibid.*, section 75(1).

(j) the President 'may at any time by proclamation prorogue or dissolve Parliament;'[279]
(k) the President may by proclamation recall a dissolved Parliament when 'an emergency arises of such a nature that, in the opinion of the Prime Minister it is necessary to recall Parliament';[280]
(l) when dissolving Parliament, the President acts on the advice of the Prime Minister except in the case of the three exceptions listed in section 76(5)(a) to (c);
(m) a general election is 'held at such time within three months after every dissolution of Parliament as the President acting in accordance with the advice of the Prime Minister, shall by proclamation appoint';[281]
(n) Parliament cannot confer functions on the President;[282]
(o) the President, by Proclamation, declares that a period of public emergency exists;[283]
(p) general elections are held on such date as the President by proclamation appoints;[284]
(q) the Attorney General may be removed from office by the President 'upon an address by the House supported by the votes of not less than two-thirds of all the members thereof';[285]
(r) the President also removes judges of the Superior Courts upon an address by the House supported by the votes of not less than two-thirds of all the members of the House;[286]
(s) the President may remove a Magistrate from office upon an address by the House supported by the votes of not less than two-thirds of all members thereof. A Magistrate is removed from office on the same grounds as those of the Attorney General or a judge, that is, 'on the ground of proved inability to perform the functions of his office (whether arising from infirmity of body or mind or any other cause) or proved misbehaviour';[287]
(t) the Auditor General is appointed by the President 'in accordance with a resolution of the House of Representatives supported by the vote of not less than two-thirds of all the members of the House';[288]
(u) the Auditor General may 'at any time be removed or suspended from his office by the President, upon an address from the House of Representatives supported by the vote of not less than two-thirds of all members of the House, praying for such removal on the ground of proved inability to perform the functions of his office (whether arising from infirmity of body or mind or any other cause) or proved misbehaviour';[289]
(v) the President may suspend the Auditor General when Parliament is not in session, 'in accordance with his own deliberate judgment, for inability to perform the

279. *Ibid.*, section 76(1).
280. *Ibid.*, section 76(4).
281. *Ibid.*, section 77.
282. *Ibid.*, section 78(3).
283. *Ibid.*, section 47(2)(b).
284. *Ibid.*, section 77.
285. *Ibid.*, section 91(5).
286. *Ibid.*, section 97(2).
287. *Ibid.*, section 100(2).
288. *Ibid.*, section 108(2).
289. *Ibid.*, section 108(4)(a).

functions of his office or misbehaviour proved to the satisfaction of the President; but any such suspension shall not continue in force beyond two months after the beginning of the next session of Parliament'.[290] Interestingly enough, in terms of the Constitution, it is only the Auditor General (and the Deputy Auditor General) who may be 'suspended' from office[291] but not the President, the Attorney General, the Chief Justice, Judges, Magistrates, members of the PSC, the Electoral Commission, the Commission for the Administration of Justice, the Broadcasting Authority, and the Ombudsman;

(w) the provisions relating to the appointment,[292] removal and suspension from office of the Auditor General, by the President upon an address by the House,[293] and the suspension of the Auditor General by the President in his/her own deliberate judgment,[294] apply to the Deputy Auditor General;[295]

(x) the office holder of President is appointed for only one term and such term may not be renewed;[296] and

(y) the oath of office of the President is set out in the Second Schedule.[297]

§14. Powers of Participation in the Activities of the Government

197. The President carries out several functions related to the governance of the country. These comprise the following:

(a) the President may 'by proclamation amend, add to, revoke or substitute the list of countries in the Fourth Schedule to this Constitution', that is, the list of Commonwealth countries;[298]

(b) the President may, by proclamation, declare that a state of public emergency exists;[299]

(c) the President is vested with the executive authority of Malta.[300] Such authority is 'exercised by the President, either directly or through officers subordinate to him, in accordance with the provisions of this Constitution'.[301] The latter wording implies that the President cannot exercise executive authority through officers subordinate to him/her in terms of any other law bearing also in mind the provisions

290. *Ibid.*, section 108(4)(b).
291. *Ibid.*, section 108(9)(b).
292. *Ibid.*, section 109(2).
293. *Ibid.*, section 108(4)(a).
294. *Ibid.*, section 108(4)(b).
295. *Ibid.*, section 108(9)(b).
296. *Ibid.*, section 123(2).
297. *Ibid.*, Second Schedule. Whilst section 50 requires both a President and an Acting President to take the oath of office, it does not require the President or an Acting President to take the oath of allegiance.
298. *Ibid.*, section 23(4). This list however needs updating with regard to The Gambia, which severed its connection with the Commonwealth on 3 October 2013.
299. *Ibid.*, section 47(2)(b).
300. *Ibid.*, section 78(1).
301. *Ibid.*, section 78(2).

of section 79(3) which prohibits Parliament from conferring functions on the President, in addition to those already assigned to him/her by the Constitution;

(d) it is the President who appoints the Prime Minister;[302]

(e) it is also the President who appoints Ministers;[303]

(f) should Parliament be dissolved and a need arises to appoint a Prime Minister and/or Ministers, the President may still make that appointment from former members of the House;[304]

(g) in the case of a no confidence vote in the government passed by a majority of MPs in the House, the President may remove the Prime Minister from office. However, 'the President shall not do so unless three days have elapsed and he has decided not to dissolve Parliament under section 76 of this Constitution';[305]

(h) the President may make subsidiary legislation under a number of laws such as rules of court in terms of section 29(1) of the Code of Organization and Civil Procedure and section 516(3) of the Criminal Code;

(i) the President may appoint another person as Prime Minister after a dissolution of Parliament;[306]

(j) the President may revoke, in accordance with the advice of the Prime Minister, a Minister's appointment;[307]

(k) the President, in accordance with the advice of the Prime Minister, allocates portfolios to Ministers.[308] But the President cannot allocate any duty to a Minister which is by the Constitution or any other law allocated to any other person or authority;[309]

(l) the President appoints an Acting Prime Minister.[310] In doing so, he/she acts in accordance with the advice of the Prime Minister unless 'the President considers that it is impracticable to obtain the advice of the Prime Minister owing to his absence or illness';[311]

(m) the President may appoint a temporary Minister from amongst MPs when a Minister is 'unable, by reason of his illness or absence from Malta, to perform the functions of his office'.[312] Should Parliament be dissolved, a temporary Minister may be appointed from amongst those persons who, prior to dissolution of Parliament, were MPs.[313] A temporary Minister holds office until the President informs him/her that the office holder has assumed the functions of office.[314]

---

302. *Ibid.*, section 80.
303. *Ibid.*
304. *Ibid.*
305. *Ibid.*, section 81(1).
306. *Ibid.*, section 81(2)(a).
307. *Ibid.*, section 81(3)(b).
308. *Ibid.*, section 82(1).
309. *Ibid.*, section 82(2).
310. *Ibid.*, section 83(1).
311. *Ibid.*, section 83(2).
312. *Ibid.*, section 84(1).
313. *Ibid.*, section 84(1) proviso.
314. *Ibid.*, section 84(2).

When appointing a temporary Minister, the President is to act on the advice of the Prime Minister;[315]

(n) when exercising his/her functions, the President acts on the advice of Cabinet or a Cabinet Minister except in those cases where the Constitution or any other law requires him/her to act on the advice of another person or authority[316] or on his/her own deliberate judgment;[317]

(o) whenever the President acts on advice, it cannot be enquired into any court whether he/she has received or acted in accordance with that advice;[318]

(p) the Prime Minister has to 'keep the President fully informed concerning the general conduct of the Government of Malta' and the Prime Minister has to 'furnish the President with such information as he [the President] may request with respect to any particular matter relating to the Government of Malta';[319]

(q) the President, in accordance with the advice of the Prime Minister, appoints Parliamentary Secretaries to assist Ministers in the performance of their duties.[320] Should Parliament be dissolved, a Parliamentary Secretary may be appointed from amongst those persons who were, prior to Parliament's dissolution, MPs;[321]

(r) the office of Parliamentary Secretary becomes vacant if the President, acting in accordance with the advice of the Prime Minister, revokes his/her appointment;[322]

(s) the President appoints the Leader of the Opposition;[323]

(t) the President may remove the Leader of the Opposition if, after a dissolution of Parliament, the President decides to appoint another person as Leader of the Opposition;[324]

(u) the President appoints, on the advice of the Prime Minister, the Attorney General;[325]

(v) the President appoints, on the advice of the Prime Minister after the latter has consulted the PSC, Permanent Secretaries and Acting Permanent Secretaries and, in the same manner, removes from office Permanent Secretaries and Acting Permanent Secretaries;[326]

(w) the President exercises, on the advice of the government, normally of the Cabinet or of the Minister responsible for justice, the prerogative of mercy.[327] The prerogative of mercy empowers the President to:

---

315. *Ibid.*, section 84(3).
316. *Ibid.*, section 85(1).
317. *Ibid.*, section 85(1) proviso.
318. *Ibid.*, section 85(2).
319. *Ibid.*, section 87.
320. *Ibid.*, section 88(1).
321. *Ibid.*, section 88(1) proviso.
322. *Ibid.*, sections 88(2) and 81(3)(b).
323. *Ibid.*, section 90(1).
324. *Ibid.*, section 90(3)(a).
325. *Ibid.*, section 91(1).
326. *Ibid.*, section 92(3).
327. *Ibid.*, section 93(1). *See* Kevin Aquilina, 'For Mercy to Be Fair to All', *The Times of Malta*, 26 February 2013, p. 17.

- 'grant to any person concerned or convicted of any offence a pardon, either free or subject to lawful conditions';[328]
- 'grant to any person a respite, either indefinite or for a specified period, of the execution of any sentence passed on that person for any offence';[329]
- 'substitute a less severe form of punishment for any punishment imposed on any person for any offence';[330]
- 'remit the whole or part of any sentence passed on any person for an offence or for any penalty or forfeiture otherwise due to the State on account of any offence.'[331]

(x) although the Constitution still authorizes the President, on the advice of the Cabinet, to grant a pardon or respite to any person sentenced to death by any court in Malta,[332] there is no longer any provision in Maltese Law which allows the infliction of capital punishment as the death penalty was removed from Maltese Law when Malta ratified the Sixth and Thirteenth Protocols of the ECHR abolishing the death penalty;
(y) the President appoints, on the advice of the Prime Minister, the judges of the Superior Courts, that is, the Chief Justice and judges;[333]
(z) the President, in accordance with the advice of the Prime Minister, appoints an Acting Chief Justice;[334]
(aa) the President, in accordance with the advice of the Prime Minister, also appoints an Acting Judge;[335]
(ab) an Acting Judge continues to act until the period of his appointment lapses or, 'if no such period is specified, until his appointment is revoked by the President acting in accordance with the advice of the Prime Minister';[336]
(ac) Magistrates of the Inferior Courts are appointed by the President acting in accordance with the advice of the Prime Minister;[337]
(ad) the 'powers of the President under any law with regard to the subrogation of judges and magistrates shall be exercised on the advice of the Minister responsible for justice, so however that, the Minister shall, in advising the President, act in accordance with any recommendation on the matter by the Chief Justice';[338]
(ae) where the Chief Justice fails to make such a recommendation and 'in any case where the Minister deems it so appropriate, the Minister may advise the President on the matter' and in any such case the Minister 'shall immediately publish in the *Gazette*, a notice of that fact together with the reasons therefor, and he shall

328. *Ibid.*, section 93(1)(a).
329. *Ibid.*, section 93(1)(b).
330. *Ibid.*, section 93(1)(c).
331. *Ibid.*, section 93(1)(d).
332. *Ibid.*, section 93(2)(b).
333. *Ibid.*, section 96(1).
334. *Ibid.*, section 98(1).
335. *Ibid.*, section 98(2).
336. *Ibid.*, section 98(3). *See Tonio Azzopardi v. Honourable Prime Minister et*, Constitutional Court, 4 November 1992.
337. *Ibid.*, section 100(1).
338. *Ibid.*, section 101A(13).

make a statement of such fact in the House of Representatives not later than the second sitting immediately after he has so advised the President';[339]

(af) the President is to be paid such salary as may be prescribed by or under any law.[340] As a matter of fact, the salary of the President is prescribed by the President of Malta and Other Officers (Salaries) Act;[341]

(ag) the President's salary is a charge on the Consolidated Fund;[342]

(ah) after appointment, the salary of the President cannot be altered to his/her disadvantage;[343]

(ai) the Auditor General has to, before the President, subscribe to the oath of allegiance and the oath for the due execution of his/her office;[344]

(aj) the President appoints the members of the PSC in accordance with the advice of the Prime Minister given after he/she has consulted the Leader of the Opposition;[345]

(ak) the President, acting in accordance with the advice of the Prime Minister, may remove from office a member of the PSC for 'inability to discharge the functions of his office (whether arising from infirmity of mind or body or any other cause) or for misbehaviour';[346]

(al) the President, acting on the advice of the Prime Minister given after the Prime Minister has consulted the Leader of the Opposition, appoints temporary members of the PSC;[347]

(am) the President, acting on the advice of the Prime Minister, appoints Ambassadors, High Commissioners and other principal representatives of Malta in any other country;[348]

(an) the President, on the advice of the Prime Minister after the latter has consulted the Leader of the Opposition, appoints the members of the Broadcasting Authority;[349]

(ao) the President, acting in accordance with the advice of the Prime Minister, removes a member of the Broadcasting Authority, 'only for inability to discharge the functions of his office (whether arising from infirmity of mind or body or any other cause) or for misbehaviour';[350]

(ap) the President, acting on the advice of the Prime Minister after the latter has consulted the Leader of the Opposition, appoints temporary members of the Broadcasting Authority;[351]

(aq) the President appoints the members of the Employment Commission. He/she appoints the Chairman in accordance with the advice of the Prime Minister given after the latter has consulted the Leader of the Opposition; he/she appoints two

339. *Ibid.*, section 101A(13) first and second proviso.
340. *Ibid.*, section 107(1).
341. Chapter 186 of the Laws of Malta.
342. *Ibid.*, section 107(2).
343. *Ibid.*, section 107(3).
344. *Ibid.*, section 108(7).
345. *Ibid.*, section 109(2).
346. *Ibid.*, section 109(6).
347. *Ibid.*, section 109(7).
348. *Ibid.*, section 111(1).
349. *Ibid.*, section 118(2).
350. *Ibid.*, section 118(6).
351. *Ibid.*, section 118(7).

members in accordance with the advice of the Prime Minister and another two members in accordance with the advice of the Leader of the Opposition;[352]

(ar) the President removes members of the Employment Commission on the advice of the holder of the office on whose advice such member was appointed. Removal takes place on the grounds only of 'inability to discharge the functions of his office (whether arising from infirmity of mind or body or any other cause) or for misbehaviour';[353]

(as) the President, acting in accordance with the advice of the holder of the office on whose advice such member of the Employment Commission was appointed, may appoint a temporary member of the Commission;[354] and

(at) the President has to approve the appointment of his/her personal staff.[355]

§15. Powers of Participation in the Activities of the Judiciary

198. The President exercises powers in relation to the Judiciary. These comprise the following:

(a) the President, acting in accordance with the advice of the Prime Minister, appoints the judges of the Superior Courts.[356] Contrary to other European states which do not vest judicial appointment powers in the executive organ of the state, in Malta the Chief Justice and Judges are appointed by government;

(b) the President, this time acting upon an address by the House supported by the votes of not less than two-thirds of all the members thereof, removes judges of the Superior Courts 'on the ground of proved inability to perform the functions of his office (whether arising from infirmity of body or mind or any other cause) or proved misbehaviour';[357]

(c) the President, acting in accordance with the advice of the Prime Minister, appoints the Acting Chief Justice and acting judges;[358]

(d) an acting judge continues in office until 'his appointment is revoked by the President acting in accordance with the advice of the Prime Minister';[359]

(e) the President, acting in accordance with the advice of the Prime Minister, appoints Magistrates of the Inferior Courts;[360]

(f) the President upon an address by the House of Representatives supported by the votes of not less than two-thirds of all the members of the House removes Magistrates from judicial office;[361]

352. *Ibid.*, section 120(2).
353. *Ibid.*, section 120(6).
354. *Ibid.*, section 120(7).
355. *Ibid.*, section 85(1), proviso, paragraph (e) and section 110(4).
356. *Ibid.*, section 96(1). *See also* section 96(3) and (4) and 96A.
357. Constitution, section 97(2).
358. *Ibid.*, section 98(2).
359. *Ibid.*, section 98(3).
360. *Ibid.*, section 100(1).
361. *Ibid.*, section 100(4).

(g) the President chairs the Commission for the Administration of Justice;[362]
(h) the President enjoys a casting vote but not an original vote when chairing the Commission for the Administration of Justice;[363]
(i) the President, acting in accordance with his/her own deliberate judgment, appoints substitute members to Commission for the Administration of Justice members who are successfully challenged or abstain who 'in his opinion has as far as may be the same qualities and qualifications as the member substituted';[364]
(j) when a judge or a magistrate has to be elected as member of the Commission for the Administration of Justice or a person has to be appointed by the Prime Minister and/or the Leader of the Opposition and any of such members are neither elected nor appointed, the President makes such appointment 'in accordance with his own deliberate judgment' and he/she shall 'appoint members in their stead who where possible in his opinion shall have the same qualities and qualifications as such members';[365]
(k) the President removes members on the Commission for the Administration of Justice and any of its committees, 'acting in accordance with the advice of the body or the holder of the office appointing such member, but he may be removed only for inability to discharge the functions of his office (whether arising from infirmity of mind or body or any other cause) or for misbehaviour';[366]
(l) the President subrogates judges and magistrates and assigns duties to judges and magistrates on the advice of the Minister responsible for justice acting in accordance with a recommendation on both matters by the Chief Justice. Should the Chief Justice fail to make his/her recommendation, the Minister may advise the President this notwithstanding but the Minister has to publish his/her advice in the Gazette and make a statement in the House not later than the second sitting after the Minister has so advised the President;[367]
(m) the President appoints a judge sitting in the Court of Appeal and a magistrate, on the recommendation of the Chief Justice, to sit on the Rule Making Board;[368]
(n) rules of court made by the Rule Making Board established under section 29(1) of the Code of Organization and Civil Procedure have to be approved by the President to be effective;[369]
(o) the President appoints a judge ordinarily sitting in the Criminal Court on the Board to make rules of court with regard to the courts of criminal jurisdiction;[370]
(p) the President has to approve the rules made by the Board established by section 516(3) of the Criminal Code;[371]

362. *Ibid.*, section 101A(1). *See also* section 101B(12)(e).
363. *Ibid.*, section 101A(2).
364. *Ibid.*, section 101A(5)(b).
365. *Ibid.*, section 101A(5)(c).
366. *Ibid.*, section 101A(10).
367. *Ibid.*, section 101A(13).
368. Code of Organization and Civil Procedure, section 29(1).
369. *Ibid.*, section 29(4).
370. Criminal Code, section 516(3).
371. *Ibid.*, section 516(5).

(q) the President approves rules of court made by the Rule Making Board established by section 29(1) of the Code of Organization and Civil Procedure in terms of section 46(7) of the Constitution;
(r) the President approves rules of court made by the Rule Making Board established by section 29(1) of the Code of Organization and Civil Procedure in terms of section 4(6) of the European Convention Act;
(s) the President approves the rules made by the Rule Making Board established by section 29(1) of the Code of Organization and Civil Procedure concerning the election of members on the Commission for the Administration of Justice;[372]
(t) the Chief Justice may be called upon to exercise the functions of an Acting President when the President cannot discharge the functions of office;[373]
(u) the President carries out functions related to the chairmanship of the Commission for the Administration of Justice;[374]
(v) the President appoints Judicial Assistants;[375]
(w) the President is invited to attend the opening ceremony of the forensic year held on 1 October of every year at the Courts of Justice building in Republic Street, Valletta.[376]

§16. Functions Concerning International Relations

199. Although the Constitution does not devolve upon the President any function concerning international relations, he/she appoints and removes, on the advice of the Prime Minister, persons to the offices of Ambassador, High Commissioner and other principal representative in any other country.[377] He/she receives Ambassadors, High Commissioners and principal representatives of foreign states during a ceremonial function held at the Palace in Valletta where heads of diplomatic missions present their credentials to the President. A consul is appointed and removed by the President even if there is no written law to this effect.[378]

§17. Functions Concerning the Armed Forces of Malta

200. In 1970, the Malta Armed Forces Act[379] was enacted, and it assigns to the President manifold functions. Section 3 empowers the President to raise and maintain an armed force:

372. *Ibid.*, section 101A(3).
373. *Ibid.*, section 49.
374. Commission for the Administration of Justice Act, Chapter 369 of the Laws of Malta, sections 3(3)(b), 3(4), 3(7)(a), 9(1), 9(6) and 10(1).
375. Code of Organization and Civil Procedure, section 97A(1).
376. The President does not take an active role in this ceremony because it is the Chief Justice and the President of the Chamber of Advocates who delivery addresses on this occasion.
377. Constitution, section 111(1).
378. *See* Ugo Mifsud Bonnici, *supra* note 190.
379. Chapter 220 of the Laws of Malta.

> **3.** (1) It shall be lawful for the President of Malta to raise by voluntary enlistment and maintain an armed force, consisting of a regular and of a territorial force or of either of such forces (including the reserve of such forces), and consisting of such units of any arm and subject to such designation of title as may be prescribed or as the President of Malta may direct.

201. The President is empowered to make regulations or orders 'with respect to the establishment, government, and discipline of the force, or any part or unit thereof, the pay, allowances, pensions and gratuities payable to and the enlistment, the terms, conditions and extensions of service and the discharge and training of, members of the force or of any part or unit thereof, and with respect to all other matters and things relating to the force, including any matter by this Act authorized to be prescribed or expressed to be subject to regulations or orders; and may make different regulations or orders or make different provision with respect to the regular force and to the territorial force'.[380]

202. The President is also given powers 'by order to empower any member of the force to exercise, in addition to any functions, powers and duties he may have as a member of the force, all or any one or more of the functions, powers and duties as are by law vested in a member of the Malta Police Force and in an officer of the Customs'.[381] An order to this effect was made by the President in 1980, the Assignment of Powers to Armed Forces of Malta Order.[382]

203. The President may also by order signified under the hand of the Minister responsible for defence, if it appears to the President that a national danger is imminent or that a great emergency has arisen, 'provide that men who would otherwise fall to be transferred to the reserve list still continue in service'.[383] Such order has to be communicated forthwith to the House.[384] But the said order may be revoked by order of the President signified by the Minister responsible for the armed forces.

204. In terms of section 11(3) of the Malta Armed Forces Act, a man of the regular force may be discharged by the President, except in pursuance of a sentence of a court martial.

205. The President is also empowered by order signified by the Minister responsible for defence to order that 'the territorial force be called out on permanent service' if 'it appears to the President of Malta that national danger is imminent or that a great emergency has arisen'.[385] On the other hand, the President may once again by order signified under the hand of the Minister, 'order the territorial force to be disembodied'.[386] The President may also authorize 'the calling out of any reserve force on permanent service' by order signified under the hand of the Minister responsible for defence if 'it appears to the President of Malta that national danger is imminent or

380. Malta Armed Forces Act, section 4(1).
381. *Ibid.*, section 4(3).
382. Subsidiary Legislation 220.06.
383. Malta Armed Forces Act, section 10(1).
384. *Ibid.*, section 10(2).
385. Malta Armed Forces Act, section 26(1).
386. *Ibid.*, section 27(1).

that a great emergency has arisen'.[387] Such an order may be revoked by the President signified as above.[388]

206. In terms of section 92 of the Malta Armed Forces Act, a general court martial is convened by any officer authorized by the President by warrant under his/her hand. Such officer may in turn delegate his/her power to convene general courts martial to another officer under his/her command.[389]

207. The President is designated as a reviewing authority in the case of sentences of courts martial.[390]

208. Insofar as redress of complaints is concerned, if 'an officer thinks himself wronged in any matter by a superior officer or authority and on application to his commanding officer does not obtain the redress to which he thinks he is entitled, he may make a complaint with respect to that matter to the Commander in terms of section 160(1) of the Malta Armed Forces Act'.[391] If the complainant requires, the Commander shall through the Minister responsible for defence, 'make his report on the complaint to the President of Malta in order to receive the directions of the President of Malta thereon'.[392] This provision is lifted from section 180 of the British Army Act 1955.[393] The UK *Manual of Military Law* comments as follows on this section:

> It is the custom of the service to forward every complaint through the officer commanding the regiment; and an officer would not be justified in deviating from this course, unless the commanding officer should refuse, or unreasonably delay, to forward it. An officer, on addressing himself directly to the general in command, should apprise his commanding officer of his doing so, and must observe in the channel of approach to the Commander-in-Chief each intermediate gradation of command.
>
> Although the Commander-in-Chief is required to examine into the complaint and report to His Majesty, he is not debarred from expressing his own view of the case. Even an expression of opinion by the intermediate general officer will in many cases suffice to render further steps unnecessary. An officer should not be disposed to push to extremes his right to bring his complaint before the Sovereign. The report to His Majesty is to be made through the Secretary of State, the constitutional adviser of the Crown.
>
> This section does not appear to limit the right of the Sovereign to receive complaints, but only to control the manner in which officers thinking themselves wronged are to approach the Sovereign. Therefore, although there may be no

387. *Ibid.*, section 32(1).
388. *Ibid.*, section 32(3).
389. *Ibid.*, section 92(1).
390. *Ibid.*, section 114(2)(a).
391. *Ibid.*, section 160(1).
392. *Ibid.*, section 160(2).
393. 3 & 4 Eliz. 2 Chapter 18.

Commander-in-Chief, it remains open to the Sovereign to give directions as to any complaints which may be brought before him by the Secretary of State.[394]

209. Section 160 does not apply to all members of the Armed Forces of Malta but only to officers as distinct from men of the force. The latter are regulated by a different complaint's procedure, by section 161 of the Malta Armed Forces Act. But the President is not involved under section 161 for the complaint is investigated by the Commander. This means that redress in terms of section 160 can be given, if the compliant is successful by the Commander or, at the request of the officer, by the President. In communicating with the President, the Commander acts through the Minister responsible for defence.

210. On the other hand, the Ombudsman Act provides in section 12(3)(b) that it 'does not apply to the bodies listed in Part B of the First Schedule to this Act' which, *inter alia*, comprises the Armed Forces of Malta, 'unless proof to the satisfaction of the Ombudsman is produced showing that all available means of redress have been exhausted'. First, this means that the Ombudsman comes into the picture at the very end after 'all available means of redress have been exhausted'. The Ombudsman's jurisdiction on the Armed Forces of Malta is thus qualified by limiting it 'in respect only of appointments, promotion, pay and pension rights of officers and men of the force'.[395] Second, the proof has to be adduced to the Ombudsman that 'all available means of redress have been exhausted', and that it is the Ombudsman who is the final arbiter in establishing such proof. Third, the Ombudsman has to be satisfied that 'all available means of redress have been exhausted'. Fourth, although the Ombudsman is empowered to decline to investigate a complaint 'where adequate means of redress are or have been available to the complainant under any other law', he/she may still 'conduct an investigation if satisfied that in the particular circumstances it is not reasonable to expect the complainant to resort or have resorted to such means of redress'.[396] Fifth, the provision does not state that the outcome of these means of redress has to be effective, either in full or in part, or such as to provide a remedy.

§18. Power to Confer Honours

211. In terms of the *Ġieh ir-Repubblika* Act,[397] the President confers various types of honours. These honours are normally conferred on Republic Day, 13 December, of each year. The President, upon the written advice of the Prime Minister,[398] appoints as members of the society[399] known as *Ġieh ir-Repubblika* not more than three persons every two years.[400] Members of the National Order of Merit are also appointed by the

394. War Office, *Manual of Military Law*, H.M.S.O., London, 1907, p. 301.
395. Ombudsman Act, Chapter 385 of the Laws of Malta, First Schedule, Part B.
396. *Ibid.*, section 13(3). *See Chief Justice Emeritus Joseph Said Pullicino noe v Minister for Home Affairs and National Security et*, Court of Appeal, 31 October 2016.
397. Chapter 251 of the Laws of Malta.
398. *Ġieh ir-Repubblika* Act (Translation: Republic Honours Act), section 3(1).
399. Society is translated into Maltese as 'Ix-Xirka'.
400. *Ġieh ir-Repubblika* Act, section 4(1).

President on the advice of the Prime Minister.[401] The President of Malta is, by virtue of his/her office, a Companion of Honour of the National Honour of Merit whilst all former Presidents are also Companions of Honour of the Order.[402] The President may award the honour of Companion of Honour of the National Order of Merit even posthumously to a person who has served as Acting President for a period of not less than one year when the office of President is vacant.[403] A medal for bravery is also conferred by the President, on the written advice of the Prime Minister, 'to any Maltese citizen for an act of exceptional bravery'.[404] The President also awards medals for service to the Republic, on the written advice of the Prime Minister.[405] The President may also award this latter medal to a group of persons or to a voluntary organization duly enrolled with the Commissioner for Voluntary Organisations in terms of the Voluntary Organisations Act.[406] In addition, national commemorative medals are approved by the President on the advice of the Prime Minister.[407] All honours awarded are published in the *Gazette*.

212. The President of Malta is the head of the Society and of the National Order of Merit.[408] The President, acting on the advice of the Prime Minister, appoints in addition to the Secretary to the Cabinet who acts as Chancellor of the Society and of the National Order of Merit, other officials of the Society and of the Order.[409] The seals of the *Xirka* and of the Order are kept in the President's custody.[410] The President may also make rules to supplement the provisions of the *Ġieh ir-Repubblika* Act.[411]

§19. Functions of President under Other Laws

213. The President exercises other functions under other laws.[412] It is not necessary to list all these laws as there are quite a number of them, but the most salient ones relate to expropriation of property,[413] the signing of warrants for various professionals,[414] and making regulations with regard to the award of pension,[415] just to mention three such laws. In the past, the Governor-General used to exercise functions

401. *Ibid.*, section 7(1).
402. *Ibid.*, section 8(5).
403. *Ibid.*, section 8(6). Such has been the case of Dr Paul Xuereb who served in that capacity for two years and one month and a half. *See* Michael J. Schiavone, *supra* note 211, p. 1258.
404. *Ibid.*, section 10(1).
405. *Ibid.*, section 11(1).
406. Chapter 492 of the Laws of Malta.
407. *Ġieh ir-Repubblika* Act, section 15(1).
408. *Ibid.*, section 19(1).
409. *Ibid.*, section 19(3).
410. *Ibid.*, section 25(2).
411. *Ibid.*, section 26.
412. *See* Ugo Mifsud Bonnici, *supra* note 190, pp. 258–266 and p. 274, and p. 278.
413. Land Acquisition (Public Purposes) Ordinance, Chapter 88 of the Laws of Malta.
414. For instance, the warrants of advocate and legal procurator in terms of the Code of Organization and Civil Procedure, Chapter 12 of the Laws of Malta, sections 79 and 85 respectively.
415. Pensions Ordinance, Chapter 93 of the Laws of Malta.

which have not been granted to the President on becoming a republic.[416] One notable example is that the Governor-General was ex officio Chancellor of the Royal University of Malta (as it was then known) and so was the President up prior to the enactment of the Education Act 1988.

§20. President's Fora and Foundations

214. Under the presidency of Dr George Abela, a President's Forum was established. Three annual fora were held. The first dealt with contemporary Malta whilst the second and third with constitutional reform. As former President Abela wrote in the introduction to the book in which the proceedings of these two fora on constitutional reform were published:[417]

> As President of Malta and guardian of the Constitution, I felt it to be my duty to promote discussion on possible reforms to our Constitution which has served the Maltese People well but which, like all living documents in a rapidly changing world, necessarily needs to evolve and develop in order to adapt to present circumstances.[418]

215. Under the presidency of H.E. Marie Louise Coleiro Preca, a President's Foundation for the Wellbeing of Society with a Board of Governance made up of former Presidents and Prime Ministers, was officially launched on 25 June 2014. Further information is available at the Foundation's website, www.pfws.org.mt/en/home.

216. A Trade Unions National Forum was established on 23 July 2014 by the President of Malta H.E. Marie Louise Coleiro Preca. It was established as a joint venture between the Presidency and the Centre for Labour Studies at the University of Malta.[419]

§21. The President and Philanthropy: The Community Chest Fund Foundation

217. Perhaps the office of President is better known in Malta more for its philanthropy than for the exercise of its constitutional functions. Yet the office of

416. *See* Ugo Mifsud Bonnici, An Introduction to the Law of Education, Malta University Press, Msida, 2013, p. 154; and Andrew Azzopardi, *supra* note 264, pp. 81–84.
417. Department of Information, Press Release 2224, *Publication of Speeches Delivered at the President's Forum in 2012 and 2013 on 'Does Malta's Constitution Still Cater for the People's Needs?'*, Department of Information, Valletta, Valletta, 11 October 2013.
418. President George Abela, 'Foreword', in Office of the President, *The President's Forum: Does Malta's Constitution Still Cater for the People's Needs?*, Office of the President, Valletta, 2013, p. 6.
419. Department of Information Press Release, 141672, Department of Information, Valletta, 23 July 2014.

President is a very prestigious office; it symbolizes national unity and also comes with a human dimension as the President is responsible for the Community Chest Fund Foundation, a charitable state institution, administered and run by the President's Office. In this respect, the President is very much near to the people and is totally immune to the criticism that he/she is running the country from the Palace far away from, with no interaction at all with, the population.[420] Lately, by means of a deed in the Acts of Notary Pierre Attard on the 25 April 2015, the Malta Community Chest Fund was established as a Foundation. According to the deed, the 'activities which led to the establishment of the organization now named the Malta Community Chest Fund date back to the nineteen fifties (1950s) when funds were raised for the fulfilment of social purposes'.[421]

§22. Concluding Remarks on the Presidency

218. The office of President has developed, according to Ian Refalo, into one which:

> provides an element of stability to the Constitution and his office has truly developed into a symbol of national unity. His main role comes into play chiefly in situations of political crisis, where the political future is uncertain and difficult decisions need to be taken. In those circumstances he exercises a key role in ensuring stability, continuity and democratic responsiveness. It is to him that the Constitution turns where the government suffers a defeat in parliament. He has to take the necessary decisions to see that stability and order are preserved and government continued. He decides ultimately as to whether to dissolve Parliament, dismiss the Prime Minister, or appoint an alternative Prime Minister eschewing dismissal.[422]

420. For a brief history of the Community Chest Fund, *see* Ugo Mifsud Bonnici, *Konvinzjoni u Esperjenza (Translation: Conviction and Experience)*, Klabb Kotba Maltin (Translation: Malta Book Club), 2015, pp. 1135–1137.
421. Deed No. 50 of 2015 in the Acts of Notary Pierre Attard, LL.D., paragraph 1.1.
422. *See* Ian Refalo, 'The Republic of Malta' in Constantijin Kortmann, Joseph Fleuren and Wim Voermans (eds.), *Constitutional Law of 10 EU Member States: The 2004 Enlargement,* Kluwer Law International, Deventer, The Netherlands, 2006, p. VII-21.

Chapter 3. The Structure of Parliament

§1. The Unicameral System: An Introduction

219. The Maltese Parliament consists of only one house, the House of Representatives, even if, in colonial times, there was an instance where the crown colony of Malta had a bicameral parliamentary system consisting of an upper house – the Senate – and a lower house – the Legislative Assembly.

220. The unicameral House of Representatives is composed only of elected Members of Parliament although there are two exceptions to this rule:

(a) the Speaker need not necessarily be elected from amongst MPs. He/she may be elected 'from among members who are not members of the House of Representatives and are qualified for election as members thereof'.[423] Such was the case, for instance, of Dr Lawrence Gonzi who was appointed Speaker of the House from outside its membership;[424] and
(b) a person may be co-opted in the House without being elected if it is not possible to fill in a vacancy in the House following a bye-election. Notable persons who became MPs through co-option are: Dr Eddie Fenech Adami,[425] Dr Karmenu Mifsud Bonnici,[426] Dr Alfred Sant[427] and Dr Joseph Muscat.[428]

221. All these four MPs, who began their parliamentary life through a co-option, ended up Prime Ministers and Leaders of their respective political party.

222. The matter related to co-option of an MP is not regulated by the Constitution but by an Act of Parliament, the General Elections Act,[429] in Part IV of the General Elections (Sorting of Ballot Papers, Casual Elections and Co-options) Regulations, 1991 contained in the Thirteenth Schedule to the General Elections Act and the Annex to such Schedule.[430] The said Part IV 'may only be deleted, amended or substituted by a bill for an Act of Parliament passed in the manner specified in sub-article (2) of

423. Constitution, section 59(2)(b).
424. *See* Michael J. Schiavone, *supra* note 211, p. 650 and p. 697.
425. Dr Eddie Fenech Adami was co-opted on 7 October 1969 following the demise of Ġorġ Caruana. *See* Michael J. Schiavone, *supra* note 211, p. 463. As to how the co-option took place, *see* Eddie Fenech Adami with the assistance of Steve Mallia, *Eddie: My Journey*, Allied Publications, Valletta, 2014, in particular Chapter 6, Co-option to Parliament, pp. 33–44.
426. Dr Karmenu Mifsud Bonnici was co-opted on 2 May 1983 instead of Paul Xuereb. Michael J. Schiavone, *supra* note 211, p. 587.
427. Dr Alfred Sant was co-opted on 9 December 1987 instead of Joseph Sciberras who had passed away. Michael J. Schiavone, *supra* note 211, p. 643.
428. Dr Joseph Muscat was co-opted on 30 September 2008 instead of Joseph Cuschieri who resigned to allow Dr Muscat to become an MP. Michael J. Schiavone, *supra* note 211, p. 922.
429. Chapter 354 of the Laws of Malta.
430. *Ibid.*, section 52(3).

Article 66 of this Constitution', that is, with the support of 'not less than two-thirds of all the members of the House'.[431]

223. Parliament has a five-year life span, unless, of course, it is not dissolved earlier: 'Parliament, unless sooner dissolved, shall continue for five years from the date of its first sitting after any dissolution and shall then stand dissolved.'[432] Once again, there are exceptions to this rule, namely:

(a) when Malta is at war, 'Parliament may from time to time extend the period of five years ... for not more than twelve months at a time: Provided that the life of Parliament shall not be extended under this sub-article for more than five years';[433]
(b) when Parliament has been dissolved but general elections have not taken place as 'an emergency arises of such a nature that, in the opinion of the Prime Minister, it is necessary to recall Parliament';[434]
(c) when Parliament intends to extend its own life span by amending section 76(2) of the Constitution. Moreover, for Parliament to be able to do so, it requires not only the support of the votes of at least two-thirds of all the members of the House but also a majority vote of electors on a bill during a referendum.[435]

224. The House can be dissolved by the President: 'The President may at any time by proclamation prorogue or dissolve Parliament.'[436] Once Parliament rests dissolved, a 'general election of members of the House of Representatives shall be held at such time within three months after every dissolution of Parliament as the President acting in accordance with the advice of the Prime Minister, shall by proclamation appoint'.[437]

225. Although the House is a political body, it does enjoy judicial powers. Such is the case, for instance, with regard to:

(a) the removal of the Attorney General;[438]
(b) the removal of judges of the Superior Courts;[439]
(c) the removal of magistrates of the Inferior Courts;[440] and
(d) contempt of, and other offences against, Parliament in terms of the House of Representatives (Privileges and Powers) Ordinance.[441]

---

431. *Ibid.*, section 66(2).
432. *Ibid.*, section 76(2).
433. *Ibid.*, section 76(3).
434. *Ibid.*, section 76(4).
435. *Ibid.*, section 66(3).
436. *Ibid.*, section 76(1).
437. *Ibid.*, section 77.
438. *Ibid.*, section 91(5).
439. Constitution, section 97(2).
440. *Ibid.*, section 100(4).
441. Chapter 113 of the Laws of Malta, section 11(3)(b) and (12).

§2. THE ELECTORAL SYSTEM

226. Elections are governed by the following laws:

(a) the Constitution insofar as elections to the House of Representatives are concerned;[442]
(b) the General Elections Act;[443]
(c) the European Parliament Elections Act;[444] and
(d) the Local Councils Act insofar as local government authorities' elections are concerned;[445]
(e) the Constitution insofar as referenda to amend the Constitution are concerned.[446]

227. Malta adopts the principle of proportional representation[447] with regard to all forms of voting, be it to the House of Representatives, the EU Parliament, Local Councils and Administrative Committees. The single transferable vote is used whereby it is possible to vote for the candidates of one's choice even if need be from different political parties, that is, by resorting to cross-party voting. Candidates are selected in order of preference, with the number one being the first preference, number two being the second preference, and so on and so forth. Contrary to the party list, where parties rather than candidates are elected, in the single transferable vote electoral system, it is candidates who are voted and elected, if successful, to Parliament. The single transferable vote system is akin to the Irish system.[448] On the whole, it can be safely stated that the way the electoral system has worked out has produced a stable government.

§3. ELECTORAL DIVISIONS

228. A very contentious electoral matter over time has been the review of electoral boundaries of the electoral divisions. According to the Constitution, 'the House of Representatives shall consist of such number of members, being an odd number and divisible by the number of electoral divisions, as Parliament shall from time to time by law determine'.[449] Members of Parliament are 'elected in the manner provided by or under any law for the time being in force in Malta in equal proportions from the electoral divisions referred to in Article 56 of the Constitution'.[450] The law which establishes thirteen electoral divisions is the General Elections Act.[451] One such division is specifically listed in the Constitution. Indeed, the organic law requires the

442. Constitution, sections 52–58; and 60–63.
443. Chapter 354 of the Laws of Malta.
444. Chapter 467 of the Laws of Malta.
445. Chapter 363 of the Laws of Malta. Elections are held for local councils, administrative committees and chairmen of regional committees.
446. Constitution, section 66(3).
447. *Ibid.*, section 56(1).
448. For a discussion of the workings of the single transferable vote system in Malta, *see* Michael Schiavone, *supra* note 211, pp. 1251–1252.
449. Constitution, section 52(1).
450. *Ibid.*, section 52(1).
451. Chapter 354 of the Laws of Malta.

Electoral Commission to 'establish the Island of Gozo together with the Islands of the Maltese Archipelago other than the Island of Malta as one electoral division'.[452] As a matter of fact, the thirteenth division consists of two other inhabited islands of the Maltese Archipelago, other than Malta, these being Gozo and Comino. Malta is then divided into twelve electoral divisions. In terms of section 56(1) of the Constitution, the electoral divisions have to be 'an odd number and not less than nine and not more than fifteen, as Parliament shall from time to time approve'.[453]

229. Once established, electoral divisions may be changed in terms of law. According to section 61(1) of the Constitution, the Electoral Commission is tasked by the Constitution to review the boundaries of the electoral divisions, 'at intervals of not less than two nor more than five years and may, in accordance with the provisions of this article, alter such boundaries to such extent as it considers desirable in the light of the review'.[454] In addition, the Electoral Commission is empowered to carry out such a review whenever Parliament alters the number of electoral divisions.[455] Furthermore, the Commission may also alter the said boundaries 'to such extent as it considers desirable in consequence of the holding of a census of the population in pursuance of any law',[456] that is, in pursuance of the Census Act.[457] The constitutional procedure to be followed whenever an alteration of boundaries is made is found in section 61(3)-(5).

230. One last point relating to the alteration of the boundaries is that 'such alteration may be made in such manner that the number of voters in that division is, at the time when the Electoral Commission carries out its review, greater or less than the electoral quota multiplied by the number of members to be so returned, but in no case more than five *per centum*, in order to take account of geographical vicinity, differences in density of population and other relevant factors' but all the islands, other than Malta, are 'treated as one electoral division and may not be divided between two or more electoral divisions'.[458] The expression 'electoral quota' is defined in the Constitution as 'the number obtained by dividing the total electorate of Malta (as ascertained from the electoral register in force at the time when the Commission carries out that review) by the total number of members to be returned to the House of Representatives at the general election following the next dissolution of Parliament'.[459]

231. Lastly, Maltese living abroad are not allowed to cast their vote at an Embassy or High Commission but have to come over to Malta to collect their voting document and to cast their vote. Voting documents cannot be collected less than twenty-four hours before polling day. Voting by proxy is prohibited though it is allowed to vote on a date prior to polling day.[460]

452. Constitution, section 61A(2)(a).
453. *Ibid.*, section 56(1).
454. *Ibid.*, section 61(1).
455. *Ibid.*, section 61(1) proviso.
456. Constitution, section 61(1) proviso.
457. Chapter 118 of the Laws of Malta.
458. Constitution, section 61(4) proviso.
459. *Ibid.*, section 61(5).
460. General Elections Act, section 77(3A).

§4. Suspension of a General Election

232. It is a principle of electoral law that the 'election of members of the House of Representatives shall be free of illegal or corrupt practices and foreign interference'.[461] Should this not be the case, serious consequences derive. Indeed, the Electoral Commission is empowered 'to suspend the election, either in all electoral divisions or in any one or more of such divisions, if it has reasonable ground to believe that illegal or corrupt practices or other offences connected with the elections have been committed or there has been foreign interference and such practices, offences or interference have so extensively prevailed or have been of such nature that they may reasonably be expected to affect the result of the election, in all or in any one or more of the electoral divisions'.[462] Should the election be suspended as aforesaid, the Chief Electoral Commissioner is duty bound to refer the matter to the Constitutional Court for its decision.[463] The Constitution does not state what procedure the Constitutional Court is to follow in arriving at its decision. It might nonetheless happen that no such reference is made by the Electoral Commission to the Constitutional Court and still grounds for suspension of an election subsist. In such case, 'any person entitled to vote at that election may, not later than three days after the publication of the official result of the election refer the matter to the Constitutional Court for its decision'.[464]

233. The powers of the Constitutional Court in this respect are wide ranging: 'On any such reference the Court shall, without prejudice to any other powers, have power to annul the election, in all or in any one or more of the electoral divisions, ... and to give directions and orders and to provide such redress and other remedies as it may deem appropriate in the circumstances and in particular to ensure that a free election, in place of any one that may have been annulled, be held at the earliest possible opportunity.'[465]

§5. Provisions Related to Conduct of Elections

234. The Constitution does contain a handful of provisions related to the conduct of elections[466] although, admittedly, it is the General Elections Act[467] which regulates in greater detail such conduct. Insofar as the Constitution is concerned, it provides that:

461. Constitution, section 56(2). Anon, 'Pursuits, Half a century ago, Times of Malta', *The Times of Malta*, 11 April 2016, p. 22 reporting on a report in the *Times of Malta* of Monday, April 11, 1966, 'MLP requests Vatican to declare Malta elections unfair: resolution at public meeting'.
462. *Ibid.*, section 56(3)
463. *Ibid.*, section 56(4).
464. *Ibid.*, section 56(5).
465. Constitution, section 56(6).
466. These are discussed by David Joseph Attard, *supra* note 25, pp. 73–80.
467. Chapter 354 of the Laws of Malta.

(a) no person can vote 'at the election of members of the House of Representatives for any electoral division who is not registered under any law for the time being in force in Malta as a voter in that division';[468]
(b) 'voting shall be by ballot and shall be carried out in such a manner as not to disclose the way in which the vote of any particular voter is given';[469]
(c) voting by proxy is prohibited: 'no person shall be permitted to vote on behalf of another.'[470] However, 'provision may be made by law whereby, if a person is unable, by reason of blindness, other physical cause or illiteracy to mark on his ballot paper, his ballot paper may be marked on his behalf and on his directions by some other person officially supervising the poll at the place of voting'.[471] This provision is in fact supplemented by sections 49 and 72 of the General Elections Act;
(d) a recent amendment to the Constitution allows a blind person to mark his/her ballot paper through adequate and special means 'independently and without the need of assistance';[472]
(e) ballot papers have to be drawn up such as 'to enable illiterates to distinguish between the political parties to which candidates belong';[473] and
(f) election candidates and their agents have to be given by the Electoral Commission 'facilities to watch the transportation of ballot boxes and the sealing and unsealing thereof'.[474]

§6. The Election of the House of Representatives

235. Although Malta uses the single transferable vote as its electoral system, which places more emphasis on candidates rather than on political parties, the Constitution has had to be amended on a number of occasions to ensure that the political party obtaining the highest number of votes obtains a corresponding number of MPs in the House of Representatives. For instance, in the 1981 general election, the PN obtained 114,132 votes equivalent to 50.92% of the popular vote, and the MLP obtained 49.07% of the popular vote. Yet in terms of MPs, the PN obtained thirty-one seats to the thirty-four seats of the MLP. The latter's electoral vote of 49.07% translated itself into 52.3% of MPs, and the PN electoral vote of 50.92% translated itself into 47.7% of MPs.[475] This was a historical first where democracy was not respected with the political party which gained a majority of votes ending up obtaining a minority of MPs. A similar result obtained in the following general election of 1987 with the difference that this time round, the PN were compensated by the addition of another four MPs over and above those obtained so that they could now govern the country

468. Constitution, section 56(9).
469. *Ibid.*, section 56(10)(a).
470. *Ibid.*, section 56(10)(b).
471. *Ibid.*, section 56(10)(b) proviso.
472. *Ibid.*, section 56(10) proviso.
473. *Ibid.*, section 56(11).
474. *Ibid.*, section 56(12).
475. Michael Schiavone, *supra* note 211, pp. 565–566.

as they had won an absolute majority of votes.[476] Such compensation was brought about through amendments to the Constitution which now allowed for the party obtaining a majority of votes in the House to govern. Act No IV of 1987 was the law which amended the Constitution introducing what is referred to as the corrective mechanism. Section 52(1) was amended through the insertion of a new proviso which provides that where:

> at any general election, a single political party obtains in the aggregate more than fifty per centum of all valid votes cast at that election, as credited to its candidates by the Electoral Commission at the first count of all the votes, but the number of its candidates elected at such election is less than fifty per centum of the total number of members composing the Parliament to be elected, the number of members of the House of Representatives shall be increased by as many members as may be necessary, so that the Party obtaining more than fifty per centum as aforesaid shall have one member more than the total of the other members elected from any other party or parties; and in any such case, such candidates shall be declared by the Electoral Commission to be elected to fill the additional seats created under this proviso, who, being candidates of the party obtaining more than fifty per centum of the valid votes as aforesaid, were credited by the Electoral Commission at the last count with the highest or next highest number of votes without being elected, irrespective of the electoral division in which such highest or higher number of votes occurs.

236. This amendment was nevertheless found to be lacking as it contemplated only one scenario: where a political party obtains an absolute majority of votes but a minority of seats in the House with only two political parties being returned to the House. Indeed, a situation could develop where both parties do not obtain an absolute majority, but the political party which gains lesser votes ends up with a majority of MPs returned to the House. Thus, the Constitution had to be amended again in 1996 in order to cater for such an eventuality. The new amendment made by section 2 of the Constitution (Amendment) Act, 1996[477] provided that:

(1) at any general election, a political party obtains in the aggregate more than fifty per centum of all the valid votes cast at that election, as credited to its candidates by the Electoral Commission at the first count of all the votes, but the number of its candidates elected at such election is less than the total of all the other candidates so elected; or

(2) at a general election which is contested by more than two political parties and in which only candidates of two of such parties are elected, a political party obtains a percentage of all the valid votes cast at such election, as credited to its candidates by the Electoral Commission at the first count of all the votes, which is greater than that obtained by any one other party, but the number of its candidates elected at such election is less than the number of the other candidates so elected, the number of members of the House of Representatives shall be increased by as

476. *Ibid.* p. 644.
477. Section 2 of Act No. XI of 1996.

many members as may be necessary in order that the party obtaining more than fifty per centum, or the larger percentage, of all the valid votes, as the case may be, shall have one member more than the total of the other candidates elected at that election; and, in any such case, such persons shall be declared by the Electoral Commission to be elected to fill the additional seats created by this proviso who, being candidates of the party last mentioned at such elections, were credited by the Electoral Commission at the last count, with the highest or next higher number of votes without being elected, irrespective of the division in which such highest or higher number of votes occurs.

237. A final amendment to the corrective mechanism occurred in 2007 through the Constitution of Malta (Amendment) (No. 2) Act, 2007,[478] which gives the position of the law as it stands today:

(1) at any general election, a political party (hereinafter referred to in this article as the 'absolute majority party') obtains in the aggregate more than fifty per centum of all the valid votes cast at that election, as credited to its candidates by the Electoral Commission at the first count of all the votes; or
(2) at a general election which is contested by more than two political parties and in which only candidates of two of such parties are elected, a political party obtains a percentage of all the valid votes cast at such election, as credited to its candidates by the Electoral Commission at the first count of all the votes (hereinafter also referred to in this article as the 'relative majority party'), which is greater than that obtained by any one other party (hereinafter referred to in this article as the 'minority party'),

and the proportion which the number of the elected candidates credited to the absolute majority party or to the relative majority party (as the case may be) represents in relation to the total number of elected members of the House of Representatives is less than the proportion which the number of votes credited to such candidates at the first count of all the votes represents in relation to the total of the votes credited at the same first count of all the votes to all the candidates of all the parties electing candidates, the number of the elected candidates of such party shall be increased (as the case may be) by a number of additional candidates in the circumstances as determined by and in accordance with the provisions of Part IV of the General Elections (Sorting of Ballot Papers, Casual Elections and Co-opting) Regulations 1991 in the Thirteenth Schedule to the General Elections Act and the Annex to such Schedule (hereinafter referred to as 'the relevant regulations') as in force on 30 September 2007 or as subsequently amended or substituted in the manner provided in sub-article (3):

Provided further that:

478. Section 4 of Act No. XXI of 2007.

(i) in the eventuality of an election result as provided for in sub-paragraph (i) of the first proviso to this sub-article but provided there is only one minority party; or

(ii) in the eventuality of an election result as provided for in sub-paragraph (ii) of the first proviso to this sub-article and the proportion which the number of elected candidates credited to the minority party represents in relation to the total number of elected members of the House of Representatives is less than the proportion which the number of votes credited to all its candidates at the first count of all the votes represents in relation to the total of the votes credited at the same first count of all the votes to all the candidates of all the parties electing candidates, the number of the elected candidates of the minority party shall be increased by a number of additional candidates as determined by the relevant regulations as in force on 30 September 2007 or as subsequently amended or substituted in the manner provided in sub-article (3).

In any case as foreseen in the first and second proviso to this sub-article, such persons shall be declared by the Electoral Commission to be elected to fill the additional seats created by the said provisos who, being candidates of the party which is to be credited with the additional seats, were credited by the Electoral Commission at the last count with the highest or next higher number of votes without being elected, irrespective of the division in which such highest or higher number of votes occurs.

§7. Election Campaign Laws

238. When a general election is called, certain provisions in the Broadcasting Act which would previously be in hibernation mode come to life. These include the following:

(a) the Broadcasting Authority issues a directive governing general elections which typically provides for all broadcasting stations to submit their programme schedules to the Broadcasting Authority for its approval. Such requirement is compulsory during an election campaign period. On the other hand, during other periods of the year, the Authority only approves the programme schedule of the public broadcasting service's nationwide television station, Television Malta. For the election campaign period, all broadcasting stations have to provide also details of programme presenters, participants and producers in the case of current affairs programmes, discussion programmes, investigative journalism programmes and other programmes which include guests who air opinions on current affairs and programmes of a similar nature. Where election candidates participate in programmes, the Authority has to be informed accordingly. This measure is intended to ensure that insofar as possible balance is maintained with regard to airtime allotted to different political parties so that there be a fair apportionment of broadcasting time. Once the Authority approves the programme schedule, no changes can be made by broadcasters unless they seek and obtain the prior approval of the Authority. Nor can promotional material concerning the news programmes be aired, once such programmes are still in the process of approval;

(b) the directive also provides that programmes and advertisements cannot encourage people to vote in a particular way. Moreover, care has to be taken to ensure that all programmes and all advertisements are free of material which can be interpreted as favouring or giving undue exposure to any political party or candidate, or which can be reasonably considered as being directed towards a political end.

239. The aim behind this directive is to ensure that no political party or a candidate of such party gets an undue advantage over another political party/candidate. This directive was first issued in connection with the 2003 referendum on the accession of Malta to the EU. Since then, it has become standard practice in the field of broadcast regulation.[479]

240. Reference has also to be made to the Financing of Political Parties Act.[480] It refers to campaign expenses made by candidates for general elections, local council elections and European Parliament elections.[481]

§8. Qualifications of Members of Parliament

241. Not everybody can be elected an MP. This is because the Constitution provides for a number of cases whereby a person cannot qualify for membership of the House. These House membership disqualifications are listed in section 54 of the Constitution and are exhaustive. Apart from these cases of disqualification, there can be no other case for disqualification in ordinary law as this would otherwise run counter to the Constitution, and the latter would lose its supremacy if such an unconstitutional situation were to be allowed to prevail. These disqualification instances are the following:

(a) If he 'is a citizen of a country other than Malta having become such a citizen voluntarily or is under a declaration of allegiance to such a country'.[482] This first disqualification made a lot of sense when Malta did not recognize dual or multiple citizenship as was the situation in 1964 when the Constitution came into existence. Since then, the Constitution recognizes the possibility for a Maltese citizen to enjoy dual or multiple citizenship in section 22(2): 'Dual or multiple citizenship

479. *Direttiva Ta' L-Awtorità tax-Xandir Dwar Programmi U Reklami Mxandra Matul Il-Perijodu 7 Ta' Jannar Sad-9 Ta' Marzu 2013* (Translation: Broadcasting Authority Directive on Programmes and Advertisements Broadcast during the Period 7 January to 9 March 2013), Broadcasting Authority, Ħamrun, 2013.

480. Financing of Political Parties Act, Chapter 544 of the Laws of Malta.

481. *Ibid.*, section 2.

482. Provided that the President is a citizen of Malta, he/she is not debarred from being under a declaration of allegiance to a foreign country, contrary to the position of an MP who is precluded from having dual or multiple citizenship.

is permitted in accordance with any law for the time being in force in Malta.' The first disqualification for membership of the House under consideration is anachronistic. This means that if a Maltese citizen enjoys a dual or multiple nationality but subsequently assumes the office of an MP, he/she has to renounce the non-Maltese citizenship/s even if, in terms of section 22(2) he/she is entitled to more than one citizenship. On the other hand, the President is allowed to retain dual or multiple citizenship. Uniformity should prevail in the selection criteria for appointment to offices of state and the rule should be that the President, like MPs, should not be entitled to dual or multiple citizenship but only to Maltese citizenship.

(b) 'Save as otherwise provided by Parliament, if he holds or is acting in any public office or is a member of the armed forces of the Government of Malta.' Maltese Constitutional Law does allow a public officer but not a member of a disciplined force to carry out his/her duties of an MP at one and the same time, provided that he/she does not form part of the top echelon of the public service, that is, from salary scales 1 to 5. This is because being an MP in Malta is a part-time job, which allows an MP to combine an MP's job with that of a public officer, and such a situation is not only tolerated but sanctioned by law. Such is the case with the Member of Parliament (Public Employment) Act[483] and the Functions of Members of Parliament (Various Laws) Amendment Act, 2013.[484] A person is not treated as holding, or acting in, a public office:

- 'if he is on leave of absence pending relinquishment of a public office'; or
- 'if he is a teacher at the University of Malta who is not by the terms of his employment prevented from the private practice of his profession or called upon to place his whole time at the disposal of the Government of Malta'.

(c) 'If he is a party to, or is a partner with unlimited liability in a partnership or a director or manager of a company which is a party to, a contract with the Government of Malta being a contract of works or a contract for the supply of merchandise to be used in the service of the public and has not, within one month before the date of election, published in the Gazette a notice setting out the nature of any such contract, and his interest, or the interest of any such partnership or company, therein.'

(d) 'If he is an undischarged bankrupt, having been adjudged or otherwise declared bankrupt under any law in force in Malta.'

(e) 'If he is interdicted or incapacitated for any mental infirmity or for prodigality by a court in Malta, or is otherwise determined in Malta to be of unsound mind.'

(f) 'If he is under sentence of death imposed on him by any court in Malta or is serving a sentence of imprisonment (by whatever name called), exceeding twelve months imposed on him by such a court or substituted by competent authority

483. Chapter 472 of the Laws of Malta. Section 3 states that a public officer 'whose office, substantive or otherwise, in the Public Service is not on a salary scale which is higher than salary scale 6, or such other salary scale as the House may by Resolution from time to time determine, shall be qualified to be elected as a member of the House'.

484. Act No. X of 2013.

for some other sentence imposed on him by such a court.' As to the death penalty, it must be noted that although capital punishment is referred to on more than one occasion in the Constitution, there is no provision of ordinary law which permits it. Furthermore, where:

- 'two or more sentences that are required to be served consecutively shall be regarded as separate sentences if none of them exceeds twelve months, but if any one of them exceeds that term they shall be regarded as one sentence'; and
- 'no account shall be taken of a sentence of imprisonment imposed as an alternative to, or in default of, the payment of a fine'.

(g) 'If he holds or is acting in any office the functions of which involve any responsibility for, or in connection with, the conduct of any election of members of the House of Representatives or the compilation or revision of any electoral register.'
(h) 'If he is disqualified for membership of the House of Representatives by or under any law for the time being in force in Malta by reason of his having been convicted of any offence connected with the election of members of the House of Representatives.'

§9. Tenure of Office of MP

242. The fact that a person qualifies for membership of the House and is so elected does not necessarily mean that there might be no impediment in the future which might bring his/her term of office to a premature end. This is because the Constitution specifically contemplates situations where the tenure of office of an MP comes to an abrupt termination with the consequential vacation of the seat of an MP. Such situations, which are once again exhaustive in nature, are the following:

(a) upon the next dissolution of Parliament after his election;
(b) if he resigns his seat by writing under his hand addressed to the Speaker or, if the office of Speaker is vacant or the Speaker is absent from Malta, to the Deputy Speaker;
(c) if he becomes a party to a contract with the Government of Malta being a contract of works or a contract for the supply of merchandise to be used in the service of the public, or if any partnership in which he is a partner with unlimited liability or a company of which he is a director or manager becomes a party to any such contract, or if he becomes a partner with unlimited liability in a partnership or a director or manager of a company that is a party to any such contract: Provided that he shall not vacate his seat under the provisions of this paragraph if before becoming a party to the contract or before, or as soon as practicable after, becoming otherwise interested in the contract (whether as a partner with unlimited liability in a partnership or as a director or manager of a company) he discloses to the Speaker the nature of the contract and his interest or the interest of the partnership

or company therein and the House of Representatives by resolution exempts him from the provisions of this paragraph;

(d) if he is absent from the sittings of the House of Representatives for such period and in such circumstances as may be prescribed by the Standing Orders of the House;[485]

(e) if he ceases to be a citizen of Malta;

(f) if he ceases to be qualified for registration as a voter for the election of members of the House of Representatives;

(g) if any circumstances arise that if he were not a member of the House of Representatives, would cause him to be disqualified for election thereto.

243. Such circumstances arise:

(a) Because any member of the House of Representatives is under sentence of death or imprisonment, interdicted or incapacitated or adjudged to be of unsound mind, adjudged or otherwise declared bankrupt or convicted of an offence connected with elections and if it is open to the member to appeal against the decision (either with the leave of a court or other authority or without such leave), he shall forthwith cease to perform his functions as a member of the House but, subject to the provisions of this article, he shall not vacate his seat until the expiration of a period of thirty days thereafter: Provided that the Speaker may, from time to time, extend that period for further periods of thirty days to enable the member to pursue an appeal against the decision, so however that extensions of time exceeding in the aggregate one hundred and fifty days shall not be given without the approval, signified by resolution, of the House.

(b) If, on the determination of any appeal, such circumstances continue to exist and no further appeal is open to the member, or if, by reason of the expiration of any period for entering an appeal or notice thereof or the refusal of leave to appeal or for any other reason, it ceases to be open to the member to appeal, he shall forthwith vacate his seat.

(c) If at any time before the member vacates his seat such circumstances as aforesaid cease to exist, his seat shall not become vacant on the expiration of the period referred to in paragraph (a) of this sub-article and he may resume the performance of his functions as a member of the House of Representatives.

(d) For the purposes of this sub-article 'appeal' means, 'in the case of an order by a court of voluntary jurisdiction for the interdiction or incapacitation of a member of the House of Representatives, the taking of any action for the review of that order before the Civil Court, First Hall'.

§10. Officers of the House of Representatives

244. The officers of the House consist in:

485. The matter falls to be regulated by Standing Orders 155–161 of the Standing Orders of the House of Representatives Order, Subsidiary Legislation Const. 02.

(a) the Speaker;[486]
(b) the Deputy Speaker;[487]
(c) the Chairman of Committees;[488]
(d) the Deputy Chairman of Committees;[489]
(e) Members of Parliament,[490] whether Ministers, Parliamentary Secretaries, government, opposition or independent backbenchers who are grouped within their respective parliamentary group, including the Prime Minister and the Leader of the Opposition;
(f) Parliamentary Officers (the Auditor General, the Deputy Auditor General, the Ombudsman and the Commissioners for Administrative Investigation);
(g) the Leader of the House;[491]
(h) Parliamentary Whips;
(i) the Clerk of the House;[492] and
(j) staff of the Clerk of the House.[493]

§11. Parliamentary Privilege

245. The Constitution allows for the making of a law where Parliament may 'determine the privileges, immunities and powers of the House of Representatives and the members thereof'.[494] The Constitution has taken on board a pre-independence law, the House of Representatives (Privileges and Powers) Ordinance[495] which came into force on 15 October 1942 and which is still in force till the present day. In addition, the Constitution does establish three important privileges which MPs enjoy:

486. Constitution, section 59(1).
487. *Ibid.*, section 69(3).
488. The Deputy Speaker is the Chairman of Committees in terms of Standing Orders 1(1) and 154 of the Standing Orders of the House of Representatives Order, Subsidiary Legislation Const. 02.
489. Standing Order 154 of the Standing Orders of the House of Representatives Order, Subsidiary Legislation Const. 02.
490. Members of Parliament are elected by popular suffrage. Constitution, section 52(1). Michael Frendo makes the case of enhancing the role played by individual MPs. *See* Michael Frendo, 'A Strong Parliament – A Mature Democracy' in Office of the President, *supra* note 418, pp. 99–101.
491. The Leader of the House is the Minister responsible for parliamentary affairs (Standing Order 1(1) of the Standing Orders of the House of Representatives Order, Subsidiary Legislation Const. 02.).
492. The office of Clerk to the House is a constitutional office, established by section 64(1) of the Constitution. According to section 64(2) of the Constitution: 'The Office of the Clerk to the House of Representatives and the offices of the members of his staff shall be public offices.'
493. Although the Constitution, in section 64(2) refers to staff of the Clerk of the House, it does not state who these staff are. Standing Order 163 of the Standing Orders of the House of Representatives Order, Subsidiary Legislation Const. 02, identifies one such member of staff, the Clerk Assistant whilst Standing Order 168 refers to the Serjeant at Arms.
494. Constitution, section 65(2).
495. Chapter 113 of the Laws of Malta.

(a) 'no civil or criminal proceedings may be instituted against any member of the House of Representatives for words spoken before, or written in a report to, the House or a committee thereof or by reason of any matter or thing brought by him therein by petition, bill, resolution, motion or otherwise';[496]
(b) for 'the duration of any session members of the House of Representatives shall enjoy freedom from arrest for any civil debt except a debt the contraction of which constitutes a criminal offence';[497]
(c) no process 'issued by any court in exercise of its civil jurisdiction shall be served or executed within the precincts of the House of Representatives when the House is sitting or through the Speaker, the Clerk or any officer of the House'.[498]

246. The House of Representatives (Privileges and Powers) Ordinance[499] was enacted in 1942 'to establish the privileges of the House of Representatives, to give the House of Representatives certain powers and to provide for other matters connected therewith'.[500] It is divided into three categories: immunities from legal proceedings; privileges; and powers.

§12. Standing Orders

247. Section 67(1) of the Constitution states that: 'Subject to the provisions of this Constitution, the House of Representatives may regulate its own procedure.' According to Raymond Mangion:

> The Standing Orders are the written regulations that govern the proceedings and conduct of any Legislature. They constitute the second main basis of procedure of the Legislature. They are to be read in juxtaposition with the practice of the House and do not form a complete code of procedure. They are principally meant to expedite the progress of business of the House by reducing opportunities and checking luxuriance for debate.
>
> A Standing Order is enacted, modified, substituted and revoked by the Legislature itself. It does not require for its passage any special procedure although it differs from every other order of the House in having an express duration beyond the end of the session in which it is passed. It only necessitates a motion so that the House agrees to it and a further motion so that the House declares it to be a Standing Order. Besides, a Standing Order is not safeguarded by any special procedure against its enactment, modification, and so on, whether explicitly or by an order contrary to its purport.[501]

496. Constitution, section 65(3). *See also* Press Act, Chapter 248 of the Laws of Malta, section 33.
497. *Ibid.*, section 64(4).
498. *Ibid.*, section 65(5).
499. Chapter 113 of the Laws of Malta.
500. House of Representatives (Privileges and Powers) Ordinance, long title.
501. Raymond Mangion, *supra* note 193, p. xvii.

§13. Pairing of Members of Parliament

248. A constitutional practice which has evolved over time is that of pairing Members of Parliament. Godfrey A. Pirotta explains the historical origins of this practice as follows:

> The practice of pairing, whereby the absence on business of a Member of Parliament on one side, normally the majority side, is balanced by the absence or withdrawal during a vote, of a member of the Opposition, became a common practice in Britain in the early part of the 1900s. In Malta the idea of pairing was broached for the first time in 1928 when a member on the Government side, Prof. Galea, and the Leader of the Opposition, Dr Ugo Mifsud, were making preparations to attend the Empire Parliamentary Association conference in Canada. Not unnaturally, the issue was raised by Lord Strickland, the Head of Ministry, in July 1928, that in view of the imminent departure of this delegation a Standing Order be passed 'to the effect that when an invitation comes from the Empire Parliamentary Association the members who go are to be considered as having paired, independently of whether they have signed a letter or not'. Mifsud stated that he saw no need for this … Consequently, the first attempt at pairing had failed to materialise and the practice was not to become established until the 1970s.[502]

§14. House Committees

249. House Committees[503] are divided into three types: (a) Committees of the whole House;[504] (b) Standing Committees[505] and (c) Select Committees.[506] House Committees have been in existence since 1921. Up till 1995, the House of Representatives could not boast of any Committee of the House apart from a handful of committees which had been established following independence and the Committee of the whole House or the Committee of Supply referred to respectively in the Standing Orders 109 and 71(1) of the House of Representatives Order. In 1995, however, following an agreement reached between the Speaker Dr Lawrence Gonzi, the Government and the Opposition, it was decided to establish a number of permanent committees of the House.[507] The Standing Orders were amended to allow for the establishment of such

502. Godfrey A. Pirotta, *Malta's Parliament: An Official History*, Office of the Speaker of the House of Representatives and the Departmjent of Information, Valletta, 2008, p. 95. For further developments, *see also* Godfrey A. Pirotta, *ibid.*, pp. 114, 206, 215–216, 221, 223, 255 and 262.

503. House Committees are regulated by Standing Orders 108–139 of the Standing Orders of the House of Representatives Order, Subsidiary Legislation Const. 02.

504. *Ibid.*, Standing Orders 108 to 120 regulate Committees of the whole House.

505. *Ibid.*, Standing Committees of the House are regulated by Standing Orders 120A to 120J.

506. *Ibid.*, Standing Orders 121 and 122 regulate select committees of the House.

507. *See* House of Representatives, *Kumitati Permanenti tal-Kamra tad-Deputati* (Translation: Permanent Committees of the House of Representatives), House of Representatives, Valletta, 2005.

permanent committees known as Standing Committees as distinct from Select Committees which are established on an ad hoc basis. Standing Order 120A establishes the following permanent Standing Committees which are regulated by subsequent Standing Orders:

(a) the Standing Committee on House Business;
(b) the Standing Committee on Privileges;
(c) the Standing Committee on Public Accounts;
(d) the Standing Committee on Foreign and European Affairs;
(e) the Standing Committee on Social Affairs;
(f) the Standing Committee on Family Affairs;
(g) the Standing Committee on Economic and Financial Affairs; and
(h) the Standing Committee on Health.

250. Standing Order 120B establishes a Committee for the Consideration of Bills[508] whilst other laws establish other Standing Committees such as the National Audit Office Accounts Committee,[509] and the Environment and Development Planning Committee.[510] Select Committees have been appointed since independence on:

(a) Strengthening of Democracy;
(b) Medically Assisted Procreation;
(c) Re-codification and Consolidation of Laws;
(d) Black Dust Precipitation; and
(e) Appointment of a Commissioner and a Standing Committee on Standards, Ethics and Proper Behaviour in Public Life.

251. The PAC is the only Committee which is chaired by an Opposition MP. However, in all Committees, including the PAC, the Government enjoys always a majority of MPs amongst the membership of those Committees.

§15. Visitors to the House of Representatives

252. Godfrey A. Pirotta recounts the various visits to the House by foreign heads of state and other dignitaries: 'It is the custom in any Parliament that distinguished visitors are welcomed to the House and treated with the courtesy that their status deserves. In 1976 Col. Gaddafi, Head of the Libyan Arab Republic had visited the House as part of the State Visit programme. But it is very rarely the custom that such

508. Although by means of Motion 22 adopted by the House on 18 April 2013, a Permanent Committee for the Consideration of Bills was appointed, by means of Motion 293 of 11 December 2015, the House appointed on 15 December 2015 an Adjunct Permanent Committee for the Consideration of Bills to consider bills and other business referred to it by the House. *See* Office of the Clerk to the House of Representatives, Valletta, Minutes of the House dated 15 December 2015, paragraph 294.
509. Auditor General and National Audit Office Act, Chapter 396 of the Laws of Malta, Second Schedule, Part IV, paragraph 13.
510. Environment and Development Planning Act, Chapter 504 of the Laws of Malta, section 34(1).

visitors are invited to address the House. One such occasion was when Mr Javier Perez De Cuellar, Secretary General of the United Nations, visited Parliament in 1988.'[511]

§16. Direct Broadcasting of Parliamentary Sittings

253. Godfrey A. Pirotta observes that from 'time to time the House approved that debates of the House should be broadcast live on radio and television. It had become almost a tradition, for example, to transmit the reading of the budget and a number of the associated debates. Foreign affairs also tended to be a topic of such transmissions. In July 1995 the Leader of the House moved a Motion to amend Standing Order No 173 so that all the Sittings of the House, unless specifically prohibited, should be transmitted live on one of the State's radio channels.'[512] Dr Alfred Bonnici states that television transmission of House sittings begun during the 1981–1986 Legislature.[513] The matter is today addressed by Standing Order 173A related to the broadcasting of Parliamentary proceedings:

> 173A. (1) The House authorises on such terms, conditions and regulations as may be determined by the House Business Committee from time to time, both live and recorded audio/video broadcasts of the sittings of the House of Representatives in plenary and of the Committees appointed by the House in their entirety over radio, television, the internet or any other medium that may be deemed appropriate by the House Business Committee.
>
> 2. The sittings of the House of Representatives in plenary shall be broadcast in their entirety on radio by live transmission by the Public Broadcasting Services.
>
> 3. The Speaker may order the interruption of such transmissions whenever, in his opinion, such interruption is necessary.
>
> 4. In the case of sittings held behind closed doors, such sittings shall not be broadcast.

511. *See* Godfrey A. Pirotta, *supra* note 502, p. 252. For other visitors to the House, *see* Godfrey A. Pirotta, *ibid.*, pp. 266–267 and 277–282.
512. Godfrey A. Pirotta, *supra* note 502, pp. 263–264. *See also* pp. 155, 206, 223, 227, 231, 241, 244, and 247–249.
513. House of Representatives, *90 Years of the Parliament of Malta 1921-2011: Commemorative Sitting Held on the 90th Anniversary from the Holding of the First Sitting of the Legislative Assembly and Senate following the Grant of the Amery-Milner Constitution in 1921, Wednesday 2 November 2011, The Palace, Valletta*, House of Representatives, Valletta, 2011, p. 13.

254. The Parliamentary Services Act amended the Broadcasting Act[514] to sanction retroactively the parliamentary sittings broadcast on the Parliament channel.[515]

§17. International Relations

255. The House of Representatives participates in various meetings of the Commonwealth Parliamentary Association, the Presidents of Parliaments of Small European States, Parliamentary Assembly of the Council of Europe, Parliamentary Assembly of the Mediterranean, the Parliamentary Assembly of the Union for the Mediterranean, the Inter-Parliamentary Union, the Parliamentary Assembly of the Organization for Security and Cooperation in Europe, and others.[516]

514. Chapter 350 of the Laws of Malta.

515. Section 21 of the Parliamentary Services Act, 2016, Act No. XLII of 2016 amending section 10 of the Broadcasting Act.

516. For the latest published list of such parliamentary groupings, *see* House of Representatives, *House of Representatives Parliament of Malta Annual Report 2013*, House of Representatives, Valletta, 2014, pp. 44–60.

Chapter 4. Parliament Its Activities

§1. The Pre-parliamentary Stage

256. Prior to a bill being tabled in the House, consultation may take place by the competent Ministry. Normally it takes place either through a Green Paper or a White Paper, through both or through any other form of consultation document. Consultation can take place also with stakeholders without the involvement of the public at large and without the publication of a Green Paper or a White Paper but through a consultation document with restricted circulation. The document can consist in a draft bill or in a write up of the proposal which the Government intends to present at a future date in legislative form before the House. All the documents mentioned above (Green Papers, White Papers, draft bills and other forms of consultation documents) would first be discussed and approved at Cabinet level before their contents are disclosed to the public or to stakeholders.

§2. The Passing of Laws

257. Laws are passed by Parliament which consists of the President of Malta and a unicameral House of Representatives.[517] The procedure followed is that the House passes bills which are then assented to by the President.[518] A bill becomes law following the President's assent.[519] The procedure followed by Parliament in passing laws is not detailed in the Constitution but is contained in the Standing Orders of the House of Representatives Order.[520]

§3. The Incorporation of Laws in a Revised Edition of the Laws of Malta

258. It is the task of the Law Commission under the Statute Law Revision Act, 1980[521] to publish, from time to time, a revised edition of the laws of Malta. The format of the Revised Edition was set out by the British Colonial Office during colonial

517. Constitution, section 51.
518. *Ibid.*, section 72(1).
519. *Ibid.*, section 72(3).
520. Subsidiary Legislation Const. 02.
521. Act No. IX of 1981. This enactment is not given a chapter number in the Revised Edition of the Laws of Malta but instead is 'printed at the commencement of a revised edition' – Statute Law Revision Act, 1980, section 10.

times.[522] There have been, to date, two revised editions, one in 1942 and another in 1984.

§4. The Different Procedures for Considering Bills

259. There are two procedures for considering bills, that related to government bills and that related to private members' bills. In Malta, it is the custom that bills are drawn up and approved by the Cabinet, after being vetted by the Attorney General rather than the House drawing up its own bills as is the situation, for instance, in the USA which follows strict separation of powers unknown in Malta.[523] On the other hand, there do exist exceptional cases, few in number, where an MP presents a private member's bill. Such type of bills, in terms of convention, are not presented by Ministers or Parliamentary Secretaries but by government backbenchers or Opposition MPs. Of course, there is no rule which debars a Minister or a Parliamentary Secretary from presenting a private member's bill.

§5. The Promulgation and Publication of Laws

260. Once the President assents to a bill, the law is published, without delay, in the *Gazette*. It 'shall not come into operation until it has been so published, but Parliament may postpone the coming into operation of any such law and may make laws with retrospective effect'.[524] However, not all laws can have retrospective effect.

I. Postponement of Coming into Operation

261. A law can be postponed from coming into operation on the date of its publication. In such case, the competent minister or other bodies or persons responsible therefor would be empowered by law to establish by means of regulations the date of entry into force of that law. Unless such a legal notice is published, that law will remain inoperative. Sometimes it can take more than a few days for a law to come into force. There have been instances where laws were never brought into force and subsequently

522. As to the format of a revised edition, *see* the 'Recommendations in connection with the Preparation and Printing of Revised Editions, Annual Volumes, etc.' in Alison Russell, *Legislative and Other Forms*, Butterworths & Co., London, 1924, pp. 75–78.

523. *See* Robert A. Carp and Ronald Stidham, *Outline of the American Legal System*, Bureau of International Information Programs, United States Department of State, Washington, 2004, pp. 7–11.

524. Constitution, section 72(4).

repealed. Such was the case of the Town and Country Planning Act, 1969[525] and the Marine Pollution (Prevention and Control) Act, 1977.[526]

II. Laws with Retrospective Effect

262. The Constitution, in section 72(4), does not prohibit the making of laws with retrospective effect. However, this provision should not be construed as a blanket power for Parliament to make any law with retrospective effect. This is because Parliament's powers in this respect are not absolute but curtailed. This, once again, indicates that Parliament – a creature of the Constitution – is subservient thereto. Section 39(8) of the basic law disallows Parliament from making retroactive criminal law. There is indeed nothing new in this provision which dates back to Roman Law – *lex non habet oculus retro* – the principle of non-retroactivity of the Criminal Law.

263. This principle is enshrined in the two legal maxims of *nullum crimen sine lege* and *nulla poena sine lege.*[527] The principle of non-retroactivity of the Criminal Law applies also to fiscal laws insofar as these also contain provisions of a penal character. Section 39(8) of the Constitution reads as follows:

> No person shall be held to be guilty of a criminal offence on account of any act or omission that did not, at the time it took place, constitute such an offence, and no penalty shall be imposed for any criminal offence which is severer in degree or description than the maximum penalty which might have been imposed for that offence at the time when it was committed.

264. The *Interpretation* Act[528] makes the same point with regard to subsidiary legislation and also clarifies that criminal subsidiary law cannot be retroactive:

> Any law made after the commencement of this Act by virtue of a power conferred by any Act passed either before or after the commencement of this Act may, unless the contrary intention appears in the Act conferring that power, be made to operate retrospectively to any date which is not earlier than the commencement of such Act or, where different provisions of such Act come into operation on different dates, the commencement of the provision under which the subsidiary law is made:

525. Act No XXXV of 1969, repealed by the Statute Law Revision (Amendment) Act, 1981, Act No XLIX of 1981.

526. Act No. XII of 1977, Chapter 271 of the Laws of Malta, repealed by the Laws (Amendment and Repeal) Act, 2015, Act No II of 2015.

527. For a study of these legal principles, *see* Kevin Aquilina, 'The Human Right Principle of Legality: *Nullum Crimen/Nulla Poena Sine Lege*', in David E. Zammit (ed.), *Maltese Perspectives on Human Rights*, Valletta, Foundation For International Studies, University of Malta, March 2009, pp. 52–75.

528. Chapter 249 of the Laws of Malta, section 9.

> Provided that no person shall be made or shall become liable to any punishment in respect of anything done or omitted to be done before the commencement of the subsidiary law.

§6. The Legislative Process of Constitutional Laws

265. The Constitution does not establish any particular procedure to be followed when the House is discussing a constitutional law. Such a law can be in the form of an amendment to the Constitution, including its repeal and substitution thereof, or the introduction, amendment or repeal of a constitutional law (other than the Constitution). The ordinary constitutional law need not necessarily amend or repeal the Constitution.

266. There is, nonetheless, one exception to the above rule where a special procedure has to be followed and that concerns the taking of certain financial measures. The matter is regulated by section 73 of the Constitution which provides as follows:

> Except upon the recommendations of the President signified by a Minister, the House of Representatives shall not:
>
> a. proceed upon any bill (including any amendment to a bill) that, in the opinion of the person presiding, makes provision for any of the following purposes, that is to say, for imposing or increasing any tax, for imposing or increasing any charge on the revenues or other funds of Malta or for altering any such charge otherwise than by reducing it, or for compounding or remitting any debt due to Malta;
>
> b. proceed upon any motion (including any amendment to a motion) the effect of which, in the opinion of the person presiding, would be to make provision for any of the purposes aforesaid; or
>
> c. receive any petition which, in the opinion of the person presiding, requests that provision be made for any of the purposes aforesaid.

§7. Laws Delegating Legislative Powers

267. Parliament may also delegate its law-making function. Unfortunately, the Constitution does not establish the criteria which ought to be followed by Parliament when delegating its powers.[529]

§8. Subsidiary Legislation Made under the Constitution

268. The Constitution allows the making of subsidiary legislation thereunder in the same way that ordinary laws empower a person or body to make delegated legislation. The subsidiary legislation made under the Constitution is the following:

(a) Subsidiary Legislation Const. 01 – Public Service Commission General Regulations;
(b) Subsidiary Legislation Const. 02 – Standing Orders of the House of Representatives Order;
(c) Subsidiary Legislation Const. 03 – Disciplinary Procedure in the Public Service Commission Regulations;
(d) Subsidiary Legislation Const. 04 – Commission for the Administration of Justice (Election of Members) Rules; and
(e) Subsidiary Legislation Const. 05 – Public Service Commission Appointments Regulations.

§9. Language of Laws

269. Laws are published in the *Gazette* both in the Maltese and in the English languages. Nevertheless, the Interpretation Act does allow 'an Act of Parliament … [to] be enacted, in whole or in part, in the Maltese or in the English language only if the bill for that Act of Parliament, or part of such bill, is presented to the Clerk of the House and published in one only of the said languages and if the Act when passed contains a provision authorising the enactment thereof, or any one or more of its parts, as the case may require, in that language only'.[530] Normally laws are published in the English language only where technical language is used which is not possible to translate into Maltese. Instances of such occurrence exist under the Merchant Shipping Act[531] and the Environment and Development Planning Act.[532]

529. Such criteria have been drawn up and are contained in the Draft Administrative Code, 7 May 2012, available at http://www.parlament.mt/sc-codification. Last accessed on 31 March 2016. The draft has never been adopted. *See* , in particular, clauses 28–31.
530. Interpretation Act, Chapter 249 of the Laws of Malta, section 14.
531. Merchant Shipping Act, Chapter 234 of the Laws of Malta, section 374(5).
532. Environment and Development Planning Act, Chapter 504 of the Laws of Malta, section 61(3).

§10. Conflict Between Texts of the Law

270. Should there be a conflict between the Maltese and English texts of a law, the Constitution solves this difficulty by stating that it is the Maltese text which always prevails over the English, including those cases where, for instance, a law might have been drafted in the English language or is relying heavily upon the text of an English law, EU Law or another law which nevertheless is written in English such as where the domestic law is incorporating an international convention. Section 74 of the Constitution provides that: 'Save as otherwise provided by Parliament, every law shall be enacted in both the Maltese and English languages and, if there is any conflict between the Maltese and the English texts of any law, the Maltese text shall prevail.' Parliament has also established in section 8(3) of the Statute Law Revision Act that: 'If there is any conflict between the Maltese and the English text of any revised edition [of the laws of Malta], the Maltese text shall prevail.'

§11. Political Control on the Government's Political Activities in Parliament

271. Apart from its deliberative and legislative functions, the House has other functions to deliver such as that of controlling the operation of the government. This is done:

(a) through the House sitting in plenary session;
(b) through its Committees;
(c) through its Parliamentary Officers – the Ombudsman and the Auditor General; and
(d) through annual reporting to the House by various persons and bodies.

272. In its deliberations, the House approves (or rejects or approves with amendments) motions, resolutions, allows the tabling and answering of parliamentary questions, and empowers MPs to deliver adjournment speeches. The PAC scrutinizes the work of government and so do Parliamentary Officers who report back to the House on their findings. In the case of the Auditor General, he/she audits the accounts of Government; in the case of the Ombudsman, he/she audits good administration. Government departments compile annual departmental reports and the House scrutinizes their performance especially during the budget discussion on each Ministry's vote.

§12. Parliamentary Enquiries

273. The House has in the past set up various Select Committees to enquire into a certain aspect of government and to report to it. Section 67(3) of the Constitution provides for such power: '... Committees of the House to enquire into matters of general public importance shall be designed to secure that, so far as it appears practicable to the House, any such Committee is so composed as fairly to represent the House.'

Indeed, Standing Order 121 of the Standing Orders of the House of Representatives Order[533] provides that: 'The House may appoint a Select Committee of its members for the purpose of investigating any subject. It shall be competent for the Speaker to be appointed a member of any Select Committee of the House.'[534]

§13. Parliamentary Hearings

274. The House, through its Committees, invariably invites various persons and bodies to attend and, in certain cases, address Committee members. Such invitees can be public officers as well as representatives of interest groups such as civil society associations and non-governmental organizations depending on the topic being examined by those Committees. For instance, the Social Affairs Committee is an excellent forum where such participation takes place. Interest groups provide relevant and pertinent information and feedback to House Committees, especially in the discussion of policy formulation and legislative measures.

§14. Links Between the House, the EU and Other International Organizations

275. The House, following Malta's accession to the EU has had to take on board the EU *acquis*. But as the EU is constantly discussing new laws and initiatives, and revising or updating existing ones, the Foreign and European Affairs Committee of the House has been tasked with discussing EU pipeline *acquis*. It is also a constitutional practice for the Prime Minister to deliver statements in the House after having attended major EU gatherings so as to keep the House abreast of developments and of Malta's stand on those issues under consideration.

533. Subsidiary Legislation Const. 02.
534. For the history of such Committees *see* , Godfrey A. Pirotta, *supra* note 502, pp. 26, 31, 49–50, 77–81, 84, 94, 98, 109, 111, 117, 119, 128, 130, 135, 138–139, 151–152, 170–171, 174, 186, 217, 229–232, 244, 249–251, 255–258 and 261.

Chapter 5. The Executive

§1. The Government: An Introduction

276. Chapter VIII of the Constitution is appropriately entitled 'The Executive'. It declares the President to be vested with the executive authority of Malta.[535] It establishes the Cabinet, provides for the appointment of a Prime Minister, Ministers, an Acting Prime Minister, Temporary Ministers, Parliamentary Secretaries, the Attorney General, Permanent Secretaries, Heads of Government Departments and the Secretary to the Cabinet. The Leader of the Opposition is included in the chapter on the Executive and not in the chapter dealing with Parliament.

277. Different laws use diverse terms to refer to the Executive organ of the state. Sometimes the term 'government'[536] or 'public administration'[537] are used. At other times, dissimilar meanings are ascribed to the same term such that the term 'government' is used to refer to Cabinet only[538] whilst at other times it refers to the public administration.[539] A classic instance where the words 'government' and 'cabinet' are distinguished is section 79(2) of the Constitution which reads as follows: 'The Cabinet shall have the general direction and control of the Government of Malta and shall be collectively responsible to Parliament.' Although the Cabinet leads the government of Malta, there are other components of government such as the public service, local councils and other non-public office bodies established or appointed by the government of the day.

278. This provision makes it quite clear that the Cabinet is the most important organ of the Government of Malta, but it is not the sole organ. Cabinet is the organ which has the 'general direction and control', but there are other institutions of government which have the day-to-day operation of government such as those mentioned in the previous paragraph. Furthermore, new terms are sometimes used such as 'heads of public offices' as in the case with the National Archives Act,[540] 'public authority' as in the case of the Freedom of Information Act,[541] and 'government entity' as used in the Public Administration Act.[542] Hence, one has to be very wary of the nuance in meaning attributed by law to these terms.

279. Included in the term 'government' is the public service[543] and ambassadors, high commissioners and principal representatives who perform government-related

535. *Ibid.*, section 78(1).
536. *Ibid*, section 12.
537. Public Administration Act, Chapter 497 of the Laws of Malta, section 2(1).
538. Constitution, section 76(5) proviso paragraph (a) and section 81(1) and section 76(5) proviso paragraph (c).
539. *Ibid.*, section 108(3)(c) and (5)(a) and (b), section 110(6) and section 121(1).
540. Chapter 477 of the Laws of Malta, section 2 which defines 'heads of public offices'.
541. Chapter 496 of the Laws of Mata, section 2 which defines 'public authority'.
542. Chapter 497 of the Laws of Malta, section 2(1) which defines 'government entity'.
543. Chapter X of the Constitution deals with the public service.

diplomatic duties. The public service comprises the Principal Permanent Secretary[544] who is the head of the civil service, the Secretary to the Cabinet, Permanent Secretaries[545] and heads of government departments.[546] A more recent entity is a government agency which is established under the Public Administration Act.[547]

§2. Structure of Government

I. The Cabinet of Ministers

280. The Constitution does not regulate in detail the Cabinet of Ministers. For instance, it does not state who is responsible for the drawing up of its agenda and how cabinet business is transacted.[548] What it nevertheless does is that it provides for its composition, function and relationship to Parliament. The Constitution thus states:

> There shall be a Cabinet for Malta which shall consist of the Prime Minister and such number of other Ministers as may be appointed in accordance with article 80 of this Constitution.[549]

281. This means that the Cabinet is composed solely of Ministers, the Prime Minister being a Minister in his/her own right. This unique composition of the Cabinet excludes from its membership junior ministers known as Parliamentary Secretaries.[550] Only Ministers have a right to vote in Cabinet. That is why the Cabinet is sometimes referred to as the 'Cabinet of Ministers' due to its exclusive formation. That said, however, this does not mean that only Ministers attend Cabinet meetings. Invariably, Parliamentary Secretaries are called to attend that part of a cabinet meeting which relates to their governmental duties. Furthermore, Cabinet can also request the presence of any public officer, chairman of a body corporate established by law or a government consultant whose presence might be needed during the discussion of a particular item on Cabinet's agenda. All Ministers are Cabinet Ministers irrespective of whether they are assigned a particular portfolio or are without portfolio.

282. As to functions, the Constitution provides that the Cabinet 'shall have the general direction and control of the Government of Malta'.[551] These are the terms of reference of Cabinet as set out in the Constitution. Needless to say, although the Cabinet has wide ranging powers – 'general direction and control of Government' – this does not mean that the Cabinet has absolute powers. This is because even Cabinet is bound

544. The office of 'Principal Permanent Secretary' is not established by the Constitution but by Article 14(1) of the Public Administration Act.
545. Constitution, section 92(3).
546. *Ibid.*, section 92(4).
547. Chapter 497 of the Laws of Malta.
548. For an insight into these matters, *see* David Joseph Attard, *supra* note 25, p. 61.
549. Constitution, section 79(1).
550. The office of Parliamentary Secretary is established in section 88 of the Constitution.
551. Constitution, section 79(2).

by the provisions of the Constitution and has to operate within the law. Powerful at it may be, Cabinet is a creature of the Constitution and therefore subject thereto. In addition, Cabinet is not only subordinate to the Constitution but it is also responsible to Parliament. Its workings are thus supervised by Parliament. This is because section 79(2) of the Constitution specifically provides that the Cabinet 'shall be collectively responsible therefor to Parliament'. This makes it quite clear that Parliament is supreme over Cabinet. The Constitution also contemplates instances where a public officer or body is not subject to the 'direction or control' of government. Apart from the obvious cases of MPs and the judiciary, although in the case of MPs one still have to bear in mind the whip parliamentary group structure, there are other cases established by the Constitution and by ordinary law where Cabinet cannot give directions, nor is it in control.[552]

II. The Prime Minister

283. The Prime Minister is appointed by the President.[553] It is one of the few instances where the President enjoys powers and exercises it, unadvised, on his/her own deliberate judgment. The Constitution directs the President how to appoint a Prime Minister: the former has to select such MP 'who, in his judgment, is best able to command the support of a majority of the members of that House'.[554] It is up to the President to establish that MP who is in a good position to form a government. In a two-party system, more often than not, it is quite clear who is the winner of a general election and who is the loser.

III. Ministers

284. Ministers are, like the Prime Minister, also appointed by the President but with the sole difference that they are appointed 'in accordance with the advice of the Prime Minister' and 'from amongst the members of the House of Representatives'.[555] Contrary to the Speaker, Ministers cannot be appointed from outside the House. A number of Prime Ministers consider this latter restriction imposed by the Constitution upon them when forming the Cabinet as an impediment to making the best choice as non-parliamentarians who might have better credentials for ministerial office are simply excluded by the Constitution.[556] The same procedure also applies to the appointment of a Minister following dissolution of the House as it applies to the Prime Minister.[557]

---

552. Such is the case with the Information and Data Protection Commissioner appointed in terms of section 36 of the Data Protection Act, Chapter 440 of the Laws of Malta.
553. Constitution, Article 80.
554. *Ibid.*
555. Constitution, section 80.
556. David Joseph Attard, *supra* note 25, p. 56.
557. Constitution, section 80 proviso.

As the Constitution does not set out any criteria for appointment of Ministers, the matter is left to the entire discretion of the Prime Minister.[558]

IV. Acting Prime Minister

285. Occasion does arise, from time to time, where the Prime Minister cannot perform the functions of office, either because he/she is abroad or on vacation or ill. In such cases, an Acting Prime Minister is appointed by the President on the advice of the Prime Minister, unless the President considers it impracticable to obtain the Prime Minister's advice.[559] Normally it is the Deputy Prime Minister or the most senior amongst Deputy Prime Ministers, if there are two in office, who is appointed Acting Prime Minister or, also in their absence, the most senior minister available at that given time. Essentially, the matter is determined on the basis of seniority. Indeed, whenever:

> the Prime Minister is absent from Malta or is unable by reason of illness to perform the functions of his office, the President may authorise any other member of the Cabinet to perform those functions (other than the functions conferred by this article) and that member may perform those functions until his authority is revoked by the President.[560]

V. Temporary Ministers

286. Insofar as Ministers are concerned, the Constitution does not refer to the appointment of an Acting Minister but to the appointment of a Temporary Minister. The Constitution states that the President may appoint, on the advice of the Prime Minister, an MP as a Temporary Minister.[561] The practice has evolved in the direction that another Minister assumes the functions of the Minister who is ill or absent from Malta. Should such a vacancy arise when Parliament is dissolved, a Temporary Minister has to be selected from amongst those MPs, including Ministers, who were MPs before the House was dissolved.[562]

VI. Parliamentary Secretaries

287. In terms of the Ministers (Delegation of Functions) Act,[563] a Minister 'may delegate to a Parliamentary Secretary assisting him in the performance of his duties, any functions which in virtue of his office are conferred on him by or under any law'.[564]

558. David Joseph Attard discusses these criteria, *supra* note 25, pp. 57–60.
559. *Ibid.*, section 83(2) proviso.
560. *Ibid.*, section 83(1).
561. *Ibid.*, section 84(1).
562. *Ibid.*, section 84(1) proviso.
563. Chapter 324 of the Laws of Malta.
564. Ministers (Delegation of Functions) Act, section 3(1).

288. A Parliamentary Secretary is appointed by the President on the advice of the Prime Minister.[565] Again, if the House is dissolved and there is an occasion to appoint a Parliamentary Secretary, the President acting on the advice of the Prime Minister, appoints as a Parliamentary Secretary – a Junior Minister – a person who has served as MP before the House was dissolved.[566]

VII. Permanent Secretaries and Heads of Government Departments

289. The Prime Minister is responsible for assigning departments of government to Permanent Secretaries.[567] A Permanent Secretary is tasked with the supervision of a department of government whilst the Minister exercises 'general direction and control over the department'.[568] Note that the words 'general direction and control' are the same words used in section 79(2) of the Constitution. Section 92(1) is therefore enshrining by necessary intendment the principle of individual ministerial responsibility even though the words 'individual responsibility' are not spelt out as 'collective responsibility' is in section 79(2).

290. When the President comes to appoint a public officer as Permanent Secretary or Acting Permanent Secretary, or to remove such a Permanent Secretary from office, he/she has to act 'in accordance with the advice of the Prime Minister given after the Prime Minister has consulted with the Public Service Commission'.[569] In this particular instance, the Prime Minister does not need to take the advice of the PSC. On the other hand, in terms of the Constitution of Malta:

> power to make appointments to public offices and to remove and to exercise disciplinary control over persons holding or acting in any such offices shall vest in the Prime Minister, acting on the recommendation of the Public Service Commission.[570]

291. This provision, therefore, deals with the appointment, promotion, removal and taking of disciplinary proceedings, against a public officer.[571] Although the Constitution vests these fourfold powers in the Prime Minister, as a matter of fact, the Prime Minister is obliged to act on the recommendation of the PSC and *not* after consultation with the PSC. This means that the Prime Minister is bound by the recommendation of the PSC. The Constitution does contemplate situations where the Prime Minister consults the PSC rather than acts on its recommendation. Such is the case with regard to:

565. Constitution, section 88(1).
566. *Ibid.*, section 88(1) proviso.
567. *Ibid.*, section 92(1) proviso.
568. *Ibid.*, section 92(1).
569. Constitution, section 92(3).
570. *Ibid.*, section 110(1).
571. For a discussion on the regulation of the public service in Malta, *see* Oliver Gulia, *The Public Servant in Maltese Law*, Progress Press Co. Ltd., Valletta, undated.

(a) the appointment of Permanent Secretaries;[572]
(b) the appointment of heads of departments of government other than those whose manner of appointment is specifically provided in the Constitution;[573] and
(c) the appointment and transfer to diplomatic offices.[574]

292. Another exception is that of Secretary to the Cabinet who is designated (not appointed) by the Prime Minister with no involvement whatsoever of the PSC.[575] However, all these exceptions to the general rule that the Prime Minister has to act on the recommendation of the PSC relate to appointments, which includes also promotions insofar as promotions are in themselves appointments to a new office. Nonetheless, the removal and the taking of disciplinary proceedings find no exception to the general rule. Hence, the Prime Minister is bound by the recommendation of the PSC with regard to removal and discipline of public officers. Moreover, it is to be observed that the Constitution is referring to public officers and not to officers employed by parastatal non-public office bodies referred to in section 110(6) of the Constitution. These latter three entities enjoy their own separate and distinct disciplinary procedure where neither the PSC nor the Prime Minister, as Minister responsible for the public service, has a stake in those proceedings.

293. No criteria are set out as to the competency needed for a public officer to be appointed Permanent Secretary. This is not the situation with regard to the appointment of a Head of Department where the Constitution specifically states that:

> Heads of department of government other than those whose manner of appointment is specifically provided for in this Constitution shall be appointed from amongst senior public officers by the Prime Minister acting after consultation with the Public Service Commission.[576]

294. The *Constitution* fails however to define the term 'senior public officer' in relation to the salary scales of public officers.

VIII. Secretary to the Cabinet

295. The Secretary to the Cabinet is appointed by the Prime Minister and is selected from amongst public officers. Up till a few years ago, the duties of Secretary to the Cabinet were not performed by the Principal Permanent Secretary but by a public officer specifically designated as 'Secretary to the Cabinet'. The duties of Secretary to the Cabinet follow:

> The Secretary to the Cabinet shall be responsible, in accordance with such instructions as may be given to him by the Prime Minister, for arranging the

572. Constitution, section 92(3).
573. *Ibid.*, section 92(4).
574. *Ibid.*, section 112.
575. *Ibid.*, section 94.
576. *Ibid.*, section 92(4).

business for, and keeping the minutes of, the meetings of the Cabinet and for conveying the decisions of the Cabinet to the appropriate person or authority, and shall have such other functions as the Prime Minister may from time to time direct.[577]

IX. Cabinet Committees

296. Sometimes Cabinet appoints a Cabinet Committee to deal with a particular issue. Not much information is available on the composition, functions and workings of Cabinet Committees. This is because Cabinet meetings are held behind closed doors, Cabinet minutes are not in the public domain except for those going back more than thirty years and scant information is released on the functioning of Cabinet government. 'Cabinet committees help to ensure that government business is processed more effectively by relieving pressure on Cabinet. The committee structure also supports the principle of collective responsibility, ensuring that policy proposals receive thorough consideration without an issue having to be referred to the whole Cabinet. Cabinet committee decisions have the same authority as Cabinet decisions.'[578]

§3. Government Formation

297. Although the Cabinet is appointed by the President, the latter acts on the advice of the Prime Minister when appointing Cabinet Ministers (and Parliamentary Secretaries) except for the appointment of a Prime Minister (and the Leader of the Opposition), where the President acts on his/her own individual judgment. The Constitution does however provide the President with guidance as how to go about in filling these two latter offices of State. Insofar as the appointment of a Prime Minister is concerned, the President has to select that 'member of the House of Representatives who, in his judgment, is best able to command the support of a majority of the members of the House'.[579] The sole criterion in appointing a Prime Minister is majority support in the House of Representatives. If an MP enjoys majority support in the House, he is appointed Prime Minister.

298. After the Prime Minister is appointed by the President, his/her first task would be that of forming a Cabinet where ministries have to be established and MPs chosen to head those ministries. In Malta, the law does not provide for the establishment of any fixed Ministries, but government business is divided as best as the Prime Minister considers relevant for the governance of Malta at that particular day the decision is taken. Before calling MPs to offer them a ministerial or parliamentary secretariat office, the Prime Minister distributes portfolios amongst ministries and identifies

577. *Ibid.*, section 94(2).

578. Sir Gus O'Donnell, *The Cabinet Manual: A guide to laws, conventions and rules on the operation of government*, Cabinet Office, London, October 2011, p. 32.

579. Constitution, section 80.

potential political heads of such ministries. In doing so, the Prime Minister may consult with his deputy, with his consultants or with trusted party officials.[580]

299. Once the distribution of ministries is arrived at, ministries are allocated government business (including government departments and agencies falling under that Ministry), ministers and parliamentary secretaries are approached and agree to their appointment, then the actual swearing in ceremony is organized. It normally takes place at the President's Palace in Valletta. An oath of allegiance and an oath of office are taken by Ministers and Parliamentary Secretaries. These oaths are reproduced in the Third Schedule and Second Schedule, paragraph (b), respectively of the Constitution.

300. A new Government comes into being when the new Prime Minister subscribes to the oath of office. This is because until this takes place, strictly speaking, it is the previous Prime Minister heading the caretaker government who is actually ruling the country together with his/her cabinet. Although a general election is called, the incumbent Prime Minister and Cabinet continue to govern: they do not resign their office; nor are they appointed in an Acting capacity. Contrary to the situation of a dissolution of Parliament where MPs no longer remain in office, in the case of the Cabinet a dissolution of Parliament does not affect them: it only exempts them from being MPs and being responsible to Parliament, once Parliament is no longer in session. This is perhaps the worst deficiency of the principle of collective and individual ministerial responsibility insofar as it is suspended following dissolution of Parliament normally to resurrect on the summoning of a new Parliament. The taking of the oaths of allegiance and of office by the new Prime Minister brings to an end the caretaker government and the new Prime Minister, even in the absence of a Cabinet, until it is formed and the oaths of allegiance and office are subscribed to, begins to govern. There is no need for the caretaker government to resign or for the new Prime Minister to sack the caretaker government ministers: once the new Prime Minister subscribes to both the said oaths, the caretaker government comes to an automatic end, its period of appointment lapses and no further action is required for the caretaker government to be dissolved.

301. Concurrent with the appointment of Ministers and Parliamentary Secretaries, the President acting on the advice of the Prime Minister, allocates portfolios to Ministers and duties to Parliamentary Secretaries. Hence, when during the ceremony held at the President's Palace, in Valletta, the President appoints Ministers and Parliamentary Secretaries, they are appointed in terms of seniority and their respective portfolios are allocated and duties assigned. Normally, the ceremony starts by the Secretary to the Cabinet reading out the name of the first Minister to be appointed, the Deputy Prime Minister – or the senior of the Deputy Prime Ministers if there is more than one – and the portfolio allocated to him/her. During the thirteenth legislature, this could not take place right from the very beginning as the Labour Party did not have in place a Deputy Leader for parliamentary affairs. Dr Chris Fearne was appointed Deputy Leader on 16 July 2017 and, in terms of Government Notice 809 of 2017, Deputy Prime Minister on 19 July 2017. The Deputy Prime Minister would then subscribe to the oaths of allegiance and office to be followed by the same rigmarole by all other Ministers in order of seniority and then followed by Parliamentary Secretaries. Seniority is determined

580. The criteria for Cabinet formation adopted by diverse Prime Ministers is discussed by David Joseph Attard, *supra* note 25, pp. 57–60.

on the basis of whether a Minister has already served and the duration of that service in the office of Minister and/or Parliamentary Secretary.

I. Caretaker Government

302. There is no provision in the Constitution referring to, let alone setting out the role of, a caretaker government. However, it can safely be stated that a constitutional practice has emerged over the years and has been observed since independence to the effect that when Parliament is dissolved and a general election is called, a caretaker government comes into being

II. Recall of Parliament

303. Once Parliament is dissolved, it can be recalled only during a period of public emergency.

§4. The Status and Responsibilities of Government Members

304. Malta cannot have a technocratic government unless all the technocrats are elected to Parliament or MPs are requested to resign and, as a matter of fact, do so, so that technocrats could be co-opted in their stead. This is because all Ministers and Parliamentary Secretaries have to be chosen from amongst MPs.

305. Furthermore, Ministers and Parliamentary Secretaries enjoy immunities from legal proceedings and privileges under the House of Representatives (Privileges and Immunities) Ordinance[581] in virtue of their parliamentary office. However, there are certain provisions in the Constitution which apply to MPs who are Ministers and not to backbenchers. Foremost amongst these is the doctrine of collective and individual ministerial responsibility. Second, Ministers are answerable at law for their executive decisions. They may thus be sued in a court of law. Their decisions can be challenged on the basis of judicial review of administrative action whilst any damages which they may cause is also subject to tortious liability. From a political and not a judicial perspective, ministers can also be held politically liable through a vote of no confidence either in the whole government or in one particular Minister. A no confidence resolution is regulated by section 81 of the Constitution. Although in Malta motions of no confidence in the government as a whole do take place in the House, motions of no confidence in a Minister are less frequent.

§5. Government Competencies

306. Over time, the competences of government change to reflect the realities of a country. For instance, prior to 1993, Malta did not have a system of local government

581. Chapter 113 of the Laws of Malta.

except for sporadic instances in the past. In 2004, Malta joined the EU and hence a new reality had to be taken on board. The most relevant activities for the House are the following:

(a) exercising scrutiny over the executive;
(b) making and replying to parliamentary questions;
(c) laying of papers on the Table of the House;
(d) presenting motions for discussion in the House;
(e) approving resolutions;
(f) making statements;
(g) approving financial estimates during the budget process;
(h) appointing parliamentary officers – Ombudsman, Auditor General, Deputy Auditor General;
(i) appointing other officers e.g., through the Social Affairs Committee – Commissioner for Children;
(j) appointing the President, Speaker, and Deputy Speaker;
(k) reviewing EU pipeline acquis;
(l) discussing reports by the Ombudsman, Auditor General and several annual reports and estimates submitted to it by various public corporations or public officers;
(m) receiving petitions;
(n) the making of laws;
(o) amending subsidiary legislation, including the Standing Orders of the House of Representatives Order or annulling subsidiary legislation;
(p) broadcasting its own proceedings;
(q) publishing its own proceedings in the forms of agenda, minutes, motions, resolutions, debates, annual reports, Speaker's rulings and speeches, and other papers laid on the table of the House;
(r) removing members of the judiciary;
(s) deciding contempt of the House and breaches of privilege;
(t) receiving foreign heads of state and other dignitaries who visit Parliament, notably UN Secretary Generals, Presidents, EU Commissioners, etc.;
(u) approving the transfer of land;
(v) receiving messages from, and sending messages to, the President;
(w) approving the Structure Plan, now substituted by the Strategic Plan for the Environment and Development; and
(x) participating in the membership of international, European, Commonwealth and Mediterranean Parliamentary assemblies.

§6. Government and Political Parties

307. Political parties are the lifeblood of a democracy. No proper democracy can function without a system of political parties struggling against each other to acquire power to implement their ideological beliefs and political electoral manifesto. The Constitution barely mentions political parties let alone regulates their behaviour. It refers to them in the following provisions:

(a) in section 52(1) related to general elections;
(b) in section 56(11) to 'enable illiterates to distinguish between the political parties to which candidates belong';
(c) in section 90 related to the Leader of the Opposition in relation to the numerical strength of the opposition party from which the President is to appoint the Leader of the Opposition;
(d) in section 119(1) related to the fair apportionment of broadcasting facilities and time 'between persons belonging to different political parties'.

308. The Standing Orders of the House of Representatives Order do not even mention or refer to political parties.

309. When the Constitution was enacted in 1964 by the British Parliament, the emphasis in the Constitution was not so much on political parties who were, at that time, not the subject of the provisions where reference was made to a 'political party' but were considered to be more the object of those provisions. This implies that as objects, political parties were not considered recipients of any rights. The 1964 independence Constitution referred to political parties in the following provisions:

(a) in section 57(4), now renumbered as section 56(11), which states that – 'Ballot papers shall be drawn up in such a way as to enable illiterates to distinguish between the political parties to which candidates belong';
(b) in section 91(2) and (4), now renumbered as section 90(2) and (4), related to the appointment of the Leader of the Opposition where reference is made to opposition political party or parties: the Leader of the Opposition is chosen from (a) the member of the opposition party which has a numerical strength greater than any other opposition party; or (b) if the opposition parties are equal in strength in the House, the Leader of the Opposition is appointed if he/she commands the support of the largest single group of MPs. If any of these two circumstances change, the appointment of the Leader of the Opposition is revoked; and
(c) in section 122(1), now renumbered as section 119(1), whereby broadcasting facilities and time have to be fairly apportioned between persons belonging to different political parties.

310. In these three provisions, the subject of the provision in section 57(4) is a general election candidate, in section 91(2) and (4) the subject is the Leader of the Opposition and in section 122(1) the subject is a person who is granted broadcasting time and facilities. This means that as the independence Constitution was originally enacted, the rights afforded in these three provisions were not granted directly to political parties even though they benefit indirectly therefrom.

311. It all began to change in 1987. The 1964 Constitution did not refer to 'political parties' in section 52(1), but when the Constitution was amended in 1987, reference to political parties was introduced therein. Subsequently new concepts were added through amendments made in 2007 related to political parties – the 'absolute majority party', the 'relative majority party' and the 'minority party'. In the 1987 and 2007 amendments to section 52(1) of the Constitution, it can be said that for the first time the status of 'political party' moved from that of an object to a subject, and it was no longer an object dependant on a subject, the subject being the candidate at a general election. The political party gained electoral rights in its own name independent of its electoral candidates.

312. The discussion on the need of a law to regulate the financing of political parties has been long ongoing before it culminated in the enactment of the Financing of Political Parties Act.[582]

313. Whilst the Constitution refers to political parties in the above-mentioned four provisions, it refrains from defining the term. The Financing of Political Parties Act affords a definition of 'political party' as 'a free association of persons, the aims of which include the participation in the formation of the political will of the people by securing the election of one or more of its members to the House of Representatives, the European Parliament or Local Council, and ensuring a continuing active relationship between the people and the state institutions'.[583] The definition is not a comprehensive one insofar as the word 'include' is used. It also does not refer to Administrative Committees under the Local Councils Act the members whereof are elected following an election and where candidates for election to Administrative Committees may contest the election on behalf of a political party.

314. A political party must pursue 'a legitimate aim and shall conform to the Constitution and the laws of the State'.[584] Political parties may lawfully have as their aim amendments to the Constitution and to the laws of Malta, but all these amendments have to be brought about by legal means.[585] If they attempt to bring about change to the Constitution or to the laws of Malta through an insurrection or a *coup d'état* or other unlawful means, they will end up in breach of the Criminal Code, for instance, of section 56 thereof.[586]

315. The Financing of Political Parties Act sets out a number of political rights not hitherto enshrined in the Constitution or in any other law related to political parties. Section 5 sets out the principle of equal treatment of political parties, section 6 allows persons to associate in a political party whilst section 7 regulates members' rights in a political party. Section 8 regulates the legal status of political parties. They enjoy a legal personality, have the right to sue and be sued, and enjoy freedom of expression. As to the latter point, there have been instances in the past where freedom of expression was denied to political parties[587] and political organizations such as the PN Youth Movement[588] and the Christian Democrat Students Organization.[589]

316. The law further regulates their internal regulation, through a statute, and respect for the rights of defence in any internal disciplinary procedures taken against

582. Chapter 544 of the Laws of Malta.

583. Financing of Political Parties Act, Chapter 544 of the Laws of Malta, section 2.

584. *Ibid.*, section 4.

585. *Ibid.*

586. For a study of this provision *see* , Kevin Aquilina, *Treason and Sedition in Maltese Law*, Msida, Doctor of Laws Thesis, Faculty of Laws, University of Malta, 1988, pp. 40–60.

587. *See Dr Eddie Fenech Adami pro et noe v. Commissioner of Police et*, Constitutional Court, 18 November 1987.

588. *See Advocate Dr Tonio Borg et v. Minister of Foreign Affairs and Culture et*, Constitutional Court, 17 February 1988.

589. *See John Lateo et v. Commissioner of Police*, Constitutional Court, 18 November 1987.

members.[590] No definition is however afforded of the term 'rights of defence'. The Financing of Political Parties Act[591] further regulates the dissolution of political parties[592] and their registration with the Electoral Commission.[593] The enactment then deals in great detail with the financing of political parties.[594]

590. Financing of Political Parties Act, Chapter 544 of the Laws of Malta, section 9.
591. Chapter 544 of the Laws of Malta.
592. Financing of Political Parties Act, Chapter 544 of the Laws of Malta, section 10.
593. *Ibid.*, section 11.
594. *Ibid.*, sections 22–45.

Chapter 6. Confidence in Parliament: The Relationship of Confidence

§1. A Motion of No Confidence

317. In Malta, once a government is formed, no vote of confidence in the Government is needed in the House. But if a government backbencher or an opposition MP wants to challenge the government, he/she presents a vote of no confidence in the government. Such procedure is regulated by the Constitution. In terms of section 81(1), the House may be called upon to pass a resolution of no confidence in the Government. If such a resolution is carried, 'supported by the votes of a majority of all the members thereof', that is, by an absolute majority, 'that it has no confidence in the Government, the President may remove the Prime Minister from office: provided that the President shall not do so unless three days have elapsed and he has decided not to dissolve Parliament under section 76 of the Constitution'.[595] Apart from requiring an absolute majority, the provision refers to 'all the members thereof'. The question which arises is whether the Speaker is a member thereof and therefore eligible to vote. If there are sixty-nine MPs in all, a two-thirds majority amounts to forty-six votes. If there are seventy MPs with the Speaker included, an absolute majority would amount to forty-seven votes. According to section 71(2) of the Constitution, the 'Speaker shall not vote unless on any question the votes are equally divided, in which case he shall have and exercise a casting vote'.[596] The Speaker is allowed only a casting vote and no original vote. But 'any other person shall, when presiding in the House of Representatives, retain his original vote as member and, if upon any question, the votes are equally divided, in which case he shall have and exercise a casting vote'. Thus the Deputy Speaker (or when another MP is presiding) is granted an original and a casting vote. But even if the Speaker does not enjoy an original vote, should he be included in the number of MPs for the purpose of voting? The answer is in the negative because: (a) the Speaker does not have an original vote in terms of section 71(2), and (b) for the purposes of ascertaining that there is a quorum in the House, 'the person presiding at the sitting of the House shall not be included in reckoning whether there is a quorum present'.[597] On the other hand, section 52(2) provides that: 'If any person who is not a member of the House of Representatives is elected to be Speaker of the House he shall, by virtue of holding the office of Speaker, be a member of the House in addition to the other members: provided that in any such case the Speaker shall not be treated as a member of the House for the purposes of establishing the number of votes required to support a bill for any of the purposes of section 66 of this Constitution.'[598]

595. Constitution, section 81(1).

596. *Ibid.*, section 71(2). *See also* Standing Order 21 of the Standing Orders of the House of Representatives Order, Subsidiary Legislation Const. 02.

597. Constitution, section 70(2)(b).

598. *Ibid.*, section 52(2).

318. Legislative power and certain appointments are shared between Government and the Opposition. The Government has called votes of confidence in itself[599] whilst the Opposition has called votes of no confidence in government as a whole.[600] There have also been cases of votes of no confidence in Ministers,[601] and a call for the removal from office of Malta's Permanent Representative to the EU.[602] There have also been instances where the government of the day was defeated because one of its backbenchers voted with the Opposition, where the Government enjoyed only a majority of one seat in the House, thereby bringing the downfall of the political party in government.[603]

§2. A Contrary Vote on Government's Proposal

319. Not every defeat which Government sustains in the House of Representatives amounts to a vote of no confidence. On the contrary, when the government loses a vote in Parliament, that vote is normally followed by a vote of confidence in the Government.

320. In terms of section 76(5)(a) of the Constitution, the President acts in accordance with his/her own deliberate judgment to dissolve Parliament 'if the House of Representatives passes a resolution, supported by the votes of a majority of all the members thereof, that it has no confidence in the Government, and the Prime Minister does not within three days either resign from his office or advice a dissolution'. Before the President, following a vote of no confidence in the government of the day, passes on to dissolve Parliament, he/she has to verify whether there is another Member of the House who is capable of forming a new Government. If this course of action is not possible, then the President will have no other option but to dissolve the Parliament. However, dissolution is a remedy of last resort and if this can be avoided, the President should entrust another MP with the object of forming a new government. With a two-party system where political parties tend to entrench themselves in rigid unmovable positions, this behaviour makes it relatively straight forward for the President to take the bold decision to dissolve Parliament. In this circumstance, the President has to

599. For an example of a vote of confidence in the Government, *see* Michael Schiavone, *supra* note 211, pp. 948–949.

600. For examples of votes of no confidence in the Government, *see* Michael Schiavone, *supra* note 211, p. 752 and pp. 948–949; and Godfrey A. Pirotta, *supra* note 502.

601. For an example of a vote of no confidence in Ministers, *see* Michael Schiavone, *supra* note 211, pp, 948–949. Nationalist MP The Hon. Dr Franco Debono presented a motion of no confidence in a Nationalist Government Minister, Dr Austin Gatt. *See* Michael Schiavone, *supra* note 211, p. 977.

602. For an example of a vote of no confidence in a Permanent Representative, *see* Michael Schiavone, *supra* note 211, pp, 966–969.

603. Labour MP The Hon. Dominic Mintoff brought about the downfall of the Labour Government. *See* Michael Schiavone, *supra* note 211, pp, 749–763 whilst Nationalist MP The Hon. Dr Franco Debono brought about the downfall of the Nationalist Government. *See* Michael Schiavone, *supra* note 211, pp, 980–983. In the case of Dr Debono, the vote related to a money bill; in the case of Mr Mintoff, it was Prime Minister Dr Alfred Sant who turned the vote in question into one of confidence in the Labour government. *See* David Joseph Attard, *supra* note 25, p. 55.

carry a heavy burden by him/herself and does not have any person or institution such as a Council of State[604] to consult. Thus a resolution of no confidence carried by the House tends to lead to dissolution of the House and to a general election.

§3. The Question of Confidence

321. Whilst the Opposition, or a government backbencher, is always free to bring a vote of no confidence in the government, it might be the government itself which requests a vote of confidence.

604. *See* Kevin Aquilina, 'The Case for a Council of State', *The Times of Malta*, 16 November 2012, p. 14 and 'Why a Second Republic for Malta?', in Office of the President, *supra* note 418, pp. 162–164.

Chapter 7. The Judicial Power

§1. The Judiciary is Subject Only to the Constitution, Laws and Customs of Malta

322. When a member of the judiciary (Chief Justice, Judge and Magistrate) is appointed, he/she subscribes to two oaths, the oath of allegiance in terms of section 101 and the Third Schedule of the Constitution, and the oath of office in terms of section 10(1) of the Code of Organization and Civil Procedure.[605] When a member of the judiciary subscribes to the oath of allegiance, he/she declares that he/she will 'bear true faith and allegiance to the people and the Republic of Malta and its Constitution'. Hence he/she swears or affirms that he/she will comply with the provisions of the Constitution which, includes amongst other things, the right to a fair trial in terms of section 39 of the Constitution and, embedded in this right, is the independence and impartiality of the judiciary. In terms of the oath of office, a member of the judiciary subscribes to a more detailed oath than the oath of allegiance which can be broken down into five constitutive ingredients:

(a) he/she performs the duties of office 'without favour or partiality, according to justice and right, and in accordance with the laws and customs of Malta';
(b) he/she has to 'honour God and the Republic of Malta';[606]
(c) he/she cannot 'hold, either directly or indirectly, any communication with any suitor in any of the Courts or with any other person on behalf of such suitor, in regard to any suit pending or about to be commenced or prosecuted in any of the said Courts, except in open court, saving the cases expressly provided for by law';
(d) he/she 'will disclose in open court and make known to the President any such communication' as may be made to him/her; and
(e) he/she will not 'act, either directly or indirectly, as an Advocate, or arbitrator, nor give in any case counsel or advice to any person in regard to any suit already commenced or to be commenced in any of the said Courts, saving the cases excepted by law, without the permission of the President of Malta first had and obtained upon an application to that effect'.

323. The Maltese judiciary is thus subject to the Constitution and to the laws whilst being independent of any other authority, in particular, the executive organ of the State. Although the doctrine of separation of powers tends to be blurred when considering the relationship between the legislature and the executive, the same cannot be said with regard to the relationship between the judiciary, on the one hand, and the legislature and the executive, on the other hand, even if the legislature may remove a

605. Chapter 12 of the Laws of Malta.
606. The reference to God has to be seen in the light of the fact that Malta is a confessional state constitutionally speaking but very much of a secular state in practice.

member of the judiciary from office and the executive appoints the judiciary and partakes in – not to say actively pursues – their removal process in the legislature.

324. The main function of the judiciary is to apply the laws enacted by Parliament or subsidiary legislation made by the public administration. Nevertheless, the judiciary does have other subsidiary functions, some of which are of great constitutional and legal purport. The judiciary interprets the law. In the latter case, it is called upon to determine disputes where the law is lacking, unclear, ambiguous or even conflicting. Moreover, judges sitting in the courts of constitutional competence have the power to review legislative acts, that is, to declare void or invalid legislation that is inconsistent with the Constitution,[607] Emergency Powers Act,[608] the Diplomatic Immunities and Privileges Act,[609] the European Convention Act,[610] and the European Union Act.[611] The courts are also called upon to review subsidiary legislation when this goes beyond the powers given in the parent act for the making of that subsidiary law, that is, where it is *ultra vires*. The judiciary also sit on international courts and tribunals and other boards such as the Commission for the Administration of Justice and Rule Making Boards.

§2. The 'External' Independence of the Judiciary: Composition and Functions of the Commission for the Administration of Justice

325. The Constitution provides for a twofold independence of the judiciary: the external and the internal independence. The external independence, albeit limited, ensures that the judiciary as a collective body is shielded from external or outside pressures coming from the executive or the legislature. The independence of the judiciary is guaranteed through the Commission for the Administration of Justice set up by the Constitution in section 101A(1).[612] A majority of votes on the Commission are enjoyed by sitting members of the judiciary, these being the Chief Justice (who is the Deputy Chairman and chairs the Commission in the absence of the Chairman) and in the case of judicial discipline, two elected judges and two elected magistrates, both the judges and magistrates being elected by and from their own class. Out of a membership of ten, five of its members hail from the judiciary. As to the other five members, one of them – the Commission's chairman (the President of Malta) does not enjoy an original vote but only a casting vote and the other four non-judicial members enjoy an original vote. As the Chairman enjoys only a casting vote, this means that he/she is not always called upon to vote and that where no casting vote is of the essence and all the judiciary who are members of the Commission are present and voting, they would enjoy a majority when voting on that issue.

607. Constitution, section 6.
608. Chapter 178 of the Laws of Malta, section 7.
609. Chapter 191 of the Laws of Malta, section 13.
610. Chapter 319 of the Laws of Malta, section 3(2).
611. Chapter 460 of the Laws of Malta, section 3(2). Reference is also made to the proposed amendments to the Equal Opportunities (Persons with Disability) Act.
612. For a discussion of the Commission for the Administration of Justice, *see* David Joseph Attard, *supra* note 25, pp. 66–70.

§3. The Internal Independence of the Judiciary

326. As to the internal independence of the judiciary, every single member of the judiciary within the judicial system is independent from interference by other members of the judiciary either on a singular basis or on a collegiate basis. No member of the judiciary may interfere in the way another member of the judiciary disposes of cases before him/her. Not even the Chief Justice, the Senior Administrative Judge, the Senior Magistrate or the Commission for the Administration of Justice may direct a member of the judiciary as to how to decide a case pending before him/her. This is because the oath of office of a member of the judiciary requires him/her to perform the duties of office 'without favour or partiality, according to justice and right and in accordance with the laws and customs of Malta'. The oath of allegiance also requires the judiciary to 'bear true faith and allegiance ... to the Constitution'.

327. The independence of the judiciary is also guaranteed by the Constitution and by Article 6 of the ECHR.[613]

§4. The Powers of the Minister Responsible for Justice

328. The Minister responsible for justice has limited powers over the courts and the judiciary. This is because the courts and the judiciary are not organs of the executive and, due to their independence from government, the Minister is not in a position to direct or control the courts and the judiciary in their judicial duties. Although the Constitution does consider judges and magistrates to be public officers,[614] yet they are not public officers in the sense that they fall under the direction and control of the executive. Indeed, section 110 of the Constitution gives the Prime Minister, acting on the recommendation of the PSC, 'power to make appointments to public offices and to remove and to exercise disciplinary control' over public officers. But, in terms of section 110(5)(a) of the Constitution, this power does not extend to the judiciary. Though public officers, the judiciary are a sui generis type of public officers. Thus the Minister's control or direction of the judiciary, in terms of law, is inexistent, not to say unconstitutional and illegal. This does not, of course, mean that the Minister has no role to play in the judicial field. For he/she can still exercise certain powers which are conducive to bringing about a proper and more efficient administration of justice. In practice, the Minister responsible for justice is, *inter alia*, responsible for:

(a) drawing up policy in the justice sector. This policy is then submitted to Cabinet for its approval, with or without amendments. It is then implemented through legislation drawn up by the Ministry responsible for justice, enacted by Parliament or through subsidiary legislation made by the Minister responsible for justice or through administrative action. Such policy making which need not be drawn up by the Minister responsible for justice but he/she may be aided in this respect through Commissions or Boards which are established for this purpose, whether

613. The judiciary enjoy security of tenure in terms of the Constitution. *See* , for example, sections 97(2) and 107(1)(2) and (4).

614. Constitution, section 124(2).

on a general level or a sectoral level, through advice given by public officers falling within the Ministry responsible for justice and through external consultants and advisors;

(b) advising Cabinet as to the appointment and promotion of new members of the judiciary;
(c) initiating discussion in cabinet with regard to the presentation in the House of motions for the removal of a member of the judiciary;
(d) providing in Parliament information on the workings of all departments and entities falling under his/her Ministerial portfolio;
(e) representing Malta abroad in various committees including EU Commission meetings related to the justice sector;
(f) piloting bills in the House of Representatives;
(g) making subsidiary laws;
(h) advising the President on the subrogation of judges and magistrates and assignment of duties to judges and magistrates in terms of section 101A(13) of the Constitution;
(i) overseeing the implementation of government policy in the justice sector either personally or through public officers, or both;
(j) appointing the board of governors of the Arbitration Centre and the Mediation Centre and chairpersons and board members of quasi-judicial boards falling within the Minister's portfolio;
(k) meeting on a regular basis the Chief Justice and the Association of the Judiciary;
(l) meeting on a regular basis various public officers such as the Attorney General, the Permanent Secretary and others to address certain issues of concern to the Ministry; and
(m) carrying out several duties assigned to him/her by law such as the Criminal Code and the Code of Organization and Civil Procedure, including the preparation of warrants of advocates and legal procurators for the President's signature and the award by the Minister of the warrants.

§5. The Organization of Justice in Malta: Civil and Criminal Jurisdiction

329. The Maltese judicial system is divided into a civil system of law and a military system of law. The civil system of law comprises civil law and procedure, administrative law and procedure, commercial law and procedure, public law and procedure and criminal law and procedure. The civil system of law is divided into two principal jurisdictions: the civil jurisdiction and the criminal jurisdiction. On the other hand, the military system of law is regulated by only one law – the Malta Armed Forces Act.[615] The civil and criminal jurisdictions are exercised by both courts and tribunals.[616] Courts are divided in four civil courts and four criminal courts. Tribunals, mainly in the civil field, supplement the civil courts and tend to be specialized, normally addressing

615. Chapter 220 of the Laws of Malta.
616. For a discussion of the organization of the courts, *see* Kevin Aquilina and Paul Edgar Micallef, *A Profile of the Maltese Courts of Justice*, Department of Information, Valletta, March 1992, and David Joseph Attard, *supra* note 25, pp. 131–188.

one sector of the law. Courts are invariably presided by full-time members of the judiciary. The Criminal Court also consists of a judge, nine jurors and three supplementary jurors whilst the Juvenile Court consists of a Magistrate and two Assistants. The jurors and Juvenile Court assistants are neither full timers nor members of the judiciary. On the other hand, tribunals may be composed of both members of the judiciary and non-members of the judiciary or mixed together with the member of the judiciary presiding the tribunals whilst sitting with two non-members of the judiciary. Again, the non-members of the judiciary may be extracted from the legal profession or from other professions depending much on the nature of the tribunal in question. For instance, the chairperson of the Environment and Planning Tribunal is not presided by an advocate but by a person versed in planning or the environment.

330. Although the Constitution recognizes only the Chief Justice, Judges and Magistrates as forming part of the judiciary, a new class of judiciary is emerging and is also being recognized by law. This is the class of the *emeriti*, the retired members of the judiciary, who are appointed to various public offices after they retire from the bench in view of the experience they would have garnered in judicial office. This has to be contrasted with the case of the Chief Justice and judges who, in terms of section 48(2)(b) of the Constitution are expressly precluded from being appointed, on retirement, to the Presidency. Furthermore, the Constitution also provides that in the case of the PSC,[617] the Broadcasting Authority[618] and the Employment Commission,[619] a member of these three constitutional entities 'shall not, within a period of three years commencing with the day on which he last held office or acted as a member, be eligible for appointment to or to act in any public office'.[620]

331. The difference between appointing a retired judge or magistrate and an incumbent judge or magistrate lies in security of tenure for retired members of the judiciary enjoy none in terms of the Constitution unless in terms of the law under which they are appointed they enjoy some form of security of tenure. The advantage of appointing retired members of the judiciary to public office comprise integrity and experience in public administration. As to the latter point, although the judiciary are not, strictly speaking, administering a department, they are exercising judicial review of administrative action, applying the laws which the public administration applies in its day-to-day duties and interpreting administrative law, including circulars and other decisions taken by the public administration. Furthermore, retired judiciary are appointed to chair Boards of Inquiry and to perform administrative non-judicial work such as chairing regulatory authorities (the Broadcasting Authority, the Embryo Protection Authority and so on and so forth).

---

617. Constitution, section 109(4).
618. *Ibid.*, section 118(4).
619. *Ibid.*, section 120(4).
620. Common provision to the Public Service Commission, the Broadcasting Authority and the Employment Commission – *see* sections 109(4), 118(4) and 120(4) respectively. No such requirement however exists in the case of the Electoral Commission (established by sections 60(1) of the Constitution) and the Commission for the Administration of Justice (established by section 101A of the Constitution).

§6. Citizen Participation in the Administration of Justice

332. Citizen participation in the administration of justice is not that widespread in Malta as in other jurisdictions. For instance, in Malta, contrary to the position in the UK and the USA, there is no system of jury trials for civil cases. In Malta, jury trial is limited only to cases brought before one court – the Criminal Court.[621] It is only in this court that jurors – nine in all and three supplementary (i.e., substitute) ones are empanelled. Jurors have a decision-making role as they decide whether an accused person is guilty or not guilty – the so-called verdict[622] – or whether sane or insane.[623] The jury's decision is of vital importance to the proper administration of criminal justice in general and to the judge presiding the Criminal Court in particular as the latter is bound, when awarding sentence, by the jury's findings of guilt.[624] At a lower level of the court hierarchy, there are also lay persons who act as Assistants to the Juvenile Court but, contrary to jurors, these Assistants do not partake in the decision-making process as the decision is taken exclusively by the Magistrate presiding the court, even though he/she may still consult the Assistants.[625] But their advice, like that of Court Experts, does not bind the court. Indeed, in section 681 of the Code of Organization and Civil Procedure, it is stated that: 'The court is not bound to adopt the report of the referee [court expert] against its own conviction.' A similar provision is found in the Juvenile Court Act.[626]

333. Other instances where lay persons are involved in the judicial process is when they are appointed as court experts, when they give evidence in court and when they are appointed on panels of a tribunal as is the case with the Administrative Review Tribunal,[627] the Rent Regulation Board, the Rural Leases Control Board, the Land Arbitration Board, and various other appeal boards and tribunals.

334. According to section 95(6) of the Constitution, 'the office of a judge of the Superior Courts shall not, without his consent, be abolished during his continuance in office'. No corresponding provision is made in the Constitution for a Magistrate which therefore appears to imply at face value that the office of Magistrate of the Inferior Courts may be abolished during his/her continuance in office without the Magistrate's consent. The Magistrate's security of tenure is, in this respect, dented and diluted when compared to that of a judge. If this power were to be applied by the legislature, this would mean that Magistrates are very much unprotected if their office were to be abolished at whim by the Legislature. One hopes that this *lacuna* in the Constitution is addressed to ensure that there can be no abolition of office of a Magistrate whilst he/she holds such office unless the Magistrate consents to such abolition.

621. For a study of jury trials in Malta *see* J.J. Cremona, 'The Jury System in Malta', *The American Journal of Comparative Law*, Vol. 13, No. 4 (Autumn, 1964), pp. 570–583; and *Zarb Adami v. Malta*, ECtHR, application no. 17209/02, 20 June 2006. *See* Mark A. Sammut et al., *supra* note 205, p. 244.

622. Criminal Code, Chapter 9 of the Laws of Malta, in particular, sections 466 and 467.

623. *Ibid.*, in particular, sections 620–628.

624. *Ibid.*, in particular, sections 487 and 490.

625. Juvenile Court Act, Chapter 287 of the Laws of Malta, section 4(2) and (3).

626. *Ibid.*, section 4(3).

627. Administrative Justice Act, Chapter 490 of the Laws of Malta, section 10.

Furthermore, the fact that a judge – or a magistrate if the provision is extended thereto – were to consent to such abolition of office (for instance he/she is assigned duties in an international court where the remuneration is by far greater than that received in Malta) that decision might benefit the individual in question but not necessarily the common good and the proper administration of justice.

335. The judiciary cannot be removed from office by the Executive and their removal from office can take place, in terms of the Constitution only, by the Legislature, although it is very much doubted how much this constitutional judicial removal power is consonant with the right to a fair and public trial both under the Constitution and the European Convention Act.

336. For the legislature to remove a member of the judiciary from office, it cannot act on its own motion but has to await a report from the Commission for the Administration of Justice that would have investigated a motion submitted to it by the Speaker of the House declaring that there is a prima facie case for such removal. Moreover, for such judicial removal to succeed there must be at least a two-thirds vote in the House in favour of judicial removal out of the total membership of the whole House, excluding the Speaker though he/she is an MP.[628] Furthermore, the judiciary cannot be transferred from one court to another or have their duties changed by the government because the Constitution allows the President of Malta to exercise such power on the advice of the Chief Justice. Should the Chief Justice fail to make such a recommendation, then the Minister responsible for justice may step in to advise the President.

337. Contrary to a number of jurisdictions on the continent, judicial discipline and removal does not vest in a special body independent of the legislature and the executive but in Parliament.

§7. Special Courts and Tribunals

338. In Malta, there are no special courts in existence at the current moment in time within the civil justice system. According to the Emergency Powers Act,[629] it is possible to 'provide for the apprehension, trial and punishment of persons offending against the regulations'.[630] This includes the power to establish special courts. However, this law comes into operation only when a 'public emergency exists'.[631] Although the Emergency Powers Act does not define what constitutes a 'public emergency', this term is nevertheless explained in section 47(2) of the Constitution.[632]

---

628. As to the Speaker's voting entitlement, *see* Constitution, section 71(2).

629. Chapter 178 of the Laws of Malta.

630. Emergency Powers Act, section 4(2)(g).

631. *Ibid.*, section 3(1).

632. Section 47(2) of the Constitution defines 'period of public emergency' as meaning 'any period during which – (a) Malta is engaged in any war; or (b) there is in force a proclamation by the President declaring that a state of public emergency exists; or (c) there is in force a resolution of the House of Representatives supported by the votes of not less than two-thirds of all the Members of the House declaring that democratic institutions in Malta are threatened by subversion'.

339. Periods of public emergency apart, there are no special courts established by the Criminal Code or by the Code of Organization and Civil Procedure – the two main ordinary primary laws which establish courts in Malta[633] – as such court, if and when established, will be so established under regulations to be made under the Emergency Powers Act. Special courts, therefore, come into being only during a period of public emergency.

340. At this juncture, a distinction should be drawn between 'special courts' and 'special tribunals'. A special tribunal is a tribunal which has been established for a special reason, such as the Rent Regulation Board, the Rural Leases Control Board, the Land Arbitration Board, the Small Claims Tribunal, the Industrial Tribunal, the Administrative Review Tribunal and other appeal boards and tribunals established by a special law, a *lex specialis*. These special tribunals are established with the purpose of determining disputes relating to a particular area of the law and which would essentially replace the courts such that in these instances the courts would no longer enjoy jurisdiction to determine those types of disputes. This does not necessarily mean that the jurisdiction of the courts is ousted because in a number of cases, the courts would still enjoy jurisdiction where the special law in question allow the courts to review or hear appeals from decisions of these special tribunals.

341. It must also be borne in mind that the Ecclesiastical Tribunal, though not a court established by the law of Malta, does exercise jurisdiction in Malta over marriages contracted in terms of the Code of Canon Law. The Ecclesiastical Courts (Constitution and Jurisdiction) Law[634] provides that: 'Ecclesiastical courts and judges established or appointed, or that may be established or appointed in Malta, to decide cases regarding the laws of the Roman Catholic Church shall have no jurisdiction and shall not make, or attempt to make any judicial act having civil, other than purely spiritual, effect except as may be provided by law.'[635] However, an exception to this law is contained in the Marriage Act[636] which recognizes the jurisdiction of the Ecclesiastical Tribunal over Catholic marriages.[637]

342. Therefore, in sum, the court system in Malta is divided as follows:

(a) the civil courts;
(b) the criminal courts;
(c) the disciplinary courts;
(d) the military courts; and
(e) the special courts.

343. The courts of justice of civil jurisdiction are fourfold:

---

633. Other laws are the Juvenile Court Act, Chapter 287 of the Laws of Malta, which establishes the Juvenile Court and the Notarial Profession and Notarial Archives Act, Chapter 55 of the Laws of Malta, which establishes the Court of Revision of Notarial Acts.
634. Chapter 1 of the Laws of Malta.
635. *Ibid.*, section 2.
636. Chapter 255 of the Laws of Malta. *See also* the Procedure regarding information required by any Court of Civil Jurisdiction from the Ecclesiastical Tribunal Regulations, Subsidiary Legislation 255.03.
637. A 'catholic marriage' is defined in section 2 of the Marriage Act.

(a) the Constitutional Court, composed of three judges;
(b) the Court of Appeal: it has a superior competence, composed of three judges and an inferior competence, composed of one judge;
(c) the Civil Court, composed of one judge. The Civil Court has three sections: the Civil Court, First Hall; the Family Section and the Voluntary Jurisdiction Section; and
(d) the Court of Magistrates, one for Malta and one for Gozo, composed of one Magistrate.[638]

344. The courts of justice of criminal jurisdiction are fourfold:

(a) the Court of Criminal Appeal: it has a superior competence, composed of three judges, and an inferior competence, composed of one judge;
(b) the Criminal Court, composed of one Judge and nine jurors;
(c) the Court of Magistrates, one for Malta and one for Gozo, composed of one Magistrate with a twofold jurisdiction: a court of criminal judicature and a court of inquiry; and
(d) a Juvenile Court, consisting of one Magistrate, who can consult two Juvenile Court Assistants, though the court is not bound by their opinion.[639] The Juvenile Court also enjoys a twofold jurisdiction like the Court of Magistrates and also two branches, one in Malta and one in Gozo.[640]

345. There is only one disciplinary court – the Court of Revision of Notarial Acts, composed of 'a retired Judge or a retired Magistrate or a retired advocate who has practised his profession for over twelve years'.[641] Although it is designated as a 'court', it is the only court in Malta which is not presided by sitting judges or sitting magistrates. A similar tribunal of a disciplinary nature is the Administration Review Tribunal which has a panel, the Professions' Regulation Panel, to deal with professional warrants.[642]

346. There is only one military court, the court martial. There is a right of appeal from a decision of a court martial to the Court of Criminal Appeal.

---

638. It must be noted that the Court of Magistrates (Gozo), before the enactment of the Code of Organization and Civil Procedure, Act No XXIV of 1995, was composed of three Magistrates to hear appeals from the same court composed by one Magistrate. This appellate composition of the Court of Magistrates (Gozo) was abolished in 1995. A proposal to further amend the composition of the Gozo Courts is still pending. *See* Kevin Aquilina, 'A Bill to reform the Courts in Gozo and to simplify proceedings between the Courts in Malta and those in Gozo', *Gozo Observer: Journal of the University of Malta – Gozo Campus*, No. 27, December 2012, pp. 21–27.
639. Juvenile Court Act, Chapter 287 of the Laws of Malta, section 4(1)-(3).
640. *Ibid.*, Chapter 287 of the Laws of Malta, sections 3(2)-(4) and 5.
641. Notarial Profession and Notarial Archives Act, Chapter 55 of the Laws of Malta, section 110(2).
642. Administrative Review Tribunal (Establishment of Panels) Regulations, Subsidiary Legislation 490.04, regulation 3(7).

§8. Officers of the Criminal Justice Sector

347. Three important public officers in the criminal justice sector are:

(a) the Inquiring Magistrate;
(b) the Attorney General; and
(c) the Advocate for Legal Aid.

I. The Inquiring Magistrate

348. The Inquiring Magistrate normally holds an inquiry *in genere* with regard to any offence liable to the punishment of imprisonment exceeding three years.[643] He/she also draws up a *repertus*, that is, a report relating to the discovery of any document relating to any offence.[644] He/she also holds inquests in cases of 'sudden or violent or suspicious death or of death whereof the cause was unknown'.[645] An inquest is also held when a 'person dies while he is imprisoned or detained in any place of confinement contemplated in the Prison Act[646] or while he is in police custody'[647] and 'whenever a person dies in Mount Carmel Hospital while he is kept there under an order of a court … or for the purpose of his being examined by experts appointed by the court to report on the plea of insanity'.[648]

II. The Attorney General

349. The second public officer of relevance in the criminal justice sector is the Attorney General[649] who carries out the duties of a Director of Public Prosecutions or of a Prosecutor General as this office is also known in other foreign jurisdictions. Section 91(3) of the Constitution sets out the criminal functions of the Attorney General when it provides as follows:

> (3) In the exercise of his powers to institute, undertake and discontinue criminal proceedings and of any other power conferred on him by any law in terms which authorise him to exercise that power in his individual judgment the Attorney General shall not be subject to the direction or control of any other person or authority.

350. The Attorney General, in Malta, has a very important role to play in the prosecution of criminal offenders. He is considered to be the Chief Prosecutor who

643. Criminal Code, section 546(1).
644. *Ibid.*, section 558.
645. *Ibid.*, section 551.
646. Chapter 260 of the Laws of Malta.
647. Criminal Code, section 551(2).
648. *Ibid.*, section 551(3).
649. For a discussion of the Attorney General, *see* David Joseph Attard, *supra* note 25, pp. 119–125.

prosecutes in the name of the Republic of Malta before the Criminal Court and who appears before the Court of Criminal Appeal, both in its superior and inferior competences. He is also the legal advisor to the Malta Police Force. The Commission for the Holistic Reform of the Justice Sector has recommended that the constitutional function of the Attorney General, be hived off from this office and assigned to a newly created office, that of Prosecutor General.[650] In this way, criminal functions will be performed by the Prosecutor General and the Attorney General continues to retain duties concerning that of chief legal advisor to government. At the moment of writing, this recommendation has yet to be implemented.

III. The Advocate for Legal Aid

351. The Advocate for Legal Aid, though this office in not established by the Constitution, is indirectly mentioned in the Constitution, in Article 39(6)(c) where it is provided that every person who is charged with a criminal offence 'shall be permitted to defend himself in person or by a legal representative and a person who cannot afford to pay for such legal representation as is reasonably required by the circumstances of his case shall be entitled to have representation at the public expense'. Both the Criminal Code,[651] the Code of Organization and Civil Procedure[652] and other special laws[653] contain provisions allowing recourse to the benefit of legal aid.[654]

§9. Military Courts

352. The Constitution does not establish military courts. Indeed, the only court it establishes is the Constitutional Court. On the contrary, the Constitution excludes military courts from its provisions when, in section 47(1), it defines the expression 'court' as 'any court of law in Malta other than a court constituted by or under a disciplinary law'. In turn, the Constitution defines 'disciplinary law' as 'a law regulating the discipline – (a) of any disciplined force; or (b) of persons serving prison sentences'.

353. It is the Malta Armed Forces Act[655] which establishes military courts for the purpose of prosecution of military personnel before such courts. Court martials come in three variegated forms:

650. Commission for the Holistic Reform of the Justice Sector, *Final Report*, Ministry for Justice, Valletta, 30 November 2013, measure 148 at pp. 95–96.
651. Criminal Code, section 570.
652. Code of Organization and Civil Procedure, Chapter 12 of the Laws of Malta, sections 911–928H.
653. For instance, Reletting of Urban Property (Regulation Ordinance), Chapter 69 of the Laws of Malta, section 36; Agricultural Leases (Reletting) Act, Chapter 199 of the Laws of Malta, section 16; and Administrative Justice Act, Chapter 490 of the Laws of Malta, section 18.
654. For a study on the Advocate of Legal Aid, *see* Chapter 8 and Appendices III, IV and V of the Final Report of the Commission for the Holistic Reform of the Justice Sector, *supra* note 650, pp. 106–128, and 197–284.
655. Chapter 220 of the Laws of Malta.

(a) a general court martial;[656]
(b) a district court martial;[657] and
(c) a field general court martial.[658]

354. The Court of Criminal Appeal has jurisdiction to hear and determine appeals from courts martial.[659] Moreover, the Malta Armed Forces Act allows a review of findings and sentence of court martials. Such function is entrusted to the President of Malta or to a judge designated for the purpose by the President of Malta.[660]

§10. The Revisionary Function of Special Tribunals

355. When the Administrative Justice Act[661] was enacted in 2007, the Administrative Review Tribunal was established in order to do away with various administrative tribunals which had proliferated over time and to rationalize administrative tribunals into one tribunal – the Administrative Review Tribunal.[662] This is a process which takes time to implement to the full, and several administrative tribunals have, since 2007, ceased to exist with their functions being reassigned to the Administrative Review Tribunal. The exercise is still far from complete.

§11. Judicial Activities and Constitutional Rights of Citizens

356. Citizens enjoy several rights within the judicial process. Such rights are given by the Constitution and by the European Convention Act[663] (which incorporates into Maltese Law the ECHR). Reference should also be made to the EU Charter of Fundamental Rights insofar as it applies to Malta in relation to EU Law. The constitutional rights which citizens enjoy are safeguarded by the judiciary which upholds these rights in favour of citizens. These include:

(a) the right to a fair hearing;[664]
(b) the right to a public hearing;[665]
(c) the right to a trial within a reasonable time;[666]

656. Malta Armed Forces Act, section 91(1).
657. *Ibid.*, section 91(2).
658. *Ibid.*, section 91(3).
659. *Ibid.*, section 116(1).
660. *Ibid.*, section 114(1) and (2).
661. Chapter 490 of the Laws of Malta.
662. *See* Kevin Aquilina, 'Empowering the Citizen Under the Law: The Administrative Justice Bill', *Law & Practice*, Issue 14, December 2006, pp. 6–14; and Caroline Farrugia, *The Implications of the Administrative Justice Act – Chapter 490 of the Laws of Malta*, Doctor of Laws Thesis, Faculty of Laws, University of Malta, Msida, 2008.
663. Chapter 319 of the Laws of Malta.
664. Constitution, section 39(1) and (2).
665. *Ibid.*, section 39(3).
666. *Ibid.*, section 39(1) and (2).

(d) the right to an independent and impartial court established by law;[667]
(e) in criminal cases:

- the right to be presumed innocent until proven guilty;[668]
- the right to be informed in writing in a language which one understands and in detail, of the nature of the offence;[669]
- the right to adequate time and facilities for the preparation of one's defence;[670]
- the right to legal representation;[671]
- the right to examine and cross-examine witnesses and to obtain their attendance;[672]
- the right to have without payment the assistance of an interpreter;[673]
- the right to be present during one's trial and that it takes place in one's absence if one misbehaves;[674]
- the right to have access within a reasonable time after judgment is delivered of a copy for the use of the accused person of any record of the proceedings made by or on behalf of the court;[675]
- the nullum crimen sine lege legal maxim;[676]
- the nulla poena sine lege legal maxim;[677]
- the ne bis in idem legal maxim;[678]
- the right against self-incrimination.[679]

(f) the right to institute an action for a declaration of invalidity of a law on any grounds other than inconsistency with the provisions of sections 33–45 of the Constitution.[680]

357. These rights ensure that the judiciary protects citizens' rights not only from the other two organs of the state – the Legislature and the Executive – but even from the judicial organ.

§12. Principles of Good Administrative Behaviour

358. Citizens' rights are also protected through the principles of good administrative behaviour which have to be followed by various tribunals established by law. Indeed,

667. *Ibid.*
668. *Ibid.*, section 39(5).
669. *Ibid.*, section 39(6)(a).
670. *Ibid.*, section 39(6)(b).
671. *Ibid.*, section 39(6)(c).
672. *Ibid.*, section 39(6)(d).
673. *Ibid.*, section 39(6)(e).
674. *Ibid.*, section 39(6).
675. *Ibid.*, section 39(7).
676. *Ibid.*, section 39(8).
677. *Ibid.*
678. *Ibid.*, section 39(9).
679. *Ibid.*, section 39(10).
680. *Ibid.*, section 116.

the right to a fair trial has to be observed not only by the courts but even by tribunals which determine civil rights and obligations. The principles of natural justice, in turn, are applicable to any tribunal which determines a dispute, irrespective of whether that dispute is a civil right and obligation or otherwise. The principles of good administrative behaviour read as follows:

(a) an administrative tribunal shall respect the parties' right to a fair hearing, including the principles of natural justice, namely:

- nemo judex in causa sua; and
- audi et alteram partem.

(b) the time within which an administrative tribunal shall take its decision shall be reasonable in the light of the circumstances of each case. The decision shall be delivered as soon as possible, and for this purpose the tribunal shall deliver one decision about all matters involved in the cause whether they are of a preliminary, procedural or of a substantive nature;
(c) an administrative tribunal shall ensure that there shall be procedural equality between the parties to the proceedings. Each party shall be given an opportunity to present its case, whether in writing or orally or both, without being placed at a disadvantage;
(d) an administrative tribunal shall ensure that the public administration makes available the documents and information relevant to the case and that the other party or parties to the proceedings have access to these documents and information;
(e) proceedings before an administrative tribunal shall be adversarial in nature. All evidence admitted by such a tribunal shall, in principle, be made available to the parties with a view to adversarial argument;
(f) an administrative tribunal shall be in a position to examine all of the factual and legal issues relevant to the case presented by the parties in terms of the applicable law;
(g) save as otherwise provided by law, the proceedings before an administrative tribunal shall be conducted in public;
(h) reasons shall be given for the judgment. An administrative tribunal shall indicate, with sufficient clarity, the grounds on which it bases its decisions. Although it shall not be necessary for a tribunal to deal with every point raised in argument, a submission that would, if accepted, be decisive for the outcome of the case, shall require a specific and express response.[681]

681. Administrative Justice Act, Chapter 490 of the Laws of Malta, section 3(2).

Chapter 8. Judicial Control of Administrative Action

§1. Introduction

359. Administrative Law deals with judicial control over the public administration and, although it is indirectly referred to in the Constitution, is of paramount importance to the governance of the state.[682] Section 46(2) proviso of the Constitution empowers a court of constitutional jurisdiction to decline to exercise its powers related to the hearing and determination of a human rights complaint where the said court 'is satisfied that adequate means of redress for the contravention are or have been available to the person concerned under any other law'.[683] Judicial review of administrative action is one such case.

§2. Evolution of the Principle of Administrative Justice in Malta

360. The historical evolution of the principle of administrative justice has already been discussed elsewhere.[684]

§3. Powers and Limits of the Ordinary Judge Over the Public Administration

361. The ordinary judge exercises judicial review of administrative action, in the Maltese legal system, in three ways, namely through:

(a) section 32(2) of the Code of Organization and Civil Procedure;
(b) section 469A of the Code of Organization and Civil Procedure; and
(c) review of administrative action by various boards and tribunals and, on appeal, where this is permitted by law, to the Superior Courts of civil jurisdiction.

I. Section 32(2) of the Code of Organization and Civil Procedure

362. Section 32(2) of the Code of Organization and Civil Procedure provides that:

682. For a summary of Administrative Law cases, *see* Ian Refalo, Cases in Administrative Law, available at http://www.statecareandmore.eu/images/documents/prof%20refalo%20administrative_lawrevisedtext2012january2012.pdf. Last accessed on 31 March 2016.
683. Giuseppe Mifsud Bonnici, *Constitutional Procedure Relative to Fundamental Rights and Freedoms*, 2nd rev. edn, Midsea Books, Sta. Venera, 2012, pp. 117–130.
684. *See* Kevin Aquilina, 'Rationalising Administrative Law on the Revocation of Development Permissions', *BOV Review*, No. 34, Autumn 2006, pp. 19–38.

> The Civil Court shall take cognizance of all causes of a civil and commercial nature, and of all causes which are expressly assigned by law to the said Civil Court.

363. The courts have interpreted this provision in the sense of granting jurisdiction to the Civil Court, First Hall, the power to enquire whether a decision of an inferior body is 'bad on the face'.[685] One of the earlier cases decided by the Civil Court, First Hall, to this effect is *Riccardo Ullo Xuereb v. Enrico Magro noe.*[686] A more recent case is *Director General Courts v. Pinu Axiaq*[687] where the Court of Appeal reiterated its jurisdiction to examine decisions of an inferior body in terms of Article 32(2) notwithstanding the fact that, in the meantime, that provision had been amended in 2004 and section 469A had been specifically introduced in the Code of Organization and Civil Procedure in 1995 regulating judicial review of administrative action. This is because the right to review decisions of judicial and quasi-juridical tribunals derives from section 32(2) of the Code which confers upon the Civil Court, First Hall, the cognizance of all causes of a civil nature which are not expressly assigned by law to another court. The Court of Appeal thus concluded that the Civil Court, First Hall, had jurisdiction to exercise judicial review of administrative action under both section 32(2) and section 469A of the Code and that under section 32(2), it could review decisions of inferior bodies as to whether their decision was *ultra vires*, whether there was any breach of the principles of natural justice and where the discretion exercised was fair and honest.

II. Section 469A of the Code of Organization and Civil Procedure

364. Judicial review of administrative action is regulated by section 469A of the Code of Organization and Civil Procedure (hereinafter referred to as 'the Code'). Judicial review of administrative action comes into play in the following instances:

> 469A. (1) Saving as is otherwise provided by law, the courts of justice of civil jurisdiction may enquire into the validity of any administrative act or declare such act null, invalid or without effect only in the following cases:
>
> a. where the administrative act is in violation of the Constitution;

685. *See Advocate Anthony P. Farrugia v. Electoral Commission*, Court of Appeal, 18 October 1996; and *Norman Rossignaud v. Gontran Borg noe*, Civil Court, First Hall, 19 April 1990. For a review of the Civil Court, First Hall's residual powers, *see* Wallace Philip Gulia, 'The Residual Powers of the First Hall, Civil Court in Malta', *Id-Dritt Law Journal*, Vol. 9, 1978, p. 56.
686. 9 March 1901.
687. *Director General (Courts) v. Pinu Axiaq*, Court of Appeal, 3 March 2006. *See also Jane Gatt v. Malta Environment and Planning Authority et*, Civil Court, First Hall, per Mr Justice Joseph R. Micallef, 24 April 2013.

b. when the administrative act is ultra vires on any of the following grounds:

- when such act emanates from a public authority that is not authorised to perform it; or

- when a public authority has failed to observe the principles of natural justice or mandatory procedural requirements in performing the administrative act or in its prior deliberations thereon; or

- when the administrative act constitutes an abuse of the public authority's power in that it is done for improper purposes or on the basis of irrelevant considerations; or

- when the administrative act is otherwise contrary to law.

3. In this article:

'administrative act' includes the issuing by a public authority of any order, licence, permit, warrant, decision, or a refusal to any demand of a claimant, but does not include any measure intended for internal organization or administration within the said authority:

Provided that, saving those cases where the law prescribes a period within which a public authority is required to make a decision, the absence of a decision of a public authority following a claimant's written demand served upon it, shall, after two months from such service, constitute a refusal for the purposes of this definition;

'public authority' means the Government of Malta, including its Ministries and departments, local authorities and any body corporate established by law.

4. An action to impugn an administrative act under sub-article (1)(b) shall be filed within a period of six months from the date when the interested person becomes aware or could have become aware of such an administrative act, whichever is the earlier.

5. The provisions of this article shall not apply where the mode of contestation or of obtaining redress, with respect to any particular administrative act before a court or tribunal is provided for in any other law.

6. In any action brought under this article, it shall be lawful for the plaintiff to include in the demands a request for the payment of damages based on the alleged responsibility of the public authority in tort or quasi tort, arising out of the administrative act. The said damages shall not be awarded by the court where notwithstanding the annulment of the administrative act the public authority has not acted in bad faith or unreasonably or where the thing requested by the plaintiff could have lawfully and reasonably been refused under any other power.

7. For the purposes of this article, and of any other provision of this and any other law, service with the government is a special relationship regulated by the legal provisions specifically applicable to it and the terms and conditions from time to time established by the Government, and no law or provision thereof relating to conditions of employment or to contracts of service or of employment applies, or ever heretofore applied, to service with the government except to the extent that such law provides otherwise.

A. General Issues Relating to Judicial Review of Administrative Action

365. In an action for judicial review, Maltese courts have held that it is not allowed for the reviewing court to substitute its discretion for that of the public administration.[688] Furthermore, the court drew a distinction between an appeal and a review: in the former case, the appellate court is generally permitted to substitute its decision for that of the lower court or public authority concerned whilst in the latter case the Court of Appeal considers the decision-making process to ensure the fairness of the proceedings without substituting its opinion for that of the public authority concerned. Courts are of the view that the PSC is actionable at law for judicial review of administrative action.[689] Moreover, the courts have held that they do not have the power to substitute their discretion for that of a public authority but to verify whether the discretion exercised by the public authority went beyond the powers given by law

688. *See* , for instance, *Kevin Falzon v. Prime Minister et*, Civil Court, First Hall, 28 January 2005 (confirmed by the Court of Appeal on 6 July 2007), and *Lawrence Borg nomine v. Governor of the Central Bank of Malta*, Court of Appeal, 9 March 2007.

689. *David Gatt v. Hon. Prime Minister Dr Lawrence Gonzi et*, Civil Court, First Hall, per Mr Justice Joseph R. Micallef, 29 September 2011. The said judge delivered on the same day two similar judgments in *Ivan Portelli v. Hon. Prime Minister et*; and in *Michael Buttigieg v. Commissioner of Police et*.

to that authority.[690] For instance, in *Advocate Anthony De Gaetano v. Planning Authority*,[691] the Court of Appeal dealt with a case where Dr Anthony De Gaetano reported a breach of a stop notice to an Enforcement Officer of the Planning Authority. Dr De Gaetano was the legal advisor of the Planning Authority. His superiors interpreted this as an abuse of power committed by him and issued him a warning. Dr De Gaetano took the case to court alleging that in the disciplinary measures instituted against him he was not given the right to put his case, and that mandatory procedural requirements as set out in the Planning Authority collective agreement were not followed. The Court concurred.

B. What Constitutes an 'Administrative Act'?

366. In *Supreme Travel Limited (C-16048) v. Malta Transport Authority et*,[692] the Civil Court was called upon to examine what constitutes an 'administrative act', that is, an act which contained a decision by a public authority, whether a decision has been actually taken or could have been taken within a period of two months. However, the court decided that a contractual relationship regulated by civil law was not an administrative decision.

C. What Constitutes Any 'Measure Intended for Internal Organization or Administration Within the Said Authority'

367. In *Nikol Borg v. Permanent Secretary in the Office of the Prime Minister*,[693] Mr Borg was a public officer and retired in the grade of Principal. He had complained with the Ombudsman that he was not granted by his Head of Department the increments due to him. In the meantime, prior to his retirement from the public service, he was transferred to another department, the Permanent Law Reform Commission, which declared that he was performing well his duties and awarded him the increments due. However, the increments were not given retroactively. This case thus concerned the granting of retroactive increments and the issue which arose before the court was whether the granting or refusing of such increments amounted to 'any measure intended for internal organization or administration within the said authority'. The court concluded that the withholding of an increment was an administrative act and did not fall under 'any measure intended for internal organization or administration within the said authority'.

690. *Dr Emmanuel Borda v. Professur Roger Ellul Micallef nomine*, Civil Court, First Hall, per Mr Justice Joseph R. Micallef, 30 January 2003. This point was confirmed on appeal by the Court of Appeal on 29 May 2009.
691. Court of Appeal, 28 April 2008.
692. Civil Court, First Hall, per Mr Justice Joseph R. Micallef, 18 January 2011.
693. Civil Court, First Hall, per Mr Justice Joseph R. Micallef, 17 October 2002, confirmed on appeal by the Court of Appeal on 27 January 2006.

D. *What Constitutes a 'Public Authority'?*

368. In *Dr Emmanuel Borda v. Professor Roger Ellul Micallef nomine,*[694] the court held that a judicial or quasi-judicial tribunal does not fall under the definition of a public authority.[695] On the other hand, the University of Malta fell under the term of a 'public authority'.

E. *Section 469A(3)*

369. In *Rodney and Judith Metters v. MEPA et,*[696] the court noted that the development permission was issued on 26 August 2008, whereas the case was filed on 4 October 2010. So more than six months had passed when plaintiffs filed their case. However, the court observed that the provision does not state that the six months should elapse from the date of the issue of the development permission but 'from the date when the interested person becomes aware or could have become aware of such an administrative act, whichever is the earlier'.

F. *Section 469A(4)*

370. In *Jupiter Co. Ltd. et. v. Malta Environment and Planning Authority,*[697] plaintiffs had appealed a decision of the MEPA before the Planning Appeals Board which proceedings were still pending before the said Board when the judicial review proceedings were instituted. In its judgment, the court applied Article 469A(4) and declared the judicial review proceedings invalid. It further applied the legal maxim of *electa una via non datur recursus ad alteram.*

G. *Section 469A(5)*

371. The distinction between judicial review of administrative action and an action in tort lies in the fact that in the latter case the court may award damages to the plaintiff whilst in the former case no such remedy is given. Judicial review of administrative action can only provoke a declaration of nullity of an administrative act. In *Buttigieg v. Rector, University of Malta et,*[698] the Civil Court, First Hall, held that the damages referred to in section 469A(5) excluded non-material damages as such type of damages were not allowed under the Civil Code. This pronouncement therefore meant that the action in tort under section 469A(5) did not enjoy a separate and autonomous existence of its own but was regulated by the provisions on tort as contained in the Civil Code. The court further declined to award material damages in this case as it had not been proven that the University had acted in bad faith or

694. Civil Court, First Hall, per Mr Justice Joseph R. Micallef, 30 January 2003. This point was confirmed on appeal by the Court of Appeal on 29 May 2009.
695. *See Pinu Axiaq v. Direttur Generali Qrati, supra* note 687.
696. Court of Magistrates (Gozo) (Superior Jurisdiction, per Magistrate Dr Anthony Ellul, 15 February 2011.
697. Civil Court, First Hall, per Mr Justice Raymond C. Pace, 30 November 2006.
698. *Denise Buttigieg v. Rector, University of Malta et,* Civil Court, First Hall, 22 December 2003.

unreasonably. In *Satariano v. Planning Authority*,[699] the Civil Court, First Hall, decided that when the Planning Authority took direct action to demolish an illegal structure, it had demolished certain parts of the building which were not covered by the enforcement notice. Damages were sustained to the cave, well and swimming pool which could have been avoided. Hence, the court liquidated the damages *arbitrio boni viri* at EUR 4,000 as the plaintiffs had not produced any evidence as to the quantum of damages suffered.

H. Section 469A(6)

372. In *C. Magri v. Commissioner of Police et*,[700] the court stated that although this sub-subsection excludes the application of the Civil Code and of employment legislation to service with the government, the special law which it resorts to applies to conditions of employment of public officers. This provision binds both the government and public officers.

---

699. *Albert Satariano et v. Planning Authority*, Civil Court, First Hall, 19 April 2010. On 28 March 2014, the Court of Appeal confirmed the Civil Court's judgment whilst increasing damages payable to plaintiffs to EUR 5,825.

700. Court of Appeal, 5 October 1998. For a study of judicial review of administrative action, *see* Ivan Mifsud, *Judicial Review of Administrative Action in Malta: An Examination of Article 469A COCP and of Judicial Review in General*, Book Distributors Limited, San Ġwann, 2017.

Chapter 9. The Constitutional Court

§1. Functions of the Constitutional Court

373. The Constitutional Court is established by the Constitution, not by ordinary law as is the position with all the other courts established in Malta, even if the Constitution does sanction the establishment of such courts by ordinary law in sections 95(1)[701] and 99.[702] The Constitutional Court is the highest court of Malta because it is established by the organic law of the Republic. Whilst the President is the guardian of the Constitution,[703] the Constitutional Court considers itself also to be the guardian of the Constitution[704] because it is specifically established to rule on questions as to the validity of laws,[705] the interpretation of the Constitution[706] and the validity of the membership of the House of Representatives[707] and of general elections.[708] The Constitutional Court also hears appeals from decisions of the Civil Court, First Hall, sitting in its constitutional competence, in relation to constitutional actions including human rights and fundamental freedoms' actions. The Constitutional Court thus has a number of important functions entrusted to it by the Constitution, some of which may, in certain cases, also bring it in a collision course with other organs of the state. Nevertheless, the Constitution gives the Constitutional Court the necessary powers to overrule the other organs of the state in those occurrences.

§2. Composition of the Constitutional Court

374. The Constitution provides that the Constitutional Court is composed of three judges who have the necessary qualifications to compose the Court of Appeal.[709] However, when the Constitution was enacted by the UK Parliament in 1964, it was then composed of five judges – 'the Chief Justice and four other judges of the Superior Courts'.[710] The independence Constitution further provided in section 96 that:

701. Section 95(1) reads as follows: 'There shall be in and for Malta such Superior Courts having such powers and jurisdiction as may be provided by any law for the time being in force in Malta.'
702. Section 99 reads as follows: 'There shall be in and for Malta such inferior Courts having such powers and jurisdiction as may be provided by any law for the time being in force in Malta.'
703. Constitution, Second Schedule.
704. *Dr Wenzu Mintoff et in the name of Alternattiva Demokratika v. Chairman, Broadcasting Authority*, Constitutional Court, 31 July 1996.
705. Constitution, section 95(2)(e).
706. *Ibid.*, section 95(2)(d).
707. *Ibid.*, section 95(2)(a).
708. *Ibid.*, section 95(2)(b).
709. *Ibid.*, section 95(2).
710. 1964 Constitution, section 96(2).

5. The Chief Justice shall be the President of the Constitutional Court, and there shall be a Vice-President of the Court, who shall be appointed from among the other judges of the Superior Courts in such manner as may be provided by law; and the Vice-President shall among those judges take precedence next to the Chief Justice.

6. If the Chief Justice is precluded by law from performing the functions of President of the Constitutional Court or is otherwise unable to perform those functions, those functions shall be performed by the Vice-President.

7. If the office of Vice-President is vacant or if the Vice-President is for any reason unable to perform the functions of his office, those functions shall be performed by such one of the other judges of the Superior Courts as may be designated in that behalf in such manner as may be provided by law.

375. The Constitutional Court was not appointed for a number of years and, therefore, was not in a position to hear, let alone determine, cases pending before that court.[711]

376. Following the amendments made to the Constitution in 1974, when Malta became a republic, the office of Vice-President of the Constitutional Court was abolished and the number of judges was reduced to three. Insofar as its composition is concerned, the Constitutional Court lost its singularity, thereby becoming similar to the other two appellate courts – the Court of Appeal and the Court of Criminal Appeal – all of which are composed of three judges with the Chief Justice presiding. The judges who sit on the Constitutional Court are appointed in the same manner as judges of the Superior Court. In this connection, the Commission for the Holistic Reform of the Justice Sector has proposed that the judges appointed to sit on the Constitutional Court should not carry out any other judicial duties on other courts other than the Constitutional Court, that it should not be presided by the Chief Justice but by a new public officer – the President of the Constitutional Court, that this court should have its own separate budget and functions from its own premises which should not be the same as those of the other courts in Republic Street, Valletta.[712]

---

711. *See* Joseph M. Pirotta, *L-Istorja Kostituzzjonali u L-Isfond Storiku (1942-2004)* (Translation: Constitutional History and the Historical Background 1942-2004), Independence Publications – PIN, Pjetà, 2005, pp. 229–230; Michael J. Schiavone, *supra* note 211, p. 504; and Nationalist Party Information Office, *Is Malta Burning*, Nationalist Party Information Office, Pietà, August 1981, pp. 5–8.

712. Commission for the Holistic Reform of the Justice Sector, *supra* note 650, measure 405, p. 171.

§3. The Origins of Constitutional Review of Legislation

377. The Maltese Constitution has as its model the Westminster Constitution which – unlike the Maltese version – does not admit, in the light of the British doctrine of the sovereignty of Parliament, the possibility of judicial review of legislation enacted by the UK Parliament.[713] In the UK – contrary to the USA – it is not possible for a court of law to annul a statute enacted by Parliament at Westminster. However, the position in Malta is different. Indeed, in this respect, Malta does not follow the British model but the American, where the Supreme Court can declare an act of the US Congress unconstitutional. This doctrine was asserted in the famous judgment of Chief Justice John Marshall, *Marbury v. Madison.* In Malta, the Constitutional Court has held that in the Constitution, the privileges and immunities applicable to the Parliament at Westminster, including that whereby the courts do not enjoy the power to judicially review legislation, have not been taken on board here.[714] As a consequence, the courts of constitutional competence have declared void laws enacted by Parliament either because they were inconsistent with the Constitution[715] or with the ECHR as incorporated in the European Convention Act.[716]

378. A constitutional question, both in terms of the Constitution and the European Convention Act, can be raised in either of two ways, either through a reference[717] or through an application[718] and sometimes it has also been raised through both procedures.[719] The reference is an indirect method of raising a constitutional question before a court seized of a case whilst the application is a direct way of raising the constitutional question.[720]

§4. The Constitutional Reference

379. The constitutional reference has to be distinguished from the reference which a court or a tribunal may make to the European Court of Justice for a preliminary

713. The doctrine of sovereignty of Parliament in Britain is discussed in Colin Turpin and Adam Tomkins, Cambridge University Press, Cambridge, 2011, pp. 58–96.

714. *Dom Mintoff v. Giorgio Borg Olivier noe,* Her Majesty's Constitutional Court, 5 November 1970.

715. *His Grace Mgr. Joseph Mercieca pro et noe v. The Hon. Prime Minister et,* Civil Court, First Hall, per Mr Justice Stephen Borg Cardona, 24 September 1984.

716. Chapter 319 of the Laws of Malta. *See* , for instance, *Advocate Dr Lawrence Pullicino v. Commander in Chief of the Armed Forces of Malta,* Constitutional Court, 12 April 1989.

717. For a discussion of the reference procedure, *see* Giuseppe Mifsud Bonnici, *Constitutional Procedure Relative to Fundamental Rights and Freedoms*, 2nd rev. edn, Midsea Books, Sta. Venera, 2012, pp. 65–82.

718. For a discussion of the application, *see* Giuseppe Mifsud Bonnici, *ibid.*, pp. 18–28.

719. As to the application/reference dichotomy, *see* Giuseppe Mifsud Bonnici, *ibid.*, pp. 83–115.

720. The constitutional reference procedure has to be distinguished from the preliminary reference to the CJEU.

ruling.[721] In the case of a constitutional reference all courts – not tribunals[722] – can refer proceedings before them before the Civil Court, First Hall, sitting in its constitutional competence and, on appeal, before the Constitutional Court. However, the following rules apply to the reference:

(a) the reference is made only to the Civil Court, First Hall, and not directly to the Constitutional Court;
(b) the Civil Court, First Hall, and the Constitutional Court are precluded from making a reference insofar as they are already competent in terms of the Constitution and the European Convention Act to determine a constitutional issue were it to be raised before them; and
(c) the constitutional reference applies only to human rights and fundamental freedoms and not to other provisions of the Constitution.

380. The constitutional reference is an indirect way of instituting proceedings before a court of constitutional competence. It is envisaged in the Constitution[723] and in the European Convention Act[724] which follows the same wording of the constitutional provision. The constitutional provision incorporating the reference procedure reads as follows:

> If in any proceedings in any court other than the Civil Court, First Hall, or the Constitutional Court any question arises as to the contravention of any of the provisions of the said articles 33 to 45 (inclusive), that court shall refer the question to the Civil Court, First Hall, unless in its opinion the raising of the question is merely frivolous or vexatious; and that court shall give its decision on any question referred to it under this sub-article and, subject to the provisions of sub-article (4) of this article, the court in which the question arose shall dispose of the question in accordance with that decision.

§5. The Constitutional Application

381. The constitutional application is the direct manner to proceed before the Civil Court, First Hall, sitting in its constitutional competence where the said court exercises its original jurisdiction. Although the constitutional reference is an effective way how to raise a constitutional question once a case is being heard by a court and have it referred to the Civil Court, First Hall, sitting in its constitutional competence, it still remains a secondary way how to raise a human rights and fundamental freedoms

---

721. On the preliminary reference mechanism, *see* Ivan Sammut, 'Effectiveness of EU Law at the National Level: The Maltese Experience So Far', in Eugène Buttigieg (ed.), *Enforcing One's Rights Under EU Law*, Gutenberg Press, Tarxien, 2011, pp. 17–35.
722. *See* , for instance, *Joseph Fenech v. Planning Authority*, Planning Appeals Board, PAB 109/97 KA, 12 October 2001; and *Citadel Insurance plc v. Kenneth Brincat*, Small Claims Tribunal, notice no. 476/01AE, per Dr Anthony Ellul, 5 September 2001.
723. Constitution, section 46(3).
724. European Convention Act, section 4(3).

question and there is no guarantee that the reference will succeed. The applicable provision regulating the constitutional application is section 46(1) of the Constitution and section 4(1) is the corresponding provision in the European Convention Act. The former provision reads as follows:

> any person who alleges that any of the provisions of articles 33 to 45 (inclusive) of this Constitution has been, is being or is likely to be contravened in relation to him, or such other person as the Civil Court, First Hall, in Malta may appoint at the instance of any person who so alleges, may, without prejudice to any other action with respect to the same matter that is lawfully available, apply to the Civil Court, First Hall, for redress.

382. Apart from the Constitution, reference has also to be made to Rules of Court made in terms of section 46(7) of the Constitution which regulate in more detail both the procedure related to the constitutional application and to the reference.[725]

§6. Effects of the Constitutional Court's Decision

383. There is a great doctrinal debate as to whether judgments of the Constitutional Court have *erga omnes* effect. This is discussed elsewhere in greater depth.[726]

§7. Interpretative and Manipulative Judgments

384. The Constitutional Court has had occasion to go beyond a strictly interpretative appreciation of a legal provision by offering a manipulative interpretation of the law, that is, a judgment whereby the Constitutional Court fills in a legislative vacuum in a law. In this case, the court not only interprets a legal provision but also goes beyond that and states what the law ought to be. Such is the case, for instance, of *Ruth Debono Sultana et v. Department for Social Welfare Standards et.*[727]

§8. Disputes Between State Powers

385. It is very rare in Malta for one organ of the state to institute judicial proceedings against another organ of the state. However, there have been cases where

725. Court Practice and Procedure and Good Order Rules, Subsidiary Legislation 12.09, rules 2–5.
726. *See* Kevin Aquilina, 'Do Pronouncements of the Constitutional Court Bind *Erga Omnes*? The Common Law Doctrine of *Stare Decisis* versus the Civil Law Doctrine of Nonbinding Case Law within a Maltese Law Context' in Vernon Valentine Palmer, Mohamed Y. Matar and Anna Koppel (eds.), *Mixed Legal Systems: East and West*, Ashgate Publishing Limited, Surrey, 2015, pp. 43–53.
727. Decided by the Civil Court, First Hall, sitting in its constitutional competence, per Mr Justice Giannino Caruana Demajo on 14 October 2008. Confirmed on appeal by the Court of Appeal on 3 April 2009.

one organ of local self-government instituted court proceedings against another organ of the state. See for instance, *Kirkop Local Council v. Attorney General et*[728] *and Marsascala Local Council v. Attorney General et.*[729] There has also been a case where the Ombudsman instituted a case against a Minister and a Permanent Secretary[730] and another case where the Prime Minister in his capacity as an MP filed court proceedings against departments falling under the political responsibility of the same Prime Minister.[731]

§9. Decisions on the Admissibility of Referenda

386. There has been only one decision delivered by the Constitutional Court related to an abrogative referendum, that is, whether spring hunting should have been abolished. In the *application of Mark Mifsud Bonnici et nomine*[732] and the application of *Joseph Perici Calascione et nomine,*[733] the Constitutional Court rejected all the grounds brought by applicants why the spring hunting referendum should not be held and passed on to decree in favour of the holding of the said referendum.

---

728. Constitutional Court, 16 April 2004.
729. Constitutional Court, 28 June 2012.
730. *See* paragraph 396.
731. *See Prime Minister Joseph Muscat in his capacity of Member of the House of Representatives and the Attorney General v. Mark Gaffarena, Josielle Gaffarena, the Commissioner for Land and the Land Registrar*, Case No. 53/2016.
732. Constitutional Court, 9 January 2015.
733. Constitutional Court, 9 January 2015.

Chapter 10. The Public Administration in the Constitution

§1. Duties and Powers of the Public Administration

387. The public administration is a conglomeration of various entities of the state which are assigned by the Constitution and by ordinary law specific duties to perform. There is no doubt that, since independence, over a period of fifty-one years, the public administration has continued to grow and it is the biggest employer in Malta employing more than 40,000 employees. The services which it provides are varied ranging from acting as a regulator in diverse fields to a service provider. The public administration comprises the public service and other parastatal non-public office bodies listed in section 110(6) of the Constitution. The functions of the public administration over time have been expanded so that it does no longer restrict itself to classic state functions such as those related to national security, defence, public order, infrastructural projects, conduct of international relations or the budget. In the world as we experience it today, the public administration carries out a multifarious list of duties ranging from economic, social, cultural, philanthropic and other functions which indicate how things have changed from since Malta became an independent state fifty-one years ago. Not only has the public administration's functions been enlarged but so have the legislative, executive and judicial controls on the public administration been augmented to curb corruption, abuse, maladministration, administrative secrecy and unaccountability. The public administration enjoys powers which go beyond executive functions such as law-making exercised through delegated legislation and dispute settlement exercised through administrative tribunals. Gone are the days of absolute discretion where the decisions of the public administration could not be challenged or reviewed. The public administration has over time become more citizen friendly and its powers are subject to various controls.

§2. The Constitutional Principles Regulating Public Administration Activities

388. There are a number of principles enshrined in the Constitution which apply to the public administration and which have already been discussed above. Other principles applicable to the public administration not discussed above comprise the following:

I. The Principle of Legality

389. The principle of legality implies that an administrative act has to be within the powers conferred upon the public administration and can therefore not exceed those powers. If the administrative act goes beyond these powers, then the administrative act in question is said to be *ultra vires* the powers conferred upon the public administration by the Constitution. One example of the application of the principle of legality as enshrined in the Constitution is contained in section 6 of the Constitution which stipulates that no ordinary law, which could also include a subsidiary law made by the public administration, may run counter to the Constitution. Another instance is where the *actio popularis* is exercised by any person to request a court of constitutional competence to invalidate a law made by the public administration on any grounds other than inconsistency with the human rights and fundamental freedoms provisions of the Constitution.[734] A further example is the power of the Civil Court, First Hall, sitting in its constitutional competence, and of the Constitutional Court to annul a law made by the public administration which is inconsistent with human rights and fundamental freedoms.[735] A similar provision is found in section 4(2) of the European Convention Act.[736]

II. The Principle of Full Respect to International Law

390. The principle of full respect of international law is contained in section 65(1) of the Constitution which mandates that when Parliament is legislating, it has to do so 'in conformity with full respect for … generally accepted principles of international law and Malta's international and regional obligations'. This provision has already been discussed above, *see* note 111.

III. The Principles of Public Finance Law

391. The principles of Public Finance Law which emerge from a study of Maltese Public Finance Law can be gathered under five headings, these being the following:

(a) *The principle of no taxation without representation*: It is only Parliament which can impose taxes. As it has been put: 'Perhaps no principle is more characteristic of our political system than the doctrine that there shall be no taxation without representation. Long and bitter controversies between the people and the Crown made this a fundamental rule of English law. Accordingly, after the American Revolution the states uniformly adopted constitutions which vested the taxing power primarily in legislative bodies.'[737] The same position applies in the case of the Constitution where tax measures have to be approved by Parliament.[738]

---

734. Constitution, section 116.
735. *Ibid.*, section 46(2).
736. Chapter 319 of the Laws of Malta.
737. Anon, 'Delegation of the Taxing Power', *Harvard Law Review*, Vol. 26, No 3 (January 1913) pp. 257–259 at p. 257. As to how this principle originated in the United States of America, *see* Keith W. Olson, *An Outline of American History*, Washington, United States Information Agency (undated), pp. 27–31.
738. Constitution, section 73. A similar provision is also found in Standing Order 69 of the Standing Orders of the House of Representatives Order, Subsidiary Legislation Const. 02.

(b) *The principle of public administration generation of revenue and expenditure thereof*: The expression 'revenue' though undefined in the Constitution is construed in the Financial Administration and Audit Act[739] as 'all taxes, imposts, rates, and duties and all other moneys collected or received for or on account of the Consolidated Fund'.[740] On the other hand, neither the Constitution nor ordinary law defines the expression 'expenditure'. Black's Law Dictionary defines it as '1. the act or process of paying out; disbursement. 2. a sum paid out'.[741]

(c) *The principle that public money can be spent by the Government only when so authorized to do by Parliament*: Once again, although the expression 'public money' is not defined in the Constitution, the term is explained in the Financial Administration and Audit Act referred to in the previous paragraph as meaning 'all revenue, loan, trust and other funds received or managed or held by, for or on account of the Government, including moneys which the Government pays out or disburses from funds received from any international or supranational organization or body or from any of its institutions or bodies'.[742]

(d) *The principle that public money can be spent by the public administration only following authorization by an appropriation law or by a law which specifically declares that money can be spent through a specific provision of a law without requiring the enactment by Parliament of an Appropriation Act.*

(e) *Principles of fiscal responsibility*, namely:

- *the principle of transparency*[743] 'whereby in setting out the budgetary targets and objectives and in carrying out its fiscal and budgetary policies, the Government has the obligation to make public all the information necessary to allow the assessment of the implementation of such fiscal and budgetary policies, the respective outcomes and the stance of central and local finances';[744]
- *the principle of stability*[745] 'whereby Government shall carry out its fiscal and budgetary policy in a manner that will ensure medium-term predictability, consistent with the objective of maintaining macro-economic stability';

739. Chapter 174 of the Laws of Malta.
740. Financial Administration and Audit Act, section 2.
741. Bryan A. Garner (ed.), *Black's Law Dictionary*, 8th edn, West, a Thomson business, St. Paul MN, 2004, p. 617.
742. Financial Administration and Audit Act, section 2.
743. Fiscal Responsibility Act, Chapter 534 of the Laws of Malta, section 3(a).
744. This provision further provides that, 'in furtherance of this principle, Government shall, at the time of the presentation of its annual budget, disclose in statement form: (i) any significant changes in the accounting standards, policies and practices affecting or likely to affect the computation of the prescribed fiscal indicators; (ii) as far as is practicable and, consistent with the protection of the public interest, the contingent liabilities created by way of guarantees, the actual liabilities arising out of borrowings by Public Sector Undertakings and Special Purpose Vehicles and other equivalent instruments where liability for repayment is on the Government; all claims and commitments made by Government having potential budgetary implications, including revenue demands raised but not realised'.
745. Fiscal Responsibility Act, Chapter 534 of the Laws of Malta, section 3(b).

- *the principle of fiscal responsibility*[746] 'whereby Government shall carry out its fiscal and budgetary policy and manage budgetary resources, obligations and fiscal risks in a manner that ensures the sustainability of the fiscal position in the medium and long term such that the Government is able to manage financial risks and unforeseen events in future periods without having to introduce economically or socially destabilizing expenditure or revenue adjustments';
- *the principle of equity*[747] 'whereby Government shall conduct its budgetary and fiscal policies taking into account the potential financial impact on current and future generations as well as the impact on medium and long term economic development while ensuring that the current generation funds the costs of its services';
- *the principle of efficiency*[748] 'whereby the Government's fiscal and budgetary policies shall be aimed at achieving an efficient use of scarce public resources requiring that economic efficiency is considered in defining fiscal policies and that public investment decisions, including those related to EU funded initiatives or other donors, are based inter alia on an economic appraisal as well as the assessment of the capacity to absorb the relevant funding levels';
- *the principle of effective management of personnel spending*[749] 'whereby public sector employment and pay policies in respect of Ministries, Departments, public sector authorities, entities and agencies and Local Councils, except where expressly excluded by the Minister for Finance, shall be consistent with the fiscal and budgetary targets set out in the fiscal strategy';
- *the principle of effective financial and asset management*[750] 'whereby Government shall implement its fiscal and budgetary policies according to the best practices for sound and effective financial and asset management. In furtherance of this principle, there shall be instituted a system of performance management and reporting, asset registers and the policies and procedures regulating the acquisition, use and disposal thereof, policies regulating funding decisions and risk management policies and practices'.

392. The latter set of principles – that is, the principles of fiscal responsibility – apply equally to 'Local Councils, public sector authorities, entities and agencies that are fully or partially financed from the Consolidated Fund'.[751]

IV. The Principle of Acting in the Public Interest

393. All state officers and bodies are appointed on the premise that they act in the public interest, not in their own interest or in the interest of a third party. This

746. *Ibid.*, section 3(c).
747. *Ibid.*, section 3(d).
748. *Ibid.*, section 3(e).
749. *Ibid.*, section 3(f).
750. *Ibid.*, section 3(g).
751. *Ibid.*, section 4.

principle is enshrined in the oaths of office and allegiance contained in the Second and Third Schedules of the Constitution where the President, Prime Minister, Ministers, Parliamentary Secretaries and the Judiciary swear to perform their duties in accordance with the Constitution. Other ordinary laws have also similar oaths. In addition, the exceptions to human rights and fundamental freedoms are dictated only by public interest. The common good is served by the public interest as opposed to the private interest.

§3. Administrative Organs with Advisory and/or Control Functions

394. There exist administrative organs which have an advisory or control function or both.

I. Advisory Administrative Organs

395. Advisory administrative organs comprise:

(a) the National Forum established by section 16(1) of the Cultural Heritage Act;[752]
(b) the Council for Children established by section 12(1) of the Commissioner for Children Act;[753]
(c) the Council for Maltese Living Abroad established by section 3(1) of the Council for Maltese Living Abroad Act;[754]
(d) the Council for Older Persons established by section 12(1) of the Commissioner for Older Persons Act.[755]

II. Control Administrative Organs

396. The Arts Council Malta, which is established by section 3(1) the Arts Council Malta Act,[756] is an example of a control administrative organ.

III. Advisory and Control Administrative Organs

397. Advisory and control administrative organs comprise:

752. Chapter 445 of the Laws of Malta.
753. Chapter 462 of the Laws of Malta.
754. Chapter 515 of the Laws of Malta.
755. Chapter 553 of the Laws of Malta.
756. Chapter 542 of the Laws of Malta.

(a) the National Commission Persons with Disability established by section 21 of the Equal Opportunities (Persons with Disability) Act;[757]
(b) the Malta Crafts Council established by section 4 of the Malta Crafts Council Act;[758]
(c) the Malta Council for Economic and Social Development established by section 3 of the Malta Council for the Economic and Social Development Act;[759]
(d) the Committee of Guarantee established by section 14 of the Cultural Heritage Act;[760]
(e) the National Commission for the Promotion of Equality for Men and Women established by section 11(1) of the Equality for Men and Women Act;[761]
(f) the National Council of the Maltese Language established by section 4(1) of the Maltese Language Act;[762] and
(g) the Malta Film Commission established by section 3(1) of the Malta Film Commission Act.[763]

§4. Independent Administrative Authorities

398. There are a number of administrative authorities which enjoy some form of independence from the government. These administrative authorities are established by the Constitution or by an Act of Parliament. Such is the case of the constitutional commissions, the Broadcasting Authority and public corporations. Examples of public corporations comprise the Central Bank of Malta and the Malta Financial Services Authority.

§5. Hierarchy of Independence of Regulators

399. Not all regulators in Malta are on the same footing insofar as their degree of independence from Government is concerned. There are some which are more independent than others. For instance, there is no comparison between the constitutionally established Broadcasting Authority and the ordinary law established Malta Communications Authority or Mineral Resources Authority. Independence from governmental control thus varies from one regulator to another. A hierarchy of independence of regulators can be divided as follows: totally independent regulators; independent regulators; quasi-independent regulators; and government dependent regulators.

757. Chapter 413 of the Laws of Malta.
758. Chapter 421 of the Laws of Malta.
759. Chapter 431 of the Laws of Malta.
760. Chapter 445 of the Laws of Malta.
761. Chapter 456 of the Laws of Malta.
762. Chapter 470 of the Laws of Malta.
763. Chapter 478 of the Laws of Malta.

Chapter 11. The Budget Process

§1. Fiscal Law versus Finance Law

400. Chapter IX of the Constitution is entitled 'Finance', that is, it deals with Financial Law, and has therefore a broader meaning than fiscal law. A financial measure comprises both revenue and expenditure whilst fiscal measures are more aimed at the generation of money in favour of the state, whether through taxation, receipt of donations or the imposition of charges howsoever designated. Section 102 of the Constitution deals with revenues (or fiscal measures) whilst section 103 deals with both revenue and expenditure (or financial measures). Once revenue is of a fiscal nature, then financial measures comprise fiscal measures but the same cannot be said for the obverse situation for fiscal law can never comprise financial law due to the former's limited meaning as contrasted with the latter's wider interpretation.[764]

401. This chapter deals with financial law which comes in various forms. There are a number of financial laws which are related to the budget;[765] to the taking of loans

764. For the distinction between 'financial law' and 'fiscal law', *see* Kevin Aquilina, 'Can the Maltese Citizenship (Amendment) Act, 2013 – Act No. XV of 2013 – be the subject of an abrogative referendum?', in *ELSA Malta Law Review*, 4th edn, 2014, pp. 55–71.

765. These comprised, over the years, the Budget Measures Implementation (2004) Act, Chapter 469 of the Laws of Malta; Budget Measures Implementation (2005) Act, Chapter 475 of the Laws of Malta; Budget Measures Implementation (2007) Act, Chapter 489 of the Laws of Malta; Budget Measures Implementation (2008) Act, Chapter 494 of the Laws of Malta; Budget Measures Implementation (2009) Act, Chapter 498 of the Laws of Malta; Budget Measures Implementation (2011) Act, Chapter 509 of the Laws of Malta; Budget Measures Implementation (2012) Act, Chapter 519 of the Laws of Malta; Budget Measures Implementation (2013) Act, Chapter 526 of the Laws of Malta; and Budget Measures Implementation (2014) Act, Chapter 531 of the Laws of Malta; the Budget Measures Implementation Act, 2016 (Act XV of 2016).

by the public administration;[766] establishing taxes,[767] imposing fees,[768] regulating financial administration,[769] providing for audit of government moneys and properties;[770] and establishing the financial year.[771] In this chapter, specific reference is made to the budget as the most important instrument of finance law.

§2. The Budget

402. Like all modern democracies, the budget is approved by Parliament. The Constitution contains a whole chapter – Chapter IX – which deals with finance. One important aspect of Financial Law is naturally the budget. Before however discussing the budget, it is of paramount importance to refer to the concept of the Financial Year and that of the Consolidated Fund because the purpose of the budget is to authorize the receipt of revenue and expenditure of money from the Consolidated Fund within a financial year.

§3. Other Financial Laws

403. The Constitution's provisions are supplemented by various other financial laws, notable amongst which are the Financial Administration and Audit Act, the Central Bank of Malta Act, the Fiscal Responsibility Act, the Participation and Guarantees under the European Financial Stability Facility Act, the Participation and Granting of Financial Stability Support under the European Stability Mechanism Act, the Participation within the Single Resolution Fund and Granting of Financial Support

766. These comprised, over the years, the Local Loan Act, Chapter 329 of the Laws of Malta; Local Loan Act, Chapter 338 of the Laws of Malta; Local Loan Act, Chapter 346 of the Laws of Malta; Local Loan Act, Chapter 357 of the Laws of Malta; Local Loan Act, Chapter 361 of the Laws of Malta; Local Loan Act, Chapter 366 of the Laws of Malta; Local Loan Act, Chapter 384 of the Laws of Malta; Local Loan Act, Chapter 388 of the Laws of Malta; Local and Other Loans Act, Chapter 393 of the Laws of Malta; Local Loan Act, Chapter 401 of the Laws of Malta; Local Loan Act, Chapter 407 of the Laws of Malta; Local Loan Act, Chapter 428 of the Laws of Malta.
767. Customs Ordinance, Chapter 37 of the Laws of Malta; Spirits Ordinance, Chapter 41 of the Laws of Malta; Revenue (Safeguard) Act, Chapter 62 of the Laws of Malta; Income Tax Act, Chapter 123 of the Laws of Malta; Import Duties Act, Chapter 337 of the Laws of Malta; Duty on Documents and Transfers Act, Chapter 364 of the Laws of Malta; Income Tax Management Act, Chapter 372 of the Laws of Malta; Bunkering (Fuels) Tax Act, Chapter 381 of the Laws of Malta; Excise Duty Act, Chapter 382 of the Laws of Malta; Customs and Excise Tax Act, Chapter 395 of the Laws of Malta; Commercial Banks (Special Tax) Act, Chapter 402 of the Laws of Malta; Value Added Tax, Chapter 406 of the Laws of Malta and the Eco-Contribution Tax Act, Chapter 473 of the Laws of Malta.
768. Fees Ordinance, Chapter 35 of the Laws of Malta.
769. Financial Administration and Audit Act, Chapter 174 of the Laws of Malta.
770. Constitution, section 108; Financial Administration and Audit Act; and Auditor General and National Audit Office Act, Chapter 396 of the Laws of Malta.
771. Financial Year Act, Chapter 282 of the Laws of Malta.

under the Single Resolution Mechanism Act, the Malta Membership of the International Monetary Fund Act, the Membership of International Financial Organizations Act, the Malta Membership of the Asian Infrastructure Investment Bank Act and the Standing Orders of the House of Representatives Order.

§4. The Financial Institutional Framework: The Competent Authorities in Constitutional Public Finance Law

404. In order to operate all the diverse Public Finance Laws, various officers and entities of Government are established by law with the specific aim of administering one or more sections falling under Public Finance Law. These include the Minister responsible for finance, the Auditor General and the Deputy Auditor General, the Accountant General, the Internal Audit and Investigations Board and the House of Representatives.

§5. Public Procurement

405. Public procurement is a very important financial management function insofar as the public administration is purchasing services from third parties which can amount to hundreds of thousands of euros. The greater the sum involved, the greater the temptation to abuse and the higher that the amount of supervision should be. Hence, the law regulates public procurement through a number of regulations, these being:

(a) Public Procurement Regulations;[772]
(b) Public Procurement of Entities operating in the Water, Energy, Transport and Postal Services Sectors Regulations;[773]
(c) Public Procurement of Contracting Authorities or Entities in the Fields of Defence and Security Regulations;[774]
(d) Procurement (Energy and Fuels) Appeals Board Regulations,[775] and
(e) Definition and Use of Compatible Technical Specifications for the Procurement of Air Traffic Management Equipment and Systems Regulations.[776]

§6. Relevant EU Law to Public Procurement

406. An aspect of Constitutional Public Finance Law which should not be ignored is the heavy influence of EU Law on this branch of the law. A number of

772. Subsidiary Legislation 174.04.
773. Subsidiary Legislation 174.06.
774. Subsidiary Legislation 174.08.
775. Subsidiary Legislation 497.06.
776. Subsidiary Legislation 499.17.

Maltese Finance Laws specifically refer to EU Law.[777] It is not the intention of this monograph to carry out a study of EU Law relevant to Constitutional Law as that would require a separate study in its own right. The point being made here is that one cannot understand Maltese Public Finance Law without examining also EU Law relevant to public finance law.

§7. Remedies: Review and Supervisory Authorities

407. The public administration's powers are wide enough to require it to be constantly kept in check in order to ensure that there is no abuse. Abuse is countered by ensuring that remedies are provided to ensure that public money is managed in the same way that a *bonus pater familias* manages his accounts – with due diligence. These remedies comprise the following:

(a) investigations by the Internal Audit and Investigations Directorate referred to above;
(b) judicial review of administrative action which is regulated by Article 469A of the Code of Organization and Civil Procedure. This provision kicks in only where the mode of contestation or of obtaining redress, with respect to any particular administrative act before a court or tribunal is not already provided for in any other law;[778]
(c) proceedings before the Administrative Review Tribunal are very much relevant insofar as tax legislation is concerned. The Administrative Review Tribunal is established by section 5(1) of the Administrative Justice Act.[779] This Tribunal hears appeals with regard to the following fiscal laws:

    - the Income Tax Act;[780]
    - the Import Duties Act;[781]
    - the Duty on Documents and Transfers Act;[782]
    - the Income Tax Management Act;[783]
    - the Excise Duty Act;[784]
    - the Customs and Excise Tax Act;[785] and
    - the Value Added Tax Act.[786]

777. On public procurement rules and implementation, *see* http://ec.europa.eu/growth/single-market/public-procurement/rules-implementation/index_en.htm. Last accessed on 31 March 2016.
778. Code of Organization and Civil Procedure, section 469A(4).
779. Chapter 490 of the Laws of Malta.
780. Chapter 123 of the Laws of Malta.
781. Chapter 337 of the Laws of Malta.
782. Chapter 364 of the Laws of Malta.
783. Chapter 372 of the Laws of Malta.
784. Chapter 382 of the Laws of Malta.
785. Chapter 395 of the Laws of Malta.
786. Chapter 406 of the Laws of Malta.

(d) proceedings before special appeal boards such as the Public Contracts Appeals Board established by regulation 15 of the Public Service (Procurement) Regulations,[787] the Public Contracts Review Board established by regulation 34(1) of the Public Procurement Regulations,[788] and the Procurement (Energy and Fuels) Appeals Board;[789]
(e) investigations carried out by the Auditor General. In terms of the Constitution, the Auditor General has powers to investigate the administration of public finance and, in terms of the Auditor General and National Audit Act, the Auditor General enjoys the powers of a Chairman of a Board of Inquiries under the Inquiries Act.[790] As an Officer of Parliament, he has direct access to the House and his/her reports are submitted to the Speaker for laying on the Table of the House and for any action thereupon by the House;
(f) pressure can be put on the public administration in the House through parliamentary questions and adjournment speeches. Both government backbenchers and Opposition MPs can use these two parliamentary tools to ensure that the public administration is administering public finances in terms of law and proper accounting standards as contained in various Public Finance Laws referred to in this chapter;
(g) Boards of Inquiry established under the Inquiries Act.[791] The Prime Minister may appoint a Board of Inquiry to investigate the conduct of public officers and of any officer of a statutory body. Such inquiry may relate to financial impropriety, and it is of an administrative nature. However, a Board of Inquiry may make recommendations for the criminal prosecution of such officer or for the taking of disciplinary, administrative or civil measures against the said officer;
(h) consideration of grievances by the House of Representatives' Committee of Supply. In terms of Standing Order 71(1) of the Standing Orders of the House of Representatives Order:

> On the occasion of a motion that the House do resolve itself into a Committee of Supply for the consideration of the General Estimates or of any Supplementary Estimate (whether consisting of one or more heads) redress of grievances may be considered and general discussion of the policy of the Government may take place and amendments may be moved to the formal question that the Speaker should leave the Chair;

i. supervision at EU level by the European Commission's Anti-Fraud Office (OLAF) insofar as EU Law related to public finance laws is concerned.

787. Subsidiary Legislation 174.02.
788. Subsidiary Legislation 174.04.
789. Subsidiary Legislation 497.06.
790. Auditor General and National Audit Office Act, Chapter 396 of the Laws of Malta, section 4.
791. Chapter 273 of the Laws of Malta.

Part III. The State and Its Subdivisions

Chapter 1. Local Government

§1. The Origins of Maltese Local Self-Government

408. Malta does not have a system of devolution of power as the UK has with Scotland, Wales and Northern Ireland. Instead it has a system of government whereby Parliament has devolved powers and responsibilities previously enjoyed by central government upon local self-government entities. Local self-government, in its current form, dates back to 1961, even though instances of local self-government in Malta vary in content and time.[792] Ordinance No. XI of 1961 – the Gozo Local Government Ordinance, 1961 – made provision for local government in Gozo, the second most populated island in the Maltese archipelago.[793] The Gozo Civic Council was a statutory

792. For a discussion of the various forms of local self-government over time, *see* Henry Frendo, 'Il-Gvern Lokali fil-Gżejjer Maltin: L-Ewwel Pass' (Translation: Local Government in the Maltese Islands: The First Step), in *Politika: Pubblikazzjoni tal-Partit Nazzjonalista* (Translation: Politics: A Publication of the Nationalist Party), Nationalist Party, Pietà, No. 4, December 1994, pp. 29–35; Louis C. Debono, 'Il-Gvern Lokali f'Għawdex' (Translation: Local Government in Gozo), in Institute of Public Administration, *L-Amministrazzjoni Pubblika f'Pajjiżna* (Translation: Public Administration in our Country), Department of Information, Valletta, 1968, pp. 72–78; Abigail Maria Caruana, *The Gozo Civic Council: An Experiment in Devolution in Gozo*, LL.D. thesis, Faculty of Laws, University of Malta, Msida, 2010, pp. 16–43; Rolan Borg, *An Analysis and Evaluation of the Powers and Competences of the Local Wardens and the System of the Local Tribunals*, LL.D. thesis, Faculty of Laws, University of Malta, Msida, May 2008, pp. 16–24 and Henri Darmanin, *The European Charter of Local Self-Government: Political and Legal Implications on Maltese Legislation*, LL.D. thesis, Faculty of Laws, University of Malta, Msida, May 2008, pp. 31–41.

793. For a history of the Gozo Civic Court *see* Joseph Bezzina, *The Gozo Civic Council: The Story of a Regional Government*, Victoria, Gozo, Committee Fiftieth Anniversary Celebrations Gozo Civic Council, 2011; Annalisa Debono, *Governance in Malta: The Dimension of Local Government*, LL.D. thesis, Faculty of Laws, University of Malta, Msida, May 2011; Edward Warrington, 'Gozo Civic Council: Past Experience or Model for the Future?', in *50 Sena mill-Kunsill Ċiviku ta' Għawdex – Esperjenza tal-Passat jew Mudell għall-Futur?* (Translation: Fifty Years Since the Establishment of the Gozo Civic Council: An Experience of the Past or a Model for the Future?), Proceedings of a conference organized by the Organisational Committee – 50 Years since the Gozo Civic Council, held at Hotel Kempinski, St. Lawrence, Gozo, on Tuesday, 14 June 2011, pp. 15–18.

local government enjoying a distinct legal personality and capable of entering into contracts, of suing and being sued, and of doing all such things and entering into such transactions as are incidental or conducive to the exercise and performance of its functions under the Ordinance.[794]

409. However, this experience of local self-government was short lived as the Gozo Local Government Ordinance, 1961, was repealed by the Gozo Local Government (Repeal) Act, 1973.[795] All assets of the Gozo Civic Council passed in favour of the Government of Malta.[796] Malta thus continued between 1973 and 1993, for a twenty-year period, solely with a system of central government. In August 1989, 'Cabinet approved the setting up of an Inter-Departmental Committee under the Chairmanship of the Deputy Prime Minister and Minister of the Interior and Justice in order to make suggestions on the setting up of Local/Municipal Councils; study the implications of efficient and cost-effective transfer of manpower attached for duties with the Councils; determine the proper financing of Councils; and to suggest a time-frame for implementation'.[797] In January 1992, a White Paper entitled *Kunsilli Lokali*: *Iċ-Ċittadin jersaq iżjed lejn il-poter*[798] was published by Government.[799] The Local Government Bill[800] followed the White Paper which was subsequently enacted into law as the Local Councils Act.[801] The 1993 enactment came into force over a three-year period.[802] A White Paper on the strengthening of decentralization was published in June 1999,[803] and one month earlier methods for estimating local councils' funding needs was approved.[804] The next historic milestone in local government law occurred in 2001 when section 115A was added to the Constitution. In the meantime, several other

794. *Ibid.*, section 3(2).
795. Act No. XLIII of 1973.
796. Gozo Local Government (Repeal) Act, 1973, section 4.
797. Natalino Attard, *The Role of Local Authorities within the Framework of the European Union Institutions*, Magister Juris in European and Comparative Law dissertation, Faculty of Laws, University of Malta, Msida, September 1995, p. 86.
798. Translation: Local Councils: Bringing the Citizen Closer to Power.
799. Department of Information, Valletta, January 1992.
800. Bill No. 30 was published in *The Malta Government Gazette* of 19 February 1993.
801. Act No. XV of 1993. For s study of the origin and enactment of the Local Councils Act, *see* Henri Darmanin, *supra* note 792, pp. 41–53.
802. Phase One came into force on 1 January 1994; Phase Two on 1 January 1995; and Phase Three on 1 January 1996. For the distribution of local councils' functions per phase *see Pajjizna: Il-Kunsill Tiegħek* (Translation: Our Country: Your Councils), Department of Information, Valletta, Issue 22, 1993, pp. 4–5. For a discussion on the introduction of local councils in Malta, *see* Saviour Micallef, *The Introduction of Local Councils in Malta*, LL.D. thesis, Faculty of Laws, University of Malta, Msida, 1994.
803. Ministry for Justice and Local Government, *White Paper on Local Government – The Strengthening of Decentralisation: Your Council for You*, Ministry for Justice and Local Government, Valletta, June 1999.
804. Local Councils Department, *Methods for Estimating Local Councils' Funding Needs,* Local Councils Department, Valletta, May 1999.

developments took place in local self-government through the report of the state of local democracy in Malta of 1999[805] and the 2009[806] proposals for reform.[807]

410. The Gozo Civic Council did not have any legislative powers. Indeed, although the Council did have the authority to make by-laws,[808] they were 'subject to the approval of the Governor, who before approving may amend the same'.[809]

411. Contrary to Local Councils, the Gozo Civic Council had to comply with two very interesting provisions which do not find a counterpart in the Local Councils Act. First, the Gozo Civic Council had the power to levy an annual rate 'on the annual rateable value of each rateable tenement in Gozo' for 'the purpose of raising revenue for the discharge of its functions'.[810] Second, the Council was required to ensure that it complies with a self-balancing budget:

> In any financial year, the ordinary and recurrent revenue and expenditure relating to any matter in respect of which the Council has any functions under this Ordinance shall be self-balancing, and no provision for works, supplies or servicing shall be made by the Council which cannot be met from the revenue of the Council.[811]

§2. Legal Principles Inspiring Local Self-Government Law

412. A study of the Constitution and of the Local Councils Act indicates that Maltese Law enshrines the following principles inspiring Local Self-Government Law:

(a) *the principle of popular representation and enhancement of democracy at local level*: Local Councils are elected by the population residing within the boundaries of a local community;[812]
(b) *the principle of electing directly the Mayor and Deputy Mayor*: the Mayor and Deputy Mayor are elected directly by the locality voters and not by the Councillors from amongst themselves;[813]
(c) *the principle of proportional representation*: Local Councils and Administrative Committees are elected in terms of the principle of proportional representation by means of the single transferable vote;[814]

805. A White Paper preceded these reforms.
806. Office of the Prime Minister, *Biex il-Kunsill Jaghtik l-Aqwa Servizz: Tiġdid tal-Kunsilli Lokali b'riżultat ta' proċess ta' konsultazzjoni* (Translation: Receiving the Best Service from your Council: Renewal of Local Councils as a result of a consultation process), Valletta, 2009.
807. *See* Henri Darmanin, *supra* note 792, pp. 68–95.
808. Gozo Local Government Ordinance, 1961, section 28(1).
809. *Ibid.*, section 28(2).
810. *Ibid.*, section 30(1).
811. *Ibid.*, section 48.
812. Local Councils Act, section 8.
813. *Ibid.*, sections 8 and 25.
814. *Ibid.*, section 8(1).

(d) *the principle of direct democracy*: the possibility of subjecting bye-laws made by Local Councils to an abrogative referendum;[815]
(e) *the principle of decentralization*: the State of Malta is divided into a system of central government and of local self-government and that certain powers vest uniquely in local self-government;[816]
(f) *the principle of hierarchical organizational division of self-government functions*: local self-government consists in three tiers, Regional Committees, Local Councils and Administrative Committees;[817]
(g) *the principle of seeking judicial redress*: local self-government institutions can seek judicial redress in court against any decision interfering with the free exercise of Local Councils' powers;[818]
(h) *the principle of acting within the powers conferred by law (the principle of legality)*: the three tiers of local self-government cannot go beyond the powers conferred upon them by the Local Councils Act;[819]
(i) *the principle of non-encroachment by central government on the functions assigned by law to local self-government*: central government is debarred from exercising those functions which are assigned by the Local Councils Act and subsidiary legislation made thereunder to local self-government institutions, that is, to Regional Committees, Local Councils and Administrative Committees;[820]
(j) *the principle of proportionality*: the exercise of supervision over local self-government has to be proportional;[821]
(k) *the principle of subsidiarity*: decisions are taken at a level which is closer to the people of the region, locality or community, as the case may be;[822]
(l) *the principle of autonomy*: Local Councils are independent in their decision-making and autonomous from central government;[823]
(m) *the principle of public consultation*: residents are consulted by Local Councils on matters related to the locality whilst residents may petition their respective council;[824]
(n) *the principle of public participation in the running of the country at local level*: once all the three tiers of local self-government are representatives of residents

815. *Ibid.*, section 36A.
816. *Ibid.*, section 33.
817. *Ibid.*, sections 3, 37A and 47A.
818. *Ibid.*, section 38.
819. *Ibid.*, sections 33, 37A and 47A, the Regional Committees Regulations (Subsidiary Legislation 363.160) and Administrative Committees For Communities Regulations (Subsidiary Legislation 363.149).
820. *Ibid.*
821. Local Councils Act, section 80(a) and (c).
822. *Ibid.*, sections 33, 37A and 47A. For a discussion of the principle of subsidiarity within a local self-government context, *see* Paul Borg Olivier, *Local Councils in Malta: Some Considerations of the Law from a Comparative Perspective*, LL.D. thesis, Faculty of Laws, University of Malta, Msida, June 1995, pp. 1–19 and Annalisa Debono, *supra* note 793, pp. 16–21.
823. Local Councils Act, sections 3(2), and 80(a) and (c).
824. *Ibid.*, section 71.

living within a region, locality or community, they are all participating in the running of the region, locality or community within which they live;[825]

(o) *the principle of political partisan divisiveness*: the elections to Local Councils are contested by the main political parties such that even at Local Council level there is an element of partisan politics which brings about divisiveness within the locality;[826]

(p) *the principle of openness*: the public has access to Local Council documents and may attend Local Council meetings, including sub-committees thereof, contrary to central government where secrecy predominates at Cabinet level;[827]

(q) *the principle of accountability*: Local Councils are accountable for their operations to the three organs of the State;[828]

(r) *the principle of limiting freedom of expression of Local Councils from broadcasting*: a restriction on the functions of Local Councils, which resents of a violation of freedom of expression, is the absolute ban on Local Councils from owning broadcasting stations, both radio and television, without however prohibiting them from owning other media such as press or new media;[829] and

(s) *the principle of allowing local authorities to form associations*: in terms of this principle Local Councils may form their own association. This principle has been given flesh through the incorporation of the Local Councils (Association) Regulations.[830]

§3. Local Self-Governing Authorities in the Maltese Constitution

413. The Constitution divides Government into two main types: central government and local government. Although the Constitution, in 1964, did refer to local government authorities, there was no organized system of local government covering both Malta and Gozo. In 1964, the sole self-government system that existed in the Maltese islands covered only Gozo. Local government was formally established by Parliament, through an ordinary law, and not through a constitutional provision. It was only in 2001 that the Constitution was amended whereby a new Chapter was introduced – consisting of only one provision – recognizing the local self-government system established by ordinary law. Indeed, the Constitution recognizes local self-government in the following

825. *Ibid.*, sections 8, 25, 37A and 47A.
826. *Ibid.*, Third Schedule.
827. *Ibid.*, sections 44–46.
828. Throughout the Local Councils Act there are various provisions where a Regional Committee, Local Council or an Administrative Committee is accountable towards the Minister responsible for local government and the Director for Local Government. Moreover, central government can exercise the power of dissolution of a Regional Committee in terms of regulation 11 of the Regional Committees Regulations, Subsidiary Legislation 363.160 and of local councils in terms of section 22 of the Local Councils Act.
829. Local Councils Act, section 77 and Broadcasting Act, Chapter 350 of the Laws of Malta, section 10(6D).
830. Local Councils Act, section 37(3) and the Local Councils Association, Subsidiary Legislation 363.06.

provisions, even if local self-government was as a matter of fact limited only to Gozo when the Constitution was given to Malta in 1964:

(a) section 38(2)(c) that authorizes a department of the Government of Malta, or a local government authority, or a body corporate established by law for a public purpose, to enter on the premises of any person in order to inspect those premises or anything thereon for the purpose of any tax, rate or due or in order to carry out work connected with any property or installation which is lawfully on those premises and which belongs to that Government, that authority, or that body corporate, as the case may be;
(b) section 45(5) which provides that nothing contained in any law is held to be discriminatory either of itself or in its effects with respect to qualifications (not being qualifications specifically relating to sex) for service of a local government authority;
(c) section 101A(4)(a) in terms of which a person is not qualified to be appointed or continue to hold office as a member of the Commission for the Administration of Justice if he/she is a member of a local government authority;
(d) sections 109(3), 118(3) and 120(3) whereby a person is unqualified to hold office as a member of the PSC, the Broadcasting Authority and the Employment Commission, if he/she is a member of a local government authority.

§4. Local Self-Government Authorities in the Local Councils Act

414. In Malta, local self-government was introduced by the Local Councils Act.[831] It was only subsequent to this enactment that in 2001, the Constitution was amended by section 4 of Act No. XIII of 2001 to introduce a new Chapter in the Constitution, Chapter XA, entitled 'Local Councils'. A new provision was added by the 2001 amendments, section 115A, to the Constitution, which reads as follows: 'The State shall adopt a system of local government whereby the territory of Malta shall be divided into such number of localities as may by law be from time to time determined, each locality to be administered by a Local Council elected by the residents of the locality and established and operating in terms of such law as may from time to time be in force.' Hence local self-government has been expressly declared in the Constitution since 2001. But the provision refers to Local Councils and not to regions and communities. This is because it was at a later stage that Malta moved from a one-tier system of local self-government to a three-tier level of local self-government. This constitutional provision is supplemented by the Local Councils Act which allows the setting up of Regional Committees, Local Councils, and Administrative Committees and their regulation. Regional Committees have limited functions when compared to local councils.[832] Decisions taken by Administrative Committees of the communities have to be approved by the Local Council under whose jurisdiction they fall. Administrative

831. Act No. XV of 1993, renumbered as Chapter 363 of the Laws of Malta.
832. Regional Committees are governed by section 37A of the Local Councils Act and the Regional Committees Regulations, Subsidiary Legislation 363.160.

Committees are more of a sub-committee of a Local Council for a particular community established by law.[833] In all, there are five regions, sixty-eight localities and sixteen communities, one of which borders into two localities. The geographic regions group the following localities: Northern Region (twelve localities); Central Region (thirteen localities); Southern Region (fifteen localities); South Eastern Region (fourteen localities); and Gozo Region (fourteen localities).

§5. The Creation of Regional Committees and Local Councils

415. The creation of Regional Committees came at a very late stage in the evolution of local self-government. This is because the 2001 constitutional provision does not refer to Regional Committees but to Local Councils. Regional Committees had, up till 2011, not even been considered important within local self-government. Even the Local Councils Act did not refer to Regional Committees except since 2011 when this enactment was amended to introduce regional government within local self-government. Section 37A now refers to Regional Committees, and this provision is supplemented by the Regional Committee Regulations.[834] On the other hand, the creation of Local Councils in 1993 came before both the creation of the regions and the recognition of Local Councils by the Constitution.

§6. Organizational Structure of Local Self-Government

416. The organization structure of local self-government in Malta is threefold:

(a) Regional Committees;
(b) Local Councils (and Joint Committees of Local Councils); and
(c) Administrative Committees.

§7. The Organization of the Regions, Local Councils and Communities

I. Organization of Regional Government

417. The Local Councils Act establishes five Regional Committees.[835] Four are for Malta (Northern Region; Central Region; South Eastern Region; and Southern Region) and one for Gozo.[836] The Gozo Regional Committee established under the Local Councils Act should not be confused with the Gozo Regional Committee

833. Administrative Committees are governed by section 47A of the Local Councils Act and the Administrative Committees for Communities Regulations, Subsidiary Legislation 363.149.
834. Subsidiary Legislation 363.160.
835. Local Councils Act, section 37A.
836. *Ibid.*, Eleventh Schedule.

established by section 6A of the Malta Council for the Economic and Social Development Act.[837] Contrary to Local Councils, Regional Committee members are not elected by the residents of the region. Instead, the Regional Committee Chairman is elected from amongst all Councillors of the localities forming the region,[838] whilst each locality appoints a representative to form part of the Regional Committee.[839] Even the Regional Deputy Chairman is not elected by the inhabitants of the region – he/she is elected from among the members of the Regional Committee.

II. Organization of Local Councils

418. 'One feature common to local authorities is their corporate status.'[840] Local Councils are composed of a Mayor, a Deputy Mayor and Councillors. The Mayor[841] and the Deputy Mayor[842] are elected directly by the residents of the locality. In the past, the position used to be that Councillors, after being returned to office, would appoint from amongst them a Mayor and a Deputy Mayor, and it can well be that the Mayor and Deputy Mayor were not necessarily those Councillors who would have polled 'the highest number of votes in the first count amongst the candidates of the political party which at such election obtained the absolute majority of Councillors in such Council'.[843] With the changes made in 2005, by means of amendments made to the Local Councils Act by section 10 of the Local Councils (Amendment) Act, 2005,[844] the position changed and it is the locality voters who decide who is to be elected Mayor and Deputy Mayor.[845] The number of Councillors per locality is determined in terms of the population size of each locality in terms of section 4 of the Local Councils Act.

III. Organization of Communities

419. Sixteen Communities are established and listed in the Ninth Schedule of the Local Councils Act. They are a sub-set of a locality. Yet they enjoy their own Administrative Committee which is elected for a four-year period.[846] The Chairman of the Administrative Committee is entitled to attend the Local Council meetings of the locality in which that community is geographically situated and to take part in the discussions but has no right to participate in the decisions.[847] In the case of one

837. Chapter 431 of the Laws of Malta.
838. *Ibid.*, section 37A(2)(a).
839. *Ibid.*, section 37A(2)(b).
840. Stephen Bailey, *Cross on Principles of Local Government Law*, Sweet and Maxwell, London, 1992, p. 2.
841. Local Councils Act, section 4(3).
842. *Ibid.*, section 4(4).
843. *Ibid.*, section 25(1).
844. Act No. I of 2005. In the Bill, this clause was number 11 (*see* Local Councils (Amendment) Act, 2004, Bill No. 38, published in *The Malta Government Gazette* on 14 January 2005).
845. Local Councils Act, section 25(1).
846. *Ibid.*, section 47A(6).
847. *Ibid.*, section 47A(7).

community – Is-Swatar – it is located within the boundaries of two localities (Birkirkara and Imsida) whilst the remaining fifteen communities are situated in only one locality.[848] Administrative Committees – contrary to the Regional Committees and Local Councils – do not have the right to make bye-laws. The Administrative Committee is composed of five persons. The Chairperson of the Administrative Committee is not elected directly by the residents registered in that community but by the elected members of the Administrative Committee who, during the first meeting, appoint a Chairperson from amongst themselves.[849] This is, however, not the situation with the election of Mayor (and Deputy Mayor) of a Local Council.[850]

§8. Competence of Regional Committees, Local Councils and Administrative Communities

420. Contrary to Local Councils, the competence of Regional Committees is not set out in the Local Councils Act but in subsidiary legislation made thereunder. Indeed, section 37A(5) of the Local Councils Act provides that the 'functions of Regional Committees shall be those established by the Minister by regulations to be made following consultation with the Local Councils Association'. Through this provision, Parliament has delegated its power of establishing the functions of regional government to central government. This, once again, shows that regional government is considered by Parliament to be of lesser status and importance than Local Councils. In the latter instance, the functions of Local Councils are set out in the Local Councils Act.

I. Functions of Regional Committees

421. According to regulation 19(1) of the Regional Committees Regulations,[851] the functions of Regional Government are the following:

(a) to provide for the proper upkeep and maintenance of street lighting in accordance with national and international standards;
(b) the enforcement of laws delegated to the Committees and the provision of warden services for all localities for which the Committee is responsible, including those functions as are necessary so as to prosecute following enforcement;
(c) to organize cultural activities that promote the locality in every possible way;
(d) to protect the natural and urban environment of the locality and take all necessary measures to ensure the more efficient use of energy, good waste management and climate change initiatives;
(e) to enter into agreements with any public body or government department for the delegation to the Committee of any of the functions of that public body or

848. *Ibid.*, Ninth Schedule.
849. *Ibid.*, section 47A(6).
850. *Ibid.*, section 4(3) and (4).
851. Subsidiary Legislation 363.160.

department: Provided that any such delegation shall only come into effect after the Minister has made the relevant order in the Gazette;

(f) to perform any other function which shall be delegated to it by the Government through the Minister by means of an order published in the *Gazette*;

(g) to provide for all such other works, things, matters and services which are not excluded from a Council's competence by any law for the time being in force nor assigned to any other authority.

II. Functions of Local Councils

422. The functions of Local Councils are enumerated in section 33(1) of the Local Councils Act.

423. An analysis of the functions of local councils reveals that they can be, broadly speaking, classified under the following general headings:

(a) upkeep and maintenance of the locality;[852]
(b) provision of advice to central government;[853]
(c) provision of information to residents;[854]
(d) promotion of initiatives within the locality;[855] and
(e) assumption of new functions not listed in the Local Councils Act.[856]

424. Various other new functions may be vested in Local Councils. Each function is devolved when the Central Government is convinced that Local Councils are prepared to take on such responsibility.[857] In such a case, such new functions are first devolved on to a small number of Local Councils, possibly of various sizes, to serve as a test.[858]

III. Functions of Communities

425. The Local Councils Act does not list down the functions of Communities. However, it is evident from a reading of section 47A of the Local Councils Act that an Administrative Committee does have certain functions to carry out. These comprise:

(a) attending Local Council meetings and participation by its Chairperson during the discussions;[859]

(b) representing the residents registered in the community during Local Council meetings;[860]

852. Local Councils Act, section 33(1)(a), (b), (c), (d), (j), (k) and (u).
853. *Ibid.*, section 33(1)(e), (f), (i) and (l).
854. *Ibid.*, section 33(1)(h).
855. *Ibid.*, section 33(1)(m), (n), (o), (p), (q), (r), (s), (t) and (v).
856. *Ibid.*, section 33(1)(w) and (x) and section 33(3)(a) and (b).
857. *Ibid.*, section 33(3)(a).
858. *Ibid.*, section 33(3)(b).
859. *Ibid.*, section 47A(7).
860. *Ibid.*, section 47A(7).

(c) using funds allocated to it, following approval by the Local Council of the locality in question;[861]

(d) applying for EU funds;[862] and

(e) obtaining financing from special funds and other funds to carry out initiatives and projects in its zone.[863]

426. In addition, the Administrative Committees For Communities Regulations[864] state that the matters 'to be discussed during the Administrative Committee meetings shall be those pertaining to the particular community'.[865]

§9. General Aspects of Regional and Local Legislative Autonomy

427. Regional committees enjoy the same legislative powers of Local Councils in terms of sections 34, 35, 36 and 36A of the Local Councils Act.[866] The Minister responsible for local government has concurrent legislative powers with Local Councils which are deemed to be made by all the Councils. A legal fiction is thus introduced by the law which equates the Minister's law-making function exercised through the making of regulations to that of an assembly of Local Councils meeting together and all making the same set of bye-laws. A Regional Committee, like a Local Council, has the power to 'make, amend and revoke bye-laws for the purpose of carrying out its functions and for the prevention and suppression of nuisance in its locality'.[867] Once bye-laws are approved by a Regional Committee or a Local Council, they have to be submitted to the Director for Local Government.[868] The Minister enjoys a six-week period from the receipt of the proposed bye-laws by the Director to propose any amendments to the Council.[869] The Council is required by law to discuss the Minister's proposed amendments. Nevertheless, the Council is not obliged by law to take on board the Minister's proposals or proposed amendments.[870] However, the Minister has 'the right to object to any bye-law approved by the Council' and must 'signify such objection and the justification thereof in writing to the Council'.[871] Nonetheless, there is no requirement imposed upon the Minister to publish his objection; nor is there a legal obligation imposed upon the Regional Committee or Local Council to reconsider the Minister's objection following the communication to the Regional Committee or Local Council of the Minister's objection and justification for such objection. Bye-

861. *Ibid.*, section 47A(9).
862. *Ibid.*
863. *Ibid.*
864. Subsidiary Legislation 363.149.
865. Administrative Committees For Communities Regulations, Subsidiary Legislation 363.149, regulation 7.
866. Local Councils Act, section 37A(6).
867. *Ibid.*, section 34(1).
868. *Ibid.*, section 35(3).
869. *Ibid.*, section 35(4).
870. *Ibid.*, section 35(6).
871. *Ibid.*, section 35(7).

laws, once made, may however be subject to an abrogative referendum in terms of Part V of the Referenda Act.[872]

§10. The Administrative Autonomy of Regional Committees and Local Councils from Central Government

I. The Administrative Autonomy of Regional Committees

428. It cannot be said that Regional Committees are administratively autonomous from central government insofar as the appointment of their Executive Secretary is concerned. The same can be said, as will be seen below, with regard to Local Councils. This is because a Regional Committee may appoint an Executive Secretary – 'the executive, administrative and financial head of the Committee'[873] – only after approval from the Minister responsible for local government[874] and only from amongst those persons forming part of the pool referred to in section 49 of the Act, that is, from amongst public servants'.[875] Should the Committee refuse or fail to appoint an Executive Secretary or a Deputy Executive Secretary, then such task falls upon the Minister to make an appointment of an Acting Executive Secretary.[876] The Committee also nominates 'a Deputy Executive Secretary to perform the duties instead of the Executive Secretary whenever the Executive Secretary cannot for any reason perform his functions or whenever the office of the Executive Secretary is vacant'. This appointment comes into force after the Regional Committee has obtained the approval of the Minister.[877] Insofar as employees are concerned, Regional Committees may 'appoint such other employees as the Committee may deem necessary for the efficient discharge of the functions of the Committee so however that the Committee may not employ without the approval of the Director' for Local Government.[878]

II. The Administrative Autonomy of Local Councils

429. The administrative autonomy of Local Councils is also curtailed by central government. The appointment of an Executive Secretary can be made by a Local Council, subject to the approval of the Minister,[879] and from amongst public officers

872. *Ibid.*, section 36A.
873. Regional Committees Regulations, Subsidiary Legislation 363.160, regulation 26(1). An identical provision is found in section 52(1) of the Local Councils Act in relation to local council Executive Secretaries.
874. Regional Committees Regulations, Subsidiary Legislation 363.160, regulation 49(2).
875. *Ibid.*, regulation 6(1).
876. *Ibid.*
877. *Ibid.*, regulation 6(2).
878. *Ibid.*, regulation 25.
879. Local Councils Act, section 49(2).

chosen from a pool of persons for this purpose.[880] Should the Local Council fail to appoint an Executive Secretary or a Deputy Executive Secretary, the Minister has the power to appoint an acting Executive Secretary or an Acting Deputy Executive Secretary from the said pool.[881] The Minister may also remove or transfer an Executive Secretary from one Local Council to another.[882]

430. A Local Council may also employ its own employees. However, the number of employees that can be employed is capped in terms of the number of residents of a locality. Currently the law provides for one employee for 2,500 residents but where their amount is less than 2,500 residents, it may still be possible to employ two employees.[883] Yet a Local Council is precluded from purchasing any clerical services.[884] It may, nonetheless, seek the Minister's approval to employ clerical personnel in excess of the above limit.[885] The Minister, after consultation with the Local Councils Association, also prescribes 'the qualifications to be possessed by, the remuneration payable to and the technical administrative and office procedures to be followed by' such employees.[886]

III. The Administrative Dependence of Administrative Committees on Local Councils

431. Communities do not enjoy any administrative autonomy. According to section 47A(8), Administrative Committees are dependent on Local Councils insofar as the communities' administration is concerned: 'The Executive Secretary of the Local Council shall be the Executive Secretary of the Administrative Committee and shall be responsible for the financial management thereof.'[887] Not only that, but the Mayor of the respective locality – or a representative of the Local Council – has the right to attend and participate during Administrative Committee meetings.[888] The representative need not be an elected Councillor. It could be, for instance, the Local Council's lawyer who could be so appointed.

IV. Regulation of Human Resources

432. In addition to the above-cited provisions of the Local Councils Act and subsidiary legislation made thereunder related to the Executive Secretary, the Deputy Executive Secretary and employees, note must also be taken of the Local Councils

880. *Ibid.*, section 49(3).
881. *Ibid.*, section 49(4).
882. *Ibid.*, section 49(5). The reasons upon which such removal or transfer may take place are contained in section 49(6) of the Local Councils Act.
883. *Ibid.*, section 53(1)(a).
884. *Ibid.*, section 53(1)(c).
885. *Ibid.*, section 53(1)(b).
886. *Ibid.*, section 53(2).
887. *Ibid.*, section 47A(8). This provision is repeated in regulation 8 of the Administrative Committees for Communities Regulations, Subsidiary Legislation 363.149.
888. Local Councils Act, section 47A(7) and regulation 8 of the Administrative Committees For Communities Regulations, Subsidiary Legislation 363.149.

(Human Resources) Regulations.[889] These regulations further prescribe the qualifications and remuneration of Executive Secretaries and the qualifications, remuneration, and conditions of work of other employees. Certain provisions of the Local Councils (Human Resources) Regulations also apply to Executive Secretaries and other employees employed by Regional Committees.[890]

§11. The Financial Autonomy of the Regions and of Local Councils and Audit Functions

I. Financial Autonomy of Regional Committees

433. There are three main sources of revenue for Regional Committees, these being through the funds generated from the local enforcement system,[891] through funds allocated on an annual basis by the Minister responsible for finance[892] and through raising its own funds. In the latter instance, the Committee may, after consulting the Director of the Department for Local Government, and 'with the unanimous approval of the members present for the Committee meeting discussing the motion, raise funds by means of a scheme providing for the collection of contributions by Local Councils'.[893] Regional Committees, like Local Councils and Administrative Committees, do not have taxing powers.

II. Financial Autonomy of Local Councils

434. Local Councils receive a financial allocation through Parliament by way of an Appropriation Act. However, it is the Minister responsible for finance who decides upon the exact amount of the financial allocation[894] and whether to allocate it in full or in part.[895] It is worked out on the basis of a formula determined in terms of the Eighth Schedule to the Local Councils Act.[896] In addition to such an allocation, a second source of funding for Local Councils is through the receipt, each year, from the Minister responsible for finance, of 'a fund to compensate for the co-financing of European Union projects'.[897] A third source of funding is through the raising of additional funds by means of a scheme instituted by bye-laws.[898]

889. Subsidiary Legislation 363.20.
890. Regional Committees Regulations, Subsidiary Legislation 360.160, regulations 27(3) and 28.
891. *Ibid.*, regulation 29(1).
892. *Ibid.*, regulation 29(2).
893. *Ibid.*, regulation 30.
894. Local Councils Act, section 55(1).
895. *Ibid.*, section 55(3).
896. *Ibid.*, section 55(2).
897. *Ibid.*, section 55(4).
898. *Ibid.*, section 60.

III. Financial Autonomy of Administrative Committees

435. Administrative Committees are given a financial allocation computed on the basis of the same funding formula for local councils.[899] However, 'any decision on the use of these funds shall be implemented after ratification by the Local Council of the locality'.[900] In other words, the Administrative Committee has to first seek and second obtain the approval of the Local Council to which it appertains before it can embark upon spending money allotted to it. Further, an Administrative Committee may apply for EU funds or other funds to carry out projects within the community.

IV. Local Self-Government Financial Regulations

436. The financial regulations which regulate the financing of the three tiers of local self-government are found in the Local Councils Act, mainly – though not exclusively – in sections 55–68, and in the following regulations:

(a) Local Councils (Financial) Regulations;[901]
(b) Local Councils (Audit) Regulations;[902]
(c) Local Councils (Tendering) Regulations;[903] and
(d) Local Councils (Procedures) Regulations.[904]

437. The Auditor General supervises the financial workings of local self-government. Two important audits carried out by the Auditor General are a performance audit of contract management capabilities across local councils[905] and an audit of the workings of local government.[906] Both reports indicate a number of financial management shortcomings, and the latter report, for instance, has identified the following main common shortcomings encountered in Management Letters:

(a) accounting records not properly updated, with the result that the Financial Statements drawn up, do not reflect a true and fair view of the actual financial situation;
(b) income and expenditure accounted for on cash rather than accrual basis;
(c) payments made not substantiated by a proper invoice and/or fiscal receipt;
(d) fixed Assets Register either lacks necessary details or not maintained at all;

899. *Ibid.*, section 47(9). The funding formula is set out in the Eighth Schedule to the Local Councils Act.
900. *Ibid.*
901. Subsidiary Legislation 363.01.
902. Subsidiary Legislation 363.02.
903. Subsidiary Legislation 363.03.
904. Subsidiary Legislation 363.12.
905. National Audit Office, *Performance Audit: Contract Management Capabilities across Local Councils*, National Audit Office, Floriana, April 2012.
906. Anthony C. Mifsud, Auditor General, *Report by the Auditor General on the Workings of Local Government, Public Accounts 2013*, National Audit Office, Floriana, 10 December 2014.

(e) budgeted expenditure for certain categories of expenditure exceeded;
(f) procurement not in line with the pertinent regulations.[907]

438. Local self-government as it currently obtains is financially unsustainable as has been indicated by the Auditor General in his 2014 report and as has been acknowledged by Government.[908]

§12. The Relationship Between Central Government and Regional Committees, Local Councils and Administrative Committees

439. The relationship between central government on the one hand, and Regional Committees, Local Councils and Administrative Committees, on the other hand, is mainly – though not exclusively – through the Minister responsible for local government. *In subsidium*, this relationship is also, at times, exercised through the Minister responsible for finance. But the main link between central government and local government is the Director of the Department for Local Government who is, in turn, responsible to the Minister responsible for local government. The Director is in continuous contact with the Mayor and the Executive Secretary. The relationship between both forms of government is exercised through the powers vested in the Minister responsible for local government, the Minister responsible for finance and the Director of the Department for Local Government.

§13. The Electoral Process for Local Self-Government

440. As all three tiers of local self-government are elected, sometimes directly[909] and at other times indirectly,[910] the law provides for the conduct of elections for local self-government. Detailed provisions are found in the Local Councils Act. Essentially, without labouring this point, the three tiers of institutions which compose local self-government are elected very much in the same way as Parliament is elected. Council elections are normally held every four years by adopting the system of proportional representation using the single transferable vote.[911] Elections are administered by the Electoral Commission.[912] The regulations which govern local self-government elections are found in the Third Schedule to the Local Councils Act, the Local Councils (Elections) Regulations, 1993. These provisions are supplemented by section 37A(2) and (3)

907. *Ibid.*, pp. 6–7.
908. Stefan Buontempo, Parliamentary Secretary for Local Government, Ministry for Justice, Culture and Local Government, 'Making Councils Sustainable', *The Times of Malta*, 14 December 2014, p. 22.
909. As in the case with Local Councils and Administrative Committees which are elected directly by the residents of the locality and community respectively.
910. As in the case with Regional Committees where the chairman is elected from among all councillors of the localities forming the region.
911. Local Councils Act, section 8(1).
912. *Ibid.*, section 8(2).

insofar as Regional Committees are concerned and section 47A(5) insofar as Administrative Committees are concerned.

§14. Local Self-Government Complaints Mechanism

441. The Sixth Schedule to the Local Councils Act sets out the Standing Orders of Local Councils. Standing Order 39 deals specifically with complaints:

> The Council shall deal with complaints of maladministration allegedly committed by the Council or by any officer or member in the manner which the Minister may by regulations prescribe.

442. The Minister responsible for local government has made the Local Councils (Complaints) Regulations.[913] These regulations apply to all three tiers of local self-government[914] and define a 'complaint' as 'any concern, accusation, criticism, grievance, charge or protest or any other negative information addressed to or received by the Council or any Council employee whether directly or indirectly'.[915] The Executive Secretary handles complaints which are then decided by the Local Council. This is of course an internal mechanism for complaints handling. There is another procedure for lodging a complaint against a Local Council without going directly to the Local Council itself. This is because a complaint can always be lodged with the Local Governance Board. The latter had jurisdiction to decide upon:

(a) any alleged abuse or bad decision or maladministration committed by any elected representative, Executive Secretary, or any other official, which offence is not one of a criminal nature;
(b) any alleged breach of the Code of Ethics for Elected Representatives in force at the time of the alleged breach;[916]
(c) any complaint by any member of the public against any Elected Representative, Executive Secretary or any official with respect to any maladministration;
(d) any complaint from any public official or private entity against any Elected Representative, Executive Secretary or any official of any maladministration;
(e) any complaint from a member of the public, public official or any public or private entity against any decision of a local government on any decision which he deems to constitute any irregularity, injustice or abuse not being of a criminal nature.[917]

443. Maladministration is defined in the Local Governance Board Regulations as including 'decisions taken by any elected representative or any official of any

913. Subsidiary Legislation 363.04.
914. Local Governance Board, regulation 2 which defines 'Elected representative', 'Executive Secretary' and 'official' as applying to all three tiers of local self-government.
915. Local Councils (Complaints) Regulations, regulation 2.
916. *See* Department for Local Government, Office of the Prime Minister, *Code of Ethics for Local Government Elected Representatives*, Valletta, 2010.
917. Local Governance Board Regulations, Subsidiary Legislation 363.150, regulation 5.

Regional Committee, Local Council or Administrative Committee that are taken after an unreasonable time without any justification, inconsistent procedures adopted under similar circumstances, the provision of wrong information or documentation, or decisions that are not according to law or statutory procedures, any action the implementation of which causes undue inconvenience or any abuse of discretion'.[918]

444. The jurisdiction of the Local Governance Board overlaps with that of the Ombudsman. Between 25 July 1995 and 1 February 2010, the Ombudsman used to deal with complaints concerning maladministration in terms of section 12(1)(c) of the Ombudsman Act which provides for jurisdiction to hear complaints related to 'local councils and any committee thereof, mayors, councillors and members of staff of all local councils'.[919] Since 2 February 2010 – the date when the Local Governance Board was established – the Ombudsman continues to exercise his jurisdiction over complaints of maladministration over Local Councils (but not over Regional Committees, their officers and staff, and Administrative Committees). However, the Ombudsman does so after the Local Governance Board would not have provided any remedy to the complainant.

§15. Local Self-Government Twinning Agreements

445. Twinning, that is, 'a friendship agreement, co-operation or association between two communities in different countries or a friendship agreement, co-operation or association between Maltese Local Councils, even though this agreement is not expressly called twinning',[920] is regulated by the Local Councils Act and by the Local Councils (Twinning) Regulations. The former provides that a Local Council has 'the right to make twinning arrangements with any city, town, village or other locality in any other country'. But such twinning agreements require the Minister's approval and such approval, when given, would have been preceded by the Local Councils Association's opinion on such proposed twinning.[921] The Minister is empowered to make regulations to regulate twinning agreements between Local Councils.[922] The Local Councils (Twinning) Regulations supplement the provisions of the Local Councils Act by making further provision in relation to giving preference to twinning with a community within the EU rather than from a third country, the preparation of a report which has to be first submitted to the Director of the Department for Local Government for approval, the evaluation procedure of such a report, the signing of the twinning agreement, the budget, funding and expenses related to travelling abroad and the validity of signing of the twinning agreement.

918. *Ibid.*, regulation 2.
919. Chapter 385 of the Laws of Malta. Interestingly enough, this provision does not cover complaints related to Regional Committees and their officers and staff and Administrative Committees. In these instances, it is the Local Governance Board which enjoys jurisdiction, not the Ombudsman.
920. Local Councils (Twinning) Regulations, regulation 2.
921. Local Councils Act, section 79(1).
922. *Ibid.*, section 79(2).

§16. Delegation of Functions to Local Self-Government

446. Central government may delegate to Local Councils functions which are performed by the former to the latter. This enabling power is found in section 33(1)(w) and (x) of the Local Councils Act. However, such delegation comes into effect after the Minister has made the relevant order in the Gazette.

§17. Dissolution of Regional Committees and Local Councils

447. Unfortunately, there are certain situations listed in the Local Council Act where a drastic action has to be taken by central government favouring the dissolution of a Regional Committee or a Local Council. Such a measure is carried out by the President through an order published in the *Gazette*, acting in accordance with the advice of the Prime Minister, in the following cases:

(a) a report of the Auditor General for persistent breach of financial responsibilities; or
(b) persistent non-regard to the provisions of this Act after formal notice has been given by the Minister; or
(c) lack of agreement in electing the Mayor; or
(d) lack of agreement by the Council in approving its annual estimates; or
(e) a recommendation to that effect in a report by a board appointed under the Inquiries Act.[923]

448. Cases where the central government had to have recourse to such measure were in the case of the local councils of Sannat, in Gozo,[924] and Paula,[925] Mtarfa,[926] and Sliema,[927] in Malta.[928]

449. To an extent, such measure is undemocratic because it is not the residents of the locality in question who recall their democratically elected representatives but central government which imposes its will over the democratically elected representatives of the locality. There might also be situations where the local council is acting at the request and with the backing of the residents of the locality at issue.

450. A similar provision is contained in regulation 11 of the Regional Committees Regulations which applies to Regional Committees. No corresponding provision is however contained in the Local Councils Act which empowers the Minister responsible for local government to dissolve an Administrative Committee, nor even in the Administrative Committees for Communities Regulations.[929]

923. Local Councils Act, section 22.
924. Dissolution of the Sannat Local Council Order, Subsidiary Legislation 363.21.
925. Dissolution of the Paola Local Council Order, Subsidiary Legislation 363.33.
926. Dissolution of the Mtarfa Local Council Order, Subsidiary Legislation 363.137.
927. Dissolution of Tas-Sliema Local Council Order, Subsidiary Legislation 363.168.
928. There are no reported instances where Regional Committees have been dissolved.
929. Subsidiary Legislation 363.149.

§18. Joint Committees of Local Councils

451. The Local Councils Act allows two or more Local Councils to 'discharge any of their functions jointly and they may also arrange for the discharge of these functions by a joint committee of theirs or by an officer of one of them'.[930] Joint Committees have to be distinguished from Regional Committees because whilst in the latter case the membership of Regional Committees is selected from a pre-established list of Local Councils with the choice being one of geographical proximity, in the case of Joint Committees, these need not necessarily be established by Local Councils from within the list of Local Councils forming a Regional Committee. In all, there are nine Joint Committees.[931] Moreover, Joint Committees are established at a horizontal level while Regional Committees are established at a vertical level, that is, they are superior to Local Councils from a hierarchical point of view.[932]

§19. Local Self-Government Enforcement System

452. The Local Enforcement System Committee Regulations[933] establishes a Management Committee for the local self-government enforcement system, the functions whereof are:

(a) to draw up and implement a general policy regarding the local enforcement of any law, regulation or bye-law, the enforcement of which has been delegated to local councils; such policy may include parameters for the operation of any local enforcement;
(b) to review the workings of local enforcement in all localities, and to give such orders which it may deem appropriate to any Joint Committee, local council, operator or contractor appointed by the Committee or by the council for the carrying out of local enforcement, in all matters that are related to local enforcement;
(c) to ensure that wherever local enforcement is in place, the minimum requirements of service are followed as envisaged in the [Commissioners for Justice] Act, in the Private Guards and Local Wardens Act, in the Local Councils Act, and in the Local Councils (Delegation of Enforcement) Order;[934]
(d) to review the workings of the operation of local tribunals, and the procedures before such tribunals, and without prejudice to the rights and powers of the

930. Local Councils Act, section 37(1).
931. For a list of the nine Joint Committees, *see* Rolan Borg, *An Analysis and Evaluation of the Powers and Competences of the Local Wardens and the System of the Local Tribunals*, LL.D. thesis, Faculty of Laws, University of Malta, Msida, May 2008, pp. 80–81.
932. *See Protokoll Lokali u Reġjonali: Kodiċi li jirregola l-preċedenza u l-istatus tal-President tar-Reġjun, tas-Sindku, Viċi Sindku u l-Kunsillieri fil-Lokalità u Membri tal-Kumitati Amministrattivi* (Translation: Local and Regional Protocol: Code to regulate the order of precedence and the status of the President of the Region, the Mayor, Deputy Mayor, and Councillors of a Locality and Members of Administrative Committees), Department of Information, Valletta (undated).
933. Subsidiary Legislation 291.06.
934. Subsidiary Legislation 363.41.

Commissioners for Justice, to give orders and, or directives in this field to any person who is involved in these proceedings, except to the said Commissioners for Justice;

(e) to set up a Disciplinary Board which shall have the power to remove from service local wardens and private guards, and any other operator;

(f) to give its consent to, following an evaluation of all the circumstances, local councils regarding the places where, the times of operation and the purposes for which speed cameras and, or other traffic cameras may be installed; and

(g) to take such initiatives and measures as are required to improve coordination between all parties involved in the local enforcement of laws, regulations and bye-laws.

453. In February 2014, Government announced a reform of the local enforcement system through the publication of a White Paper entitled 'Reform of the Local Enforcement System'. A Local Enforcement System Agency (LESA) has recently been established on 1 October 2015.[935] 'This agency is the new regulator of the field and has taken over the responsibilities that were delegated to regional committees for the previous four years.'[936] The LESA was established after the government 'looked at the economies of scale of running such a system, and it was evident that the system was not sustainable, given that five different entities were tasked with running such a complex operation without having the proper resources, both in terms of manpower and financial capacity'.[937]

§20. Local Self-Government Machinery of Justice

454. There is a system of local tribunals which was originally set up in 2000 by means of the Local Councils (Delegation of Enforcement) Order.[938] Local Councils have been delegated enforcement functions through this Order. It is supplemented by the Local Tribunals (Delivery of Summons) Regulations,[939] the Local Tribunals (Establishment of Tribunals and Designation of Registry, Registrar and Other Officers) Regulations[940] and the Petitions (Local Tribunals) Regulations.[941]

455. Competent persons involved in the running of the local enforcement system comprise Authorized Officers who administer local tribunals, Commissioners for Justice who decide upon depenalized administrative offences brought before them by Prosecutors, and the Tribunal's Registrar and employees. In all, there are seven local

935. Local Enforcement System (Establishment As An Agency) Order, Subsidiary Legislation 497.14.
936. Stefan Buontempo, 'Enforcement agency's 100 days', *The Times of Malta*, 8 January 2016, p. 14.
937. *Ibid.*, 'Of Regional Committees and Devolutions', *The Times of Malta*, 29 December 2015, p. 40.
938. Subsidiary Legislation 363.41.
939. Subsidiary Legislation 291.01.
940. Subsidiary Legislation 291.02.
941. Subsidiary Legislation 291.04.

tribunals.[942] Finally, a word should be said about local wardens who enforce the local enforcement system. Local wardens are regulated by the Private Guard and Local Wardens Act.[943] It is Local Wardens who are responsible for issuing citations against those persons who would have contravened laws and regulations which fall within the competence of Local Wardens. Citations issued by a Local Warden may be contested before a Commissioner for Justice with an appeal to the Court of Magistrates in terms of the Commissioners for Justice Act.[944] A re-trial is also possible before the Court of Magistrates.[945] A Petitions Board also exists to hear petitions related to the local enforcement system.[946]

§21. Local Councils Association

456. The Local Councils Association is not specifically mentioned in the Local Councils Act. However, this enactment does provide that Local Councils are obliged to 'form part of an association recognized as such by the Government for the protection and promotion of their common interests'. Local Councils can also belong to international associations of local government authorities.[947] The Local Councils (Association) Regulations[948] establish the Local Councils Association; and regulate the appointment of the Association's Executive Committee; the office of Chairman of the Association; functions of the Association, its procedure and meetings; its officers and employees; its finances; and its Auditors.

457. The Local Councils Association is a consultant to Government on local self-government. Such function results from various provisions in the Local Councils Act such as sections 37A(4) and (5), 53(2), 72(4), and 79(1). At other times, it has to agree to a government measure as is the case with section 3(2A) of the Local Councils Act, before that measure can have effect.

§22. Local Councils and the Development Planning Process

458. In Malta, local self-government does not enjoy the duty of licensing development permissions within its region, locality or community; nor does it assume any responsibility for development planning for the land falling within its region, locality or community. Such a matter is regulated by central government through the MEPA. The three tiers of local self-government, nonetheless, do enjoy certain rights in relation to the development planning process limited to objecting against development

942. *See* https://les.gov.mt/tribunalinfo.aspx. Last accessed on 31 March 2016.
943. Chapter 389 of the Laws of Malta.
944. Commissioners for Justice Act, Chapter 291 of the Laws of Malta, section 11(1).
945. *Ibid.*, section 11A.
946. Petitions (Local Tribunals) Regulations, Subsidiary Legislation 291.04.
947. Local Councils Act, section 37(3).
948. Subsidiary Legislation 363.06.

permissions, appealing from the grant of a development permission or being consulted within the planning process.[949]

§23. Prohibition of Broadcasting by Local Councils

459. It is not allowed, in terms of law, for a Local Council to own a broadcasting station. This rule is set out both in the Local Councils Act and in the Broadcasting Act.

460. There is no prohibition against broadcasting by Regional Committees and Administrative Committees.

§24. The EU Dimension of Local Self-Government: The Committee of the Regions

461. The EU has got its own regional policy.[950] Malta, being a EU Member State, has a role to play within the EU.[951] This is because it is represented in the Committee of the Regions. Such role is recognized in the Local Councils Act:

> The Minister may also, after consulting the Local Councils Association, make regulations providing for the representation of Maltese Local Councillors on the Committee of Regions of the European Union and on any other international forum or institution requiring representation of local Councillors.[952]

§25. Concluding Remarks on Local Self-Government

462. Local self-government in Malta has not developed to the extent that it has done so within Europe. It is still very much subjugated to central government which still enjoys a very tight grip on local self-government to such an extent that the latter remains very much in a relationship of dependence. Although the functions of local self-government have, since 1993, increased incrementally, they still remain limited

949. For a discussion of local self-government in the context of development planning law, *see* Kevin Aquilina, *Development Planning Legislation: The Maltese Experience*, Mireva Publications, Msida, May 1999, and Kevin Aquilina and Isabelle Calleja Ragonesi, 'The Relations Between States and Local Authorities in the Context of Development Planning', in Stéphane Guérard and Algirdas Astrauskas (eds), *Local Autonomy in the 21st Century: Between Tradition and Modernisation*, Institut Universitaire Varenne, Paris, 2016, pp. 205–231.

950. For a study of the European Union's regional policy, *see* Didier Lhomme. 'La Politique Régionale Européenne: De L'Ancrage À L'Adaptation. Plaidoyer Pour Une Gouvernance Simplifiée?', in Emmanuel Cherner and Stéphane Guérard (eds), *La Régionalisation En Europe Regards Croisés*, Editions Bruylant, Brussels, 2014, pp. 65–111.

951. For a study of Maltese local self-government and the European Union, *see* Kevin Aquilina and Isabelle Calleja, 'Local Government in Malta', in Ángel Manuel Moreno Molina (ed.), *Local Government in the Member States of the European Union: A Comparative Legal Perspective*, Madrid, National Institute of Public Administration, Spain, 2012, pp. 435–458 at pp. 454–456.

952. Local Councils Act, section 72(4).

in purport. Suffice it to state that local self-government is heavily regulated by central government, has no taxing powers such that it has to rely predominantly on central government for its financial needs, and recruitment of its employees is prescribed by law-making it difficult for local self-government institutions to recruit personnel without central government approving requests for additional human resources which go beyond the statutory limited number. In addition, although Regional Committees have been established recently, they are in turn very limited in their functions when compared to Local Councils. Perhaps the situation should have been the obverse where central government devolves powers unto Regional Committees with the latter delegating powers to Local Councils. The time is now ripe to revisit local self-government in Malta to bring it more akin to the European experience so as to ensure that the Maltese system of local self-government does not remain a weak experience, devoid of proper powers, lacking the necessary clout, human resources and finances to be able to carry out at local level self-government functions on the same lines as their counterparts abroad.[953]

953. A latest report on local self-government making concrete contributions for reform is Centre of Expertise for Local Government Reform, *Peer Review on Local Government Reform in Malta*, Council of Europe, Strasbourg, Peer Review Report, 3 November 2014. A relevant document on local self-governance is Parliamentary Secretariat for Public Dialogue and Information, *Malta Policy for Local Governance 2009*, Valletta, undated.

Part IV. Citizenship and Fundamental Rights

Chapter 1. Citizenship

§1. Introduction to Maltese Citizenship Law

463. The most important link between a citizen and his/her state is citizenship. This point was made in the ICJ's judgment in the Nottebohm Case, *Liechtenstein v. Guatemala.*[954] The Court held that a genuine national link ties a citizen to his/her state:

> According to the practice of States, to arbitral and judicial decisions and to opinions of writers, nationality is a legal bond having as its basis a social fact of attachment, a genuine connection of existence, interests and sentiments, together with the existence of reciprocal rights and duties. It may be said to constitute the juridical expression of the fact that the individual upon whom it is conferred, either directly by the law or as the result of an act of the authorities, is in fact more closely connected with the population of the State conferring nationality than with that of any other State. Conferred by a State, it only entitles that State to exercise protection vis-á-vis another State, if it constitutes a translation into juridical terms of the individual's connection with the State which has made him its national.

464. Needless to say, the most serious crime a citizen can commit against his/her state is treason. For a subject or citizen to be naturalized in an enemy state during war is considered to be an act of treason.[955] Since independence, this bond has been breached with Britain, and Maltese citizens now owe their allegiance to the Republic of Malta, its organs, institutions and officers of the state.

465. Citizenship is regulated by Chapter III of the Constitution. As a matter of fact, the 1964 Constitution had ten provisions, but in the last twenty-five years, amendments were made to this Chapter to such an extent that only three provisions

954. *I.C.J. Reports* 1955, p. 4.

955. *Rex v. Lynch*, King's Bench Division, cited in *His Majesty the King v. Roberto Mallia et*, Criminal Court, 5 October 1946, *Collection of Decision of the Superior Courts of Malta*, Government Printing Press, Valletta, p. 631.

remain on citizenship in the Constitution. This chapter is however supplemented by an ordinary Act of Parliament, the Maltese Citizenship Act[956] which delves into greater detail with regard to citizenship as will be explained in this Chapter. In turn, this enactment is supplemented by three subsidiary laws which give flesh to the constitutional provisions, namely:

(a) the Citizenship Regulations;[957]
(b) the Deprivation of Maltese Citizenship (Committee of Inquiry) Rules;[958] and
(c) the Individual Investor Programme of the Republic of Malta Regulations.[959]

§2. The Constitutional Regulation of Citizenship

466. Eugène Buttigieg and Daniela DeBono have discussed in depth Maltese Citizenship Law. They opine that:

> Malta's legal regime on citizenship is relatively young as it came into being on the day of Malta's acquisition of independence from British rule in 1964. Throughout these years, however, particularly over the past 25 years, it has undergone extensive alterations marking changes in the governing principles. Malta's first citizenship provisions were a combined application of the ius soli and ius sanguinis principles with a strict prohibition of dual/multiple citizenship and in certain respects manifested a degree of gender inequality. Reforms in 1989, 2000 and 2007 bought about a radical change of policy regarding citizenship by in particular (i) reversing the prohibition against dual/multiple citizenship, in certain instances, even retrospectively, and extending dual citizenship not only to those who had been Maltese citizens by birth in Malta and lost this Maltese citizenship on emigrating but also to first, second and subsequent generations of Maltese born outside Malta and living abroad whose Maltese citizenship derived from descent rather than birth in Malta; (ii) shifting to a rule based more on ius sanguinis than on jus soli; and (iii) removing gender inequality. Apart from the existing routes by naturalisation and registration, a more recent reform in 2013 introduced a new route for the acquisition of Maltese citizenship through an investment scheme. This reform took many by surprise, in part because there was no other citizenship-by-investment scheme in existence up until then, but also because, as a policy, it marks a radical shift from the 'protectionist', 'arbitrary' and 'discretionary' policy of citizenship acquisition by naturalisation.[960]

956. Chapter 188 of the Laws of Malta.
957. Subsidiary Legislation 188.01.
958. Subsidiary Legislation 188.02.
959. Subsidiary Legislation 188.03.
960. Eugène Buttigieg and Daniela DeBono, *Country Report on Citizenship Law: Malta*, Revised and updated January 2015, European University Institute, Florence, Robert Schuman Centre for Advanced Studies and EUDO Citizenship Observatory, San Domenico di Fiesole, 2015, p. 1.

467. Section 22 of the Constitution states that the 'acquisition, possession, renunciation and loss of Maltese citizenship shall be regulated by law'. In other words, this provision simply sets out the framework within which citizenship law is to operate. But the details regulating the matters listed in this subsection are reserved to the Maltese Citizenship Act and to subsidiary legislation made thereunder. These aspects of citizenship law will be dealt with sequentially below.

§3. ACQUISITION OF CITIZENSHIP

468. Citizenship is according to the Maltese Citizenship Act acquired in different modes namely, through birth, marriage, adoption, descent, registration and naturalization. When it is acquired through birth, it is referred to as *jus soli* – acquisition of nationality by birth in the territory of a state – and when it is acquired through descent it is referred to as *jus sanguinis* – acquisition of nationality by descent whereby 'as a rule, an illegitimate child acquires at birth the nationality of the mother, a legitimate child that of his parents or, if the parents are of different nationalities, that of the father'.[961] The rules related to illegitimate, adopted children and foundlings are discussed below.

I. Birth

469. Birth may give rise to citizenship on two particular occasions:

(a) on or after the appointed day; or
(b) before the appointed day.

470. The appointed day for the purposes of the Constitution of Malta and of the Maltese Citizenship Act is the day on which the UK colony of Malta became an independent state. The 21 September 1964 was established as the appointed day by Her Majesty the Queen of the UK, Queen Elizabeth II, in terms of section 2 of the Malta Independence Order 1964. The latter Order was made under the UK Malta Independence Act, 1964.

A. On or After the Appointed Day

471. According to section 5(1) of the Maltese Citizenship Act, every person born in Malta on or after the appointed day 'shall be deemed to have become or shall become a citizen of Malta'. Three exceptions are however made to this rule:

(a) if a person is born on or after 31 July 1989, such person is not deemed to have become a Maltese citizen if at the time of his birth, neither of his parents were Maltese and his father possessed immunity from suit due to being an envoy of a

961. Paul Weis, *Nationality and Statelessness in International Law*, The Netherlands, Sijthoff & Noordhoff International Publishers B.V., 1979, p. 95.

sovereign power accredited to Malta, or his father was an enemy alien and the birth occurred in a place then under occupation by the enemy;

(b) if a person is born on or after 1 August 1989, such person is not deemed to have become a citizen of Malta unless at the time of birth, his father or mother was or is a citizen of Malta or was a person who had emigrated from Malta before, on, or after 21 September 1964, who was a citizen of Malta but ceased to be such a citizen; or who emigrated from Malta before 21 September 1964, ceased to be a citizen of the UK and Colonies but became a citizen of Malta in terms of the Maltese Citizenship (Amendment) Act, 2000;

(c) the provisions of paragraphs (a) and (b) above do not apply to 'a newborn infant found abandoned in any place in Malta who would in virtue thereof be stateless, and any such infant shall remain a citizen of Malta until his right to any other citizenship is established'.

B. Before the Appointed Day

472. In the case of those persons born in Malta before the appointed day who were citizens of the UK and Colonies, were in terms of section 3 of the Maltese Citizenship Act, 'deemed to have acquired Maltese citizenship on the appointed day'. But if neither of his/her parents were born in Malta, then such person would not have acquired Maltese citizenship on the appointed day.

II. Marriage

473. As in the case of birth, the Maltese Independence Act regulates acquisition of Maltese citizenship through marriage either on or after the appointed day, or before the appointed day.

A. On or after the Appointed Day

474. A person may be registered as a Maltese citizen because he/she marries a Maltese citizen. However, this registration is not automatic, and certain conditions have to be satisfied. First, the Minister must be satisfied that 'the grant of citizenship to such person is not contrary to the public interest'. Second, the applicant for registration must on the date of application still be married 'to a citizen of Malta or is the widow or widower of a person who was a citizen of Malta at the time of his/her death'. Third, no person is entitled for registration unless on the date of application he/she is still married to a citizen of Malta and has been so married for at least five years and on that date had been living with that citizen or, if on that date had been de jure or de facto separated, had lived with such citizen of Malta for at least five years after the celebration of the marriage, or is the widow or widower of such citizen and at the time of his/her death had been married to that person for at least five years and was still living with him/her or who would, 'but for the death of that person, have been so married on the date of the application or, if on the date of death of such citizen had been de jure or de facto separated from such citizen, had lived with such citizen of Malta for at least five years after the celebration of marriage'.[962]

B. Before the Appointed Day

475. Another provision relating to the acquisition of citizenship by marriage is found in section 4 of the Maltese Citizenship Act dealing with persons who before 21 September 1964 were married to a person who become on the appointed day a citizen of Malta or who would have so become were it not that he died before 21 September 1964.

III. Illegitimate Children, Adopted Children and Foundlings

476. In the case of a person born out of wedlock, that is, an illegitimate child, who has not been legitimated, the illegitimate child takes the citizenship of the mother.[963] In the case of a person who was lawfully adopted before 1 January 1977, the adopted child takes the nationality of the adopter and, in the case of a joint adoption, the adopted child takes the nationality of the male adopted.[964] In the case of a person under the age of 10 years who was lawfully adopted on or after 1 August 1989, his/her parents are the adopters.[965] If a newborn infant is 'found abandoned in any place in Malta, that infant shall, unless the contrary is shown, be deemed to have been born in Malta'.[966] With regard to posthumous children, the Maltese Citizenship Act provides that in the case of a person who is born after the death of his father, reference has to be made to the national status of the child's father at the time of the child's birth. If the father's death occurred before the appointed date but the child was born after the appointed date, the child takes the national status of the father as if the father would have died on the appointed date.[967]

IV. Descent

477. A person may acquire Maltese citizenship through descent where he/she has not been born in Malta but outside Malta. However, he/she does still have a connection with Malta through his/her parents or through one of such parents who were Maltese citizens or could have so become had he/she not emigrated from Malta before 21 September 1964. In this case, citizenship is said to be acquired by descent and is regulated by sections 3 and 5 of the Maltese Citizenship Act. Section 3 relates to birth outside Malta before the appointed date, and section 5 concerns birth outside Malta on or after the appointed day.

962. Maltese Citizenship Act, section 6(2).
963. *Ibid.*, section 17(1)(a).
964. *Ibid.*, section 17(1)(b).
965. *Ibid.*, section 17(1)(c).
966. *Ibid.*, section 17(3).
967. *Ibid.*, section 18.

V. Registration

478. Registration applies in a number of cases:

(a) in terms of sections 4 and 6 of the Maltese Citizenship Act where the applicant for registration:

- is married to a citizen of Malta; or
- the widow or widower of a person who was a citizen of Malta at the time of his/her death; or
- the widow or widower of a person who would, but for his/her death, have become a citizen of Malta; and
- has been so married for at least five years and is still living with his spouse; or
- is separated from his/her spouse with whom he/she had lived for at least five years after the celebration of marriage; or
- had lived with his/her spouse for at least five years after the celebration of marriage; or
- was still living with his/her spouse at the time of his/her death and a period of at least five years had elapsed from the date of his/her marriage.

(b) in terms of section 4(4) of the Maltese Citizenship Act where the applicant for registration:

- has been a citizen of Malta but has ceased to be such a citizen after emigrating from Malta; or
- having emigrated from Malta before the appointed day and would have become a citizen of Malta by birth in Malta before the appointed day and both of his/her parents were born in Malta but has ceased to be a citizen of the UK and Colonies before the appointed day.

(c) in terms of section 8 of the Maltese Citizenship Act where the applicant for registration has been a citizen of Malta and has ceased to be such a citizen;
(d) in terms of section 3(2) of the Maltese Citizenship Act where the applicant for registration was born outside Malta before the appointed day and his/her mother who became, or would, but for her death have become, a citizen of Malta in accordance with the provisions of section 3(1) of the Maltese Citizenship Act;
(e) in terms of section 5(2) of the Maltese Citizenship Act where the applicant for registration was born outside Malta on or after the appointed day, and before 1 August 1989 and that at the date of his/her birth his/her mother was a citizen of Malta otherwise than by section 3(2) or 5(2) of the Maltese Citizenship Act;
(f) in terms of section 3(3) or section 5(3) of the Maltese Citizenship Act where the applicant for registration was born outside Malta:

- before the appointed day or on or after the appointed day; and

- is the descendant in the direct line of an ascendant born in Malta of a parent likewise born in Malta.

VI. Naturalization

479. Naturalization can take place is several ways:

(a) in terms of section 10(4) of the Maltese Citizenship Act where the applicant for naturalization is a descendant of a person born in Malta;
(b) in terms of section 10(1) of the Maltese Citizenship Act where the applicant for naturalization has resided in Malta throughout the period of twelve months immediately preceding the date of application, and, during the six years immediately preceding the said period of twelve months, he or she has resided in Malta for periods amounting in the aggregate to not less than four years, is of good character and has adequate knowledge of Maltese or English;
(c) in terms of section 10(2) of the Maltese Citizenship Act where the applicant for naturalization:

- became a citizen of Malta by virtue of section 22(2) of the Maltese Citizenship Act; or
- would but for his death have become a citizen of Malta by virtue of section 3(2) of the Maltese Citizenship Act; or
- was at the time of his/her birth a citizen of Malta by virtue of section 5(2) of the Maltese Citizenship Act; or
- would but for his death have been at the time of his/her birth a citizen of Malta by virtue of section 5(2) of the Maltese Citizenship Act.

(d) in terms of section 10(3) of the Maltese Citizenship Act where the applicant for naturalization:

- has been a citizen of Malta by virtue of section 3 or section 5(1) of the Maltese Citizenship Act and has ceased to be such a citizen after emigrating from Malta; or
- has emigrated from Malta before the appointed day and would have become a Maltese citizen by virtue of section 3(1) of the Maltese Citizenship Act, were it not for having ceased to be a citizen of the UK and Colonies before that day, and have returned to, and taken up permanent residence in, Malta.

(e) in terms of section 10(6) of the Maltese Citizenship Act where the applicant for naturalization:

- has always been a stateless person, was born in Malta, was ordinarily resident in Malta and had been so resident throughout the period of five years ending with the date of application, and was not convicted in any country of an offence against the security of the State or was not sentenced in any country to a punishment restrictive of personal liberty for a term of not less than five years; or

- has always been a stateless person, either his/her father was a citizen of Malta at the date of his/her birth by virtue of the provisions of section 3 or section 5(2) of the Maltese Citizenship Act or his/her mother was at the date of her birth a citizen of Malta, was ordinarily resident in Malta and had been so resident throughout the period of three years ending with the date of application, and was not convicted in any country of an offence against the security of the State.

(f) in terms of section 10(9)(a) of the Maltese Citizenship Act where the applicant for naturalization is a spouse of any citizen of Malta when either the spouse or the said citizen has rendered exceptional services to the Republic of Malta or to humanity;
(g) in terms of section 10(9)(b) of the Maltese Citizenship Act 'to any person who is an applicant, or is a spouse or an eligible dependant of such applicant, under the individual investor programme of the Republic of Malta, and satisfies the requirements as prescribed under the [Maltese Citizenship] Act';
(h) in terms of section 11(1) of the Maltese Citizenship Act where the applicant for naturalization is the parent of a minor child where the parent is a citizen of Malta or where the applicant is the tutor of a minor child who is the son or daughter of a citizen of Malta.

§4. Possession of Citizenship

480. Citizenship continues to be possessed until the citizen opts to renounce it or else is deprived thereof.

§5. Renunciation of Citizenship

481. Renunciation of citizenship is regulated by section 13 of the Maltese Citizenship Act. Renunciation takes place by any Maltese citizen of full age and capacity, who is also a national of a foreign country, who makes a declaration renouncing Maltese citizenship.[968] Cases where the Minister may refuse to register such a declaration are when 'it is made during any war in which Malta may be engaged or if, in his opinion, it is otherwise contrary to public policy'.[969]

§6. Deprivation of Citizenship

482. Likewise, the Maltese Citizenship Act, in section 14, regulates loss of or deprivation of citizenship. What is however interesting to note about this provision is

968. *Ibid.*, section 13(1).
969. *Ibid.*, section 13(2).

that deprivation of citizenship can take place only in the case of registration or naturalization. Thus, if a person has obtained his/her citizenship through birth, such person's citizenship cannot be withdrawn. The list of cases listed above through which citizenship can be obtained by registration and naturalization is of the essence to determine whether a person can lose his/her citizenship.

I. Grounds for Deprivation of Citizenship

483. A further limitation on the competent Minister's power to deprive citizenship of registered and naturalized citizens arises only in the following cases where the citizen:

(a) has shown himself by act or speech to be disloyal or disaffected towards the President or the Government of Malta; or
(b) has, during any war in which Malta was engaged, unlawfully traded or communicated with an enemy or been engaged in or associated with any business that was to his knowledge carried on in such a manner as to assist an enemy in that war; or
(c) has, within seven years after becoming naturalized, or being registered as a citizen of Malta, been sentenced in any country to a punishment restrictive of personal liberty for a term of not less than twelve months; or
(d) has been ordinarily resident in foreign countries for a continuous period of seven years and during that period has neither:

  - been at any time in the service of the Republic or of an international organization of which the Government of Malta was a member; or
  - given notice in writing to the Minister of his intention to retain citizenship of Malta.

II. Procedure for Deprivation of Citizenship

484. The procedure for deprivation of citizenship is laid down in section 14(3)-(5) of the Maltese Citizenship Act and in subsidiary legislation made under section 14(5) as follows:

(a) section 14(3): the Minister cannot deprive a person of his/her citizenship 'unless he is satisfied that it is not conducive to the public good that that person should continue to be a citizen of Malta and, … it appears to him that that person would not thereupon become stateless';
(b) section 14(4): the person whose citizenship is proposed to be deprived has to be informed of the ground therefor and of his right to an inquiry whereby the Minister refers 'the case to a committee of inquiry consisting of a chairman, being a person possessing judicial experience, appointed by the Minister and of such other members appointed by the Minister as he thinks proper';

(c) section 14(5): the Minister may make rules 'for the practice and procedure to be followed in connection with a committee of inquiry appointed under this article, and such rules may, in particular, provide for conferring on any such committee any powers, rights or privileges of any court, and for enabling any powers so conferred to be exercised by one or more members of the committee'; and
(d) the Deprivation of Maltese Citizenship (Committee of Inquiry) Rules[970] which set out the procedure to be followed by the Committee of Inquiry when considering cases referred to it by the Minister.

§7. Statelessness

485. The term 'stateless' is defined in section 2 of the Maltese Citizenship Act as being destitute of any nationality, and a stateless person is a person with no nationality.

§8. Dual or Multiple Citizenship

486. When dealing with dual or multiple citizenship, the 1964 Constitution expressly excluded the possibility of a Maltese citizen enjoying a dual nationality. Section 28 of the independence Constitution did not contemplate the possibility of multiple citizenship. It simply excluded dual citizenship thereby prohibiting, without the need of saying it, multiple citizenship. Things changed in the year 2000 when the Constitution was amended to allow not only dual but even multiple citizenship: 'Dual or multiple citizenship is permitted in accordance with any law for the time being in force in Malta.'[971] The law which permits dual or multiple citizenship is the Maltese Citizenship Act. Part IV of the Maltese Citizenship Act is entitled 'Multiple Citizenship' consisting in three provisions. The first has it that it shall be 'lawful for any person to be a citizen of Malta, and at the same time a citizen of another country'.[972] This provision is stating nothing new but is simply repeating the principle laid down in the Constitution of dual and multiple citizenship. The second provides that any person who in the past had to renounce his/her Maltese citizenship in favour of a foreign citizenship simply because Malta did not accept dual or multiple citizenship can now apply to be registered as a Maltese citizen. Such re-acquisition of Maltese citizenship may, nonetheless, not be allowed if the Minister responsible for citizenship is satisfied that it is 'contrary to the public interest'.[973] No definition is however afforded as to what constitutes the 'public interest'. The third states that when any person was a Maltese citizen prior to the coming into force of the provision allowing dual and multiple citizenship, he/she is deemed not to have ever ceased to be a citizen of Malta simply because he/she has 'resided in any country outside Malta for an aggregate period of at least six years and acquired or retained the citizenship of any other country'.[974]

970. Subsidiary Legislation 188.02.
971. Constitution, section 22(2).
972. Maltese Citizenship Act, section 7.
973. Maltese Citizenship Act, section 8.
974. *Ibid.*, section 9.

§9. Commonwealth Citizens

487. Maltese citizens are automatically, by operation of the Constitution, Commonwealth citizens. Malta is a member of the Commonwealth of Nations and by virtue of that membership, Malta can afford a provision in its Constitution stating that Maltese citizens are Commonwealth citizens. The Constitution does not state, nevertheless, what are the advantages of being a Commonwealth citizen and what protection, benefit or privilege does a Maltese citizen enjoy by virtue of being a Commonwealth citizen. Section 23 of the Constitution deals with Commonwealth citizenship. Subsection (1) reads as follows:

> 1. Every person who under the Constitution or any Act or Parliament is a citizen of Malta or under any enactment for the time being in force in any country to which this article applies is a citizen of that country shall, by virtue of that citizenship, have the status of a Commonwealth citizen.

488. In terms of the above provision, there is no need for a Maltese citizen to apply to obtain Commonwealth citizenship. Furthermore, the citizens of those countries listed in the Fourth Schedule to the Constitution benefit from Commonwealth citizenship. But to enjoy Commonwealth citizenship, a person must be a citizen of Malta or one (or more) of the countries listed in the Fourth Schedule. However, other statutes which a person may enjoy, even concurrent with citizenship, such as permanent residence, habitual residence, residence and domicile do not qualify for Commonwealth citizenship: it is only nationality which does. However, an exception to this rule is found in subsection (2) which does allow a non-citizen to be a Commonwealth citizen:

> Every person who is a British subject without citizenship under the British Nationality Act, 1948, or who continues to be a British subject under article 2 of that Act shall by virtue of that status have the status of a Commonwealth citizen.

489. According to subsection (3), this provision applies to those countries listed in the Fourth Schedule to the Constitution. Subsection (4) then empowers the President, by Proclamation, to 'amend, add to, revoke or substitute the list of countries in the Fourth Schedule to this Constitution'.[975]

§10. Criminal Liability of Commonwealth Citizens

490. The Constitution contains a provision dealing with the criminal liability of Commonwealth citizens. A Commonwealth citizen who:

(a) is not a citizen of Malta; nor
(b) is not a citizen of the Republic of Ireland and also not a citizen of Malta,

975. Constitution, section 23(4). The list of Commonwealth countries in found in the Fourth Schedule.

is not guilty 'of an offence against any law in force in Malta by reason of anything done or omitted in any part of the Commonwealth other than Malta or in the Republic of Ireland or in any foreign country' unless two conditions are satisfied. First, the act or omission would constitute an offence if he were an alien, that is, a person who is not a Commonwealth citizen, a British protected person – that is, 'a person who is a British protected person for the purposes of the British Nationality Act, 1948, or any other law of the United Kingdom replacing that Act', or a citizen of the Republic of Ireland. The second condition which also has to be satisfied is that 'in the case of an act or omission in any part of the Commonwealth or in the Republic of Ireland, it would be an offence if the country in which the act was done or the omission made were a foreign country'. By 'foreign country', it is meant a country (other than the Republic of Ireland) that is not part of the Commonwealth.

§11. European Union Citizenship

491. Article 20 of the TFEU states that: 'Citizenship of the Union is hereby established. Every person holding the nationality of a Member State shall be a citizen of the Union. Citizenship of the Union shall be additional to and not replace national citizenship.'[976] EU citizenship has a practical bearing, for instance, insofar as local councils elections are concerned. This is because in terms of section 5(2) of the Local Councils Act, every person 'who is a national of a Member State of the EU who, after the publication of the last revised European Union Electoral Register, attained or shall attain the age of sixteen years up to the day and including the day preceding the date on which the election of 2015 onwards of the Local Council or the Administrative Committee is to be held, and who has not been convicted of any offence connected with the election of members of Local Councils or of the Administrative Committee shall be entitled to vote in elections of the Local Councils and of the Administrative Committees'.

§12. The Individual Investor Programme

492. The Individual Investor Programme is regulated by the Maltese Citizenship Act and by the Individual Investor Programme of the Republic of Malta Regulations.[977] The former empowers the President of Malta to make regulations 'for prescribing the requirements for and administration of the individual investor programme and for the granting of a certificate of naturalization as a citizen of Malta to an applicant, and spouse and eligible dependants of such applicant, meeting the requirements as may be prescribed'.[978]

493. Section 25 empowers the Prime Minister, after consulting the Leader of the Opposition, to appoint a Regulator 'for the purposes of the correct implementation

976. Official Journal, C 326, 26 October 2012, pp. 47–390.
977. Subsidiary Legislation 188.03.
978. Maltese Citizenship Act, section 24(1)(j).

and monitoring of the individual investor programme'. Such person has to be selected from amongst:

(a) retired judges, magistrates and Attorney Generals;
(b) Permanent Secretaries; or
(c) advocates who have practised their profession in Malta for a period of at least twelve years.

494. Should there be no regulator in office, it shall be the Ombudsman who shall be appointed Regulator. The law does not set out the duration of office of Regulator or whether it is renewable and for how many terms. It simply states that the Regulator 'shall hold office in accordance with the terms of his appointment'.[979] No remuneration is established in the law, but it is left in the hands of the Prime Minister to determine. The Regulator has to 'keep under review all aspects of the individual investor programme'[980] and in the discharge of his/her functions, he/she acts in 'his individual judgment and shall not be subject to the direction and control of any other person or authority'.[981] Persons involved in the administration of the individual investor programme are bound to 'disclose or give to the Regulator such documents or information as he may require for the purpose of enabling him to discharge his functions'.[982] The Regulator must draw up an annual report and it has to be laid on the table of the House.[983] Finally, the Regulator is entrusted with the investigation of complaints on the individual investor programme.[984] A Monitoring Committee is established by the Maltese Citizenship Act to monitor the workings of the individual investor programme.[985]

495. The Individual Investor Programme of the Republic of Malta Regulations establish the said programme which allows for 'the grant of citizenship by a certificate of naturalization to foreign individuals and their families who contribute to the economic development of Malta'.[986] The regulations set out the qualifications and general requirements for naturalization,[987] the eligibility criteria,[988] the ineligibility criteria,[989]

979. *Ibid.*, section 25(2).
980. *Ibid.*, section 25(3).
981. *Ibid.*, section 25(5).
982. *Ibid.*, section 25 (6).
983. *Ibid.*, section 25(8) and (9). Two such reports have already been laid on the Table of the House. *See* Godwin Grima, Office of the Regulator, Individual Investor Programme, *First Annual Report of the IIP Programme of the Government of Malta*, Valletta, October 2014 (Papers Laid, Sitting No. 239 of 17 February 2015) and *Second Annual Report on the IIP Programme of the Government of Malta*, Valletta, October 2015 (Papers Laid 5897, Sitting No. 314 of 26 October 2015).
984. Maltese Citizenship Act, section 25A.
985. *Ibid.*, section 25B.
986. Individual Investor Programme of the Republic of Malta, Subsidiary Legislation 188.03, regulation 3.
987. *Ibid.*, regulation 4.
988. *Ibid.*, regulation 5.
989. *Ibid.*, regulation 6.

the application process,[990] refund of fees and contributions,[991] dissemination of information,[992] deprivation of citizenship,[993] forms and procedural guidelines,[994] maximum number of admissions,[995] the National Development and Social Fund,[996] disclosure[997] and fees.[998]

990. *Ibid.*, regulation 7.
991. *Ibid.*, regulation 8.
992. *Ibid.*, regulation 9.
993. *Ibid.*, regulation 10.
994. *Ibid.*, regulation 11.
995. *Ibid.*, regulation 12.
996. *Ibid.*, regulation 13.
997. *Ibid.*, regulation 14.
998. *Ibid.*, regulation 15.

Chapter 2. The General Aspects of Fundamental Rights and Freedoms

§1. Introduction

496. Chapter IV of the Constitution contains a detailed 'Bill of Rights', consisting in sixteen provisions, from sections 32–47. These provisions encapsulate the so-called civil and political rights. Chapter 2 of the Constitution, on the other hand, relates to the social, economic and cultural rights, contained in sections 7–21.

497. The very first provision of the Constitution, as amended in 1974, declares Malta to be 'a democratic republic founded on work and on respect for the fundamental rights and freedoms of the individual'. Section 65(1) of the Constitution obliges Parliament to make laws 'in conformity with full respect for human rights'.

498. The Constitution refers to human rights both in section 1(1) and in section 32 – the preamble to the human rights and fundamental freedoms provisions of the Constitution – as 'fundamental rights and freedoms of the individual'.

499. Five points need to be made at this juncture.

500. First, fundamental rights and freedoms are restricted to civil and political rights as contained in Chapter IV, sections 33–46, of the Constitution.

501. Second, although section 65(1) refers to 'human rights', that expression should be interpreted in a wide manner, that is, by applying it not only to fundamental rights and freedoms of the individual but to all types of human rights and fundamental freedoms and of whatever generation they might be. This is because the Constitution does not exclude any human right from its purview.

502. Third, the provisions of section 1(1) of the Constitution do not apply to the social, economic and cultural rights as the words used are not 'human rights' as in section 65(1) but 'fundamental rights and freedoms of the individual', that is Chapter IV rights.

503. Fourth, although the term 'individual' is used in Chapter IV of the Constitution, this does not mean that fundamental rights and freedoms are restricted only to individuals and cannot be enjoyed by legal persons. Indeed, in Chapter IV, the Constitution refers to a 'person'. This term is not defined in the interpretation provision of Chapter IV, nor in the interpretation provision of the Constitution. Recourse thus has to be had, in terms of section 124(14) of the Constitution to the Interpretation Act.[999] The latter defines the expression 'person' in section 4(d) as including 'a body or other association of persons whether granted legal personality, in accordance with the provisions of the Second Schedule to the Civil Code, or not'.

504. Fifth, the human rights and fundamental freedoms' provisions of the Constitution are not exhaustive. This is because they are supplemented by other human rights and fundamental freedoms' provisions contained in ordinary law. Whilst Chapter IV of the Constitution can be considered to be Malta's Bill of Rights as J.J. Cremona

999. Chapter 249 of the Laws of Malta.

calls it, Malta has a second Bill of Rights in the form of the European Convention Act and a third Bill of Rights in the form of the EU Charter of Fundamental Rights. Therefore, there is a fourfold set of legislation enunciating human rights and fundamental freedoms in Maltese Constitutional Law consisting as follows:

(a) Chapter IV of the Constitution;
(b) the European Convention Act;
(c) the EU Charter of Fundamental Rights; and
(d) other ordinary legislations encompassing human rights and fundamental freedoms legislation.

505. As noted below, apart from Chapter IV of the Constitution, there are other provisions in the organic law of the Republic which refer to human rights and fundamental freedoms such as sections 1(1) and 65(1).

506. As to the European Convention Act, at least at the moment of writing, Malta has signed and ratified Protocol No. 12 to the ECHR which came into effect in Malta on 1 April 2016. But legislation still needs to be drawn up to have it incorporated into Maltese Law so that it can be enforced by domestic courts as part of the law of the land.

507. Insofar as other ordinary laws providing for human rights and fundamental freedoms' provisions are concerned, there are several such provisions which, contrary to Chapter IV of the Constitution, do not attract the primacy of protection as those rights and freedoms contained in Chapter IV of the Constitution do. The latter laws can therefore be altered by a simple majority vote in the House. Furthermore, when referring to ordinary laws which afford protection to human rights and fundamental freedoms, reference is being made to those rights and freedoms which emerge from Chapter IV of the Constitution and not to those rights and freedoms enjoyed by persons in Malta which are totally alien to Chapter IV rights and freedoms. For instance, the protection of journalistic sources in terms of the Press Act is a civil right which derives from section 41 of the Constitution – freedom of expression. But the right to divorce in the Civil Code does not derive from a human right in the Constitution. Hence a distinction is appropriate at this juncture between human rights and civil rights. Human rights are those rights contained in the Constitution, the ECHR and the EU Charter of Fundamental Rights and in ordinary laws which are derived from Chapter IV, the ECHR and the EU Charter whilst civil rights in this context are all those rights which are afforded by ordinary law but which are not contained in the Constitution, ECHR or EU Charter but derived from these three set of legal instruments. The ordinary laws which derive from, or supplement, Chapter IV of the Constitution include the following:

(a) the Gender Identity, Gender Expression and Sex Characteristics Act[1000] insofar as gender identity has been included in the 2014 constitutional amendments to sections 32 and 45 of the Constitution related to discrimination on the basis of gender identity;

1000. Chapter 540 of the Laws of Malta.

(b) freedom of expression insofar as broadcasting is concerned in terms of section 11(1)(a) of the Broadcasting Act[1001] and in relation to freedom of reception and freedom of retransmission in section 16(1)(a) and (b) of the same enactment;
(c) non-discrimination provisions contained, for instance, in the Criminal Code,[1002] Press Act,[1003] the Equal Opportunities (Persons with Disability) Act[1004] and the Equality for Men and Women Act;[1005]
(d) freedom of expression in relation to journalistic freedoms as enshrined in section 46 of the Press Act;[1006]
(e) Articles 5 and 6 rights of the ECHR as incorporated both in the Criminal Code and in the Code of Organization and Civil Procedure;
(f) freedom of expression insofar as freedom of information is concerned in the Freedom of Information Act;[1007]
(g) children's rights as contained in the Commissioner for Children Act;[1008]
(h) human rights of older persons in terms of the Commissioner for Older Persons Act;[1009]
(i) patients' rights in terms of the Health Act;[1010] and
(j) privacy rights in terms of the Data Protection Act.[1011]

§2. The Preambular Status of Section 32 of the Constitution

508. Although fundamental rights and freedoms are contained in Chapter IV of the Constitution, it must be pointed out that section 32 – the very first provision of Chapter IV – is more in the nature of a non-binding preamble. Indeed, in terms of section 46 of the Constitution – the enforcement provision for fundamental rights and freedoms – no reference is made in that provision to section 32. Instead, reference is made to sections 33–45, both inclusive. In other words, the protective mechanism in the Constitution does not extend to the preamble to Chapter IV.

509. The Preamble to Chapter IV limits fundamental rights and freedoms to the individual when it provides that 'every person in Malta is entitled to the fundamental rights and freedoms of the individual', the same wording which as a matter of fact is used in section 1(1) of the Constitution. The person is thus qualified in these two provisions as referring only to an 'individual', that is, to a physical not to a legal person. Yet sections 33–45 do not refer to an 'individual' but to a person and, in very limited

1001. Chapter 350 of the Laws of Malta.
1002. Chapter 9 of the Laws of Malta.
1003. Chapter 248 of the Laws of Malta.
1004. Chapter 413 of the Laws of Malta.
1005. Chapter 468 of the Laws of Malta. This Act is being proposed to be repealed by a new Equality Act. *See* Ministry for Social Dialogue, Consumer Affairs and Civil Liberties, *Towards a Robust Human Rights & Equality Framework: Consultation on Bills', Valletta, 10 December 2015.*
1006. Chapter 248 of the Laws of Malta.
1007. Chapter 496 of the Laws of Malta.
1008. Chapter 462 of the Laws of Malta, section 13(6)(a).
1009. Chapter 553 of the Laws of Malta, section 17.
1010. Chapter 528 of the Laws of Malta, sections 27–29.
1011. Chapter 440 of the Laws of Malta.

cases, to a citizen of Malta and, in one case, to a resident of Malta. The expression 'person' applies to citizens of Malta, residents in Malta and to foreigners who happen to be in Malta, all of whom can fall within the nomenclature of an 'individual'. Needless to say, 'citizen' when compared to a 'person' has a narrow meaning as it is singling out one type of person – the citizen of Malta, thereby excluding non-citizens. The same point can be made for the resident of Malta which, although it may include both citizens and non-citizens within its fold, excludes non-residents. In section 41(3) of the Constitution, there is a reference to 'anyone who is resident in Malta', whilst sections 43(3) and 44(1)-(4) refer to a 'citizen of Malta'. Strictly speaking, the Constitution grants fundamental rights and freedoms to individuals. However, although the Constitution has excluded a legal person from sections 1(1) and 32, can it be said that it has done so with regard to sections 33–45? If one were to adopt a literal approach the answer would be in the negative; if one were to interpret sections 33–45 by reference to sections 1(1) and 32, the answer would be in the affirmative. The Constitutional Court has used section 32 as an aid of construction of sections 33–45 and concluded that 'person' has to be interpreted in terms of section 124(14) of the Constitution, that is, by reference to the Interpretation Act, Chapter 249 of the Laws of Malta, which construes a 'person' both as a physical person and a legal person.[1012]

§3. The Inviolability of Constitutional Rights and Freedoms

510. Once human rights and fundamental freedoms are declared by the Constitution to be 'fundamental' this means that these rights are inviolable. Although the Constitution does not refer to the principle of inviolability of human rights and fundamental freedoms, it does so indirectly when it declares them to be fundamental and ensures their protection through the enforcement mechanism found in section 46. The same cannot however be said of the economic, social and cultural rights contained in Chapter II of the Constitution which are not justiciable in terms of section 21 and therefore their violation does not lead to any legal consequence, although it may lead to political or moral consequences. By comparing sections 21 and 32 of the Constitution, on the one hand, and sections 33–45 on the other hand, it is clear that by 'fundamental', the Constitution means inviolable. 'Fundamental' raises the status of Chapter IV rights over Chapter 2 principles, thereby ensuring respect therefor by one and all the three organs of the state and all state institutions and public officers. Fundamental rights are also protected by the alteration provision of the Constitution which mandates that they can be amended only by a vote of at least not less than a two-thirds majority of the House.[1013] The alteration provision of the Constitution ensures that the Executive cannot amend human rights and fundamental freedoms without the consent of the Opposition. On the other hand, the economic, social and cultural rights contained in Chapter II of the Constitution may be amended by an absolute majority of the members of the House and thus do not attract the same status as Chapter IV rights. Chapter II rights may be altered by

1012. A recent pronouncement to this effect by the Constitutional Court is *Commissioner of Land v. Maria Theresa Deguara Caruana Gatto et* of 6 September 2010.
1013. Section 66(2).

the Executive without the involvement of the Opposition once the party in government in a two-party duopoly enjoys a majority in the House.

§4. The Beneficiaries of Fundamental Rights and Freedoms

I. Physical Persons and Legal Persons

511. The beneficiaries of fundamental rights and freedoms are: individuals, citizens, non-citizens and residents. These four categories have however been extended by the courts of constitutional competence to include legal persons. One may argue that a legal person may, in certain circumstances embody the manifestation of the will of a person or of a plurality of individuals. For instance, a number of individuals can come together to form a non-governmental association (such as a band club, football team, foundation and social group) or a commercial association (a company, a bank or a partnership). However, one must bear in mind that once these bodies corporate are created, they enjoy their own distinct and separate personality from that of their founders, directors, managers, beneficiaries or members. In this respect, the Constitution, as such, does not appear at face value to afford fundamental rights and freedoms to legal persons, but the courts of constitutional competence have ascribed such a status to legal persons. Contrary to the Italian Constitution, the Maltese Constitution does not have a provision that guarantees fundamental rights and freedoms to the person 'both as an individual, and as a member of the social groups in which their personality finds expression'[1014] thus protecting both the individual and those legal persons in which the individual finds his/her expression. Something similar is found in section 42(1) of the Constitution which refers to a person being able 'to form or belong to trade or other unions or associations for the protection of his interests'. Implied in these words is the fact that even trade unions or other unions should enjoy the protection of freedom of assembly and association as their members do. But does this also mean that such trade unions or other unions should also enjoy the protection of all other fundamental rights and freedoms? Whilst the European Convention Act and the ECHR answer this question unhesitatingly in the positive, the constitutional provision provides no answer.

512. The courts of constitutional competence have, nevertheless, boldly, adopted a proactive stance by allowing legal persons to enjoy fundamental rights and freedoms under the Constitution even if *stricto jure* the Constitution seems very cautious in granting such protection. So legal persons and social groupings such as the family, non-governmental organizations, political parties, trade unions, employers' associations, civil society associations, foundations, trusts, companies, civil and commercial partnerships, economic associations, funds, minority organizations, interest groups, and other groupings of more than one person, howsoever designated, would be protected by the Constitution's fundamental rights and freedoms through the interpretation given by the courts of constitutional competence to the word 'person' as contained in sections 33–45 of the Constitution, where the context allows the interpretation of the term

1014. Section 2 of the Constitution of Italy.

'person' to extend to a legal person. Paragraphs 53 and 54 of the Constitutional Court's judgment in the names of *Commissioner of Land v. Maria Theresa Deguara Caruana Gatto et of 6 September 2010* is a vindication of this interpretation.

II. Citizens and Non-nationals

513. In Chapter IV, the Constitution refers to 'persons' meaning both citizens and non-citizens, the latter term including both residents who are not Maltese citizens and foreigners. Insofar as citizenship is concerned, the Constitution refers to the concept of Commonwealth citizens in section 23; and in terms of Article 20 of the TFEU, all Maltese citizens are automatically EU citizens. Yet when it refers to a citizen of Malta, it excludes from this category Commonwealth citizens and EU citizens who are not Maltese citizens.

514. Apart from the provisions of sections 43(3) and 44(1)-(4) of the Constitution, any foreigner enjoys the same fundamental rights and freedoms as a citizen of Malta, when such foreigner happens to be in Malta. This means that, barring a few exceptions, the Constitution recognizes fundamental rights and freedoms, as applicable, to every human being in Malta.

§5. The European Convention Act: An Adjunct to the Constitution

515. The Constitution is not the only piece of Maltese legislation that contains fundamental rights and freedoms. This is because the European Convention Act has incorporated into Maltese Law the text of the ECHR and relevant protocols which provide substantive human rights and fundamental freedoms provisions. Although the Convention is not incorporated in the Constitution, it is incorporated into an ordinary primary law. This ordinary law is also superior to all other ordinary laws but inferior in status to the Constitution and on the same footing as the Emergency Powers Act, the Diplomatic Immunities and Privileges Act, the European Convention Act, and the European Union Act. In this respect, the ECHR applies both to citizens and to foreigners in Malta.

516. Insofar as the European Convention Act is concerned, the law does not restrict the expression 'person' to an 'individual'. On the contrary, section 2 of the European Convention Act defines the expression 'person' as including 'any physical person, non-governmental organization or groups of individuals'. The ECHR uses the term 'everyone' which includes both physical and legal persons.

§6. Fundamental Rights under the Maltese Constitution and International Legal Norms

517. As stated above, Malta has incorporated the ECHR in its own domestic law. This, however, has been the case only since 1987. Prior to that date, although

Malta was bound by the provisions of the ECHR on an international plane since 1966,[1015] the Convention's provisions did not form part of Malta's domestic law until the Convention was incorporated into Maltese Law.[1016]

518. The EU Charter of Fundamental Rights is also part of Maltese Law in relation to EU Law in terms of the European Union Act. A number of EU Laws give effect to the Charter's provisions, and these EU Laws apply to Malta as well.

519. Malta has, in the meantime, adhered to several human rights and fundamental freedoms conventions which have also found their place on the Maltese Statute Book. David Joseph Attard provides a list of these conventions.[1017]

520. In addition, as an EU Member State, Malta is bound by several EU laws which grant human rights and fundamental freedoms such as the rights to interpretation, translation of essential documents, access to all the materials of the case, legal assistance during interrogation and others availed of during criminal proceedings.

§7. European Multi-Level System for the Protection of Fundamental Rights and Freedoms

521. Insofar as the protection of fundamental rights and freedoms at European level is concerned, regard has to be had to the ECtHR and to the Court of Justice of the European Union (CJEU). Insofar as the EU Charter is concerned, although adopted in 2000, it was only in 2009 with the Treaty of Lisbon[1018] that it achieved binding force. Like EU institutions, Malta is bound by the EU Charter insofar as EU Law is concerned. Article 6 of the Treaty on European Union reads as follows:

(1) The Union recognises the rights, freedoms and principles set out in the Charter of Fundamental Rights of the European Union of 7 December 2000, as adapted at Strasbourg, on 12 December 2007, which shall have the same legal value as the Treaties ...
(2) The Union shall accede to the European Convention for the Protection of Human Rights and Fundamental Freedoms ...
(3) Fundamental rights, as guaranteed by the European Convention for the Protection of Human Rights and Fundamental Freedoms and as they result from the constitutional traditions common to the Member States, shall constitute general principles of the Union's law.

522. At the moment of writing, the EU has not yet adhered to the ECHR.

1015. *See* Kevin Aquilina, 'The Legislative Development of Human Rights and Fundamental Freedoms in Malta: A Chronological Appraisal' in Norman A. Martínez Gutiérrez, *Serving the Rule of International Law: Essays in Honour of Professor David Joseph Attard,* First Volume, Mare Nostrum Publications, Gudja, 2009, pp. 225–247 at p. 235.

1016. *Ibid.*, pp. 235–236.

1017. *See* David Joseph Attard, *supra* note 25, pp. 141–142, note 439.

1018. O.J. 2007/C 306/01.

§8. Fundamental Rights and the European Convention of Human Rights

523. Fundamental rights and the ECHR, the contribution of Maltese judges on the ECtHR, Maltese Courts applying the ECHR and the ECtHR's decisions, and the implementation of the ECtHR decisions in Malta have already been discussed elsewhere.[1019]

§9. The Principle of Equality

524. The principle of equality is not specifically set out in the Constitution. But it can be considered to be the basis of the principle against non-discrimination protected by section 45 of the Convention. Contrary to section 14 of the ECHR, section 45 of the Constitution is not linked to the 'enjoyment of the rights and freedoms set forth' in the ECHR but may be protected without any correlation to any other rights and freedoms protected by the Constitution. A law cannot be 'discriminatory either of itself or in its effects'. This implies that laws and their effects should guarantee formal equality between all persons. The principle of equality binds the legislature which enacts the laws, the executive which gives effect to the law and the judiciary which interprets it. The law enshrining this principle is expected to change.[1020]

§10. Two Instruments for the Protection of Fundamental Rights and Freedoms

525. Fundamental rights and freedoms are regulated on a twofold basis. The first tier is contained in Chapter IV of the Constitution. The second tier is found in ordinary law. The most relevant of ordinary laws is the European Convention Act. But there are several other laws which contain civil rights which attract the protection of the law.[1021] At this stage, it is relevant to distinguish between fundamental rights and non-fundamental rights in the form of civil rights. To put it simply, a fundamental right is one which is included in either Chapter IV of the Constitution, in the European Convention Act and in the EU Charter. Fundamental rights are divided into human rights and fundamental freedoms. The former are civil rights (though not all civil rights

1019. Fundamental rights and the ECHR are discussed in Kevin Aquilina, *supra* note 1015, pp. 235–238, whilst the other aspects are discussed in Mark A. Sammut et al., *supra* note 205, pp. 314–334.

1020. *See* Ministry for Social Dialogue, Consumer Affairs and Civil Liberties, *White Paper: Towards the Establishment of the Human Rights and Equality Commission*, Valletta, 10 December 2014; Chief Justice Emeritus Joseph Said Pullicino, Ombudsman, *Reflections on the White Paper 'Towards the Establishment of the Human Rights and Equality Commission'*, Office of the Ombudsman, Valletta, July 2015; Kevin Aquilina, 'Human Rights and Equality', *The Times of Malta*, 15 October 2015, p. 16; Ministry for Social Dialogue, Consumer Affairs and Civil Liberties, *Towards a Robust Human Rights and Equality Framework: Consultation on Bills*, Valletta, 10 December 2015.

1021. *See* Mark A. Sammut, note 205, *supra* pp. 302–303.

are human rights) and the latter are political rights. Civil and political rights are first generation rights as distinguished from other generations of human rights.[1022]

§11. Judicial Remedies for the Protection of Fundamental Rights and Freedoms

526. Judicial remedies for the protection of fundamental rights and freedoms come in various ways. These include the following:

(a) the constitutional law remedy under section 46 of the Constitution;
(b) the conventional remedy under section 4 of the European Convention Act;
(c) the remedy under EU Law;[1023]
(d) the reporting machinery under various international human rights law to which Malta is a member;
(e) remedies granted under ordinary law; and
(f) remedies under section 116 of the Constitution.

527. The remedy provided by section 116 of the Constitution is ex post facto, that is, after a law which is invalid has been assented to. The issue however arises as to whether it is possible for a court to issue a warrant of prohibitory injunction so that a law is not enacted because it might be inconsistent with the Constitution. In the UK, the answer is in the negative. Owen Hood Phillips maintains that:

> Dixon C.J. later more than once expressed the opinion that an injunction to restrain the presentation of a Bill for the Royal Assent ought not to be granted at any stage of the legislative process, the proper remedy being to apply for a declaration of invalidity after the statute has been enacted (Hughes & Vale Pty. Ltd. v. Gair (1954) 90 C.L.R. 203; Clayton v. Heffron (1960) 105 C.L.R. 214). This opinion, said Lord Diplock, should be read rather as a statement of what ought to be the practice in Australian courts where there is the alternative remedy of seeking a declaration that a statute is void.[1024]

1022. *See* Kevin Aquilina and Lino Bianco, 'Editorial: The Mediterranean Environment within a Human Rights Context: Towards the Emergence of Mediterranean Environmental Human Rights Law and the Implementation of an Effective Enforcement Machinery Therefor', Special Issue of the *Mediterranean Journal of Human Rights* entitled 'Human Rights and the Environment in the Mediterranean Region', Vol. 14, No. 1, 2010, 13–33.

1023. *See* Kevin Aquilina, *supra* note 726.

1024. O. Hood Phillips, 'Judicial Intervention in the Legislative Process', *The Law Quarterly Review*, Vol. 87, July 1971, pp. 321–325 at p. 323.

Chapter 3. Key Rights Enshrined in the Constitution

§1. Introduction

528. Chapter IV of the Constitution consists in human rights and fundamental freedoms provisions. The rights and freedoms enshrined in the Constitution are the following:

(a) section 33 – protection of right to life
(b) section 34 – protection from arbitrary arrest or detention
(c) section 35 – protection from forced labour
(d) section 36 – protection from inhuman treatment
(e) section 37 – protection from deprivation of property without compensation
(f) section 38 – protection for privacy of home or other property
(g) section 39 – provisions to secure protection of law
(h) section 40 – protection of freedom of conscience and worship
(i) section 41 – protection of freedom of expression
(j) section 42 – protection of freedom of assembly and association
(k) section 43 – prohibition of deportation
(l) section 44 – protection of freedom of movement
(m) section 45 – protection from discrimination on the grounds of race, etc.

529. The above substantive human rights and fundamental freedoms are supplemented by three other provisions, a Preamble contained in section 32 whose marginal note reads 'Fundamental rights and freedoms of the individual', section 46 which is entitled 'Enforcement of protective provisions' and section 47 whose marginal note reads 'Interpretation of Chapter IV'. The rights and freedoms set out in Chapter IV of the Constitution are also supplemented by other rights contained in other provisions of the Constitution other than Chapter IV thereof, the European Convention Act,[1025] the European Union Act,[1026] the Equal Opportunities (Persons with Disabilities) Act[1027] and by other rights and freedoms contained in other ordinary laws.[1028]

530. The Constitution's rights and freedoms provisions have barely been amended during the last fifty-three years. As a matter of fact, only sections 32, 37, 40, 42, 43, 44, 45 and 46 have been so amended, and these amendments took place only four times within a fifty-three-year span of time:

1025. Chapter 319 of the Laws of Malta.
1026. Chapter 460 of the Laws of Malta.
1027. Chapter 413 of the Laws of Malta.
1028. For instance, Equality for Men and Women Act, Chapter 456 of the Laws of Malta; Commissioner for Children Act, Chapter 462 of the Laws of Malta; Mental Health Act, Chapter 525 of the Laws of Malta; and the Gender Identity, Gender Expression and Sex Characteristics Act, Chapter 540 of the Laws of Malta.

(a) in 1974 – when Malta became a republic (in the case of sections 37, 40, 42, 43, 45, 46 and 47);
(b) in 1991 (in the case of sections 45 and 47);
(c) in 2001 (in the case of section 44); and
(d) in 2014 (in the case of sections 32 and 45).

531. These amendments cannot be considered to be of a substantial nature. Contrary to the ECHR, which is kept constantly updated over time through the addition of new Protocols and the proactive interpretation of the Convention by the ECtHR, the Constitution's human rights and fundamental freedoms have remained static and there has been no statutory holistic review of the provisions contained in Chapter IV of the Constitution during the last fifty-one years, except for the piecemeal amendments above-mentioned carried on four distant and separate occasions. Perhaps the time is ripe to consider whether these provisions should be revisited or whether the ECHR and its Protocols or the EU Charter should replace the Chapter IV human rights and fundamental freedoms' provisions to avoid having three diverse human rights instruments in Maltese Constitutional Law. The matter needs to be addressed legislatively.

§2. Historical Evolution and Sources of Chapter IV of the Constitution

532. The historical evolution of human rights law in Malta has already been dealt with elsewhere.[1029]

§3. Preamble: Fundamental Rights and Freedoms of the Individual

533. The Judicial Committee of the Privy Council, when considering the equivalent provision (Article 15) of the Constitution of The Bahamas to section 32 of the Constitution of Malta, held that:

> Article 15 is in this respect no more than a preamble, as the Board held it to be in Campbell-Rodriques.[1030] There is a distinction between on the one hand Constitutions in the form adopted in The Bahamas, Jamaica and Malta, in which the equivalent article 15 is wholly or predominantly a preamble, and on the other hand Constitutions in the form adopted in Trinidad and Tobago and Mauritius, which contain instead an enacting provision. The distinction was recognised by the Board in Sociétė United Docks v. Government of Maritius[1031] as well as in

1029. Kevin Aquilina, *supra* note 1015, pp. 225–247. An updated version of this paper was published in Professor David Joseph Attard, *supra* note 25, pp. 105–136. *See also* Anne-Louise Ellul Cachia Caruana, *The Adoption of the European Convention of Human Rights into Municipal Law: A Comparative Analysis*, LL.D. thesis, Faculty of Laws, University of Malta, Msida, May 1993, pp. 146–199.
1030. *Campbell-Rodriques v. Attorney General of Jamaica* [2007] UKPC 65 (3 December 2007).
1031. [1985] 1 AC 585, 600D-G.

Campbell-Rodriques, paras 9 to 12 … The Board therefore considers that article 15 has no relevance or application in this case, save as a preamble and introduction to the subsequently conferred rights.[1032]

534. The Preamble to Chapter IV of the Constitution states that 'every person in Malta is entitled to the fundamental rights and freedoms of the individual' but stops short from defining these three key terms – 'rights', 'freedoms' and 'individual'. It further proclaims which are these fundamental rights ('life, liberty, security of the person, the enjoyment of property and the protection of the law') and fundamental freedoms ('conscience, of expression and of peaceful assembly and association') together with 'respect for his private and family life'. All these rights and freedoms are enjoyed by an individual 'whatever his race, place of origin, political opinions, colour, creed or sex' (to which list sexual orientation and gender identity were added in 2014), but all these fundamental rights and freedoms are enjoyed subject to 'respect for the rights and freedoms of others and for the public interest'. Once again, the key term 'public interest' is left undefined.[1033]

§4. Structure of the Human Rights and Fundamental Freedoms Provisions: The Clawback Clause

535. A careful review of the structure of the human rights and fundamental freedoms provisions reveals that each provision first sets out the right or freedom in question and then passes, in second instance, to restrict or limit its exercise. This is because human rights and fundamental freedoms are not absolute. The second part of each such provision consists in a 'clawback clause'. Andy Darkoh explains this clause as follows:

> There is no doubt that rights and freedoms cannot be granted in absolute terms. They must be expressed to be subject to qualification to allow for an opposing superior interest, the interest of the State and the rights of other people. Most fundamental rights contained in modern constitutions are qualified by [a] 'clawback

1032. *Gordon Newbold v. the Commissioner of Police, Shanto Curry v. the Commissioner of Police, Sheldon Moore v. the Commissioner of Police, Trevor Roberts and Devroy Moss v. The Attorney General of the Commonwealth of the Bahamas and the Government of the United States of America, Melvin Maycock Senior v. The United States of America and Another* [2014] UKPC 12 (16 April 2014).

1033. For an attempt at definition of the term, *see Dr Carmelo Vella et v. Housing Secretary et*, Court of Appeal, 30 December 1993.

clause'. Thus the right is given by one hand and a greater part of it taken back by another hand.[1034]

§5. Protection of Right to Life

536. Section 33 of the Constitution regulates the most fundamental of all human rights and freedoms – the right to life. Without the enjoyment of this right, all the other rights and freedoms are meaningless. The Constitution sets out the right to life in the following words:

> **33.** (1) No person shall intentionally be deprived of his life save in execution of the sentence of a court in respect of a criminal offence under the law of Malta of which he has been convicted.

537. Abortion is a criminal offence in Malta in terms of section 241 of the Criminal Code. Moreover, section 170 of the Civil Code protects the unborn child through the appointment of a curator *ad ventrem* when at the time of the husband's death, his wife declares that she is pregnant, 'with a view to preventing any supposition of birth, or substitution of child, and administering the property up to the day of the birth, under such directions as the court may deem it proper to give'. The Constitution respects the Criminal Code and the Civil Code and makes no allowance for abortions of whatsoever nature.

§6. Protection from Arbitrary Arrest or Detention

538. Section 34 of the Constitution protects from arbitrary arrest or detention. It proclaims in subsection (1) that no person 'shall be deprived of his personal liberty save as may be authorized by law'. Hence, although everybody enjoys security of the person, this right can be curtailed by law. The instances where such curtailment is allowed are the following:

(a) in consequence of his unfitness to plead to a criminal charge;
(b) in execution of the sentence or order of a court, whether in Malta or elsewhere, in respect of a criminal offence of which he has been convicted;
(c) in execution of the order of a court punishing him for contempt of that court or of another court or tribunal or in execution of the order of the House of Representatives punishing him for contempt of itself or of its members or for breach of privilege;

1034. Andy Darkoh, 'The Cayman Islands Constitution – An Outcry for a Bill of Rights?', *Commonwealth Judicial Journal*, Vol. 9, No. 4, December 1992, pp. 7–13 at p. 11. It is not the intention of this chapter to discuss the case law of the Maltese courts of constitutional competence as this has already been done elsewhere. *See* Tonio Borg. *A Commentary on the Constitution of Malta*, Kite, B'Kara, 2016 and David Joseph Attard, *supra* note 25 and David Joseph Attard with the assistance of Kevin Aquilina and Patricia Mallia, *The Maltese Legal System, Volume II, Constitutional and Human Rights Law*, Part B, Malta University Press, Msida (forthcoming).

(d) in execution of the order of a court made to secure the fulfilment of any obligation imposed on him by law;
(e) for the purpose of bringing him before a court in execution of the order of a court or before the House of Representatives in execution of the order of that House;
(f) upon reasonable suspicion of his having committed, or being about to commit, a criminal offence;
(g) in the case of a person who has not attained the age of eighteen years, for the purpose of his education or welfare;
(h) for the purpose of preventing the spread of an infectious or contagious disease;
(i) in the case of a person who is, or is reasonably suspected to be, of unsound mind, addicted to drugs or alcohol, or a vagrant, for the purpose of his care or treatment or the protection of the community; or
(j) for the purpose of preventing the unlawful entry of that person into Malta, or for the purpose of effecting the expulsion, extradition or other lawful removal of that person from Malta or the taking of proceedings relating thereto or for the purpose of restraining that person while he is being conveyed through Malta in the course of his extradition or removal as a convicted prisoner from one country to another.

539. The provision further provides, in subsection (2), that upon arrest or detention, the arrested or detained person has to be informed, in a language which he/she understands – and not necessarily in his/her mother tongue – of the reasons why he/she has been arrested or detained. The provision obliges the arresting or detaining authority to inform the arrested or detained person of such reason 'at the time of his arrest'. Arrest and detention are two different legal concepts. Arrest is instantaneous whilst detention is recurring: arrest takes a few minutes to materialize but detention can take up to forty-eight hours before the detained person is either released or charged in court. The Constitution does not prescribe who the arresting and/or detaining authority should be. Hence, the provision applies to any person who, under Maltese Law, has the right to arrest and to detain. Such is the case of a court, an Inquiring Magistrate, a Police Officer and a person subject to military law. The Criminal Code also allows private persons to arrest and detain[1035] whilst the Code of Organization and Civil Procedure gives a corresponding power to court executive offices.[1036] The provision, nonetheless, does not explain how the reasons should be communicated, that is, whether they should be provided in writing or by word of mouth, and what extent of detail should be given. However, since 2014, the Criminal Code does remedy the defect by providing for a letter of rights to be given to the detained person.[1037] Should an interpreter be required, then the arresting authority has to provide one, and if no interpreter is 'not readily available or if it is otherwise impracticable to comply

1035. Criminal Code, section 355W.
1036. Code of Organization and Civil Procedure, section 68(3).
1037. Criminal Code, Schedule E (added by the Various Laws (Criminal Matters) (Amendment) Act, 2014, Act No. IV of 2014) introduces section 534AB of the Criminal Code related to the letter of rights which obliges the Police and the Court to issue such letter but not any other arresting or detaining authority.

with the provisions of this subsection at the time of the person's arrest or detention, such provisions shall be complied with as soon as practicable'.[1038]

540. The reasons for arrest and detention are set out in section 34(3) and can be either in compliance with a court order so that he/she is brought before it, as instructed, or 'upon reasonable suspicion of his having committed, or being about to commit, a criminal offence'. Interestingly the provision does not require a suspicion but 'upon reasonable suspicion'. Not any suspicion therefore can give rise to an arrest and/or detention. The arresting authority needs to establish that there is a prima facie case to warrant the arrest. The period of detention is prescribed by the Constitution in the proviso to section 34(3): it cannot exceed forty-eight hours. If a person is detained for more than forty-eight hours without being charged in court (or released), the arresting and detaining authority would fall foul of the constitutional provision. Although the Constitution allows detention up to forty-eight hours, this does not mean that once the arresting and detaining authority have concluded their interrogation of the arrested or detained person, they can still hold him/her detained up to forty-eight hours. When, on the other hand, the person arrested or detained is arraigned in court within forty-eight hours, this does not mean that the court may continue to detain the person charged or accused indefinitely. In such case, he/she has to be 'tried within a reasonable time'. If the person charged or accused is undergoing criminal proceedings, he/she may 'be released either unconditionally or upon reasonable conditions, including in particular such conditions as are reasonably necessary to ensure that he appears at a later date for trial or for proceedings preliminary to trial'. The conditions for bail are established in the Criminal Code.[1039]

541. Cases might arise where persons are 'unlawfully arrested or detained by any other person'. In such eventuality, in terms of section 34(4), it is possible for the arrested or detained person to claim compensation. Such compensation may be granted under this provision by way of moral damages or in terms of the tort provisions in the Civil Code.

542. Section 34(5)–(7) regulate arrest and detention during a period of public emergency. The pertinent provisions of the Constitution relating to such a period are contained in section 47 and are supplemented by the Emergency Powers Act.[1040] The Constitution allows, in subsection (5), for derogations from the protection from arbitrary arrest or detention, during a period of public emergency with regard to lawful measures 'that are reasonably justifiable for the purpose of dealing with the situation that exists during that period of public emergency'. Subsection (6) ensures that any person who is detained 'not earlier than six months after he last made such a request during that period', will have his/her case 'reviewed by an independent and impartial tribunal established by law'. This tribunal, which is not a court, is however to be 'composed of a person or persons each of whom holds or has held judicial office or is qualified to be appointed to such office in Malta'. Persons who hold judicial office are the Chief Justice, Judges and Magistrates.[1041] Finally, the said Tribunal is empowered by subsection

1038. Constitution, section 34(2) proviso.

1039. Criminal Code, sections 574–587.

1040. Chapter 178 of the Laws of Malta. For a study of these provisions, *see* Kevin Aquilina, 'Why a Second Republic for Malta?', in Office of the President, *supra* note 418, pp. 152–198.

1041. Constitution, sections 95(5) and 100.

(7), to 'make recommendations concerning the necessity or expediency of continuing his detention to the authority by whom it was ordered, but, unless it is otherwise provided by law, that authority shall not be obliged to act in accordance with any such recommendations'.

§7. Protection from Forced Labour

543. Section 35 deals with protection from forced labour. In subsection (1), it prohibits any person from performing forced labour. The expression 'forced labour' is defined in subsection (2) as excluding:

(a) any labour required in consequence of the sentence or order of a court;[1042]
(b) labour required of any person while he is lawfully detained by sentence or order of a court that, though not required in consequence of such sentence or order, is reasonably necessary in the interests of hygiene or for the maintenance of the place at which he is detained or, if he is detained for the purpose of his care, treatment, education or welfare, is reasonably required for that purpose;
(c) any labour required of a member of a disciplined force in pursuance of his duties as such or, in the case of a person who has conscientious objections to service as a member of a naval, military or air force, any labour that that person is required by law to perform in place of such service; and
(d) any labour required during a period of public emergency or in the event of any other emergency or calamity that threatens the life or well-being of the community.

§8. Protection from Inhuman Treatment

544. Section 36 of the Constitution proclaims that no person 'shall be subjected to inhuman or degrading punishment or treatment'.[1043] However, this right is circumscribed by a number of limitations 'contained in or done under the authority of any law' which empower the infliction of any description of punishment which was lawful in Malta immediately before independence.[1044] Furthermore, collective punishments are outlawed except in the case of members of a disciplined force in accordance with the law regulating the discipline of that force.[1045]

1042. The punishment of hard labour has been removed from the Criminal Code, Chapter 9 of the Laws of Malta.
1043. Constitution, section 36(1).
1044. *Ibid.*, section 36(2).
1045. *Ibid.*, section 36(3).

§9. Protection from Deprivation of Property without Compensation

545. According to section 37 of the Constitution, no property may be compulsorily taken possession of. Nor may any interest in or right over property of any description be compulsorily acquired. A list of exceptions to this rule follow 'where provision is made by a law applicable to that taking of possession or acquisition:

(a) for the payment of adequate compensation;
(b) securing to any person claiming such compensation a right of access to an independent and impartial court or tribunal established by law for the purpose of determining his interest in or right over the property and the amount of any compensation to which he may be entitled, and for the purpose of obtaining payment of that compensation; and
(c) securing to any party to proceedings in that court or tribunal relating to such a claim a right of appeal from its determination to the Court of Appeal in Malta'.[1046]

546. In special cases: 'Parliament may, if it deems it appropriate so to act in the national interest, by law establish the criteria which are to be followed, including the factors and other circumstances to be taken into account, in the determination of the compensation payable in respect of property compulsorily taken possession of or acquired; and in any such case the compensation shall be determined and shall be payable accordingly.'[1047]

547. The above does not, nevertheless, affect 'the making or operation of any law so far as it provides for the taking of possession or acquisition of property:

(a) in satisfaction of any tax, rate or due;
(b) by way of penalty for, or as a consequence of, breach of the law, whether under civil process or after conviction of a criminal offence;
(c) upon the attempted removal of the property out of or into Malta in contravention of any law;
(d) by way of the taking of a sample for the purposes of any law;
(e) where the property consists of an animal upon its being found trespassing or straying;
(f) as an incident of a lease, tenancy, licence, privilege or hypothec, mortgage, charge, bill of sale, pledge or other contract;
(g) by way of the vesting or administration of property on behalf and for the benefit of the person entitled to the beneficial interest therein, trust property, enemy property or the property of persons adjudged bankrupt or otherwise declared bankrupt or insolvent, persons of unsound mind, deceased persons, or bodies corporate or unincorporate in the course of being wound up or liquidated;
(h) in the execution of judgments or orders of courts;
(i) by reason of its being in a dangerous state or injurious to the health of human beings, animals or plants;

1046. Constitution, section 37(1).
1047. *Ibid.*

(j) in consequence of any law with respect to the limitation of actions, acquisitive prescription, derelict land, treasure trove, mortmain or the rights of succession competent to the Government of Malta; or
(k) for so long only as may be necessary for the purposes of any examination, investigation, trial or inquiry or, in the case of land, the carrying out thereon:

- of work of soil conservation or the conservation of other natural resources of any description or of war damage reconstruction; or
- of agricultural development or improvement which the owner or occupier of the land has been required and has without reasonable and lawful excuse refused or failed to carry out.'

548. Furthermore, section 37(1) does not affect the making or operation of any law so far as it: (a) provides 'for vesting in the Government of Malta the ownership of any underground minerals, water or antiquities',[1048] or (b) 'for the compulsory taking of possession in the public interest of any property, or the compulsory acquisition in the public interest of any interest in or right over property, where that property, interest or right is held by a body corporate which is established for public purposes by any law and in which no monies have been invested other than monies provided by any legislature in Malta'.[1049]

§10. Protection for Privacy of Home or Other Property

549. Protection from privacy of home or other property is contained in section 38 of the Maltese Constitution. It provides that, except 'with his own consent or by way of parental discipline, no person shall be subjected to the search of his person or his property or the entry by others on his premises'.[1050] The restrictions to the protection for privacy of home or other property are those laws which provide for anything:

(a) that is reasonably required in the interest of defence, public safety, public order, public morality or decency, public health, town and country planning, the development and utilization of mineral resources, or the development and utilization of any property in such a manner as to promote the public benefit;
(b) that is reasonably required for the purpose of promoting the rights or freedoms of other persons;
(c) that authorizes a department of the Government of Malta, or a local government authority, or a body corporate established by law for a public purpose, to enter on the premises of any person in order to inspect those premises or anything thereon for the purpose of any tax, rate or due or in order to carry out work connected with any property or installation which is lawfully on those premises and which belongs to that Government, that authority, or that body corporate, as the case may be; or

1048. *Ibid.*, section 37(3).
1049. *Ibid.*, section 37(4).
1050. *Ibid.*, section 38(1).

(d) that authorizes, for the purpose of enforcing a judgment or order of a court, the search of any person or property by order of a court or entry upon any premises by such order, or that is necessary for the purpose of preventing or detecting criminal offences, and except so far as that provision or, as the case may be, the thing done under the authority thereof is shown not to be reasonably justifiable in a democratic society.

§11. Provisions to Secure Protection of Law

550. The Maltese Constitution establishes a number of provisions which are intended to secure protection of law. Indeed, when a person is charged with a criminal offence, he has to be granted 'a fair hearing within a reasonable time by an independent and impartial court established by law'.[1051] The same is extended to a court or 'other adjudicating authority prescribed by law for the determination of the existence or the extent of civil rights or obligations'.[1052] Furthermore, proceedings before all courts and other adjudicating authorities as aforesaid, 'including the announcement of the decision of the court or other authority, shall be held in public'.[1053]

551. This notwithstanding, a court or other adjudicating authority may exclude from the proceedings persons (other than the parties thereto and their legal representatives) in the following cases:

(a) 'in proceedings before a court of voluntary jurisdiction and other proceedings which, in the practice of the Courts in Malta are, or are of the same nature as those which are, disposed of in chambers;
(b) in proceedings under any law relating to income tax; or
(c) to such extent as the court or other authority:

- may consider necessary or expedient in circumstances where publicity would prejudice the interests of justice; or
- may be empowered or required by law to do so in the interests of defence, public safety, public order, public morality or decency, the welfare of persons under the age of eighteen years or the protection of the private lives of persons concerned in the proceedings.'[1054]

552. The presumption of innocence is enshrined in section 39(5) of the Constitution, and it is clarified that it is not breached when a law 'imposes upon any person charged as aforesaid the burden of proving particular facts'.[1055]

553. A number of rights are afforded to every person charged with a criminal offence. Such person:

1051. *Ibid.*, section 39(1).
1052. *Ibid.*, section 39(2).
1053. *Ibid.*, section 39(3).
1054. *Ibid.*, section 39(4).
1055. *Ibid.*, section 39(5).

(a) 'shall be informed in writing, in a language which he understands and in detail, of the nature of the offence charged;
(b) shall be given adequate time and facilities for the preparation of his defence;
(c) shall be permitted to defend himself in person or by a legal representative and a person who cannot afford to pay for such legal representation as is reasonably required by the circumstances of his case shall be entitled to have such representation at the public expense;
(d) shall be afforded facilities to examine in person or by his legal representative the witnesses called by the prosecution before any court and to obtain the attendance of witnesses subject to the payment of their reasonable expenses, and carry out the examination of witnesses to testify on his behalf before the court on the same conditions as those applying to witnesses called by the prosecution; and
(e) shall be permitted to have without payment the assistance of an interpreter if he cannot understand the language used at the trial of the charge, and except with his own consent the trial shall not take place in his absence unless he so conducts himself as to render the continuance of the proceedings in his presence impracticable and the court has ordered him to be removed and the trial to proceed in his absence'.[1056]

554. Further rights given to an accused person comprise the following:

(a) a person tried for any criminal offence or any person authorized by him in that behalf has the right, 'subject to payment of such reasonable fee as may be prescribed by law, [to] be given within a reasonable time after judgment a copy for the use of the accused person of any record of the proceedings made by or on behalf of the court';[1057]
(b) the criminal law maxims of *nullum crimen sine lege,*[1058] *nulla poena sine lege,*[1059] the right against self-incrimination[1060] and *ne bis in idem*[1061] are also adopted by the Maltese Constitution. The latter double jeopardy principle also extends to situations where a person has already been pardoned for an offence[1062] except in the case of a member of a disciplined force who may be tried by a court of criminal jurisdiction for a criminal offence even if such member has been punished under a disciplinary law, though, in so doing, the court shall take into account the punishment awarded under the disciplinary law.[1063]

1056. *Ibid.*, section 39(6).
1057. *Ibid.*, section 39(7).
1058. *Ibid.*, section 39(8).
1059. *Ibid.*
1060. *Ibid.*, section 39(10).
1061. *Ibid.*, section 39(9).
1062. *Ibid.*
1063. *Ibid.*

§12. Protection of Freedom of Conscience and Worship

555. Freedom of conscience and worship are regulated by section 40 of the Maltese Constitution where it is stated that all 'persons in Malta shall have full freedom of conscience and enjoy the free exercise of their respective mode of religious worship'.[1064] That said, however, the Constitution limits the exercise of this freedom in the case of a law that 'makes provision that is reasonably required in the interests of public safety, public order, public morality or decency, public health, or the protection of the rights and freedoms of others, and except so far as that provision or, as the case may be, the thing done under the authority thereof, is shown not to be reasonably justifiable in a democratic society'.[1065]

556. In addition, no person is 'required to receive instruction in religion or to show knowledge or proficiency in religion if, in the case of a person who has not attained the age of 16 years, objection to such requirement is made by the person who according to law has authority over him and, in any other case, if the person so required objects thereto'. But such requirement is not inconsistent with or in contravention of freedom of conscience and worship 'to the extent that the knowledge of, or the proficiency or instruction in, religion is required for the teaching of such religion, or for admission to the priesthood or to a religious order, or for other religious purposes, and except so far as that requirement is shown not to be reasonably justifiable in a democratic society'.[1066]

§13. Protection of Freedom of Expression

557. Freedom of expression is regulated by section 41 of the Constitution when it provides that except 'with his own consent or by way of parental discipline, no person shall be hindered in the enjoyment of his freedom of expression, including freedom to hold opinions without interference, freedom to receive ideas and information without interference, freedom to communicate ideas and information without interference (whether the communication be to the public generally or to any person or class of persons) and freedom from interference with his correspondence'.[1067] Freedom of expression – like all the other fundamental freedoms in the Constitution – is not absolute. Laws do not infringe this freedom if they make provision:

(a) that is reasonably required:

- in the interests of defence, public safety, public order, public morality or decency, or public health; or
- for the purpose of protecting the reputations, rights and freedoms of other persons, or the private lives of persons concerned in legal proceedings, preventing the disclosure of information received in confidence, maintaining

1064. Constitution, section 40(1).
1065. *Ibid.*, section 40(3).
1066. *Ibid.*, section 40(2).
1067. *Ibid.*, section 41(1).

the authority and independence of the courts, protecting the privileges of Parliament, or regulating telephony, telegraphy, posts, wireless broadcasting, television or other means of communication, public exhibitions or public entertainments.

(b) that imposes restrictions upon public officers, and except so far as that provision or, as the case may be, the thing done under the authority thereof is shown not to be reasonably justifiable in a democratic society.[1068]

558. The Constitution empowers any person resident in Malta to 'edit or print a newspaper or journal published daily or periodically' but, once, again this freedom may be restricted by a law:

(a) prohibiting or restricting the editing or printing of any such newspaper or journal by persons under 21 years of age; and
(b) requiring any person who is the editor or printer of any such newspaper or journal to inform the prescribed authority to that effect and of his age and to keep the prescribed authority informed of his place of residence.[1069]

559. Should any edition of a newspaper be seized on the ground that it constitutes the means whereby a criminal offence has been committed, the Police are obliged, within twenty-four hours of the seizure, to inform the competent court thereof. Nonetheless, should the court be unsatisfied that there is a prima facie case of such offence, that edition has to be returned to the person from whom it was seized.[1070] Finally, a person cannot be deprived of his citizenship or of his juridical capacity only because of his political opinions.[1071]

§14. Protection of Freedom of Assembly and Association

560. Freedom of assembly and association are both the subject of section 42 of the Maltese Constitution. It provides that except 'with his own consent or by way of parental discipline no person shall be hindered in the enjoyment of his freedom of peaceful assembly and association, that is to say, his right peacefully to assemble freely and associate with other persons and in particular to form or belong to trade or other unions or associations for the protection of his interests'.[1072] Both these freedoms may be limited by any law-making provision:

(a) that is reasonably required:

1068. *Ibid.*, section 41(2).
1069. *Ibid.*, section 41(3). The Press Act, Chapter 248 of the Laws of Malta, is the applicable law.
1070. *Ibid.*, section 41(4).
1071. *Ibid.*, section 41(5).
1072. *Ibid.*, section 42(1).

- in the interests of defence, public safety, public order, public morality or decency, or public health; or
- for the purpose of protecting the rights or freedoms of other persons.

(b) that imposes restrictions upon public officers, and except so far as that provision or, as the case may be, the thing done under the authority thereof is shown not to be reasonably justifiable in a democratic society.[1073]

561. For the purposes of clarification, it is further established that 'any law prohibiting the holding of public meetings or demonstrations in any one or more particular cities, towns, suburbs or villages shall be held to be a provision which is not reasonably justifiable in a democratic society'.[1074]

§15. Prohibition of Deportation

562. Extradition is not automatic; it may be permitted only in pursuance of an extradition agreement.[1075] But such an agreement does not apply in the case of an offence of a political character.[1076] Indeed, a citizen of Malta cannot be removed from Malta except as a result of extradition proceedings or under the Extradition Act.[1077] Although no reference is made in the Constitution to the EAW, it is still comprised in the definition of extradition in terms of the Extradition (Designated Foreign Countries) Order.[1078]

§16. Protection of Freedom of Movement

563. Freedom of movement is guaranteed by section 44 of the Constitution whereby no Maltese citizen may be deprived of his freedom of movement, that is, 'the right to move freely throughout Malta, the right to reside in any part of Malta, the right to leave and the right to enter Malta'. But freedom of movement can be infringed in the case of a citizen's lawful detention[1079] and in the case of a law which makes provision:

1073. *Ibid.*, section 42(2).
1074. *Ibid.*, section 42(3).
1075. *Ibid.*, section 43(1).
1076. *Ibid.*, section 43(2).
1077. Chapter 276 of the Laws of Malta and Constitution, section 43(3). *See also* Anthony Micallef, *Terrorism and the Political Offence Exemption in International Criminal Law*, LL.D. thesis, Faculty of Laws, University of Malta, Msida, 1983, pp. 123–153.
1078. Subsidiary Legislation 276.05. *See also* regulation 16(2) of the Procedural Standards for Granting and Withdrawing International Protection Regulations, Subsidiary Legislation 420.07. Reference to the EAW are also found in the Criminal Code, Chapter 9 of the Laws of Malta. For a study of the EAW in Malta, *see* Stefano Filletti, *supra* note 53, pp. 170–176 and pp. 221–224.
1079. Constitution, section 44(2).

(a) for the imposition of restrictions that are reasonably required in the interests of defence, public safety, public order, public morality or decency, or public health and except so far as that provision or, as the case may be, the thing done under the authority thereof is shown not to be reasonably justifiable in a democratic society;
(b) for the imposition of restrictions on the freedom of movement of any citizen of Malta who is not a citizen by virtue of Article 3(1) or of Article 5(1) of the Maltese Citizenship Act as in force upon the coming into force of the Maltese Citizenship (Amendment) Act, 2000;
(c) for the imposition of restrictions upon the movement or residence within Malta of public officers; or
(d) for the imposition of restrictions on the right of any person to leave Malta that are reasonably required in order to secure the fulfilment of any obligation imposed on that person by law and except so far as that provision or, as the case may be, the thing done under the authority thereof is shown not to be reasonably justifiable in a democratic society.

§17. Protection from Discrimination on the Grounds of Race, Etc.

564. The Constitution proclaims that 'no law shall make any provision that is discriminatory either of itself or in its effect'[1080] except in the following cases:

(a) for the appropriation of public revenues or other public funds; or
(b) with respect to persons who are not citizens of Malta; or
(c) with respect to adoption, marriage, dissolution of marriage, burial, devolution of property on death or any matters of personal law not hereinbefore specified; or
(d) whereby persons of any such description as is mentioned in sub-article (3) of this article may be subjected to any disability or restriction or may be accorded any privilege or advantage which, having regard to its nature and to special circumstances pertaining to those persons or to persons of any other such description and to any other provision of this Constitution, is reasonably justifiable in a democratic society; or
(e) for authorizing the taking during a period of public emergency of measures that are reasonably justifiable for the purpose of dealing with the situation that exists during that period of public emergency:

Provided that paragraph (c) of this sub-article shall not apply to any law which makes any provision that is discriminatory, either of itself or in its effect by affording different treatment to different persons attributable wholly or mainly to their respective description by sex.

1080. *Ibid.*, section 45(1).

565. Furthermore, 'no person shall be treated in a discriminatory manner by any person acting by virtue of any written law or in the performance of the functions of any public office or any public authority[1081] except:

(a) with respect to qualifications for service or conditions of service in any disciplined force; or
(b) with respect to qualifications (not being qualifications specifically relating to sex) for service as a public officer or for service of a local government authority or a body corporate established for public purposes by any law'.

566. Discriminatory is defined as 'affording different treatment to different persons attributable wholly or mainly to their respective descriptions by race, place of origin, political opinions, colour, creed or sex whereby persons of one such description are subjected to disabilities or restrictions to which persons of another such description are not made subject or are accorded privileges or advantages which are not accorded to persons of another such description'.[1082]

567. Finally, a requirement, however made, 'that the Roman Catholic Apostolic Religion shall be taught by a person professing that religion shall not be held to be inconsistent with or in contravention of this article'.[1083]

1081. *Ibid.*, section 45(2).
1082. *Ibid.*, section 45(3).
1083. *Ibid.*, section 45(9).

Part V. Specific Issues

Chapter 1. Relations Between the State and Religious Denominations

§1. Equality of Religious Denominations and Their Different Relations with the State

568. Insofar as protection of conscience and worship is concerned, the Constitution safeguards the freedom of all persons in Malta to enjoy 'full freedom of conscience' and 'the free exercise of their respective mode of religious worship'.[1084] The latter words are indicative of the fact that, although Malta is predominantly a Roman Catholic country, it still guarantees other religious denominations the right to worship according to non-Catholic religious rites and traditions. In this respect, freedom of cult is practised and applied indiscriminately.

§2. Relations Between the State and the Catholic Church

I. Canon Law Influence on the Legal Relationship Between Church and State

569. Canon Law is not just simply the law of the Roman Catholic Apostolic Church which has been an influencing factor on Malta surely from the time of the Order of St. John onwards, if not from the time of the advent of St. Paul in the Maltese islands.[1085] As Robinson, Fergus and Gordon hold, 'canon law was more than a collection of technical rules; it was a force which shaped all society, lay and cleric alike; their membership of society made them members of the Church and subject to the rational ordering of a daily life that was seen *sub specie aeternitatis*'.[1086]

1084. *Ibid.*, section 1(1).

1085. Circa 61 A.D. *Acts of the Apostles*, 28: 1–10 in Anon, *The Jerusalem Bible* Darton, Longman & Todd, London, pp. 246–247.

1086. Olivia F. Robinson, T. David Fergus and William M. Gordon, *European Legal History*, 2nd edn, Butterworths, London 1994, p. 72.

II. The Constitution

570. The highest law of the land – the Constitution of Malta – is influenced by the 1917 Code of Canon Law. The Constitution proclaims that the 'religion of Malta is the Roman Catholic Apostolic Religion'.[1087] The implication of this declaration in the Constitution insofar as State-Church relations are concerned is that the 'authorities of the Roman Catholic Apostolic Church have the duty and the right to teach which principles are right and which are wrong'.[1088] Furthermore, religious teaching 'of the Roman Catholic Apostolic Faith shall be provided in all State schools as part of compulsory education'.[1089] The Catholic religion is not only the state adopted religion but even the Catholic Church is recognized by the Constitution, and the Catholic faith has to be thought as part of compulsory education in state schools. No such treatment is afforded in the Constitution to any other religion. Furthermore, section 45(9) provides that a 'requirement, however made, that the Roman Catholic Apostolic Religion shall be taught by a person professing that religion shall not be held to be inconsistent with or in contravention of this section'. Linked to this latter provision is section 40 dealing with the protection of freedom of conscience and worship which, in section 40(2) provides that:

> No person shall be required to receive instruction in religion or to show knowledge or proficiency in religion if, in the case of a person who has not attained the age of sixteen years, objection to such requirement is made by the person who according to law has authority over him and, in any other case, if the person so required objects thereto: provided that no such requirement shall be held to be inconsistent with or in contravention of this article to the extent that the knowledge

1087. Constitution, section 2(1).

1088. *Ibid.*, section 2(2): this provision was added to the Constitution in 1974 by section 4 of Act No. LVIII of 1974, through which enactment Malta became a Republic. Canon 1322 of the 1917 Code of Canon Law dealt with 'The Power to Teach'. It provided that: 'Our Lord Jesus Christ entrusted the deposit of faith to the Church, that under the constant guidance and assistance of the Holy Spirit, she might sacredly guard and faithfully explain this divine revelation. The Church has therefore the right and the duty, independently of any civil power, to teach all nations the full evangelical doctrine, and all men are bound by the law of God to learn this doctrine properly and to embrace the true Church of God.' *See* T. Lincoln Bouscaren and Adam C. Ellis, *Canon Law: A Text and Commentary,* 3rd rev. edn, The Bruce Publishing Company, Milwaukee, 1957, p. 723. A more developed version of this canon is found in Canon 747 of the Code of Canon Law of 1983. *See* John P. Beal, James A. Coriden and Thomas J. Green (eds), *New Commentary on the Code of Canon Law*, Paulist Press, New York, 2000, pp. 911–912.

1089. Constitution, section 2(3); Canon 1113 of the Code of Canon Law of 1917 provided that: 'Parents are bound by a most serious obligation to provide to the best of their power for the religious and moral as well as for the physical and civil education of their children, and also to provide for their temporal welfare.' *See* Bouscaren and Ellis, *supra* note 1088, p. 583. The Code of Canon Law of 1983, in Canon 226, paragraph 2, has got a similar provision when it provides that: 'Since they have given life to their children, parents have a most grave obligation and possess the right to educate them. Therefore, it is for Christian parents particularly to take care of the Christian education of their children according to the doctrine handed on by the Church.' *See* Beal, Coriden and Green, *supra* note 1088, pp. 293–295.

of, or proficiency or instruction in, religion is required for the teaching of such religion, or for admission to the priesthood or to a religious order, or for other religious purposes, and except so far as that requirement is shown to be reasonably justifiable in a democratic society.

III. Ordinary Laws

571. The legal relationship between Church and State is contained in various laws some written others not. For instance, the order of precedence which is accorded to His Grace the Archbishop and the Bishop of Gozo as well as the Auxiliary Bishop is not written down in a law but in a policy document adopted by the Ministry of Foreign Affairs. The ecclesiastical authorities are dignitaries who are given their respect by being placed nearly at the very beginning of the order of precedence. The same approach is adopted by the Education Act[1090] which provides in section 47(3) that: 'It shall be the duty of the Minister to provide for the education and teaching of the Catholic religion in State schools and to establish the *curriculum* for the education and teaching of that religion in those schools according to the dispositions in this regard of the Bishops in Ordinary of these Islands'[1091] and, further, in section 47(5) that a minor's parents have the right to opt that such minor may not receive Catholic instruction.[1092] Non-Catholic religions are not considered at par with the Catholic religion as these are not taught in school. Finally, the Education Act contains a provision regulating the Faculty of Theology at the University of Malta. In terms of Schedule 3 to the Education Act, the Archbishop has to approve all the appointment of teachers at the Faculty of Theology. This is in line with Canon 812 of the Code of Canon Law of 1983.[1093]

1090. Chapter 237 of the Laws of Malta.

1091. Canon 1381 paragraph 1 provides that 'the religious instruction of youth in schools of whatever kind is subject to the authority and inspection of the Church. In terms of paragraph 3, Ordinaries of places have also the right to approve teachers and textbooks of religion and also to demand in the interest of religion and morality that either teachers or books be removed.' *See* Bouscaren and Ellis, *supra* note 1088, p. 747.

1092. The Constitution of Malta, section 40(2) provides as follows: 'No person shall be required to receive instruction in religion or to show knowledge or proficiency in religion if, in the case of a person who has not attained the age of sixteen years, objection to such requirement is made by the person who according to law has authority over him and, in any other case, if the person so required objects thereto: provided that no such requirement shall be held to be inconsistent with or in contravention of this article to the extent that the knowledge of, or the proficiency or instruction in, religion is required for the teaching of such religion, or for admission to the priesthood or to a religious order, or for other religious purposes, and except so far as that requirement is shown not to be reasonably justifiable in a democratic society.'

1093. Canon 812 of the 1917 Code of Canon Law reads as follows: 'Those who teach theological disciplines in any institutes of higher studies whatever must have a mandate from the competent ecclesiastical authority.' *See* Beal, Coriden and Green, *supra* note 1088, pp. 966–971.

IV. Recent Trends in State: Church Relations

572. State-Church relations in Malta cannot be said to have been without difficulty. The State did have its share of feuds with the Catholic Church. Two such hostilities occurred in the last century, the first was between the Progressive Constitutional Party headed by Lord Gerald Strickland and the Church and the second between the MLP led by Dom Mintoff and the Church led by Mgr. Sir Michael Gonzi.[1094] Two other hostilities related to Church schools[1095] and Church property.[1096]

573. Inroads to the relationship between Church and State are however developing in the direction of emphasizing more the lay component of the state rather than the Catholic component of the state. This is due to the fact that the Catholic faith in Malta is on the decline and that Maltese are questioning the teachings of the magisterium especially in areas related to divorce, same-sex unions, surrogacy and other morally related issues. Recently divorce was introduced following a positive outcome in a referendum and then through a law amending the Civil Code, the enactment of legislation allowing transsexuals to marry (this being a type of same-sex marriage), and lately the introduction of a Civil Unions Act which not only allows gay and lesbian marriages but also adoption of children by such couples.[1097] The Catholic values which were very strong in Malta in the past are being eroded and evidencing a trend towards the secularization of the state. Government is also proposing the revision of the Embryo Protection Act though, at the moment of writing, no Bill has been published encapsulating Government's proposals for legislative change.[1098] Government has also stated that it will allow same-sex couples to marry as well even though civil unions are, for all intents and purposes of law, equivalent to marriage. As a matter of fact, section 4(1) of the Civil Unions Act provides that: 'Save as provided in this Act a civil union, once registered, shall *mutatis mutandis* have the corresponding effects and consequences in law of civil marriage contracted under this Act.'

1094. *See* Charles Buttigieg, *Mikiel Gonzi: Ħamsin Sena fit-Tmum* (Translation: Michael Gonzi: 50 Years a Leader), *Klabb Kotba Maltin*, 2015, pp. 5–6 and pp. 69–80; and Arthur Bonnici, *History of the Church in Malta, Volume III, Period IV – 1800-1975*, Arthur Bonnici, Veritas Press, Zabbar, 1975, pp. 266–277. *See also* Dom Mintoff, 'Priests and Politics in Malta: A Brief Analysis', in Mario Cutajar (ed.), *Mintoff: il-bniedem u l-istorja* (Translation: Mintoff: the Man and History), Pubblikazzjonijiet SKS, 2012, pp. 246–252; and Cesare Catania, *Strickland, Britain and the Vatican 1929-1932*, Agius & Agius Ltd., Ħamrun, 2011, pp. 41–62.

1095. *See* Fr Dominic Scerri O.P., *The Saga of the Church Schools in Malta (1970-1986): A Historical Portrayal of Events*, MUT Publications Ltd., Valletta, 2000.

1096. *See* Edgar Mizzi, *Malta in the Making: 1962-1987: An Eyewitness Account*, Edgar Mizzi, Malta, 1995, pp. 389–427.

1097. *See* Joseph Ellul O.P., 'The Catholic Identity of Malta after Ten Years of Membership in the European Union: Challenges and Prospects', *Reflections on a Decade of EU Membership: Expectations, Reflections, Achievements, Disappointments, The Future.* Occasional Paper 02/2004, Institute for European Studies, University of Malta, Msida, 2014; and Emmanuel Agius, 'Co-operation in Marriage-Related Legislation', *Melita Theologica*, Vol. 65, No. 2, 2015, pp. 27–51.

1098. *Conferentia Episcopalis Melitensis*, *Legislation Regulating Assisted Human Procreation: A Position Paper*, Archbishop's Curia, Floriana, November 2015.

V. Agreements with the Vatican

574. A number of agreements have been concluded with the Vatican. These include:

(a) An Agreement entered into between the Holy See and Malta, signed on the 28th day of November 1991, relative to the transfer to the State of such immovable property in Malta as is not required by the Catholic Church for pastoral purposes and on the determination of certain issues pertaining to the relations between the Church and the State as regards matters of patrimony; which Agreement was done in two originals in the English and Italian language. The text of the said Agreement (without the annexes thereto) is reproduced in the Schedule to this Act. A copy of the Agreement, was laid on the Table of the House of Representatives on 29 November 1991 and 25 May 1992 (as to the annexes).[1099]
(b) An Agreement between the Holy See and Malta on the Recognition of Civil Effects to Canonical Marriages and to the Decisions of the Ecclesiastical Authorities and Tribunals about the Same Marriages, as well as the Protocol of Application thereto, both signed in Malta on the 3 February 1993.
(c) A Third Additional Protocol thereto was signed in Malta on 27 January 2014, which Agreement and protocols are reproduced in the Schedule to the Marriage (Amendment) Act, 2014.[1100]

§3. Relations Between the State and Other Religious Denominations

575. There is a Muslim community in Malta which is made up of around 35,000 Muslims. It has its own mosque and Imam. The state helps financially the Muslim's school. There is nothing extraordinary in this as the state also assists Church schools. However, there has been a difficulty with regard to practice of religion in a mosque as the sole mosque which exists in Paola can accommodate only 1,500 Muslims and is therefore considered to be insufficient to cope with the larger religious congregation.[1101] Government has eased this problem by making available a place in Floriana where the Muslim community can pray.

1099. Ecclesiastical Entities (Properties) Act, Laws of Malta, Chapter 358.
1100. Act No. XXI of 2014.
1101. News bulletin, TVM, 8 January 2016, 8 o'clock evening news item.

Chapter 2. The Economic Constitution

§1. The Way to a Mixed Economy

576. The Constitution does not adopt a specific economic model. It does not state that the Maltese economy is a free market economy, a collectivist economy or a mixed economy. However, from the reading of the Constitution, one understands that the Constitution favours a mixed economy. That a collectivist economy is excluded emerges from section 18 of the Constitution which states that the 'State shall encourage private economic enterprise'. But such a provision, on the other hand, is not advocating a free market economy where capitalism reigns supreme. On the contrary, the Constitution encourages the social function. This is done through the encouragement of co-operatives. Section 20 states that the 'State recognizes the social function of co-operatives and shall encourage their development'. Furthermore, there is also a social function to the use of private property. Therefore, the conclusion that one arrives at when reading the Constitution, is that it opts more for a mixed economy rather than a free market or a collectivist economy, even though this is not specifically and clearly stated by the Constitution but can be arrived at by necessary implication.

§2. Economic Principles in the Constitution

577. The Constitution advocates the encouragement by the State of three economic rights. These are:

(a) the encouragement of private economic enterprise in section 18;
(b) the protection of artisan trades in section 19; and
(c) the encouragement of co-operatives in section 20.

578. The Constitution allows the compulsory taking possession of or acquisition of private property, even if this is made subject to the payment of adequate compensation.[1102] As a matter of fact, the Constitution contains a long list of instances where private property may be compulsorily taken by the State.[1103] What must nonetheless be noted about the three above-mentioned economic rights is that, strictly speaking, the Constitution does not refer to them as 'rights' but as 'principles' which, though fundamental to the governance of the country and which it is the State's duty to apply in making laws, are unenforceable. This is stated quite clearly in section 21 of the Constitution:

> The provisions of this Chapter shall not be enforceable in any court, but the principles therein contained are nevertheless fundamental to the governance of

1102. Constitution, section 37(1).
1103. *Ibid.*, section 37(2).

the country and it shall be the aim of the State to apply these principles in making laws.

579. For these principles to be translated into rights, they have to be incorporated in a law. Thus it is necessary, at this juncture, to examine how these principles have been enshrined into a legal instrument.

I. The Encouragement of Private Economic Enterprise

580. The encouragement of private economic enterprise is contained in a number of laws. Consider the following:

(a) the Business Promotion Act;[1104]
(b) the Small Enterprises (Loan Guarantee) Act;[1105]
(c) the Malta Enterprise Act;[1106] and
(d) the Small Business Act.[1107]

II. The Protection of Artisan Trades

581. There is one law in Malta which is intended to protect artisan trades. This is the Malta Crafts Council Act.[1108]

III. The Encouragement of Co-operatives

582. Co-operatives are encouraged through the Co-operative Societies Act.[1109]

§3. Freedom of Private Economic Enterprise

583. Freedom of private economic enterprise is manifested by the emphasis Maltese Law places on the implementation of the constitutional principle of the encouragement of private economic enterprise, thereby following the principle of the liberalization of economic activities. Private economic enterprise is encouraged in various ways as can be seen hereunder.

1104. Chapter 325 of the Laws of Malta.
1105. Chapter 397 of the Laws of Malta.
1106. Chapter 463 of the Laws of Malta.
1107. Chapter 512 of the Laws of Malta.
1108. Chapter 421 of the Laws of Malta.
1109. Chapter 442 of the Laws of Malta.

I. The Business Promotion Act

584. The long title of the Business Promotion Act is to 'encourage the establishment of new businesses and the expansion of existing ones, and to make ancillary arrangements in relation thereto'. It is this law which provides 'incentives and benefits'[1110] which are 'due to and obtained by any enterprise which carries on or intends to carry on, in Malta, a trade or business'.[1111] The typology of trades and businesses that are entitled to benefit under the enactment are listed in section 3(1)(a) to (k) and it is only a qualifying company, that is, 'a company which carries on, or intends to carry on in Malta, a trade or business consisting solely of any of the activities referred to in section 3(1)(a) to (k)',[1112] which is entitled to partake of such incentives and benefits. The Business Promotion Act lists, in Parts II and III, the incentives which a qualified company can benefit from. Further details are provided in the Business Promotion Regulations[1113] which, *inter alia*, also distinguish between a medium-sized enterprise,[1114] a small enterprise[1115] and a micro enterprise.[1116]

II. The Small Enterprises (Loan Guarantee) Act

585. The Small Enterprises (Loan Guarantee) Act has the main purpose, as set out in the enactment's long title as that to 'encourage the establishment of new small enterprises and the expansion of existing new ones through the provision of loan guarantees by the Malta Development Corporation' (now known as the 'Malta Enterprise').[1117] The Small Enterprises (Loan Guarantee) Act also defines the term 'small enterprise' for the purpose of that law, but the definition is in stark contrast with that afforded by the Business Promotion Act.[1118] Essentially the Small Enterprises (Loan Guarantee) Act allows a small enterprise to obtain an assisted loan from Malta Enterprise if it does not manage to 'obtain a conventional loan from an authorized bank for lack of adequate security or business track record'.[1119]

III. The Malta Enterprise Act

586. The Malta Enterprise Act was enacted, in terms of its long title, to 'make provision for the establishment of a corporation in Malta, to determine the functions

1110. Business Promotion Act, section 2(4).
1111. *Ibid.*, section 3(1).
1112. *Ibid.*, section 2(1).
1113. Subsidiary Legislation 325.06.
1114. *Ibid.*, in particular, regulation 3(1)(a).
1115. *Ibid.*, in particular, regulation 3(1)(b).
1116. *Ibid.*, in particular, regulation 3(1)(c).
1117. Malta Enterprise Act, section 43.
1118. Compare and contrast the definitions of 'small enterprise' in section 3(1)(b) of the Business Promotion Act with that in section 2 of the Small Enterprises (Loan Guarantee) Act.
1119. Small Enterprises (Loan Guarantee) Act, section 3(1).

and powers of the Corporation in order to promote enterprise and related business undertakings in Malta, to encourage the establishment of new business undertakings and the expansion of existing business undertakings in Malta, to provide for the development and administration of incentives, schemes and other forms of support for such ventures and to provide for matters ancillary or in relation thereto and to provide for powers to rationalize and update the relevant legislation in the sector'. This law requires the Government to 'cooperate with the private sector to promote private enterprise in Malta'.[1120] It further requires Government to, from time to time, 'determine Malta's principal economic policies and objectives' and to 'appropriate such funds and provide such incentives as it considers necessary to achieve such aims'.[1121] Such economic objectives and policies are to be achieved by Government through increased investment, employment and entrepreneurship; improved international competitiveness; diversification of the local industry base; the development of enterprise networking and inter-sector linkages as well as of human resources; and the promotion of industrial research, technology development and innovation, and such other strategies as may be conducive to the achievement of such objectives and policies.[1122] Support measures on the lines indicated in the law[1123] have to be established by Government to achieve the goals set out in section 4(2) of the Malta Enterprise Act. The Assistance to Small and Medium-Sized Undertakings Regulations sets out the various types of assistance which such undertakings may enjoy.[1124]

IV. The Small Business Act

587. The Small Business Act was enacted with the objective, in terms of the long title of the enactment, to 'enhance the operational environment for medium and small enterprises in order to facilitate their setting up and growth. It seeks to identify those areas where the existing regulatory environment can be improved in order to provide solutions that will benefit enterprises and make it easier for them to operate. It further sets up the Enterprise Consultative Council and the College of Regulators, two advisory bodies, which aim to provide a forum for consultation and social dialogue, advise Government on challenges faced by the business enterprise, address grievances which emanate from the business enterprise and come up with remedial action'. The enactment requires the public administration to 'endeavour to facilitate the carrying out of business activities'[1125] and sets out a number of obligations which the public administration has to comply with. The law establishes an Enterprise Consultative Council with the functions of making recommendations to Government on issues relating to the enterprise sector and on the formulation of policies in the field of small and medium enterprises; of working towards improvements in the operating environment for small enterprises; of reviewing, discussing and providing advice on legislative

1120. Malta Enterprise Act, section 3.
1121. *Ibid.*, section 4(1).
1122. *Ibid.*, section 4(2).
1123. *Ibid.*, section 4(3).
1124. Subsidiary Legislation 463.03.
1125. Small Business Act, section 3(1).

proposals that have a significant impact on the enterprise sector; of monitoring the proper implementation of government policy; and of instigating research, monitoring, evaluating and advocating measures for an environment conducive to a high level of service provision.[1126] In addition, the Council is tasked to:

(a) work on identifying issues which hinder enterprise growth, development and competitiveness;
(b) follow such policy guidelines as may be set out by Government;
(c) promote cost-conscious and effective regulation;
(d) promote synergies in the application of government policy within the Administration; and
(e) undertake research work in-house, or through outsourcing, or relevant issues.[1127]

588. The enactment also establishes a College of Regulators which, amongst other functions, has to 'ensure better use of regulation to promote efficiency, economy and competition within the enterprise sector'[1128] and to 'hold regular joint meetings with the Council and discuss topics of importance for the enterprise sector'.[1129] The College is mandated by law to 'develop measures for the promotion of efficiency, better economy and competition within the enterprise sector'[1130] and to identify regulatory barriers which hinder the growth of the enterprise sector and make recommendations to address such issues'.[1131]

§4. Co-operative Societies and Handicraft

I. Co-operative Societies

589. Co-operative Societies are regulated by the Co-operative Societies Act.[1132] The purpose of this enactment as stated in its long title is to 'provide for the constitution, registration and control of co-operative societies and for matters connected therewith or ancillary thereto'. The law establishes a Register of Co-operative Societies[1133] held by the Co-operatives Board established by section 3 of the enactment. It regulates the formation and registration of co-operative societies, their organization and duties,

1126. *Ibid.*, section 11(1).
1127. *Ibid.*, section 11(2).
1128. *Ibid.*, section 14(1)(b).
1129. *Ibid.*, section 14(1)(d).
1130. *Ibid.*, section 14(2)(a).
1131. *Ibid.*, section 14(2)(b).
1132. Chapter 442 of the Laws of Malta. For a study of co-operatives, *see* David Fabri, E.P. Delia, John Rouse, Janos Juhasz, John Millns, Egon Samler and Kyriacos Patsalos, *Reconsidering Co-operatives: Lessons for Maltese Co-ops*, APS Bank, Floriana, 2006; and Godfrey Baldacchino, 'Worker Cooperatives in Malta: Between Self-Help and Subsidy' in Ronald G. Sultana and Godfey Baldacchino (eds), *Maltese Society: A Sociological Inquiry*, Mireva Publications Ltd., Msida, 1994.
1133. Co-operative Societies Act, section 10.

rights and duties of members, operation and management of co-operative societies, property and funds of co-operative societies, their amalgamation, dissolution and liquidation and the constitution, functions and duties of the Apex organization. A Central Co-operatives Fund Committee is established by the Central Co-operative Fund Regulations[1134] responsible:

(a) to administer the Central Co-operative Fund;
(b) to promote co-operative education and training for the general development of the co-operative movement in Malta, and to carry out all activities relating thereto;
(c) to finance educational and training programmes relating to the promotion and development of the co-operative movement for members of and personnel engaged by co-operatives and other persons who may actively contribute to the promotion of the co-operative movement;
(d) to commission studies and research on particular areas of co-operative activity or any individual co-operative society in Malta, with a view to assessing past performance and discovering possible potential for future operation;
(e) to produce or publish co-operative educational material for use by members of co-operative societies, students and the general public with a view to promoting co-operative ideals and practice;
(f) to sponsor participation by co-operatives in trade fairs as specialized fairs for the promotion of co-operative societies or the co-operative movement in general;
(g) to support and intensify the participation of the Maltese co-operative movement in relevant organizations, activities and projects on an international level;
(h) to support the existence and development of co-operative societies in all sectors of the economy and society;
(i) to consider and, where deemed appropriate, to support the educational programmes proposed by the Board from time to time;
(j) to collect, recover and institute proceedings for the payment of sums to the Central Co-operative Fund.[1135]

II. Crafts

590. The Malta Crafts Council Act has, as its long title, 'the encouragement, promotion and regulation of crafts and craftsmen, in particular crafts forming part of Malta's historical heritage, for the setting up of a national crafts council to be called the Malta Crafts Council and for matters ancillary to or connected therewith'. The enactment does not provide an exhaustive list of crafts. On the contrary, it defines 'craft' as an 'art, skill or trade' but stops from listing such crafts.[1136] Instead it empowers the Ministry responsible for industry in section 3 to declare an art, skill, trade or industry to be a craft 'practised by a person or persons in the manufacture of artefacts and other products and generally requiring in their manufacturing a greater input of

1134. Subsidiary Legislation 442.03, regulation 3(1).
1135. *Ibid.*, regulation 3(1).
1136. Malta Crafts Council Act, section 2.

human skill than of machinery'.[1137] A list of forty-six arts, skills, trades and industries considered as Maltese crafts has been published by the Minister responsible for industry in terms of the Maltese Craft (Constitution) Order.[1138] A craftsman may register with the Malta Crafts Council in terms of the Registration of Craftsmen and Entrepreneurs (Malta Crafts Council) Regulations.[1139] The functions of the Malta Crafts Council are the following:

(a) 'to register craftsmen and entrepreneurs in accordance with such rules as may be prescribed;
(b) to promote a steady interest, appreciation, promotion and regulation of Maltese crafts in particular and in Maltese crafts in general among all sectors of the community both resident and foreign;
(c) to support and safeguard the interests of craftsmen through the promotion of studies for the identification of raw materials, design, market research and sales programmes;
(d) to promote the revival of traditional Maltese crafts;
(e) to promote the creation of opportunities for the production of Maltese craft products;
(f) to establish a voluntary certification system whereby the genuineness of Maltese craft products is guaranteed and to regulate and supervise such system;
(g) to advise the Minister on all aspects of Maltese crafts, generally and in particular in the formulation of a national policy on Maltese crafts, and in the making of regulations under this Act;
(h) to advise on the implementation of, and to monitor, the national policy on Maltese crafts;
(i) to establish international contacts with the aim of enhancing Maltese crafts;
(j) to perform any other function as may be assigned to it under this or any other law.'

§5. Ownership in the Maltese Constitution

591. Ownership in the Constitution is seen from the perspective of a fundamental human right, but it is not considered to be an absolute right. What the Constitution protects is not the actual right of ownership but the protection from deprivation of property without compensation. In other words, the Constitution does not protect the right to own property per se but ensures that if that property is deprived from a person, that person is duly compensated. On the other hand, the Civil Code regulates in more detail the right of ownership of private property.[1140] In terms of section 320 of the Civil Code, 'ownership is the right of enjoying and disposing of things in the most absolute manner, provided no use thereof is made which is prohibited by law'. Section 321 then provides that: 'No person can be compelled to give up his property or to permit

1137. *Ibid.*
1138. Subsidiary Legislation 421.02.
1139. Subsidiary Legislation 421.01.
1140. Chapter 16, sections 320–327.

any other person to make use of it, except for a public purpose, and upon payment of a fair compensation.' In terms of the Civil Code, 'All things which can be the subject of private or public ownership are either movable or immovable property.'[1141] The Civil Code thus makes it clear that property may be in public or private ownership. The Constitution does in no way contradict this principle.

§6. Public Ownership

592. The Constitution states that nothing in section 37 'shall be construed as affecting the making or operation of any law so far as it provides for vesting in the Government of Malta the ownership of any underground minerals, water or antiquities'. These three matters are in fact regulated by the following laws:

a. the Malta Resources Authority Act,[1142] which although it does not vest ownership of mineral resources in the State, requires a licence in connection with any activity or operation related to underground minerals and water:

Save as may otherwise be prescribed, no person shall carry out any activity or operation, or be engaged in such activity or operation, relating to energy, water and mineral resources unless such person is in possession of a licence, permit or other authorisation of the Authority under this Act: Provided that in relation to the exploration and production of hydrocarbons, power to exercise the issue of a licence under this Act shall be subject to an authorisation of the Minister in terms of the Petroleum (Production) Act;[1143] and

b. the Cultural Heritage Act[1144] with regard to movable objects:

Every movable object forming part of the cultural heritage discovered in any location within Malta, its territorial waters, and its contiguous zone whether

1141. Civil Code, section 307. *See also* the Civil Code (Amendment No. 3) Act, 2016, Act No. XXV of 2016, which regulates property in the public domain.
1142. Chapter 423 of the Laws of Malta.
1143. Malta Resources Authority Act, section 26(1).
1144. Chapter 445 of the Laws of Malta.

found in authorized or illegal excavations or exploration or accidentally in the course of any work or any other manner shall belong to the State;[1145] and

Discoveries made during a period of occupation by the Superintendent shall be the property of the Government.[1146]

593. According to section 327 of the Civil Code, vacant property belongs to the Government. However, the public administration is also a property holder, and various laws enacted by Parliament have empowered numerous entities of the public administration to own property. Quite a number of laws also regulate property owned by the Government such as:

(a) the Land Acquisition (Public Purposes) Ordinance[1147] whereby the Ordinance aims to 'regulate the acquisition of land for public purposes and to establish the procedure to be followed in relation thereto';[1148]
(b) Special Development Areas Act[1149] in terms of which 'the Government has earmarked an area within Malta for public acquisition with a view to its development for a public purpose other than merely of town planning';[1150]
(c) Commissioner of Land Ordinance[1151] in terms of which the Commissioner of Land assumed rights and liabilities 'relating to immovable property belonging to, or possessed, held or administered by the Government, or relating to the administration thereof' previously exercised by the Accountant General and for public corporations designated in the Ordinance or persons designated by the Minister responsible for land be empowered to exercise rights and responsibilities with regard to government land;[1152]
(d) UK Lands Vesting Act[1153] in terms of which provision was made 'for the vesting in or reversion to the Government of Malta of certain properties and rights which on 20 September, 1964 were vested in or belonged or pertained to or were held or were exercisable by certain departments or authorities of the Government of the UK or an authorized service organization';[1154]
(e) Land (Compulsory Eviction) Act[1155] in terms of which provision was made 'for the compulsory eviction from land and tenements owned or administered by the Government or held by Government under any other title';[1156]

1145. Cultural Heritage Act, section 43(6).
1146. *Ibid.*, section 45(5).
1147. Chapter 88 of the Laws of Malta.
1148. Long title to the Land Acquisition (Public Purposes) Ordinance.
1149. Chapter 149 of the Laws of Malta.
1150. Special Development Areas Act, section 3(1).
1151. Chapter 169 of the Laws of Malta.
1152. Commissioner of Land Ordinance, sections 2 and 3.
1153. Chapter 193 of the Laws of Malta.
1154. Long title of the United Kingdom Lands (Vesting) Act.
1155. Chapter 228 of the Laws of Malta.
1156. Long title of the Land (Compulsory Eviction) Act.

(f) Disposal of Government Land Act[1157] in terms of which provision was made to 'regulate the grant on any title of immovable property belonging to or administered by the Government, and to provide for matters ancillary thereto or connected therewith';[1158]
(g) Reversion of Certain Lands Act[1159] in terms of which provision was made 'for the restitution of land expropriated by virtue of the Building Development Areas Act';[1160]
(h) Administration of Lands Act[1161] in terms of which provision was made to provide for the administration of 'all lands belonging to foundations and administrations administered by the Government separate from the administration of other land belonging to the Government shall vest in the Government'.[1162]

594. The Civil Code also contemplates instances where property passes on to the Government. Such is the case of lost property[1163] and intestate succession.[1164] The Government can, when owning property, rent it out or dissolve a lease.[1165]

§7. Private Ownership

595. Private ownership is regulated by section 37(1) of the Constitution as stated above. It provides that 'in special cases Parliament may, if it deems it appropriate so to act in the national interest, by law establish the criteria which are to be followed, including the factors and other circumstances to be taken in account, in the determination of the compensation payable in respect of property compulsorily taken possession of or acquired; and in any such case the compensation shall be determined and shall be payable accordingly'. The matter is dealt with by the Land Acquisition (Public Purposes) Ordinance.[1166]

§8. Expropriation and Partial Expropriation

596. It is the Land Acquisition (Public Purposes) Ordinance which makes provision for expropriation and partial expropriation of immovable property. The President of Malta may declare any land to be required for a public purpose.[1167] The

1157. Chapter 268 of the Laws of Malta.
1158. Long title of the Disposal of Government Land Act.
1159. Chapter 432 of the Laws of Malta.
1160. Long title of the Reversion of Certain Lands Act.
1161. Chapter 448 of the Laws of Malta.
1162. Administration of Lands Act, section 2.
1163. Civil Code, section 564(6).
1164. *Ibid.*, sections 789 and 816.
1165. *Ibid.*, sections 1576A–1576D.
1166. Chapter 88 of the Laws of Malta.
1167. Land Acquisition (Public Purposes) Ordinance, section 3.

President may further declare that 'any land is subject to clearance rights and to subsoil rights'.[1168] The Commissioner of Land may acquire land for any public purpose either:

(a) by the absolute purchase thereof; or
(b) for the possession and use thereof for a stated time, or during such time as the exigencies of the public purpose shall require; or
(c) on public tenure.[1169]

1168. *Ibid.*, section 4.
1169. *Ibid.*, section 5.

Chapter 3. Constitutional Principles Relating to the Armed Forces

§1. The Maltese Constitution and the Deployment of the Armed Forces

597. The Constitution defines the term 'disciplined force', in section 47(1), as including 'a naval, military or air force of the Government of Malta'. The term 'disciplined force' is used mainly, though not exclusively, in Chapter IV of the Constitution dealing with fundamental rights and freedoms as follows: (a) section 35(2)(a); (b) section 36(3)(b); (c) section 39(9); (d) section 45(5)(a); (e) section 47(1) – 3 references; and (f) section 47(6). The expression is also used in section 57(c) proviso.

598. Although the expression 'disciplined force' is used in the Constitution, it must be made clear that this term is meant to include: (a) the naval, military and air forces of the Government of Malta; (b) the Malta Police Force; (c) any other police force established by law in Malta; and (d) the Malta prison service. Insofar as the police are concerned, there is only one Police Force established in Malta and that is established by law, by the Police Act.[1170] On the other hand, the definition of 'disciplined force' in the Constitution excludes another disciplined force currently in existence in Malta that is the Assistance and Rescue Force established by virtue of section 8 of the Civil Protection Act.[1171] Insofar as the Assistance and Rescue Force is concerned, that was established in 1999, quite some time after the 1964 Constitution was written, no consequential amendment was made to the Constitution to have the Assistance and Rescue Force included in the definition of 'disciplined force'. As to Customs Officers, the Customs Department has been in existence ever since 16 September 1909, the date of entry into force of the Customs Ordinance.[1172] Yet, this law does not state that Customs Officers are a disciplined force.

§2. Military Service

599. The Constitution does not refer to military service. This is because in Malta military service is not compulsory but voluntary. It is the Malta Armed Forces Act[1173] which regulates enlistment in the Armed Forces of Malta. Power to raise, maintain and regulate armed forces is vested in the President.[1174] The Armed Forces of Malta are thus made up of professional soldiers, both men and women, recruited specifically

1170. Chapter 164 of the Laws of Malta.
1171. Chapter 411 of the Laws of Malta.
1172. Chapter 37 of the Laws of Malta.
1173. Chapter 220 of the Laws of Malta.
1174. Malta Armed Forces Act, section 3.

for the job. In addition, the Malta Armed Forces Act allows the creation of a Reserve Force by the President.[1175] Calling a reserve force is an exceptional measure as it is allowed only when 'national danger is imminent or that a great emergency has arisen'.[1176]

§3. THE ORGANIZATION OF THE ARMED FORCES

600. The Constitution is silent on the organization of the Armed Forces. Indeed, the Constitution in Chapter X, entitled 'The Public Service', as its title indicates, only regulates the public service ignoring other services of the state such as the military service and the security service. These latter two services do not form part of the public service, and each service is regulated through its own law, the military service through the Malta Armed Forces Act and the Security Service through the Security Service Act.[1177] A parliamentary service will soon be established by ordinary law through Bill 137 of 2016 referred to above in paragraph 501 which will also be regulated through its own law.

601. The organization of the Armed Forces of Malta is set out in the Malta Armed Forces Act. It is organized in a Regular Force, a Territorial Force and a Reserve Force. Currently it has a Force Headquarters and five separate units – three land units, an air wing and a maritime squadron.[1178]

602. The Malta Armed Forces Act establishes military offences which are in turn tried by courts martial. The Court of Criminal Appeal has jurisdiction to hear and determine appeals from court martials.[1179]

§4. THE COMMAND STRUCTURE

603. The command structure is set out in the Designation, Command and Establishment of the Armed Forces of Malta Order.[1180] In terms of section 3(1) of that Order, the Commander of the Armed Forces of Malta is appointed by the Minister responsible for defence, currently the Minister for Home Affairs and National Security. The said Minister may also appoint a Deputy Commander of the Armed Forces of Malta. In the absence or inability to act of the Commander or Deputy Commander, the said Minister may appoint an officer to act as Commander. The Commander has the overall command of the Armed Forces of Malta whilst the Deputy Commander assists the Commander in the performance of his functions and duties.[1181] Normally

1175. *Ibid.*, section 32(1).
1176. *Ibid.*, section 32(1).
1177. Chapter 391 of the Laws of Malta.
1178. *See* www.afm.gov.mt/en/forcestructure.aspx. Last accessed on 31 March 2016.
1179. Malta Armed Forces Act, Chapter 220 of the Laws of Malta, section 116(1).
1180. Subsidiary Legislation 220.02.
1181. *Ibid.*, section 3(2) and (3).

the Commander enjoys the rank of a Brigadier.[1182] Furthermore, 'the Minister responsible for defence may place any part of the Armed Forces of Malta under a separate command and in any such case he may appoint a separate commander and in respect of such part of the Armed Forces of Malta'.[1183]

§5. Police Powers

604. It is to be noted that the Armed Forces of Malta, in addition to their military duties, enjoy police powers as is the case of Officers of Customs in terms of Certain Powers of Officers of Customs Regulations.[1184] Section 4(3) of the Malta Armed Forces Act provides that:

> (3) It shall be lawful for the President of Malta by order to empower any member of the force to exercise, in addition to any functions, powers and duties he may have as a member of the force, all or any one or more of the functions, powers and duties as are by law vested in a member of the Malta Police Force and in an officer of the Customs.

605. An order to this effect was made in terms of the Assignment of Powers to Armed Forces of Malta Order.[1185] In relevant part, the Order reads as follows:

> In the performance of patrol, guard or security duties or of duties in connection with criminal offences, assigned to him by a Commander of the Armed Forces of Malta, whether such duties are performed on land, sea or air, a member of the Armed Forces of Malta shall be empowered to exercise all such functions, powers and duties as are by law vested in an officer of the Customs or in a member of the Malta Police Force: Provided that such functions, powers and duties as are by law reserved to officers holding the rank not below that of Inspector of Police shall only be exercisable by a member who holds a commission in the Armed Forces of Malta.[1186]

1182. Paul Edgar Micallef, *Criminal Courts and Courts-Martial: A Comparative Study Relating to Jurisdiction and Procedure, with Particular Reference to the Malta Armed Forces Act, 1970*, Faculty of Laws, University of Malta, Msida, 1983, p. 25.
1183. Subsidiary Legislation 220.02, regulation 3(4).
1184. Subsidiary Legislation 37.09. Regulation 2 provides that: 'Every officer of Customs shall, in addition to the powers and duties assigned to him under the Customs Ordinance, be empowered to exercise all the powers and duties as are by law vested in an officer of the Executive Police in any place set out in the Schedule to these Regulations in connection with an offence committed or suspected of having been committed: Provided that such functions, powers and duties as are by law reserved to officers holding the rank not below that of inspector of Police shall only be exercisable by officials not below the rank of Officer I.'
1185. Subsidiary Legislation 220.06.
1186. *Ibid.*, section 2.

§6. Parliamentary Control of the Armed Forces of Malta

606. A proclamation of public emergency comprises situations when Malta is at war, declaring a state of public emergency or declaring that democratic institutions of Malta are threatened by subversion. In all these three cases, especially, the first, the Armed Forces of Malta have a crucial role of play. Such a proclamation of public emergency is made by the President on the advice of the government. Once made, it has to be forthwith communicated to the House of Representatives and, if the House is not in session, it shall be summoned to meet.[1187] The proclamation remains in force up to a period of fourteen days unless it is extended by the House for a maximum period not exceeding three months.[1188] If the resolution expires, another one can be made at or before the end of said period.[1189] The matter is also dealt with by the Emergency Powers Act.[1190]

1187. Constitution, section 47(3)(a).
1188. *Ibid.*, section 47(3)(b) and (c).
1189. *Ibid.*, section 47(4).
1190. Chapter 178 of the Laws of Malta.

Selected Bibliography

Books

Aquilina, Kevin and Micallef, Paul Edgar. *A Profile of the Maltese Courts of Justice*, Department of Information, Valletta, March 1992.

Aquilina, Kevin. *Development Planning Legislation: The Maltese Experience*, Mireva Publications, Msida, May 1999.

Aristotle (384-322 BC), *The Politics*, Bk iv, xiv, 1297b35.

Attard, David Joseph, with the assistance of Aquilina, Kevin and Mallia, Patricia. *The Maltese Legal System, Volume I: A General Introduction,* Malta University Press, Msida, 2012.

Attard, David Joseph, with the assistance of Aquilina, Kevin and Mallia, Patricia. *The Maltese Legal System, Volume II, Constitutional and Human Rights Law*, Part A, Malta University Press, Msida, 2015.

Azzopardi, Andrew. *George Abela: Qalb in-Nies* (Translation: George Abela: The Heart of, and Amongst, the People), Kite, B'Kara, 2014.

Bailey, Stephen. *Cross on Principles of Local Government Law*, Sweet and Maxwell, London, 1992.

Barnett, Hilaire. *Constitutional and Administrative Law*, tenth edition, Routledge, London, 2013.

Beal, John P., Coriden, James A. and Green, Thomas J. (eds), *New Commentary on the Code of Canon Law*, Paulist Press, New York, 2000.

Bezzina, Joseph. *The Gozo Civic Council: The Story of a Regional Government*, Victoria, Gozo, Committee Fiftieth Anniversary Celebrations Gozo Civic Council, 2011.

Bingham, Tom. *The Rule of Law*, Penguin Books, London, 2011.

Bonnici, Arthur. *History of the Church in Malta, Volume III, Period IV – 1800-1975*, Arthur Bonnici, Veritas Press, Zabbar, 1975.

Bouscaren, T. Lincoln and Ellis, Adam C. *Canon Law: A Text and Commentary,* 3rd rev. edn, The Bruce Publishing Company, Milwaukee, 1957.

Brincat, Joseph M. *Maltese and Other Languages: A Linguistic History of Malta*, Midsea Books Ltd., Sta. Venera, 2011.

Brown, E.D. *The International Law of the Sea*, Volume I – *Introductory Manual*, Dartmouth Publishing Company Limited, Aldershot, 1994.

Selected Bibliography

Buttigieg, Charles. *Mikiel Gonzi: Ħamsin Sena fit-Tmum* (Translation: Michael Gonzi: 50 Years a Leader), *Klabb Kotba Maltin*, 2015.

Carp, Robert A. and Stidham, Ronald. *Outline of the American Legal System*, Bureau of International Information Programs, United States Department of State, Washington, 2004.

Catania, Cesare. *Strickland, Britain and the Vatican 1929-1932*, Agius & Agius Ltd., Ħamrun, 2011.

Clews, Stanley J.A. *Malta Year Book 2003*, De La Salle Brothers Publications, Sliema, 2003.

Craig, P.P. *Administrative Law*, 5th edn, Sweet & Maxwell, London, 2003.

de Secondat, Charles-Louis, Baron de Montesqieu, *The Spirit of Laws*, New York, Prometheus Books, 2002.

Dicey, Albert Venn. *An Introduction to the Study of the Law of the Constitution,* 10th edn, The Macmillan Press Ltd., London.

Fabri, David, Delia, E.P., Rouse, John, Juhasz, Janos, Millns, John, Samler, Egon and Patsalos, Kyriacos. *Reconsidering Co-operatives: Lessons for Maltese Co-ops*, APS Bank, Floriana.

Fenech Adami, Eddie, with the assistance of Mallia, Steve. *Eddie: My Journey,* Allied Publications, Valletta, 2014.

Friggieri, Oliver. *Dun Karm il-Bniedem fil-Poeta* (Translation: Rev. Carm The Man in the Poet), Valletta, *Edizzjoni Klabb Kotba Maltin* (Translation: Maltese Book Club Edition), 1980.

Friggieri, Oliver. *L-Istorja tal-Innu Malti: Kif Sar U Xi Jfisser* (Translation: The History of the Maltese Anthem: Its Formulation and Meaning), Valletta, *Klabb Kotba Maltin* (Translation: Maltese Book Club), 2014.

Garner (ed.), Bryan A. *Black's Law Dictionary*, eighth edition, West, a Thomson business, St. Paul MN, 2004.

Gulia, Oliver. *The Public Servant in Maltese Law*, Progress Press Co. Ltd., Valletta, undated.

Hood Phillips, Owen, Jackson, Paul and Leopold, Patricia. *O. Hood Phillips and Jackson, Constitutional and Administrative Law,* 8th edn, Sweet & Maxwell, London, 2001.

Hull, Geoffrey. *The Maltese Language Question: A Case Study in Cultural Imperialism*, Said Publications Ltd., Valletta.

Loveland, Ian. *Constitutional Law, Administrative Law, and Human Rights: A Critical Introduction*, 5th edn, Oxford University Press, Oxford, 2009.

Mangion, Raymond (ed.). *Speakers' Rulings in the Parliament of Malta, First Volume, Part One, The Legislative Assembly, 1921-1924*, House of Representatives, Valletta, and Malta University Press, 2012.

Selected Bibliography

Mifsud, Ivan. *Judicial Review of Administrative Action in Malta: An Examination of Article 469A COCP and of Judicial Review in General*, Book Distributors Limited, San Ġwann, 2017.

Mifsud Bonnici, Giuseppe. *Constitutional Procedure Relative to Fundamental Rights and Freedoms*, 2nd rev. edn, Midsea Books, Sta. Venera, 2012.

Mifsud Bonnici, Ugo. *Il-Manwal tal-President* (Translation: The Manual of the President of the Republic), Office of the President, Valletta (undated).

Mifsud Bonnici, Ugo. An Introduction to the Law of Education, Malta University Press, Msida, 2013.

Mifsud Bonnici, Ugo. *Konvinzjoni u Esperjenza (Translation: Conviction and Experience)*, Klabb Kotba Maltin (Translation: Malta Book Club), 2015.

Mizzi, Edgar. *Malta in the Making: 1962-1987: An Eyewitness Account*, Edgar Mizzi, Malta, 1995.

Olson, Keith W. *An Outline of American History*, Washington, United States Information Agency (undated).

Pirotta, Godfrey A. *Malta's Parliament: An Official History*, Office of the Speaker of the House of Representatives and the Department of Information, Valletta, 2008.

Pirotta, Joseph M. *L-Istorja Kostituzzjonali u L-Isfond Storiku (1942-2004)* (Translation: Constitutional History and the Historical Background 1942-2004), Independence Publications – PIN, Pjetà, 2005.

Robinson, Olivia F., Fergus, T. David and Gordon, William M. *European Legal History*, 2nd edn, Butterworths, London 1994.

Russell, Alison. *Legislative and Other Forms*, Butterworths & Co., London, 1924.

Said (ed.), Philip E. *Dun Karm: Patrimonju Malti u Żebbuġi* (Translation: Rev Carm: Maltese and Zebbugian [from the village of Żebbuġ] Patrimony), Ħaż-Żebbuġ Local Council, 2012.

Sammut, Mark A., Cuignet, Patrick and Borg, David A., *Malta at the European Court of Human Rights 1987-2012,* Birkirkara, *ius melitae*, 2012.

Scerri O.P., Fr Dominic. *The Saga of the Church Schools in Malta (1970-1986): A Historical Portrayal of Events*, MUT Publications Ltd., Valletta, 2000.

Schiavone (ed.), Michael J. *Dictionary of Maltese Biographies, Volume II, G-Z*, Pubblikazzjonijiet Indipendenza, Pjetà, 2009.

Schiavone, Michael J. *L-Elezzjonijiet F'Pajjiżna Fl-Isfond Storiku 1800-2013* (Translation: Elections in our Country within a Historical Background 1800-2013), Independence Publications – PIN, Pjetà, 2013.

Schlaich, Klaus. *Das Bundesverfassungsgericht*, 3rd edn, Verlag C.H. Beck, Munich, 1994.

Shaw, Malcolm N. *International Law*, 3rd edn, Cambridge, Grotius Publications Limited, 1991.

Simma, Bruno (ed.). *The Charter of the United Nations: A Commentary*, Oxford, Oxford University Press, 1994.

Steiner, Josephine, Woods, Lorna and Twigg-Flesner, Christian. *EU Law*, 9th edn, Oxford University Press, Oxford, 2006.

Turner, John Frayn. *The Awards of the George Cross 1940-2009*, Pen & Sword Military, South Yorkshire, 2010.

Turpin, Colin and Tomkins, Adam. *British Government and the Constitution*, Cambridge University Press, Cambridge, 2011.

Vassallo, Mario Thomas. *The Europeanization of Interest Groups in Malta and Ireland: A Small State Perspective*, Palgrave Macmillan, Hampshire, 2015.

Weis, Paul. *Nationality and Statelessness in International Law*, The Netherlands, Sijthoff & Noordhoff International Publishers B.V., 1979.

Wheare, Kenneth C. *Modern Constitutions*, Oxford University Press, Oxford, 1951.

Wolf-Phillips, Leslie. *Comparative Constitutions*, The Macmillan Press Ltd., London, 1972.

Book chapters

Abela, George. 'Foreword', in Office of the President, *The President's Forum: Does Malta's Constitution Still Cater for the People's Needs?*, Office of the President, Valletta, 2013, p. 6.

Aquilina, Kevin. 'The Human Right Principle of Legality: *Nullum Crimen/Nulla Poena Sine Lege*', in David E. Zammit (ed.), *Maltese Perspectives on Human Rights*, Valletta, Foundation For International Studies, University of Malta, March 2009, pp. 52–75.

Aquilina, Kevin. 'The Legislative Development of Human Rights and Fundamental Freedoms in Malta: A Chronological Appraisal' in Norman A. Martínez Gutiérrez, *Serving the Rule of International Law: Essays in Honour of Professor David Joseph Attard,* First Volume, Mare Nostrum Publications, Gudja, 2009, pp. 225–247.

Aquilina, Kevin. 'Remedies under Maltese Law for Wrongful State Action in Breach of EU Law: A Case of Crying Over Spilt Milk?', in Eugène Buttigieg (ed.), *Enforcing One's Rights Under EU Law*, Gutenberg Press, Tarxien, 2011, pp. 87–130.

Aquilina, Kevin. 'Why a Second Republic for Malta?', in Office of the President, *The President's Forum: Does Malta's Constitution Still Cater for the People's Needs?*, Office of the President, Valletta, 2013, pp. 152–198.

Aquilina, Kevin. 'Territorial Sea and the Contiguous Zone', in Malgosia Fitzmaurice and Norman Martínez Gutiérrez (eds), *The IMLI Manual of International Maritime Law, Volume I, The Law of the Sea*, Oxford University Press, Oxford, 2014, pp. 26–70.

Selected Bibliography

Aquilina, Kevin. 'Do Pronouncements of the Constitutional Court Bind *Erga Omnes*? The Common Law Doctrine of *Stare Decisis* versus the Civil Law Doctrine of Nonbinding Case Law within a Maltese Law Context' in Vernon Valentine Palmer, Mohamed Y. Matar and Anna Koppel (eds.), *Mixed Legal Systems: East and West*, Ashgate Publishing Limited, Surrey, 2015, pp. 43–53.

Aquilina, Kevin and Calleja, Isabelle. 'Local Government in Malta', in Ángel Manuel Moreno Molina (ed.), *Local Government in the Member States of the European Union: A Comparative Legal Perspective*, Madrid, National Institute of Public Administration, Spain, 2012, pp. 435–458.

Aquilina, Kevin and Calleja Ragonesi, Isabelle. 'The Relations Between States and Local Authorities in the Context of Development Planning', in Stéphane Guérard and Algirdas Astrauskas (eds), *Local Autonomy in the 21st Century: Between Tradition and Modernisation*, Institut Universitaire Varenne, Paris, 2016, pp. 205–231.

Baldacchino, Godfrey. 'Worker Cooperatives in Malta: Between Self-Help and Subsidy' in Ronald G. Sultana and Godfey Baldacchino (eds), *Maltese Society: A Sociological Inquiry*, Mireva Publications Ltd., Msida, 1994.

Borg, Alexander. 'Language', in Henry Frendo and Oliver Friggieri (eds), *Malta: Culture and Identity*, Ministry of Youth and the Arts, Floriana, 1994, pp. 27–49.

Debono, Louis C. 'Il-Gvern Lokali f'Għawdex' (Translation: Local Government in Gozo), in Institute of Public Administration, *L-Amministrazzjoni Pubblika f'Pajjiżna* (Translation: Public Administration in our Country), Department of Information, Valletta, 1968, pp. 72–78.

Fabri, David. 'Transposition Tables, Toil and Tears ... True Tales from the Accession', in Peter G. Xuereb (ed.), *Malta in the European Union: Five Years On and Looking to the Future*, The European Documentation and Research Centre, Jean Monnet Centre of Excellence, University of Malta, Msida, 2009, pp. 85–95.

Frendo, Michael. 'A Strong Parliament – A Mature Democracy' in Office of the President, *The President's Forum: Does Malta's Constitution Still Cater for the People's Needs?*, Office of the President, Valletta, 2013, pp. 99–101.

Harding, Hugh W. 'Law', in Henry Frendo and Oliver Friggieri (eds), *Malta: Culture and Identity*, Ministry of Youth and the Arts, Floriana, 1994, pp. 205–217.

Lhomme, Didier. 'La Politique Régionale Européenne: De L'Ancrage À L'Adaptation. Plaidoyer Pour Une Gouvernance Simplifiée?', in Emmanuel Cherner and Stéphane Guérard (eds), *La Régionalisation En Europe Regards Croisés*, Editions Bruylant, Brussels, 2014, pp. 65–111.

Lowe, Vaughan. 'The Principle of Non-intervention: Use of Force', in Vaughan Lowe and Colin Warbrick (eds), *The United Nations and the Principles of International Law: Essays in Memory of Michael Akehurst*, Routledge, London, 1994, pp. 66–84.

McGoldrick, Dominic. 'The Principle of Non-intervention: Human Rights', in Vaughan Lowe and Colin Warbrick (eds), *The United Nations and the Principles of International Law: Essays in Memory of Michael Akehurst*, Routledge, London, 1994, pp. 85–119.

Mintoff, Dom. 'Priests and Politics in Malta: A Brief Analysis', in Mario Cutajar (ed.), *Mintoff: il-bniedem u l-istorja* (Translation: Mintoff: the Man and History), Pubblikazzjonijiet SKS, 2012, pp. 246–252.

Refalo, Ian. 'The Republic of Malta' in Constantijin Kortmann, Joseph Fleuren and Wim Voermans (eds.), *Constitutional Law of 10 EU Member States: The 2004 Enlargement*, Kluwer Law International, Deventer, The Netherlands, 2006, p. VII-21.

Sammut, Ivan. 'Effectiveness of EU Law at the National Level: The Maltese Experience So Far', in Eugène Buttigieg (ed.), *Enforcing One's Rights Under EU Law*, Gutenberg Press, Tarxien, 2011, pp. 17–35.

Thornberry, Patrick. 'The Principle of Self-Determination', in Vaughan Lowe and Colin Warbrick (eds), *The United Nations and the Principles of International Law: Essays in Memory of Michael Akehurst*, Routledge, London, 1994, pp. 175–203.

Warbrick, Colin. 'The Principle of Sovereign Equality', in Vaughan Lowe and Colin Warbrick (eds), *The United Nations and the Principles of International Law: Essays in Memory of Michael Akehurst*, Routledge, London, 1994, pp. 204–229.

Warrington, Edward. 'Gozo Civic Council: Past Experience or Model for the Future?', in *50 Sena mill-Kunsill Ċiviku ta' Għawdex – Esperjenza tal-Passat jew Mudell għall-Futur?* (Translation: Fifty Years Since the Establishment of the Gozo Civic Council: An Experience of the Past or a Model for the Future?), Proceedings of a conference organized by the Organisational Committee – 50 Years since the Gozo Civic Council, held at Hotel Kempinski, St. Lawrence, Gozo, on Tuesday, 14 June 2011, pp. 15–18.

Journals

Agius, Emmanuel. 'Co-operation in Marriage-Related Legislation', *Melita Theologica*, Vol. 65, No. 2, 2015, pp. 27–51.

Anon, 'Delegation of the Taxing Power', *Harvard Law Review*, Vol. 26, No. 3, January 1913, pp. 257–259.

Aquilina, Kevin. 'Rationalising Administrative Law on the Revocation of Development Permissions', *BOV Review*, No. 34, Autumn 2006, pp. 19–38.

Aquilina, Kevin. 'Empowering the Citizen Under the Law: The Administrative Justice Bill', *Law & Practice*, No. 14, December 2006, pp. 6–14.

Aquilina, Kevin. 'Judicial Appointment in Malta: A Historico-Legal Perspective', *Melita Historica*, Vol. XV, No. 3, 2010, pp. 233–254.

Aquilina, Kevin. 'Rethinking Maltese Legal Hybridity: A Chimeric Illusion or a Healthy Grafted European Law Mixture?', *Journal of Civil Law Studies*, Vol. 4, 2011, pp. 261–283.

Aquilina, Kevin. 'Non-Autochthonous Law Influences on the Maltese Legal System', *Id-Dritt*, Vol. XXII, 2011, 265–278.

Selected Bibliography

Aquilina, Kevin. 'The Parliament of Malta versus the Constitution of Malta: Parliament's Law Making Function under Section 65(1) of the Constitution', *Commonwealth Law Bulletin*, Vol. 38, No. 2, June 2012, pp. 217–249, at pp. 238–244.

Aquilina, Kevin. 'A Bill to Reform the Courts in Gozo and to Simplify Proceedings Between the Courts in Malta and those in Gozo', *Gozo Observer: Journal of the University of Malta – Gozo Campus*, No. 27, December 2012, pp. 21–27.

Aquilina, Kevin. 'The Nature and Sources of the Maltese Mixed Legal System: A Strange Case of Dr Jekyll and Mr Hyde', *Comparative Law Review*, Vol. 4, No. 1, 2013, pp. 1–38.

Aquilina, Kevin. 'Can the Maltese Citizenship (Amendment) Act, 2013 – Act No. XV of 2013 – Be the Subject of an Abrogative Referendum?', in *ELSA Malta Law Review*, 4th edn, 2014, pp. 55–71.

Aquilina, Kevin and Bianco, Lino. 'Editorial: The Mediterranean Environment Within a Human Rights Context: Towards the Emergence of Mediterranean Environmental Human Rights Law and the Implementation of an Effective Enforcement Machinery Therefor', Special Issue of the *Mediterranean Journal of Human Rights* entitled 'Human Rights and the Environment in the Mediterranean Region', Vol. 14, No. 1, 2010, 13–33.

Cremona, John J. 'The Jury System in Malta', *The American Journal of Comparative Law*, Vol. 13, No. 4, Autumn 1964, pp. 570–583.

Darkoh, Andy. 'The Cayman Islands Constitution – An Outcry for a Bill of Rights?', *Commonwealth Judicial Journal*, Vol. 9, No. 4, December 1992, pp. 7–13.

Felice-Pace, Joseph. 'Maltese Legal Jargon', *Symposia Melitensia*, Msida, University of Malta Junior College, No. 5, 2008, pp. 99–110.

Frendo, Henry. 'Il-Gvern Lokali fil-Gżejjer Maltin: L-Ewwel Pass' (Translation: Local Government in the Maltese Islands: The First Step), in *Politika: Pubblikazzjoni tal-Partit Nazzjonalista* (Translation: Politics: A Publication of the Nationalist Party), Nationalist Party, Pietà, No. 4, December 1994, pp. 29–35.

Gulia, Wallace Philip. 'The Residual Powers of the First Hall, Civil Court in Malta', *Id-Dritt Law Journal*, Vol. 9, 1978, p. 56.

Hood Phillips, O. 'Judicial Intervention in the Legislative Process', *The Law Quarterly Review*, Vol. 87, July 1971, pp. 321–325.

Official Publications

Buttigieg, Eugène and DeBono, Daniela. *Country Report on Citizenship Law: Malta*, Revised and updated January 2015, European University Institute, Florence, Robert Schuman Centre for Advanced Studies and EUDO Citizenship Observatory, San Domenico di Fiesole, 2015.

Cabinet Office, *Cabinet Manual of Procedures*, Cabinet Office, Valletta, August 2014.

Selected Bibliography

Centre of Expertise for Local Government Reform, *Peer Review on Local Government Reform in Malta*, Council of Europe, Strasbourg, Peer Review Report, 3 November 2014. A relevant document on local self-governance is Parliamentary Secretariat for Public Dialogue and Information, *Malta Policy for Local Governance 2009*, Valletta, undated.

Commission for the Holistic Reform of the Justice System, *The First Document for Public Consultation*, Parliamentary Secretariat for Justice, Valletta, 31 May 2013.

Commission for the Holistic Reform of the Justice System, *The Second Document for Public Consultation*, Parliamentary Secretariat for Justice, Valletta, 29 July 2013.

Commission for the Holistic Reform of the Justice Sector, *Final Report*, Ministry for Justice, Valletta, 30 November 2013.

Conferentia Episcopalis Melitensis, Legislation Regulating Assisted Human Procreation: A Position Paper, Archbishop's Curia, Floriana, November 2015.

Department of Information, *Protokoll Lokali u Reġjonali: Kodiċi li jirregola l-preċedenza u l-istatus tal-President tar-Reġjun, tas-Sindku, Viċi Sindku u l-Kunsillieri fil-Lokalità u Membri tal-Kumitati Amministrattivi* (Translation: Local and Regional Protocol: Code to regulate the order of precedence and the status of the President of the Region, the Mayor, Deputy Mayor, and Councillors of a Locality and Members of Administrative Committees), Department of Information, Valletta, undated.

Department of Information, Press Release 2224, *Publication of Speeches Delivered at the President's Forum in 2012 and 2013 on 'Does Malta's Constitution Still Cater for the People's Needs?'*, Department of Information, Valletta, Valletta, 11 October 2013.

Department of Information Press Release, 141672, Department of Information, Valletta, 23 July 2014.

Department for Local Government, Office of the Prime Minister, *Code of Ethics for Local Government Elected Representatives*, Valletta, 2010.

Direttiva Ta' L-Awtorità tax-Xandir Dwar Programmi U Reklami Mxandra Matul Il-Perijodu 7 Ta' Jannar Sad-9 Ta'Marzu 2013 (Translation: Broadcasting Authority Directive on Programmes and Advertisements Broadcast during the Period 7 January to 9 March 2013), Broadcasting Authority, Ħamrun, 2013.

Farrugia, Anglu. *Is-Sedja Titkellem, Collection of Decisions Delivered Between April 2013 and March 2014*, Vol. I, 2014, Office of the Speaker of the House of Representatives, Valletta.

Farrugia, Anglu. *Is-Sedja Titkellem, Collection of Decisions Delivered Between April and December* 2014, Vol. II, 2015, Office of the Speaker of the House of Representatives, Valletta.

Farrugia, Anglu. *Is-Sedja Titkellem, Collection of Decisions Delivered Between December 2014 and October 2015*, Vol. III, 2015, Office of the Speaker of the House of Representatives, Valletta.

Farrugia Anglu. *Is-Sedja Titkellem, Collection of Decisions Delivered Between November 2015 and April 2016*, Vol. IV, 2016, Office of the Speaker of the House of Representatives, Valletta.

Selected Bibliography

Grima, Godwin. Office of the Regulator, Individual Investor Programme, *First Annual Report of the IIP Programme of the Government of Malta*, Valletta, October 2014 (Papers Laid, Sitting No. 239 of 17 February 2015) and *Second Annual Report on the IIP Programme of the Government of Malta*, Valletta, October 2015 (Papers Laid 5897, Sitting No. 314 of 26 October 2015).

House of Representatives, *Kumitati Permanenti tal-Kamra tad-Deputati* (Translation: Permanent Committees of the House of Representatives), House of Representatives, Valletta, 2005.

House of Representatives, *90 Years of the Parliament of Malta 1921-2011: Commemorative Sitting Held on the 90th Anniversary from the Holding of the First Sitting of the Legislative Assembly and Senate following the Grant of the Amery-Milner Constitution in 1921, Wednesday 2 November 2011, The Palace, Valletta*, House of Representatives, Valletta, 2011.

House of Representatives, *House of Representatives Parliament of Malta Annual Report 2013*, House of Representatives, Valletta, 2014.

Local Councils Department, *Methods for Estimating Local Councils' Funding Needs,* Local Councils Department, Valletta, May 1999.

Mifsud, Anthony C. Auditor General. *Report by the Auditor General on the Workings of Local Government, Public Accounts 2013*, National Audit Office, Floriana, 10 December 2014.

Ministry for Infrastructure, Transport and Communications, *Next Generation Access Infrastructure Green Paper*, Ministry for Infrastructure, Transport and Communications, Valletta, July 2008.

Ministry for Justice and Local Government, *White Paper on Local Government – The Strengthening of Decentralisation: Your Council for You*, Ministry for Justice and Local Government, Valletta, June 1999.

Ministry for Social Dialogue, Consumer Affairs and Civil Liberties, *Towards the Establishment of the Human Rights and Equality Commission*, Ministry for Social Dialogue, Consumer Affairs and Civil Liberties, Valletta, December 2014.

Ministry for Social Dialogue, Consumer Affairs and Civil Liberties, *Towards a Robust Human Rights and Equality Framework: Consultation on Bills*, Valletta, 10 December 2015.

Nationalist Party Information Office, *Is Malta Burning*, Nationalist Party Information Office, Pietà, August 1981.

National Statistics Office, *Demographic Review 2013*, National Statistics Office, Valletta, 2015.

O'Donnell, Sir Gus. *The Cabinet Manual: A Guide to Laws, Conventions and Rules on the Operation of Government*, Cabinet Office, London, October 2011.

Office of the Prime Minister, *Biex il-Kunsill Jagħtik l-Aqwa Servizz: Tiġdid tal-Kunsilli Lokali b'riżultat ta'proċess ta'konsultazzjoni* (Translation: Receiving the Best Service from your Council: Renewal of Local Councils as a result of a consultation process), Valletta, 2009.

Pajjizna: Il-Kunsill Tiegħek (Translation: Our Country: Your Councils), Department of Information, Valletta, Issue 22, 1993.

Report of the Malta Constitutional Commission, 1960, Her Majesty's Stationery Office, London, February 1961, Cmnd. 1261.

Said Pullicino, Ombudsman Chief Justice Emeritus Joseph, *Reflections on the White Paper 'Towards the Establishment of the Human Rights and Equality Commission'*, Office of the Ombudsman, Valletta, July 2015.

War Office, *Manual of Military Law*, H.M.S.O., London, 1907.

Theses

Aquilina, Kevin. *Treason and Sedition in Maltese Law*, Msida, Doctor of Laws Thesis, Faculty of Laws, University of Malta, 1988.

Attard, Natalino. *The Role of Local Authorities within the Framework of the European Union Institutions*, Magister Juris in European and Comparative Law dissertation, Faculty of Laws, University of Malta, Msida, September 1995.

Borg, Rolan. *An Analysis and Evaluation of the Powers and Competences of the Local Wardens and the System of the Local Tribunals*, LL.D. thesis, Faculty of Laws, University of Malta, Msida, May 2008.

Borg Olivier, Paul. *Local Councils in Malta: Some Considerations of the Law from a Comparative Perspective*, LL.D. thesis, Faculty of Laws, University of Malta, Msida, June 1995.

Caruana, Abigail Maria. *The Gozo Civic Council: An Experiment in Devolution in Gozo*, LL.D. thesis, Faculty of Laws, University of Malta, Msida, 2010.

Darmanin, Henri. *The European Charter of Local Self-Government: Political and Legal Implications on Maltese Legislation*, LL.D. thesis, Faculty of Laws, University of Malta, Msida, May 2008.

Debono, Annalisa. *Governance in Malta: The Dimension of Local Government*, LL.D. thesis, Faculty of Laws, University of Malta, Msida, May 2011.

Debono, Maria Carmen. The Development of the Law on Referenda in Malta, LL.D. thesis, Faculty of Laws, University of Malta, Msida, 2008.

Ellul Cachia Caruana, Anne-Louise. *The Adoption of the European Convention of Human Rights into Municipal Law: A Comparative Analysis*, LL.D. thesis, Faculty of Laws, University of Malta, Msida, May 1993.

Fabri, David. *From Application to Accession: The Interplay between the EC Consumer Directives and Selected Areas of National Consumer Law and Policy – A Case Study From Malta (1990-2004)*, PhD thesis, Faculty of Laws, University of Malta, Msida, 2015.

Farrugia, Caroline. *The Implications of the Administrative Justice Act – Chapter 490 of the Laws of Malta*, Doctor of Laws Thesis, Faculty of Laws, University of Malta, Msida, 2008.

Filletti, Stefano. *Significant Developments in EU Criminal Law and Their Impact on Maltese Criminal Law*, PhD thesis, Faculty of Laws, University of Malta, Msida, November 2015.

Micallef, Anthony. *Terrorism and the Political Offence Exemption in International Criminal Law*, LL.D. thesis, Faculty of Laws, University of Malta, Msida, 1983.

Micallef, Paul Edgar. *Criminal Courts and Courts-Martial: A Comparative Study Relating to Jurisdiction and Procedure, with Particular Reference to the Malta Armed Forces Act, 1970*, Faculty of Laws, University of Malta, Msida, 1983.

Micallef, Saviour. *The Introduction of Local Councils in Malta*, LL.D. thesis, Faculty of Laws, University of Malta, Msida, 1994.

Spiteri, Mario. *The National Day, Standard and Flag in Maltese Legislation, 1849 to 1964*, LL.D. thesis, Faculty of Laws, University of Malta, Msida, May 2006.

Occasional Papers

Baldacchino, Godfrey. 'Malta Transformed by Multi-Level Governance: More Than Just an Outcome of Europeanisation', *Reflections of a Decade of EU Membership: Expectations, Achievements, Disappointments and the Future*, Occasional Paper No 3, Institute for European Studies, University of Malta, Msida, 2014.

Ellul O.P., Joseph. 'The Catholic Identity of Malta after Ten Years of Membership in the European Union: Challenges and Prospects', *Reflections on a Decade of EU Membership: Expectations, Reflections, Achievements, Disappointments, The Future.* Occasional Paper 02/2004, Institute for European Studies, University of Malta, Msida, 2014.

Newspapers

Anon, 'Pursuits, Half a Century Ago, Times of Malta', *The Times of Malta*, 11 April 2016, p. 22 reporting on a report in the *Times of Malta* of Monday, April 11, 1966, 'MLP requests Vatican to declare Malta elections unfair: resolution at public meeting'.

Aquilina, Kevin. 'Ambassadors at the Bar', *The Times of Malta*, 29 June 2012, p. 11.

Aquilina, Kevin. 'The Case for a Council of State', *The Times of Malta*, 16 November 2012, p. 14.

Aquilina, Kevin. 'The Consultation Process', *The Times of Malta*, 4 February 2013, p. 16.

Aquilina, Kevin. 'For Mercy to Be Fair to All', *The Times of Malta*, 26 February 2013, p. 17.

Aquilina, Kevin. 'Human Rights and Equality', *The Times of Malta*, 15 October 2015, p. 16.

Aquilina, Kevin. 'Constitutional Symbols', *The Times of Malta*, 14 August, 2015, p. 16.

Buontempo, Stefan. Parliamentary Secretary for Local Government, Ministry for Justice, Culture and Local Government, 'Making Councils Sustainable', *The Times of Malta*, 14 December 2014, p. 22.

Buontempo, Stefan. 'Of Regional Committees and Devolutions', *The Times of Malta*, 29 December 2015, p. 40.

Buontempo, Stefan. 'Enforcement Agency's 100 Days', *The Times of Malta*, 8 January 2016, p. 14.

Websites

socialdialogue.gov.mt/en/Public_Consultations/Pages?Home.aspx.

http://www.justiceservices.gov.mt/DownloadDocument.aspx?app=lom&itemid=8566&l=1.

http://www.justiceservices.gov.mt/LOM.aspx?pageid=24.

http://www.ombudsman.org.mt/wp-content/uploads/2014/10/Guidlines-for-Good-Governance.pdf.

http://www.ombudsman.org.mt/category/case-notes/.

https://opm.gov.mt/en/PSC/Pages/Documents/Annual-Reports-.aspx.

http://www.ba-malta.org.

http://www.nao.gov.mt/page.aspx?id=38.

http://www.ombudsman.org.mt/category/annual-reports/.

http://gozonews.com/15832/gharb-council-releases-the-official-results-of-the-referendum/print.

http://www.parlament.mt/sc-codification. Last accessed on 31 March 2016.

http://www.statecareandmore.eu/images/documents/prof%20refalo%20administrative_lawrevisedtext2012january2012.pdf.

http://ec.europa.eu/growth/single-market/public-procurement/rules-implementation/index_en.htm.

https://les.gov.mt/tribunalinfo.aspx.

Various

News bulletin, TVM, 8 January 2016, 8 o'clock evening news item.

Index

The numbers here refer to the paragraph numbers.

Abrogative Referendum, 155
Administrative organs with advisory and/or control functions, 394-397
  advisory administrative organs, 395
  advisory and control administrative organs, 397
  control administrative organs, 396

Budget process, 400-407
  budget, 402
  financial institutions framework, 404
  fiscal law versus financial law, 400–401
  other financial laws, 403
  public procurement, 405
  relevant EU Law to public procurement, 406
  review and supervisory authorities, 407

Characteristics of the Maltese State, 5-48
  constitutionalism, 5–24
  independence of the judiciary, 31
  national sovereignty, 32–40
  republican constitution, 154
  rule of law, 25–27
  separation of powers, 28–30
Confidence in parliament, 317-321
  contrary vote on government's proposal, 319–320
  motion of no confidence, 317–318
  question of confidence, 321
Constitutional annulment of laws, 143-152
  actiopopularis, 143
  Diplomatic Immunities and Privileges Act, 151
  Emergency Powers Act, 148
  European Convention Act, 149
  European Union Act, 150
  section 6 of the Constitution, 144
  section 46 of the Constitution, 145
  section 47 of the Constitution, 146
  section 95 of the Constitution, 147
  ultra vires delegated legislation, 152
Constitutional Court, 373-386
  composition of the Constitutional Court, 374–376
  constitutional application, 381–382
  constitutional reference, 379–380
  decisions on the admissibility of referenda, 386
  disputes between State powers, 385
  effects on the Constitutional Court's decisions, 383
  functionsof the Constitutional Court, 373
  interpretative and manipulative judgments, 384
  origins of constitutional review of legislation, 377–378
Constitutionalism, 5-40
  juridical status of the constitution of Malta, 5
  supremacy of the constitution of Malta, 6–24
Constitutional multi-level government, 62-65
  following EU accession, 65
  prior to EU accession, 62–64
Constitutional organs, institutions and public offices, 66-68
  organs of the state, 66
  public offices of the state, 68
  state institutions, 67
Constitutional principles, 139, 388-393, 597-606

Index

Constitutional review mechanisms of legislative and executive action, 69
Constitutional state affiliations, 60–61
Constitutional state symbols, 51–56
  George Cross award, 54
  national anthem, 56
  national flag, 53
  national language, 55
  national religion, 52
Cooperative societies and handicrafts, 589–590
  co-operative societies, 589
  crafts, 590

Direct democracy forms, 153–159
  popular sovereignty, 153–158
    abrogative referendum, 155
    constitutional amendment referendum, 156–157
    consultative referendum, 154
    local council referenda, 158
  public consultation, 159

Economic Constitution, 576–596
  cooperative societies and handicrafts, 589–590
  economic principles in the Constitution, 577-582
  expropriation and partial expropriation, 596
  freedom of private economic enterprise, 583–588
  mixed economy, 576
  ownership in the Maltese Constitution, 591
  private ownership, 595
  public ownership, 592–594
Economic principles in the Constitution, 577–582
  encouragement of co-operatives, 582
  encouragement of private economic enterprise, 580
  protection of artisan trades, 581
European legislation, 123–128
  Council of Europe Treaties, 128
  European Union Law, 124–127

Features of the republican constitution, 51–56
  multi-level government, 62–65
  organs, institutions and public offices, 66–68
  principles, 57
  review mechanisms of legislative and executive action, 69
  state affiliations, 60–61
  state symbols, 51–56
  typology of the constitution, 58–59
Form of government, 160–407
  activities of Parliament, 256–275
  budget process, 400–407
  confidence in Parliament, 317–321
  Constitutional Court, 373–386
  executive, 276–316
  judicial control of administrative action, 359–372
  judicial power, 322–358
  Maltese system of government, 160–165
  President, 166–218
  public administration in the constitution, 387–399
  structure of parliament, 219–255
Freedom of private economic enterprise, 58--588
  Business Promotion Act, 584
  Malta Enterprise Act, 586
  Small Business Act, 587–588
  Small Enterprises (Loan Guarantee) Act, 585
Fundamental rights and freedoms, 496–527
  beneficiaries, 511–514
  citizens and non-nationals, 513–514
  European Convention Act, 515–516
  European multilevel system, 521–522
  fundamental rights of the ECHR, 517–520
  inviolability, 510
  judicial remedies, 526–527
  physical persons and legal persons, 511–512
  Preamble, 508–509
  principle of equality, 524

two instruments for the protection of, 525

Government, 276–316
Acting Prime Minister, 285
Cabinet of Ministers, 280–282
Cabinet Committees, 296
caretaker government, 302
government and political parties, 307–316
government competencies, 306
government formation, 297–303
Ministers, 284
Parliamentary Secretaries, 287–288
Permanent Secretaries and Heads of Government Departments, 289–294
Prime Minister, 283
recall of parliament, 303
Secretary to the Cabinet, 295
status and responsibilities of government members, 304–305
structure of government, 280–296
Temporary Ministers, 286

International Law, 71–85
incorporation into domestic law, 73
incorporation of international customary law, 74–75
incorporation of international treaties, 76–85
International relations, 199
Introduction to the Maltese system of government, 160–165
outline of the Maltese system of government 160–162
political system, 163–164
social forces, 165
Investigatory functions, 69

Judicial control of administrative action, 359–372
evolution of the principle of administrative justice, 360
powers and limits of the ordinary judge over the public administration, 361–372
Judicial power, 322–372
citizen participation in the administration of justice, 332–337
composition and functions of the Commission for the Administration of Justice, 325
external independence of the judiciary, 325
internal independence of the judiciary, 326–327
judicial activities and constitutional rights of citizens, 356–357
military courts, 352–354
officers of the criminal justice system, 347–351
Advocate for Legal Aid, 351
Attorney General, 349–350
Inquiring Magistrate, 348
organisation of justice in Malta: civil and criminal jurisdiction, 329–331
powers and limits of the ordinary judge over the public administration, 361–372
section 32(2) of the Code of Organization and Civil Procedure, 362–363
section 469A of the Code of Organization and Civil Procedure, 364–372
powers of the minister responsible for justice, 328
principles of good administrative behaviour, 358
revisionary function of special tribunals, 355
special courts and tribunals, 338–346
Judicial review, 364--372
administrative act, 366
general issues relating to judicial review of administrative action, 365
measure intended for internal organisation or administration, 367
public authority, 368

Key rights enshrined in the Constitution, 528–567
clawback clause, 535

historical evolution, 532
Preamble, 533–534
prohibition of deportation, 562protection for privacy of home and other property, 549
protection from arbitrary arrest or detention, 538–542
protection from deprivation of property without compensation, 545–548
protection from discrimination on certain grounds, 564–567
protection from forced labour, 543
protection from inhuman treatment, 544
protection of freedom of assembly and association, 560–561
protection of freedom of conscience and worship, 555–556
protection of freedom of expression, 557–559
protection of freedom of movement, 563
protection of right to life, 536–537
provisions to secure protection of law, 550–554
sources of Chapter IV of the Constitution, 535
structure of the human rights and fundamental freedoms provisions, 535

Legal sources of Maltese constitutional law, 103–139
general principles of Maltese constitutional law, 139
judicial decisions, 130–136
legislation, 105–129
official publications setting out rules and procedures, 137–138
Legislation, 105–129
European legislation, 123–128
foreign national constitutional legislation, 120–122
international legislation, 129
Maltese constitutional legislation, 119
Maltese primary constitutional legislation, 107–114
Maltese subsidiary constitutional legislation, 115–118

Local Government, 408–462
administrative autonomy of regional committees and local councils from central government, 428–432
administrative autonomy of local councils, 429–430
administrative autonomy of regional committees, 428
administrative dependence on administrative committees on local councils, 431
regulation of human resources, 432
administrative committees, 431
competence of regional committees, local councils and administrative committees, 420–426
functions of communities, 425–426
functions of local councils, 422–424
functions of regional committees, 421
complaints mechanism, 441–444
creation of regional committees and local councils, 415
delegation of functions to, 446
dissolution of regional committees and local councils, 447–450
electoral process for local self-government, 440
enforcement system, 452–453
EU Committee of the Regions, 461
EU Dimension of local self-government, 461
financial autonomy, 433–438
of administrative committees, 435
of local councils, 434
of regional committees, 433
local self-government financial regulations, 436–438
general aspects of regional and local legislative autonomy, 427
in the Local Councils Act, 414
in the Maltese Constitution, 413
legal principles inspiring local self-government law, 412
local councils and the development planning process, 458
Local Councils Association, 456–457

Index

joint committees of local councils, 451
machinery of justice, 454–455
organisational structure, 416–419
organisation of communities, 419
organisation of local councils, 418
organisation of regional government, 417
origins of Maltese local self-government, 408–411
prohibition of broadcasting by local councils, 459–460
relationship between central and local governments, 439
twinning agreements, 445

Malta, 3–4
demography of Malta, 3
population of Malta, 4
Maltese Citizenship Law, 463–495
acquisition of citizenship, 468
birth, 469–472
Commonwealth citizenship, 487–489
criminal liability of Commonwealth citizens, 490
constitutional regulation of citizenship, 466–467
deprivation of citizenship, 482–484
descent, 477
dual or multiple citizenship, 486
EU citizenship, 491
illegitimate children, adopted children and foundlings, 476
Individual Investor Programme, 492–495
marriage, 473–475
naturalisation, 479
possession of citizenship, 480
registration, 478
renunciation of citizenship, 481
statelessness, 485
Maltese constitutional history, 1–2
Maltese constitutional legislation, 119
Maltese primary constitutional legislation, 107–114
Constitution, 110
constitutional laws, 111–114
Maltese subsidiary constitutional legislation, 115–118

National sovereignty, 32–40
limitations on sovereignty, 38–40
making of extra-territorial legislation, 33
meaning of sovereignty, 34–37
Non-legal sources of Maltese constitutional law, 140–142
authoritative works, 141
constitutional practice, 142

Parliament, 219–275
conduct of elections, 234
conflict between texts of the law, 270
different procedures for considering bills, 259
direct broadcasting of parliamentary sittings, 253–254
election campaign laws, 238–240
election of the House of Representatives, 235–237
electoral divisions, 228–231
electoral system, 226–227
House Committees, 249–251
incorporation of laws in a revised edition of the laws of Malta, 258
international relations, 255
language of laws, 269
laws delegating legislative powers, 267
legislative process of constitutional law, 265–266
links between the House, the European Union and other International organisations, 275
officers of the House of Representatives, 244
pairing of Members of Parliament, 248
parliamentary enquiries, 273
parliamentary hearings, 274
parliamentary privilege, 245–246
passing of laws, 257
political control on the government's political activities in Parliament, 271–272
pre-parliamentary stage, 256

promulgation and publication of laws, 260–264
qualifications of Member of Parliament, 241
Standing Orders, 247
subsidiary legislation made under the Constitution, 268
suspension of a general election, 232–233
tenure of office of Member of Parliament, 242–243
unicameral system, 219–225
visitors to the House of Representatives, 252
President, 166–218
acting on advice or on own deliberate judgment, 192–195
acting on government advice, 193–194
acting on own deliberate judgment, 195
appointment, 171–173
as guardian of the Constitution, 180
Community Chest Fund Foundation, 217
dual or multiple citizenship, 182
election of President, 167–169
electoral procedure, 170
fora and foundations, 214–216
infirmity of body or mind, 183
functions
concerning international relations, 199
concerning the Armed Forces of Malta, 200–210
under other laws, 213
oath and term of office, 174–178
permanent incapacity, 181–183
philanthropy, 217
powers
concerning the parliamentary system, 196
of participation in the activities of government, 197
of participation in the activities of the judiciary,198
to confer honours, 211–212
qualifications for appointment, 171–173
re-appointment, 188
replacement, 184–187
responsibility, 191
salary, 189–190
status as holder of multiple roles, 179
temporary incapacity, 181–183
term of office, 176–178
Promulgation and publication of laws, 260–264
laws with retrospective effect, 262–264
postponement of coming into operation, 261

Relations between State and Catholic Church, 569–574
agreements with the Vatican, 574
Canon Law influence on the legal relationship between Church and State, 569
Constitution, 570
ordinary laws, 571
recent trends in State-Church Relations, 572–573
Relations between state and religious denominations, 575

Separation of powers, 28–30
Sources of law,
domestic sources, 95–152
characteristics of Maltese constitutional law, 100–101
classification of Maltese constitutional law, 97–99
definition of Maltese constitutional law, 97–99
relevance of sources to a study of Maltese constitutional law, 96
European sources, 86–94
EU directives, 94
incorporationof EU law into domestic law, 89
reception of EU Law into the Maltese legal system, 90–93
external sources, 71–85
State territory, 41–48
definition of 'State', 42

Index

definition of 'Malta', 43–48
Supremacy of the constitution, 6–24
section 6 of the Constitution, 8–14
section 46(2) of the Constitution, 15
section 47(9) of the Constitution, 16
section 65(1) of the Constitution, 17–18
section 66 of the Constitution, 19–20
section 95(2)(e) of the Constitution, 21–22
section116 of the Constitution, 23–24

Typology of the constitution, 58–59

Made in the USA
Monee, IL
18 October 2026

66037571R10164